Their Fiery Cross of Union

A Retelling of the Creation of the Australian Federation, 1889-1914

Their Fiery Cross of Union

A Retelling of the Creation of the Australian Federation, 1889-1914

William Oliver Coleman

Connor Court Publishing Pty Ltd

Published in 2021 by Connor Court Publishing Pty Ltd.

Copyright © William Coleman

Not to be reproduced without the permission of the Copyright holders.

Connor Court Publishing Pty Ltd.
PO Box 7257
Redland Bay QLD 4165
sales@connorcourt.com
www.connorcourt.com

ISBN: 978-1-922449-66-5

Cover Design by Maria Giordano
Cover illustration: Medal – Promote Federation, Australia, 1899

Printed in Australia.

For Leo

Contents

List of tables	x
List of illustrations and maps	xii
Timeline to Federation and beyond	xiii
Acknowledgements	xviii
1 A Preamble	1
2 Was Federation economic in root?	9
The great dispersion	10
Customs unity	14
Professional Federationists	22
The organisational impulse	31
3 Was Federation nationalist in credo?	37
The British Empire nation	38
Plastic nationalists	42
The culture clue	48
'To make a nation'	53
4 Was Federation status-seeking in motive?	61
Status anxiety	61
Status soothers	65
5 Was Federation psychological in catalyst?	69
Séance power	69
The golden age ahead	73
6 The 'Sliding Plane'	77
The *modus operandi* of the master	78
His federal wand	82
Barton and the Corowa Conference	86
Reid and the Quick scheme	88

7 Five Federationists — 93
    George Reid — 94
    Edmund Barton — 104
    Bruce Smith — 119
    Henry Bournes Higgins — 124
    William Astley — 127

8 Contriving the Convention — 133
    The flawed design — 133
    The inequitable outcome — 137
    Some alternatives — 144

9 Cruelling the Constitution — 149
    The false lights — 149
    A brighter beam — 155
    The confederal alternative — 158
    Their handiwork — 161

10 The Anti-Federationists — 167
    John Dunmore Lang — 167
    John Robertson — 170
    John Henry Want — 178
    John Haynes — 184
    Thomas Joseph Byrnes — 193

11 Reading the referendums — 201
    The campaign — 202
    The results' significance and insignificance — 206
    The 1898 NSW election — 220
    The 1899 referendums — 224
    The problem of electoral fraud — 234

12 The Finale — 239
    The fox at bay — 239
    The Bill in London — 244

Tommy Cornstalk goes to war 252
Western Australia at the gates of the Commonwealth 255
The Hopetoun incident 262
A day to misremember 265
The opening round 268

13 The birth of a state 275
Some true colours 275
Installed in Melbourne 279
On the march 281
The Commonwealth empire state 283
The decline of parliamentarism 289
Labor ascendant 292
Industrial discord 296
The purity of the race 297
The High Court 302
The Post Office 307
The armed forces 310
The ending 317

14 A Codicil 321

Appendix 1   Some thumbnail biographies 329

Appendix 2   Some statistical relationships 337

Appendix 3   Authors and sources of introductory quotations 340

Abbreviations 341

Select bibliography 344

Endnotes 373

General Index 435

Names Index 441

Tables

Table 2.1: The geographical distribution of population and production across Australia	13
Table 2.2: Measures of tariffs and trade in Australia on the eve of Federation	16
Table 2.3: Immigration within Australia, net	19
Table 2.4: Politicians who transferred from free trade to protection, with their highest political office	21
Table 3.1: Immigration to NSW and Victoria	56
Table 3.2: The distribution of Victoria's population across age brackets	56
Table 7.1 Some earnings of occupations	110
Table 8.1 Measures of support for candidates in the election of the Australasian Federal Convention	138
Table 8.2: The success of tickets in the Australasian Federal Convention election	140
Table 8.3: The size of majorities in the divisions of the Australasian Federal Convention	148
Table 11.1 The results of the 1898 referendums	206
Table 11.2 Imperial Federation, Australian Federation and the status quo ranked by three outlooks	209
Table 11.3 The results of the 1898 referendums in terms of electorates	212
Table 11.4: The results of the 1899 referendums	227
Table 11.5: The results of the 1899 referendums in terms of electorates	228
Table 11.6: The total vote in Riverina electorates, 1895-1901	236
Table 12.1: The results of the WA referendum	260
Table 12.2: Turnout at the Commonwealth 1901 election vs State elections circa 1901	271
Table 12.3: Voter turnout at the national level circa 1901	271
Table 13.1: Labor members of the lower houses of Australian parliaments	293

Table 13.2: The number of strikes in Canada and Australia,
        1860-1959   296
Table 13.3: Convention delegates' voting proclivities with
        one another   306
Table A.1: Explaining candidate support in the election
        of NSW delegates to the Australasian Federal
        Convention   337
Table A.2: Explaining the Yes Vote in the NSW referendums
        by means of party support at 1898 general election   337
Table A. 3 Explaining the Yes vote in South Australia's
        referendums   338
Table A.4: Explaining the Yeses and Noes in South
        Australia's referendums   338
Table A.5: Explaining turnout in the NSW referendum of 1899   339

Illustrations

1. The 'often poetical' Henry Parkes, in poet's dress. 11
2. Cardinal Moran, inspecting the Irish Rifles. 49
3. Alfred Deakin 'hypnotising' an audience. 71
4. George Reid, in 'self-lampoon', stretches for the camera. 97
5. The Australasian Federal Convention, in Sydney. 151
6. John Robertson amid friends, on the last day of his life. 177
7. 'Jack' Want, the self-described 'arch-destroying angel' of Federation. 180
8. J. F. Archibald and 'Sunny' John Haynes, in Darlinghurst gaol. 186
9. Rose Scott. 205
10. Billy Trenwith, labour orator. 216
11. On the hustings, September 1898. 222
12. Reid in 1917, with children, and Mrs Florence Reid. 241
13. Bushmen's Contingent farewelled to South Africa, Melbourne. 252
14. The WA goldfields' Separation for Federation petition unfurled. 258
15. William Lyne conferring with a Victorian legislator. 263
16. A nation is born? 276
17. The NSW Ensign flown by volunteer fire fighters. 278
18. Victoria's Standard. 278
19. Food supplies under guard during the Brisbane general strike of 1912. 297
20. *En garde* – boy trainees, at Pulteney Street School for Boys, Adelaide. 313

Maps

1. The 1898 NSW Referendum. 213
2. The 1899 NSW Referendum. 233

Timeline to Federation and beyond

1856
New South Wales, Victoria, South Australia, Tasmania, and New Zealand obtain self-government.

1859
Queensland obtains separation from NSW, and self-government.

1886
Federal Council of Australasia first meets in Hobart. NSW and New Zealand do not join.

1889, 24 October
Henry Parkes calls for federation in an address at Tenterfield.

1890, January
WA obtains self-government.

1890, 6-14 February
Australasian Federal Conference, Melbourne.

1891, 2 March-9 April
National Australasian Convention, Sydney.

1891, 23 October
Following fall of Parkes government in NSW, George Dibbs becomes Premier, and Edmund Barton Attorney-General.

1893, 31 July-1 August
At the Corowa Conference, John Quick proposes a second, elected, convention, followed by a referendum.

1893, 14 December
Barton forced to resign as Attorney-General.

1894, 17 July
General election in NSW: George Reid becomes Premier.

1895, 31 January
Quick's scheme of a second convention adopted by a Premiers' Conference, Hobart.

1895, 24 July
General election in NSW. Reid retains government. Barton leaves parliament.

1896, 27 April
Parkes dies.

1896, 17 November
People's Federal Convention, Bathurst.

1897, 4 and 6 March
Elections of delegates to the Australasian Federal Convention: NSW, Victoria, Tasmania and SA.

1897, 22 March-23 April
Adelaide session of Australasian Federal Convention.

1897, 8 May
Barton appointed by Reid to Legislative Council of NSW.

1897, 2-24 September
Sydney session of Australasian Federal Convention.

1897, 6 December
NSW *Australasian Federation Enabling Act Amendment Act* lays down that the Convention's draft constitution must receive 80 000 Yes votes to pass.

1898, 20 January-17 March
Melbourne session of Australasian Federal Convention. A Bill 'To Constitute the Commonwealth of Australia' adopted.

1898, 4 April
John Want resigns from Reid government.

1898, 3 and 4 June
Referendums on Bill held in NSW, Victoria, Tasmania and SA. Yeses exceed Noes in all four, but fail to reach 80 000 in NSW.

1898, 27 July
General election NSW: Reid retains power and defeats Barton in Sydney-King.

1898, 22 August
Thomas Joseph Byrnes, Queensland Premier, confers with Reid in Sydney.

1898, 15 September
Barton wins Hastings Macleay by-election, and replaces William Lyne as NSW Opposition leader.

1898, 27 September
Death of J.T. Byrnes.

1899, 2 February
All premiers meet in camera in Melbourne to revise the draft Constitution Bill.

1899, 18 April
Want resigns from Reid government a second time.

1899, April to September
Referendums on revised Bill: SA, 29 April; NSW, 20 June; Victoria and Tasmania, 27 July; Queensland, 2 September. All succeed.

1899, 24 August
Lyne replaces Barton as Opposition Leader, and Reid as Premier, 14 September.

1900, May
Joseph Chamberlain, Colonial Secretary, confers with Barton, Alfred Deakin and Charles Kingston in London on the Constitution Bill.

1900, 31 July
WA referendum approves Bill and joins the Commonwealth as an 'original State'.

1900, 24 December
The Governor-General, the 7th Earl of Hopetoun, settles on Barton as Prime Minister after Lyne withdraws.

1901, 1 January
Commonwealth of Australia proclaimed, Sydney. State departments of customs and excise transferred to Commonwealth.

1901, 29-30 March
General election of both houses of Parliament of Commonwealth. Barton, the protectionist leader, confirmed as Prime Minister.

1901, 31 March

Commonwealth assumes control of military, customs and post office.

1901, 17 December

Pacific Island Labourers Act.

1901, 23 December

Immigration Restriction Act.

1902, 12 June

Commonwealth Franchise Act.

1902, 16 September

Customs Tariff Act.

1903, 24 September

Deakin succeeds Barton as prime minister.

1903, 6 October

First sitting of the High Court.

1904, 27 April

Labor leader Chris Watson replaces Deakin as prime minister.

1904, 15 August

Seat of Government Act places capital 'within seventeen miles of Dalgety'.

1904, 18 August

Reid, the free traders' leader, replaces Watson as prime minister.

1904, 15 December

Commonwealth Conciliation and Arbitration Act.

1905, 5 July

Deakin replaces Reid as Prime Minister.

1906, 12-13 October.

Isaac Isaacs and H. B. Higgins appointed to High Court.

1908, 13 November

Labor leader Andrew Fisher replaces Deakin as prime minister.

1908, 14 December

Seat of Government Act moves capital to 'the district of Yass-Canberra'.

1909, 2 June

Deakin replaces Fisher as prime minister.

1909, 13 December

Defence Act.

1910, 13 April

Labor wins general election.

Acknowledgements

I am indebted to the extensive comments on the entire manuscript of John Nethercote and Henry Ergas. I also wish to express my considerable debt to the dedication and professionalism of Michael Gilchrist in preparing my book for publication. I also gratefully acknowledge the thoughts of Greg Melleuish and Richard Pomfret on distinct chapters, and the benefit of conversations with Tim Hatton, Ged Martin, John Ruddick, Andrew Sudol, Rod Tyers and Claire Wright. Marie-Jose Le Garrec has my wholehearted thanks for her research assistance, pictorial acumen and valuable observations on several particulars. I wish additionally to express my debt to the 'Demythologising Australia's Federation Episode' conference, which took place in 2019 with the support of the University of Notre Dame, Australia, and the Mannkal Economic Education Foundation. Finally, I express my appreciation of Christina Houen's scrutiny of the manuscript.

The author and publisher gratefully acknowledge approval to reproduce the images in the illustrations: 1, 6, 7, 8, 9 and 17 (State Library of New South Wales); 13 and 18 (State Library of Victoria); 14 (State Library of Western Australia); 19 (State Library of Queensland); 20 (State Library of South Australia, PRG 280/1/44/56).

1

A Preamble

'1901' is the paramount event of Australia's political history. The integration that year into a single Commonwealth of the six political bodies occupying the Australian landmass is the foundational fact of the country's political and legal existence. From that year, it seems, all else flows: 1901 is 'the fateful date'.

How happy or hard was the fate ordained by that year? The question has received just one answer: Federation is deemed a lofty feat, a piece of progress, 'the greatest political achievement in Australian history'.[1] In this universal judgement, the Federation of 1901 was virtuous in provenance – begotten of commendable ideals of our better selves (patriotism, brotherhood, equality), led by remarkable men, and pursued to consummation by democratic processes. And it was a natural thing – fitting, functional, and almost inevitable. And it was for the good in its effects. At the very least, Federation was a mark of progress; the consequence of the development of Australian life, in everything from telegraphy to sporting fixtures.

Such are the glad responses of the keepers of Federation's flame to a question which is, in fact, rarely put. There is no need to: a faith in Federation is the first article of Australia's civic religion.

It is this contented faith in Federation that this work seeks to contest.

The truth is there was little natural about Federation. Circumstances supplied small occasion to federate in 1901; the deed bordered on the gratuitous. Chance, accordingly, looms large in its origins. Worse, those origins were more frequently mundane than elevated; its leadership was, at its very pinnacle, mediocre; its democracy was mechanical, and, at the worst moments, fraudulent; it was born as much from alienation from country as from love of it; and more from careerism than from citizenship. And the act of federating in 1901 was frequently injurious in consequence. That Federation was economically costly through inhibiting competition is likely. That it committed offences against political justice seems undeniable: by promptly introducing racially-based immigration laws of a severity not previously known; by deporting the Kanakas; and removing Aboriginals from electoral rolls. Federation – in slighting freedom while endorsing compulsion and bureaucratisation – replaced voluntarism with conscription as the basis of the defence forces. It dried the wells of democracy and parliamentarism in Australian politics. Its constitutionalising metamorphosed a slurry of quirks and crotchets of the 1890s into marble ramparts of a Constitution from which a complacent High Court provided little resort. It pinioned the country with a Constitution which was confounding, encumbering, and ultimately anti-federal. Above all else, Federation did not so much 'make a nation' as 'make a state'.

But if Federation was not a piece of progress, what was it? Rather than constituting an advance, it might be apprehended, more neutrally, as a constitutional upheaval; the downfall, and supersession, of an extant political order. Specifically, it might be interpreted as the insurgency of an agitated periphery against a heedless centre. In a more prosaic telling, Federation was simply the local release of an international political hit of the day, known as 'Progressivism' in the United States and 'New Liberalism' in Great Britain, which amounted to a certain winning formula of centralism, bureaucracy and imperialism. A more resentful judgement might construe Federation as the submission of the rest of Australia to Victoria. Alternatively, a puckish eye might conceive the constitutional episode of 1889-1914 as a prank of history: where a small circle of self-entitled bourgeoisie excitedly fashioned an exquisite device to gratify their quest for prestige and power, only to see it brusquely snatched away by unsmooth palms, and put to rough work serving the plain appetites of hatless women and men in broad-rimmed felts. One might even intuit something more shadowy behind the event, which was so unheralded, so unbeckoned by objective circumstance, and so helter-skelter; does it not bespeak an 1890s restlessness? For all its seeming prosiness, the surging crowds and heaving emotions of the Federation decade suggest something of a frantic vault. A *folie à famille* of a *folie de grandeur*.

Federation is many things, and more. No single paragraph can give justice to its nature, or to its effects. On account of this complexity this book does not attempt the unremitting degradation of Federation. Was it not entirely peaceful in method, and nearly devoid of malignity in motivation? And what can be all bad in its results? Or wholly tainted in its provenance? Neither is this work hostile to federation in general; federation with a lower case 'f'. A genuine federation – as distinct from a faux federation of unification – may have served Australia well. The flaw of Federation of 1901 is that it botched federation, and may have precluded a better one. This contention is only reinforced by the long-standing and continual impetus for closer integration in Australia before Federation: a style of governance of 19th century Australia, amounting to the imitation and co-operation of the six governments, rather than their differentiation and competition, 'federation before Federation'. This impetus would surely have resulted in some sort of federation sooner or later, though not the political organism born in 1901.

The pressure for closer political integration is so obvious in Australian history that it makes space for an entirely distinct species of criticism of '1901'. This pressure relieves the critic of affirmative history of Federation from being committed to condemning it as a misstep, a wrong turn, a blunder, a folly. An entirely different dissent from judging Federation as an 'achievement' would see Federation as, in some dimensions, a non-event. So, in this different dissent, 1901 is not so much a fork in the road, a rupture, a Year Zero, but just more of the same.[2]

Abandoning an 'affirmative history' of Federation evidently opens several alternative interpretations of the event. So what this work avows most confidently is not the character of the causes or consequences of Federation but the deficiencies of the history of the thing; a history that, despite its sophistication and bulk, amounts, at bottom, to an act of giving thanks for Federation. A history which is not just wrong, but is a legend – a public myth, inculcated to the cost of society. A history, then, which anyone who holds Federation of 1901 less than dear implicitly undertakes to challenge.

The foundation of the received history of Federation is a handful of celebratory and 'memorialising' chronicles composed between 1900 and 1950. In those years of living memory, the most literary of the Federationists – Alfred Deakin, B. R. Wise, Robert Garran and Ernest Scott – took up the pen, both to rally the public against 'this feeling of disappointment' which they conceded the new Commonwealth had met,[3] and to fashion what they hoped would endure as the authorised account of its creation.[4] Theirs was a triumphalist story, of the noble struggling against villains, clods, and a clown or two. It was a history of memory, sometimes false memory. It was, in part, a fabulist history, composed of propaganda sallies which were being fashioned even before Federation had come to pass. It was, above all, victors' history, where things happen because an elect strive to achieve them. To stylise it in mock-heroic terms: in 1889, at a village remote in a mountain recess, a venerable, bearded prophet dramatically sounds the trump of the great cause.[5] Its ruby note is heard, but does not resound as deeply as hoped . At his (political) death bed the figure anoints a younger, clean-shaven prince, who collects a band of paladins, and inspires a gathering stream of common folk to issue from another remote (but riverine) village. Together, in a series of sharp contests, they finally storm, in 1899, the last, obdurate city of the plain.

The second phase of Federation history – that crafted by professional historical investigators of the first generation after the Second World War – inevitably replaced the brilliant hues of the first phase's artistry. Browns and greys now appeared in the pallet. There was a tilt towards the anti-sentimental, as economic advantage was advanced as an explanatory factor. A marxist interpretation of the Federation drama was attempted, without much success, but also, mark, without any intention to diminish the deed.[6] The Whig presumption of the first stage of history-making – that the 1890s was a struggle between those seeking to usher in the political norms of 20th century Australia and those seeking to stall them – was crushed.[7] And the roles of hero and villain allocated by Deakin, Wise and Garran were challenged. Their casting, above all, of George Houstoun Reid as a kind of obese Richard III of the wars of Federation was repudiated.

None of the shifts of the post-war historians of Federation altered an essentially positive outlook on Federation. More generally, 'left nationalist' history (Russel Ward, Bernard Smith, Brian Fitzpatrick, Fin Crisp), so much of the backdrop of the period, was glad to make Federation and its immediate upshot something of a high point of the Australian panorama. Reinforcing the positive outlook was an innovation of the period – the inauguration of a semi-canonical gallery of 'Federation Fathers'. The politicians who were once simply known as 'makers' of the Commonwealth, and who had been experienced as creatures of flesh, were now given over to the pages of myth. This tendency might be dated from the first biography of Edmund Barton in 1948, a figure who by then had almost disappeared from national consciousness.

The third phase of Federation history – say from the Bicentenary until the present – saw a mottling of attitudes. External events were deflating of the enthusiasts of 1901. The policy regimen which Federation quickly established – tagged as the 'Australian Settlement' but in fact the 'Federation settlement' – had persisted throughout most of the 20th century. But in the post-1988 period, the repudiation, or at least disowning, of three programs inseparably associated with the Federation's policy regimen – White Australia, compulsory arbitration and tariff protection – could only impart an awkwardness to any toasting of 1901. In particular, the near obsessive racial hostility of the Federation movement to 'coloureds' is, in the present climate, rattling to any memorialist of it. In parallel, the mythology of the Australian people – important to Federationists, and even more to left nationalist history of the mid-20th century – was now dead, and smelling bad to the left. Perhaps independently, but to the same effect, the momentum of professional history continued to grind away at Federationist mythology: the myth of Parkes's 'Tenterfield oration' was deflated;[8] the myth of the cause's 'turn to the people' after 1891 was coolly reappraised; the fact that a majority of Australia's largest city in 1899, Sydney, voted No to Federation now silently crept into histories.[9]

For all this apparent edging away from affirmative history, any frank disaffection with the Federation project has been unusual.[10] To the political right, Federation was something which only an unpatriotic knocker could want to take down. And to the left, if Federation was no longer magnificent, it was still beneficent. Their censures were the censures of blemishes or shortfalls. Any suggestion that Federation wrecked the country was quite off their mental map. And, rather suddenly, '1901' reobtained an additional service to the left, in consequence of their new program to redeploy Marxist categories in racial terms. Its key substitution of 'colonisation' for the hire of labour as the essential act of exploitation meant that any neo-Europe's foundational past is reduced to 'colonisation'. The advent of Commonwealth in 1901 proved useful in marking out a boundary between the 'colonial', exploitative foundation of Australia, and the (apparently) not quite so bad successor. An upshot of the contemporary left's proclivity to affix the brand of disgrace, 'colonial', to anything that preceded 1901, is that it has implicitly revived one of earlier Australia's most fanciful illusions about Federation: that 1901 somehow amounted to the 'independence' of Australia. The New Left of the 1960s had riotously demonstrated how glad Federationists were to play lion cub to the great Britannic lioness, and that the Commonwealth which Federationists created was in every way – technically, practically, and palpably – a British colony. The pressure of the tenets of the New Left's successors has pushed this disconcerting truth to one side.

The centenary of Federation in 2001 underlined the endurance of the essentially positive consensus. A flood of federally funded scholarly studies were well content with an 'affirmative' interpretation of the history of Federation. Forthright champions of Federation added their voice.[11] And the veneration of the Federation Fathers seemed to grow only brighter, crowned by the publication of a major, charitable new biography of 'Australia's noblest son', Edmund Barton.[12]

To summarise: a plaster cast nobility of '1901' remains condoned, respected and even added to by the past generation of historians. Thus, notwithstanding some well-placed stings, the most significant single account of 1901 – John Hirst's *The Sentimental Nation* – does not baulk from its own sentimental gesture: the work is dedicated to 'the 422,778 Yes voters who have no other memorial'.[13]

Even the best history remains, at bottom, an act of giving thanks for Federation. And in the slighter historical efforts – popular, text-book, Wikipedia and 'official' history – the myth-making of first generation history remains pervasive. Thus a ritualistic, commemorative, and legendary history of Australia's Federation episode is kept in circulation.

From any affirmative and commemorative history the present work expresses, and strives to justify, its dissent. The following pages advance something that the (massive) history of Federation has barely seen: a revisionist account of Federation.[14] It is revisionist, not only in debunking myth, and telling the untold, but in its stress on contingency over necessity; on continuity as much as turning points; on the role of individuals and their networks, rather than the power of ideas, or the force of common interest. But, above all, it is revisionist in confronting what, in atmosphere, remains a thankful and grateful history of Australia's Federation episode. Other societies have been prolific in revisionist challenges to the legendary summaries of their own fateful dates. This is an attempt at an Australian one.

2

Was Federation economic in root?

There's no one so wealthy as we.
– Henry Parkes

How came Australia to federate in 1901? The question frustrates its student. No stern imperative spurred it into existence;[15] no bright lure begot it; and no dry reckoning of gain tugged it into realisation. Historians have, accordingly, granted a generous role to chance; some to providence; some even to 'miracles'.[16]

But if Federation was fortuitous, it was not, say its advocates, gratuitous. It was rationalisable; there were 'grounds' for Federation. The economic, in particular, makes sense of Federation. By 1901, suggests this thought, physical barriers to 'trade and intercourse' between the colonies had so dwindled that political divisions had become redundant and costly, and their political integration rewarding.

From these contentions, the present chapter dissents.

The Federation of 1901 was economically costly to Australia as a whole: the country faced an economic price – not a reward – for Federation.[17] If Federation profited certain economic sectors – some producers and, more importantly, the professions – Australia's interest at large cannot *justify* Federation, even if sectional interest helps to *explain* it.

And yet, if the economy as a whole was not strengthened by Federation, another sphere of life – call it 'organisation' – was accommodated. This sphere, symbolised by 'the plan' as much as 'the market' symbolises the economic, appears to present a competing, and conflicting, 'rationality' for dealing with the material side of human existence. In this sphere was Federation rooted; in Federation this sphere culminated.

The great dispersion

On Wednesday 1 May 1889 Sir Henry Parkes stood by the edge of the Hawkesbury River, Sydney's encircling necklace and collar, and declared open an 890 metre bridge spanning its tortuous currents. Sydney was finally linked by rail to Brisbane and, hence, the four capitals of eastern Australia to one other. On that day, Sir Henry exalted in the thought of the 'crimson fluid of kinship coursing through all the iron veins' of rail.[18] Parkes was expressing in his poetic way the plainest rationalisation of the Federation of 1901: the steady overpowering of the continent's great tyrant, distance. The several, original, distinct settlements had sought to depose this burdensome sovereign by assuming self-direction as soon as was practical. Accordingly, the Separation Days of Victoria and Queensland, which marked their independence from New South Wales, were a matter of jubilation, fireworks and 14-gun salutes. This not quite forgotten joy of the larger colonies' separation was awkward for Federationists.[19] But a close half-century on from the 1850s, the tyrant seemed almost chased from the land by modern technology, and the separations redundant. Every popular history of Federation pauses to remark on the creation by 1889 of a railway network connecting four colonies, and the possibility of travelling by train from Adelaide to Brisbane.

But was the creation of a semi-continental railway network so stimulative of federal union? A certain 'conquest of distance' is a technical precondition for any government to govern the Australian continent effectively. But the real question is whether that conquest would bestow the 'unity' which Parkes grandly invoked. The examples of civil wars in Europe and North America during the lifetimes of Federationists explode any pretension that railways are essentially unifying. And in the particular case of Australia, the real effect of the railways was the reverse of 'unifying'. The network's greatest significance lay not in making it easier to trade and travel between distinct colonies, but in easing trade and travel from each colony's hinterland to its ports, and thence the world. For the rail network which made it quicker to travel from Sydney to Melbourne, also made it quicker to travel from, say, Albury to Sydney. Hence the networks were as consolidating of the colonies as entities, as dissolving of them; an effect

The 'often poetical' Henry Parkes, in poet's dress

only magnified by the difference in gauges. And, with respect to the inter-colonial transport which did take place, sea passage remained ascendant over rail. 'By 1890 ... small coastal steamers dominated inter-state trade, usually undercutting the railways with heavy rail subsidies'.[20] Thus the seven robust coastal shipping lines of the day, and what one British observer described as the 'immense and incessant passenger traffic' between coastal cities in Australia.[21] The role of coastal shipping in the conquest of distance's tyranny is ignored by Federationist history, and for good reason, as coastal shipping cannot serve as any rationalisation for Federation: it had no revolution in the 1890s, and the great hey day of coastal passenger shipping came after Federation. Coastal shipping was, in the longer run, a casualty of Federation.

But the conquest of distance thesis is not disposed of by dispensing with Federationist illusions about railways. The thesis might discard the debatable benefit of being able to depart Adelaide railway station at 3.30 pm Monday and arrive Brisbane at 6.15 am Saturday,[22] and instead invoke the huge improvements in communications over the generation previous to Federation. From 6 November 1861, Brisbane, Sydney, Melbourne and Adelaide were linked by another 'chord of iron stretching thousands of miles', conveying messages almost instantly.[23] By 1890 a million telegrams each year were either sent by NSW to the rest of Australia, or received by NSW. But it is an 'Esperantist' delusion that such communication was necessarily fostering mutual sympathy and harmony. To communicate is not, at the same time, to understand. And understanding is more than a matter of words. For the bulk of humanity, to understand someone is to know that someone. 'Being there' seems far more important than just 'cabling there'. On this premise, distance was barely overcome in late 19th century Australia. If 'being there' is what matters, then 'distance' was actually *increasing* in the Federation era: not because geography was altering but because of the great dispersal of population across the continent. It may be calculated that in 1861 the average distance of the inhabitants of Australia's six capital cities from each other was 624 km. By 1901 it was 798 km. And, by 1911, 857 km.[24]

The increase in average distance of Australia's inhabitants from one another reflects a key material fact of the generation preceding the Federation decade; economic activity dispersed across the country from its mid-century concentration in the continent's south-east sixth. Whereas, in 1861, Victoria, Tasmania and South Australia had provided two-thirds of Australia's population and economic activity, over the next thirty years this share had dropped to half, or even less.

Table 2.1: The geographical distribution of population and production across Australia

(Percent of Australia's total)

		1861	1871	1881	1891	1901	1911
Population	Victoria, SA and Tasmania	65	61	55	50	46	43
	NSW and Queensland	34	38	43	48	49	51
	WA	1	1	1	2	5	6
GDP	Victoria, SA and Tasmania	69	60	52	46	39	40
	NSW and Queensland	30	39	47	52	50	52
	WA	1	1	1	2	11	8

Sources: ABS (3105.0); Sinclair (2009).

This dispersion of people and production would make the political integration of the continent still more challenging. And the corresponding dispersion within each colony, as the edges of settlement fanned outwards from their capitals, could only increase the reward for political *dis*aggregation. Thus the dispersal of population across Queensland after self-government, in 1859, would recommend carving out a 'North Queensland', and, perhaps, a 'Central Queensland', from the gargantuan parent colony of Queensland; in area greater than the combined area of California, Texas, Montana and New Mexico; and with its capital, Brisbane, 'closer to Sydney than to Mackay, closer to Melbourne than to Cairns, and closer to Hobart and Adelaide than to Burketown and Thursday Island'.[25] In the early

1890s the movement to have a North Queensland calved from the existing Queensland was on the brink of success.[26] That several prominent Federationists conceded and championed the creation of a North Queensland underlined its legitimacy.[27] But the moment passed. The impulse for disaggregation rapidly transmuted into an espousal of aggregation, as North Queensland hopefully wagered that the balance of forces in a new Commonwealth would favour what it wanted economically and racially. It was clear enough to North Queensland that Federation would, in practical terms, not tolerate the creation of new states, but a calculation of expediency overrode a value of self-government.[28]

Customs unity

If a conquest of distance had not made redundant the apportionment of the continent into six distinct political units, perhaps the particular delineations of that apportionment were proving increasingly unsuitable. If Federation pressed against the natural centrifugal impulses of a dispersion of population, its advocates could still claim it would replace the 'artificial' boundaries between the colonies by the 'natural' boundaries of the new Commonwealth. The boundaries between the colonies were, undeniably, ill-contrived. With an insouciance approaching caprice, imperial authority had settled the New South Wales-Victoria border upon the Murray, instead of the Murrumbidgee, creating a discontented region out of NSW's Riverina. And it had fixed the Queensland-NSW border on 29 degrees south, instead of 30 degrees south, creating the same for the Northern Rivers. SA's border with Victoria, NSW and Queensland, at the 141st meridian, was 'almost totally discordant with the natural character of the area'.[29] And the northern border of SA was drawn at 26 degrees south with a complete unaccountability.[30] Later mineral discoveries would make the borders still unluckier (Broken Hill). These distant margins of the colonies destabilised them, and facilitated Federation. The solution to badly drawn borders, however, would not be to abolish them, but to correct them.

But the economic grounds rallied by Federationists rested not so much on the particular path traced by borders, but on their misuse; the erection of artificial barriers by the six governments – tariffs – along their 'accidental' boundaries. It was in the abolition of intra-Australian tariffs that we have one great theme of Federationists; one where the rational and the ardent seemed conjoined, in one great roar for an end to those 'unholy barriers between brethren'.[31]

> **Charles Kingston:** *Intercolonial free trade has ever been one of the chief objects of Federation.*[32]
>
> **William Lyne:** *[Intercolonial free trade] is the main and staple thing that is inducing the people to ask for federation.*[33]
>
> **George Reid:** *Why are we preparing this Constitution? To obtain federal freedom for trade and intercourse between the different colonies of the Commonwealth.*[34]

But one may look askance at this yearning for federal freedom. Elimination of intra-Australian trade barriers did not require creation of a new level of government: it was well within the legal powers of the six parliaments to make a free trade area of Australia. Such a resolution had, in effect, abolished tariffs between NSW and Victoria between January 1867 and November 1873, and between SA and NSW throughout the 1870s.[35] Even after the re-establishment of these barriers, no colony faced significant hurdles in exporting to NSW by the close of the 1890s. By Reid's *Customs Duties Act (NSW)* of 1895, the rest of Australia could, by 1 July 1900, export to the largest economy of the six colonies any good fully free of tariff, apart from alcohol, tobacco products, tea and opium. And barriers faced in exporting to any other part of mainland Australia were minor. Even the tariffs imposed by 'protectionist Victoria' on imports from NSW averaged no more than 4.5 percent (Table 2.2).

So what was all the stir about trade barriers? Federationists might, by way of reply, invoke the benefit of ending the harassment by officialdom of travellers at colonial borders. But conferring a 'duty free' status for the small quantities travellers typically carried might have ended that just as well. And by 1895, writes the historian of the 19th century Australian tariff, 'bonding

Table 2.2: Measures of tariffs and trade in Australia on the eve of Federation
(percent)

	New South Wales	Victoria	Queensland	South Australia	Western Australia	Tasmania
Average rate of duty on 31 major imports from rest of Australia.	3.7	4.5	9.1	5.7	11.7	19.3
Average rate of duty on 31 major imports from rest of world.	3.2	12.1	16.1	12.2	22.9	34.2
Imports from the rest of Australia as a proportion of GDP, 1895-1900	15	13	12	25	19	13
Imports from the rest of the world as a proportion of GDP, 1895-1900	20	19	15	22	17	7
Exports to the rest of Australia as a proportion of GDP, 1895-1900	12	10	25	23	12	16
Exports to the rest of the world as a proportion of GDP, 1895-1900	25	21	18	27	18	10

Sources: Rows 1 and 2: Lloyd 2015. Rows 3 to 6: Commonwealth Bureau of Census and Statistics (1911), Sinclair (2009).

facilities removed the worst inconveniences for merchants and consumers: the border settlers had grown accustomed to customs houses, and many enjoyed steady employment as customs officers or smugglers'.[36] Finally, and more fundamentally, there was theoretical naivety in the joy of freetraders, at the prospect of Victoria, SA, Tasmania, etc., removing their tariffs from one another.[37] For while the well-known arguments of the economist, rooted in David Ricardo and W. S. Jevons, easily rationalise the proposition that the abolition of tariffs would benefit an economy, considered as a whole, the very same pattern of argument concludes that an economy may be harmed by abolishing the tariff on imports from one source but not from all.[38] To illustrate: while SA will certainly benefit from reducing tariffs on hops, whatever their source, SA may be harmed by reducing its tariff on Victoria's hops *alone*, while maintaining tariffs on hops imports from the rest of the world. This perhaps recondite-seeming proposition turns on the plain truth that SA loses the same amount of tariff revenue as with a non-discriminating reduction, but gains less in terms of a reduction in price, as Victoria's hops must have been uncompetitive for Victoria to value such a concession. In more intuitive terms, the logic of this proposition is that a 'discriminating' tariff reduction does not create trade – and so does not create welfare – it only diverts trade from its welfare-creating channels.

The phenomenon of 'trade diversion' lessens surprise at the failure of attempts in the late 19th century to secure intra-Australasian free trade deals, like that proposed for SA and New Zealand. Any surprise shrinks still further given a special case of this proposition: if New Zealand's supply of hops is insufficient to satisfy all of SA's demand for hops, then SA *must* be harmed by such a tariff concession to NZ only.[39] Further, and crucially, New Zealand cannot, without harming itself, provide sweeteners in return that are sufficient for SA to agree to such a concession. This implies that, if the terms of the mooted agreement were such that SA was ahead, then New Zealand must be behind, with no possibility of SA being able to compensate … and vice versa. In the light of this proposition, the failure of SA and New Zealand (or Victoria and Tasmania) to secure free trade deals prior to Federation might have been no 'failure' at all, contrary to Federationist chiding.[40] It may, indeed, have been a victory of the economic criterion, and Federation a defeat of it.

The defender of the Federationist program of 'free trade at home and protection from abroad' may retort that the possibility of free inter-colonial trade producing only costly 'trade diversion' is no more than that: a possibility. But the abolition of such barriers was only one prong of the two-pronged policy – the Federationist commitment to creating intra-Australian free trade was rigidly combined with a second commitment: the institution, around the entirety of Australia, of a barrier to trade with the rest of the world.[41] That second prong would be costly by the usual arguments of trade economics. It adds a second, perhaps surer, twist of the knife in the economic case against Federation, especially as trade with the rest of the world remained, for the three largest colonies, more important than trade with the rest of Australia (see Table 2.2, Rows 3 to 6).

The Federation advocate may ultimately rely on the contention that, if Federation trade policy had a price, it was a price the community was willing to pay. But in adopting such a hypothesis we are leaving behind any economic rationalisations of Federation.

If the economic is to have anything to do with Federation, it is not in the *justification* for it, but in the *explanation* of it. There was a price to be paid for Federation, but Federation came about because those who 'paid' the price were less politically significant than those who were paid it. Thus a sectional benefit from Federation's trade policy, not aggregate benefit, was key. What sectional interests would have benefitted from Federation's mixed dish of free trade within Australia and 'protection against the world'? Miners? 'Overall, mining towns tended to relegate economic arguments to last place'.[42] Manual labour? The huge railway and construction labour forces would not be served by such a policy formula. The land? Whatever calculation the squatter might make regarding this formula, he was now a political absentee.

But one beneficiary of a sectional benefit of the Federation was plain in expressing themselves:

Federation [is] necessary to provide new markets for Victorian goods.

– Alfred Bailes, MP for Sandhurst (Bendigo), 1886-1904[43]

For a generation prior to the 1890s, Victorian industry had sought with success to construct a tariff wall around Victoria alone. But by the early 1890s, both the efficacy and political feasibility of a Victorian tariff wall were undercut by new circumstances. For most of the 1890s Victoria was in a slump, much more seriously than the rest of Australia. The nostrum and panacea of the previous generation – to make Victoria prosperous by replacing imports with Victorian production – now seemed wanting. In the wake of the bust, Victorians might be said to have voted with their feet against the old reliance.[44]

Table 2.3: Immigration within Australia, net (000)

	NSW	Victoria	Queensland	SA	WA	Tasmania
Decade to 1891	37	-32	62	-61	7	-13
Decade to 1901	1	-101	16	-14	101	-3
Decade to 1911	25	-51	2	-10	48	-15

Source: Brosnan (1982).

The bust of the 1890s made a novel truth especially painful; that instead of serving the revenue needs of Victoria, the policy of a Victorian tariff wall was strangling its tax receipts. The government of George Turner, in consequence, legislated tariff reductions in 1894 on the assumption that a slate of goods had been tariffed so high that lower rates would, by stimulating imports, add to the revenue the government was anxious for.[45] The very success of import-replacing tariffs was now in pointed collision with the need for revenue.

Independently of the Victorian government's incentive to reduce tariff rates, the long run growth in industry was weakening, or even eliminating, the benefit of Victorian industry from a tariff wall around Victoria. By the 1890s industry had grown so much that the benefit from further shrivelling imports was small. Markets beyond Victoria were now sought, and the abolition of the smaller colonies' tariffs would supply them.

> *A large deputation from the Melbourne Chamber of Manufacture[r]s recently waited on Mr Turner, Premier of Victoria, to ask the Government to take steps to bring about intercolonial free trade.*[46]

But what the deputation was requesting was no more than free trade within Australia. And how valuable was that goal? Regarding the great prize of trade policy, the NSW market, Victoria's exporters already enjoyed virtually unimpeded access under Reid's free trade government. Hence hope for markets and profits was more definitely pinned on the establishment of a tariff wall between NSW and the rest of the world, and the exclusion of foreign competitors from the NSW market. Thus a Commonwealth 'customs union'. Victorian federalists were not shy of pointing out the nature of its benefit.

> *When a uniform tariff is established Victoria will be benefitted by being called upon to meet the demand in the other colonies which have not developed industries under protection.*
>
> – William Trenwith, Victorian delegate to the Australasian Federal Convention[47]

This would be the new course.

NSW, too, was not bereft of interests who could share Victoria's vision. NSW manufacturers would also look forward to such a tariff wall around the whole of Australia. NSW manufacturers provided one wing of the colony's protectionist party, which had been rapidly strengthening in supposedly 'free trade' NSW. In 1885 the NSW Parliament contained only four protectionists; by 1891 and 1899 protectionists formed (minority) governments. The fact that even in traditionally free trade NSW protectionists could occupy the Treasury benches by the 1890s suggests there was a rising tide of protectionism which few politicians could resist (Table 2.4).

The defection of politicians from free trade to protection

Table 2.4: Politicians who transferred from free trade to protection, with their highest political office

Person	Highest political office
Edmund Barton	Prime Minister
Alfred Deakin	Prime Minister
George Dibbs	Premier, NSW
William Lyne	Premier, NSW
John See	Premier, NSW
Thomas Waddell	Premier, NSW
Graham Berry	Premier, Victoria
James McCulloch	Premier, Victoria
Charles Gavan Duffy	Premier, Victoria
James Service	Premier, Victoria
Philip Fysh	Premier, Tasmania
B. R. Wise	Acting Premier, NSW
George Higinbotham	Attorney-General, Victoria
J. P. Abbott	Speaker, NSW
R. E. O'Connor	Vice-President of Executive Council
T. T. Ewing	Minister for Defence
Henry Copeland,	Minister for Lands, NSW
Julian Salomons	Vice-President, Executive Council, NSW

doubtless reflected the long run increase in the benefit of tariffs to industry relative to their harm to consumers. There could be no benefit to industry from protection when there was no industry to protect; a tariff would simply injure consumers. But as industry emerged and grew, its benefit from a tariff emerged and grew, and over the 19th century the balance of political significance tipped away from the consumer. The Federationist trade program – and so Federation – might be construed as part of the rising waters of protectionism, drawn by the pull of long-term structural change. Hence George Reid's rebuke of Parkes: 'when he met a parliament nearly half protectionist, and saw the tide rising, he jumped under the protectionist boat, rubbed out the motto of protection, and wrote federation on it'.[48]

And yet the significance of the interests of import-competing manufacturing as a driver of Federation should not be overworked. In the 1890s manufacturing contributed only about 12 percent of GDP. The £5.7m of manufacturing plant in NSW in 1900 palls in the face of £38.4m of capital in her railways. If manufacturing was so powerful, why were manufacturers strikingly absent from the parliaments and conventions of the 1890s? Of the 63 occupations recorded of the delegates to the Australasian Federal Convention of 1897-98, just one was a manufacturer.[49] Even in relatively industrialised Victoria, it appears only two of the 94 members of its Legislative Assembly at the time of the Federation referendums were manufacturers.[50]

Professional Federationists

The most fruitful location to search for an 'interest' animating the drive for Federation is not among producing activities, but in the professions, especially the church, the law and the army.

In the last decades of the 19th century, the professions were establishing that peculiarly prominent position they hold in Australian society:[51] swelling in numbers;[52] waxing in prestige;[53] gathering in legislatures;[54] organising their self-government;[55] recruiting the sons of squatters, capitalists and merchants;[56] and developing an ideology of self-justification. Between the Gog and Magog of Labour and Capital, there would advance a corps of professionals, conscientiously committing their expertise to the improvement of wider society.[57]

The idealism of the Federationist cause was at least consonant with professional ideology. But professionals would also benefit the most from Federation. Professionals are a natural ruling class when previous structures have been destroyed or subverted, being figures of trust and expertise, a vehicle of informal authority. Thus the 'civic or territorial nationalism' of the post-Second World War period – where the nation was defined in terms of an ex-colony – depended upon, and was almost synonymous with, the local professionals.

> *In the ex-colonies ... the lack of a developed civil society, the dominance of the state and its bureaucratic institutions and the need for communication skills ... placed the professionals in positions of leadership ... It was among these professionals (lawyers, doctors, engineers, journalists, teachers, etc.) that early civic and territorial nationalisms found their primary support.*[58]

And so it was in Australia.

The most venerable of the professions was, in general, supportive of Australian Federation, when not avid for it. Up and down the denominational scale – Congregational, Methodist, Presbyterian, Anglican and Catholic – clergymen of the 1890s proclaimed the glad tidings of the coming national union. Its palpable gratification to men of the cloth is not hard to construe. The new state would not seem forbidding. An abstract anti-clericalism was rare in Australia – Australians were a church-going people, if not religious.[59] A rigorous conception of the separation of church and state was American and foreign; did not Parkes's own *Public Instruction Act* require government schools to 'teach the cardinal principles of our common religion'?[60] Voters took no exception to an individual cleric openly involving themselves in public affairs, as distinct from a church doing so covertly. Doubtless, very few clergy of the 1890s actually saw themselves as future federal legislators, even if one did achieve that position in the inaugural parliament (J. B. Ronald, Labor, MHR). But the clergy saw itself as a valued complement to the organised expression of public life in Australia. And, more ambitiously, maintained, with respect to the approaching Commonwealth, that 'the Church' would be 'the conscience of the body corporate' and 'in the State as a power for good'.[61] A plan for a grander architecture for that state could only be gratifying.

It would take many pages even to begin to record the public pledges of clergy to the begetting of the Commonwealth, 'baptised', one declared, 'into the name of Him'.[62] Their activities including much hymn writing for the Convention and the Commonwealth; a special prayer for the Commonwealth by Cardinal Moran of Sydney, who on 'literally hundreds of occasions' had publicly advocated Federation, along with his Melbourne counterpart; the organisation of the Young Men's Federal Convention of 1897 by a Canon of St Andrew's Cathedral of Sydney; endless pro-Federation leaders of the former Methodist minister who edited the *Sydney Morning Herald* between 1886 and 1903;[63] the indiscreet Reverend Kelly's announcement to his congregation that Edmund Barton had been sent by God; and the Reverend Dr Bevan's declaration that voting Yes in federation referendums was 'a religious duty' which would 'fulfil the will of God'.[64] The unquenchable Reverend Dr was moved to compare the federal cause's tribulations with the Stations of the Cross, and the hoped for final victory to the Resurrection.[65]

The rewards which Federation would deliver to the profession of arms were more tangible. Although professional military forces in Australia were then new, the 'permanent forces' (those paid and full-time) amounted to 1 800 men, a not trivial number, and were overwhelmingly officers or specialists. And they were waxing in professional consciousness; manifested in the foundation of a United Services Institution in NSW in 1889, and by 1892 in Victoria, each with a journal and seminars. How these aspirational officers would benefit from a larger scale military force is evident. It is unsurprising that they readily co-operated with moves to federalise Australia's armed forces in the 1890s, and that their members could publicly express their frustration at capital and labour stalling over the advent of Federation.[66]

But the profession which would be most rewarded by Federation was the law, the ultimate profession of 19th century Australia; a community within a community, or, even better, a parallel community, which could easily bat away any attempt of any other profession (say, medicine) to resist its presumption.

No other profession could match the closeness of the law's self-government; the rigour of its barriers to entry; the effectiveness of its monopolisation of services; its almost hereditary lines of descent from one generation to another; its apartness from the rest of society; and the strength of its members' affective ties. The legal profession was an intense, still small, even intimate brotherhood, nourished by professional bodies, common education, shared employment history, intertwining friendships and, of course, briefs and appointments passing back and forth constantly between them.

The intensity of the law's professional solidarity was well-seen even in the least aloof of the three chapters of the legal profession, solicitors. In 1899 one prominent NSW solicitor observed of his fellow practitioners, without disapproval, 'the absolute line of demarcation that separates them from all other classes'. With a more distinct approbation, he noted 'there is something in the relations of solicitors which precludes estrangements ... [and] demands an habitual exercise of reasonable forbearance and complaisance of his fellow practitioners'. The upshot of this solidarity was that the junior branch of the legal profession was, in his words, 'singularly homogenous, united and apart'.[67]

The intensity of professional existence was still greater among barristers. They enjoyed additional barriers to entry, which were guarded by legislation, and defended by Barton and Samuel Griffith whenever an 'amalgamated' profession was proposed. An older hurdle in NSW – that an entrant to the bar be unsoiled by earning an income in any way in the twelve months prior to their admission – had been removed. But barristers in NSW remained immunised from contamination by the market by the requirement that their clients be solely solicitors. Barristers' removedness was reinforced by its own 'dress uniform' of wigs and coats, and their 'off-duty uniform' of frock coats and top hats. There were additional structures of self-management – the Bar Association from 1898, and the Bar Council from 1902, in which leading Federationist lawyers were prominent. The Bar's affective ties were strengthened by 'much bonhomie' at pleasant social fixtures, the requirement that students dine at law courts, and the congregation of barristers in three or four Chambers (no street address required), some residing there.[68] Jack Want was not mouthing pious hooey when he spoke of 'our brotherhood at the bar'. There was a brotherhood; one that would allow two enemies in politics to unite in matters of law. Thus Want, QC, could represent in court Barton, QC, in the latter's defamation case against the *Daily Telegraph*.[69] Or the free trader Reid represent the protectionist tub thumper Crick.[70] Or the conservative Josiah Symon defend the radical Kingston, when the future premier had been charged with duelling. Had they not been articled clerks together? Bonded to each other, and apart from society, 'most of the ablest barristers' were also 'identified in some degree with the government of the colony'. The second most senior cabinet ministry, the attorney-general, was reserved for barristers.

Judges comprised the most senior tier of the legal profession. A Queen's Counsel might easily out-earn a judge, but judges themselves received the highest salary inside, and perhaps outside, government. Sir Samuel Griffith was paid £3 500, compared to the equivalent £2 125 of a justice of the Supreme Court of the United States. He resided in a 'palatial' home in Brisbane 'indicative of his desire ... of remaining socially superior and aloof from most Queenslanders'.[71] Later, as justices of the High Court, Barton and O'Connor were to live, for a time, as virtual neighbours, just around from Admiralty House in Sydney. And no barrister, or cabinet minister, could expect to enjoy the particular dignities of these priest-kings of the legal profession. A judge on circuit, on the approach to a country court house, might be met and escorted by a detachment of mounted police in white helmets bearing long cavalry swords. Beyond the dignified parts of government, judges were well-acquainted with its efficient part; seven of the ten NSW supreme court justices of the 1890s had between them 67 years of membership of the NSW Parliament. Even after elevation to the bench, a judge might still assume executive function. Thus during the frequent absences of the Governor, the Chief Justice would usually assume the position of acting Governor (as Lieutenant-Governor), thereby acceding to all the vice-regal prerogatives, including chairing the Executive Council, administering oaths to new members of parliament, and sometimes opening parliament itself (as Griffith was to do in 1914). In this station, and sometimes addressed as Your Excellency,[72] a supplicant for mercy from judicial sentence might literally fall upon their knees when ushered into his presence, and worshippers would certainly rise from their pews upon his entrance to church. Of Samuel Griffith, the very epitome of the judge-governor, a loyal junior later wrote,

> *Always, it seems to me, he was in the position of St Paul's centurion, of a man who says to one 'Go' and he goeth, and to another 'Come' and he cometh, of one used to commanding ... Despite his condemnation of the existence of a master class, he himself was essentially of that class.*[73]

Australia's legal profession was indubitably a profession of unmatched wealth, power and prestige. In Australia's legal profession there was every appearance of a ruling class.

And for the legal profession the rewards of Federation were clearest and brightest. The drafting of any written constitution will draw essentially upon lawyers. Six of the ten delegates from NSW to the Australasian Federal Convention were legal practitioners, and so were six of the Victorian delegates. Federation also promised to establish a High Court, and four of those twelve lawyers would cap their careers by sitting there. It also promised a new form of law, constitutional law. The mountains of cases and opinions that would flow from the creation of a federal constitution could not have been fully foreseen; but Deakin's dictum that federalism is legalism would have been recognised. Finally, Federation meant an additional legislature, numbering 111 members, a type of body which disproportionally draws on lawyers. It is not surprising that the historian of the NSW Bar should write that, 'At no stage in the Bar's history was the influence of so many of its members exerted on behalf of the Commonwealth'.[74] To put the same thought another way, the nerve centre of the Federation movement coincided with a certain complex of barristers and judges: Barton, O'Connor, Reid, Wise, Griffith, Andrew Inglis Clark, Deakin, Isaac Isaacs, Kingston, John Downer, John Quick, Josiah Symon, Robert Garran, H. B. Higgins, Richard Baker, P. M. Glynn, Bruce Smith, W. H. James, N. E.

Lewis, Thomas Bavin, J. G. Drake and W. P. Crick. At the centre of the Australia political fish tank of the 1890s was a highly intelligent, jet-propelled, carnivorous, multi-armed tentacular organism.

Only one professional group could reasonably hope for even more from Federation than the law: civil servants. A wave of legislation in the 1890s had professionalised them by making the civil service 'independent' (that is, largely self-governing) and 'expert'. The inexpert beneficiaries of the old patronage were retrenched, and rigorous entrance examinations, set by civil servants, were instituted. This 'extremely painful' process had, from 1895, reduced the number of NSW civil servants by more than a quarter; so a new level of government would be more than consoling. Indeed, the prospects of an enhanced civil service were expressly advanced as an argument for Federation. One delegate to the Convention, J. T. Walker, commiserated that 'the colonial civil service has very little attraction to rising young men', as they were required to spend their time on 'estimates' hearings, and in answering the queries of MPs. But, he wrote, 'the establishment of the Federation should in time, make its civil service attractive to a considerable portion of the very elite of its youth'.[75]

The strength of the liaison between the civil service and Federation is well marked by the fact that of the six premiers who presided over Australia in the key period, 1895-1899, three were career bureaucrats prior to entering politics.[76]

The strength of the liaison between the civil service and Federation is further signalled by its long-standing. Half a century before Walker brandished the benefits of Federation to would-be bureaucrats, the pre-eminent civil servant of mid-19th century Australia had been directly responsible for the first moves to federate. It is acknowledged that the first person known to have proposed a 'central authority' in Australia superior to the separate governments of NSW, Victoria and other colonies was no firebrand politician, patriot statesman or visionary, but the principal public servant of NSW, Sir Edward Deas Thomson. In his thirty years of 'intimate connexion' with the government of NSW, Thomson was from 1828 until 1856, the chief advisor of all governors, the son-in-law of one, and the 'channel through which all the governor's correspondence flowed'. Historians concur that it was Thomson who, in 1846, advised Governor Fitzroy to recommend to the Colonial Office that it create 'a superior functionary' in Australia to review and possibly veto the Acts being produced by the separate legislatures in Sydney, Hobart and Adelaide.[77]

The 1890s again saw the salience of bureaucrats in the movement to Federation. The student of Federation might usefully ask: 'of all the stripes of Federationist, whose career was not only the most exclusively identified with Federation, but was also the most enduring, successful and fulfilling?' It may be argued that that person was not a politician, but Robert Garran, the longest serving 'permanent head' the Commonwealth has (so far) had. A product of Sydney Grammar School and the University of Sydney, in 1889 Garran completed a dissertation on 'federalism', nicely timed for the onset of the Federation episode. The new graduate 'pushed aside his anticipated career as an equity barrister for zealous involvement in the federation movement throughout the next decade'.[78] The clever, practical and equable young man was soon private secretary to George Reid and, with just a short pause, secretary to the drafting committee of the Australasian Federal Convention, where he found his verbal formulations 'wedging themselves into the bill'. So ubiquitous was Garran at these deliberations that he was often assumed to be a 'delegate' to the Conventions. Not simply an *éminence grise*, Garran was also an ardent public advocate of Federation; his *The Coming Commonwealth* of 1897 was read by 'everybody' and 'soon sold out'.[79] At the birth of the Commonwealth, the new polity was christened by his co-authoring the 1008 pages of *The Annotated Constitution of the Australian Commonwealth*, which, for 70 years, remained the bible of constitutional lawyers. On the first of January 1901, feeling like 'a junior barrister suddenly promoted to the final court of appeal', Garran was appointed by Alfred Deakin to be Secretary to the Attorney-General's Department – the first appointment of the new Commonwealth Government – and hurriedly issued that day, handwritten, its first Gazette. For the next 31 years Garran was the Department's permanent head, ultimately assuming, as Solicitor-General, many duties of the Attorney-General's position and, in 1919, numbered among Australia's delegates to the Paris Peace Conference.

As the Commonwealth made Garran's career, so it made the careers of other civil servants who will appear in these pages, including Atlee Hunt and Thomas Bavin. But perhaps the epitome of the mutually beneficial interdependence between Federation and the lawyer-bureaucrat is the career of Lieutenant-General James Legge. Also educated at Sydney Grammar School and the University of Sydney, he read law in the same chambers as Garran. One fruit of these years was his *Selection of Supreme Court Cases in New South Wales from 1825 to 1862*, a two-volume work, soon to be known as 'Legge's Reports', and 'constantly quoted in legal arguments'. He put aside the law to become a permanent officer in the NSW defence force, benefitting from the patronage of its commander, the imperial soldier Edward Hutton. Active in the United Services Institution, in 1899 Legge delivered a proposal for an 'Australian Defence Force', which would be 90 000 strong and based on the compulsory military training of men between 20 and 25 years of age. Shortly after, he departed for South Africa, where he was principal administrative staff officer of the 1st NSW Mounted Rifles, and intelligence officer to the Australian Brigade. The advent of the Commonwealth quickened his prospects. In 1903 he was secretary to the committee drafting the Defence Act, and in 1904 was made honorary aide-de-camp to the Governor-General. Late in 1906 he declined a lectureship in military science at Sydney University in order to begin to work directly under the Minister for Defence, as chief planner of a complete re-foundation of the Commonwealth army on the basis of compulsory military training. He was now the favourite man-at-arms of Deakin and the Minister for Defence of the period, Thomas Ewing; 'inseparable' claimed the *Melbourne Punch*. Finishing this task, the position of Military Secretary to the Military Board was created for Legge. Following his appointment to membership of the Board itself, he was made Australia's representative in England at the Imperial General Staff. And, as if Mars was looking down over him, just before the outbreak of the First World War, Legge was appointed Chief of the General Staff of the Australian Army. And then the ultimate prize: on May 1915 Legge was made commander of the Australian Imperial Force. So it was that a bureaucrat-soldier, with combat experience limited to a few weeks in South Africa, was made the captain-general of Australia's gathered legions.

But in this affinity of the bureaucrat to Federation there lay more than just palpable personal advantage; one may see at the centre of Federation the operation of an entire sphere of life, 'organisation'.

The organisational impulse

'Organisation' is a sphere of life born of an impulse to regularity; which operates through acts of 'public ordering', involving uniformity and arrangement, resulting in rules, systems, and 'plans'; where the disconnected is now connected, and arrayed in logical pattern. The epitome of organisation is the 'bureaucratic', but it encompasses far more than government administration, or those huge state enterprises which constituted Australia's largest employers in the late 19th century.[80] It includes 'organised knowledge', or science. The sphere of organisation also juts a considerable distance into the law. A certain amount of legal activity is plainly administration. Beyond the mundane motions of the suburban law firm, the codification of laws lies within the sphere of organisation. Certain senior Federationists were avid legal codifiers: thus Samuel Griffith, who industriously codified the entire criminal law for Queensland, and saw his labour inaugurated on the very day of national unity, 1 January 1901. Or Richard O'Connor, on whose initiative in May 1893 a Statute Law Consolidation Commission was established for the same organising purpose.[81] But even more signal of the kinship of the law and organisation is the legal officer who does not merely codify what exists, but who actually articulates some code – the Commissioner, that is to say, 'the bureau judge'. Such are highly kindred to bureaucracy, are salient figures in Australian life, and have been made prolific by Federation.

Organisation in its several manifestations – government, science and law – has been powerful in Australia from its genesis. Australia began as a piece of administration. The apex of the management of colonial Australia was itself a bureaucracy; the Colonial Office, which, in the key mid-century period, was presided over by James Stephen, a 'strict legalist' with a 'passion for system and uniformity'.[82] And it cannot be assumed that this style of governance receded with the advent of self-government in the 1850s. 'The most enduring feature of any colonial regime,' it has been said, 'one of the first to appear and the last to leave, is the administrator, the colonial bureaucrat, high, middle and low'.[83]

Federation, as the 'Fathers' conceived it, was congruent with the sphere of organisation, so well developed in Australia. In functional terms, the nature of Federation exhibited an essential correspondence with the three key ordering moves of the sphere of organisation: the imposition of uniformity; the construction of hierarchy; and the elimination of competition.

Federation, the 'Fathers' hoped, would be useful in inhibiting competition, the great disrupter of organisation, and the essential tool of the rival rationality, the market. It was Thomson who implored a 'federal agreement … so that the different colonies may not be found, endeavouring as it were to outbid each other'.[84] And so federalisation has remained fertile in anti-competitive schemes, ranging from weather bureaus in differing jurisdictions agreeing not to forecast the weather of their neighbours,[85] or Queensland Premier Sir Thomas McIlwraith proposing the Federal government be allocated excise tax to prevent tax competition by the colonies,[86] or Deakin airing the thought that the passing of a Commonwealth compulsory arbitration act would, by extending Victoria's labour regulations to NSW, 'mitigate' the cost disadvantage which those regulations imposed on Victoria.[87]

Federation, as construed by the 'Fathers', would also be a federation of uniformity, a quality acutely cognate with law-likeness, and thus the ordering impulse of bureaucracy, and so cherished by it. Federation was seen as a means to that uniformity, in everything from railway gauges to gambling laws.[88] The history of telegraphy provides a clinching illustration of the triangular nexus between uniformity, bureaucratisation, and Australian federation. In the generation before Federation, 'intercolonial conferences' of the six ministers of Postal and Telegraphs were frequent. Although conducted at a 'ministerial level', 'senior technical bureaucrats ... readily took the initiative in tendering advice and drafting submissions to politicians and wielded enormous influence over ministers'.[89] The most senior of these technical bureaucrats was Charles Todd, hero of the overland telegraph to Darwin, expert on all things electrical, and Postmaster-General of South Australia from 1870 to 1905. In 1893 another 'Postal and Telegraph' conference took place in Brisbane, with the aim of settling the issue of time zones. Todd held no ministerial position, but, nevertheless, was South Australia's representative. Remarkably, he persuaded that conference to resolve to establish a single time zone for the whole of Australia. This meant that in Perth, at the summer solstice, the sun would rise at 8.14 am, and, in the winter solstice, at 9.17 am. This eccentric proposal was 'strongly urged' by Todd, and adopted without dissent. It was Thomas McIlwraith, the Premier of Queensland, who pressed the rescission of this weird decision; and it was reversed in the subsequent Conference of 1894, never to be heard of again.[90] But McIlwraith was, evidently, blind to the call for 'a nation for a continent', and at the critical referendum of 1899 urged Queenslanders to vote No to putting Queensland in 'hands of men unacquainted with the past, and who cannot in full share our hopes for the future'.[91]

Federation, finally, amounted to a means of accommodating another bureaucratic value, which, on the face of it, is hostile to equality: hierarchy. Hierarchy may be considered a way of conferring order when uniformity is either unobtainable, or not useful. If everything cannot be made equal, the compulsion to order requires that any given thing be classed as unambiguously superior to, or inferior to, or 'corresponding to', every other thing. The end point of this ordering by ramification is the familiar branching hierarchy, with a single summit or fount, and might be contrasted with less hierarchical orderings such as 'the network'. Australian federation, in the caricature that prevails today, is obviously a branching hierarchy, with a 'headquarters', in Canberra, at the summit.

Hence Federation may be interpreted as a culmination of the bureaucratic impulse which seems planted so deep in Australia's *modus operandi*. And yet it would be an exaggeration to say the organisational impulse 'demanded' Federation. The impulse to organise will find other devices to pursue its ideals of monopoly, uniformity, and hierarchy. The impulse had found such devices before the Commonwealth existed: thus the Intercolonial Conferences,[92] the Premiers' Conferences, and the Federal Council of Australasia. These all had a strong flavour of the committee about their conduct; resembling more a pooling of information in the quest of a commonly acknowledged 'correct' answer, rather than a parliamentary contest of differences.

And to say Federation was a culmination of the organisational impulse is not to say that impulse has never served the country. Plausibly, Australia's context had rationally swollen the organisational sphere. The incomprehension of the country's natural resource base conferred a great utility on applied science. The total absence of property rights and customary law made for an intense demand for legalism. And the highly urbanised nature of settlement may have made social organisation especially useful.

But none of these possible uses of organisation in Australia demanded Federation. For all of these uses of organisation had been actively pursued in the 19th century by the distinct governments of the 'six Australias'. And all six had commonly cooperated when 'organisation in concert' seemed beneficial.[93] The doubter might counter by citing the co-existence in the Australia of 1901 of three distinct railway gauges. This multiplicity of gauges scandalises the organisational impulse, and was a staple of rhetorical appeals for Federation. But the differences in rail gauges amounted to a difference in capital intensity in rail transport, and, to some degree, rationally reflected the greater productivity of capital on busier routes, just as larger bridges in larger towns do. The multiplicity of gauges may have been anticompetitive by incidental consequence, and, therefore, socially costly. But before 1901 the key instrument in managing railways, for better or worse, was pricing policy. Thus the endless negotiations over railways pricing policy in devising the Constitution, while gauges themselves received only oratorical attention. In these negotiations Federationists wanted the Commonwealth to restrict the railways of NSW and Victoria from price-competing for markets – such competition was, in their language, 'jealousy'. But such competition of the different states' railways meant lower prices for everyone who used a railway, directly or indirectly. It also led to some freight being railed at greater cost than necessary, just as permitting a high cost business to compete with a low cost monopoly will mean some output is produced at 'unnecessarily' high cost. The upshot is that whether the extinction of railways' price competition by Commonwealth control would have done more good than harm is beyond any rational and confident prediction.

So we conclude were we began, with railways, and no clear economic case for Federation.

3

Was Federation nationalist in credo?

> *The moonlight of a milder clime*
> *Is round me pour'd o'er scenes sublime:*
> *But I would fly from all earth's light and grandeur*
> *to behold tonight my native land!*
>
> – Henry Parkes

If the Federation did not serve economic rationality, was it instead a recoil of the social web's centre from the intrusions of those at the margins? Was it a wish to reshape politics in conformity with that web? Was the new Commonwealth a discharge of the great political volcano of the century which followed 1848, 'nationalism'? A glancing scrutiny of Federation encourages that thought. The union of a population which was culturally homogenous but politically fragmented into distinct colonies does have the appearance of a nationalist episode. But appearances mislead. Australian Federation lacked the hallmark signs of a nationalist movement; its emotional core was not the cleansing of the community of the alien consciousness; and it did not attempt the defining deed of the nationalist mission: the conferral of sovereignty upon the nation. It was not rooted in a sense that the supreme political identity was an Australian one. On the contrary, the leading strain of Federation was, in fundamental intention, imperial: to fasten Australia more securely to the Empire.

The closest Federationists came to a nationalism was their commonly expressed aspiration to 'make a nation'. But their distance from the kind of nationalism that was shaking the world in their lifetimes remained decisive. Whereas the goal of a classical nationalism was to free a nation, the goal of these Federationists was to make one. Whereas the classical nationalist was pledged to deliver a new state to an old nation, these Federationists were undertaking to conjure up a new nation for a new state. Above all, whereas the classical nationalists saw the consummation of their endeavours as an independent and sovereign nation, in their nationalism's strange tasting brew of assertion and submission, Federationists aimed to create a colonial nation. Not a nation state, but a nation colony. This plausibly delayed an uncolonial nation. Australia's nationalist trajectory over the 20th century was, if anything, delayed by Federation.

The British Empire nation

> *I am an Englishman!*
> – John See, Federationist Premier of NSW[94]

The official Federation movement – of Conventions, Leagues and Parties – was almost devoid of the *style, incitement, program* and essential *object* of a fully-fledged classic nationalist movement.

Federation lacked the unfailing *style* of nationalist political movement. Their invocations of Australia were mechanical, even insipid; they lacked the vital rhetoric,[95] the reverent usage of symbols, the allusions to mythic history, the exalting of past heroes, and the genuflection to cultural icons which typify nationalist political movements. Illustratively, the Federation movement, as a whole, never settled on a national flag: the closest it came was the opportunistic appropriation in New South Wales and Queensland of the NSW Ensign, for 18 months from mid-1898. Such an emblem could not expect any great favour in other colonies, and it was quickly discarded by Federationists after the inauguration of the Commonwealth. But, then, who needed a national flag? The Union Jack was more than satisfactory. Thus Parkes in 1890: 'When I talk of a national flag I mean nothing that is not perfectly in accord with the flag of England'. Of the same, Reid in 1895 declared, to cheers, at a Federationist meeting that no man 'could live under a nobler flag'. In 1900 a Federationist MP in South Australia was moved to tear a flag from a Government House flag pole which was not the Union Jack, but which offensively bore local symbolism.[96]

The absence of such marks of nationalism arose from the Federationists' lack of nationalism's *incitement*: a resentment by those near the nerve centre of the social web of any society to claims of those at its margin, be they rich or poor, proud or humble, weak or strong.[97] Accordingly, the Federationist movement did not pursue the most salient marginal group in Australia: Irish Catholic immigrants and their children, who, in one protesting memory, remained for fifty years 'a breed apart, firebranded like travelling stock in a strange country so that all might know whence they came'.[98] On the contrary, the Federationist movement took care to keep this group on side. It is true that some Federationists did resent certain margin dwellers: some thickly fumed at the Chinese; almost all repudiated any rights of the Kanaka. And Barton was free in tracing Federation's tap root to a hostility to these and their like.[99] 'I say that if there is a kernel to this federation question it lies in the coloured labour question'.[100] This may bespeak a nationalist revulsion at margin dwellers. But Barton's several remarks of this kind seem more simply classifiable as racial chauvinism than nationalism. There was, he said, 'a natural antagonism between white man and black'.[101]

Federationists lacked the *program* of a nationalist movement: the ridding of foreign accretions to, and invasions of, the national soul. Concomitantly, it lacked an ideologist to ordain such a purification. The closest the Federation cause came to such was Inglis Clark. There was a strain of nationalism in the Tasmanian, and he was reminiscent of the nationalist doctrinaire: the intellectual 'little magazine', the picture of Mazzini over a fireplace, the inspiration by a power rivalrous to the imperial one – in his case the USA. But this semi-hemi-demi nationalist was awkwardly askew the Federation cause. Despite the hopeful urgings of Federationists, Clark abstained from supporting the cause in its climactic campaigns. He absented himself from its Convention, its rallies, and its hustings. A week before the 1898 Federation referendum he made it publicly known that 'It is not his intention to advise any elector on how to vote'.[102]

Above all else, Federationism lacked the defining, *supreme goal* of classical nationalism: the conferral of a sovereign state on the nation. This defining goal of the nationalist becomes particularly luminous when the nation does not even 'share' sovereignty, but has none at all; that is, when the nation is a colony. But, if there is a patent constitutional truth about the Commonwealth of Australia which was sought and secured by Federationists, it is that it would be a British colony; a 'self-governing colony', as the *Commonwealth of Australia Constitution Act* puts it. This truth was fully recognised and supported by the Convention; pressed by Federationist leaders in the inaugural Parliament; plainly articulated by the movement's 'official ideologists', Quick and Garran;[103] and underlined by Federationists' insertion in the Constitution of section 59:

> *The Queen may disallow any law within one year from the Governor-General's assent, ...*

Thus an Act may pass the two houses of the Commonwealth's Parliament, and receive the assent of the Governor-General, and yet be 'disallowed' by the Queen, on the advice, of course, of her ministers in London. So who could ultimately take charge was clear. Note that this section was not inserted, say, at the behest of the Colonial Office, and conceded by Federationists, as a (hopefully) passing price of a step forward towards sovereignty: it was inserted by the Federationists, at their own initiative, in the earliest versions of the Constitution. This makes a telling contrast to the treatment of royal 'disallowance' in the struggle for self-government of NSW in the 1850s. In accord with Wentworth's Remonstrances of 1850 and 1851, the *Constitution Act of NSW 1853* restricted the royal veto to laws concerning naturalisations, external affairs, defence and treason. The Act was, in the event, referred by the governor to Her Majesty, and her ministers were 'unable to advise her to assent' on account of these restrictions. But Wentworth did travel to London to defend the bill in all its clauses.[104]

Those who clamoured 'to see the flag of the Southern Cross flying' were not the Federationists like Parkes and Barton, but leading anti-Federationists of Parkes's parliamentary opposition – George Dibbs and his followers, who declared two-thirds of the countryside were republican, and vowed to oppose 'any system of federation that is not coupled with the glorious principles of independence'.[105]

Rather than typify the nationalist anti-colonial movement,

Federation would be better described as an exercise in Empire-ism; an attempt to achieve 'a more perfect union' between colony and its Mother Country; a step towards the 'consolidation of the Empire' in the words of one Federationist; 'a stage in the growth of the Empire' in the words of Wise, in which Australia would become an integral component of a Greater Britain dappling the globe. This aspiration was given its most pure and candid expression by 'imperial federationists', and their slogan found in Federationist demonstrations, 'One Flag, One Fleet, One Throne'.[106] The oneness was of Australia and Britain.

This Empire-ism was, unsurprisingly, supported by the Colonial Office, its Secretary of State, and the governors they appointed. This support was a manifestation of the unprecedentedly confident and, even, affectionate, relations between Imperial power and local Australian governments in the 1890s. Gone were the days of the unhappy collision of Australian governments' sense of right with the Imperial insistence on its established prerogatives. Queensland saw several such rows in the 1880s,[107] which had provoked into being a 'National Party' of Thomas McIlwraith, which won power in 1888 with a goal of 'Australia for the Australians' and, even, Federationists complained, the 'complete separation of Australia from the British Empire'.[108] But within a few years, the sources of contention were dissolved, with 'Papua' incorporated into the British Empire, governors now chosen in consultation with the local ministry, the prerogative of mercy effectively invested in the premier, and the local defence forces firmly under the direction of the minister rather than the governor. By the mid-1890s McIlwraith was politically *hors de combat*; his opposition to the Federation Bill disregarded by Queensland, and his 'right nationalism' – of himself, Douglas of Tasmania and, perhaps, Baker of South Australia – proving irrelevant to the movement to Federation, as was the fringe 'left republicanism' of NSW, with which it coincided.[109]

The upshot was that the 1890s was a period of sweet music between Governors and their ministers. Perhaps the most important of these Government House harmonies was the 'sustaining friendship' between Lord Carrington and Parkes. The third Baron Carrington 'captivated' Parkes',[110] whose 'determination in 1889 to promote Federation arose largely from their conversations'.[111] 'Carrington's diplomatic work through the governors in Victoria and South Australia was crucial in paving the way for the Conference of 1890'.[112] This effectual vice-regal busyness prompts the question: to what degree does the Commonwealth owe itself to these envoys of the Colonial Office?

Plastic nationalists

To say the Federationist movement was not a nationalist movement is not to say no publicist or politician supporting federation ever adopted a nationalist stance. But, however sincere they may have been in their own mind, these stances were inauthentic. Their nationalisms were the nationalisms of *careerism*, *proxyism* and *surrogatism*.

The Australian scene of the latter 19th century included a sprinkle of career provocateurs, who could draw the eyes of the crowd by a stance of Australian rebellion.[113] Their falsity need not be laboured; these were not serious politicians. A greater significance lay in the arrival in Australia of political adventurers from afar, who felt they found in local nationalism a propellant for their own career. The distribution of this species of careerist in the Age of Nationalism was worldwide, and has been well-described by Charles King:

> *Peripheral nations attract committed intercessors. Over the last two centuries, the cause of almost every sizeable cultural group from Central Europe to the Arabian Peninsula and beyond has been taken up by one or another traveller, journalist, adventurer, or ne'er-do-well intent on finding in the often disorganized resistance to imperial rule a germ of national sentiment that might be put to some political use. ... they also brought with them a clear and often inflated sense of their own importance on the ground. ... Some ascribed to themselves the role of nation-maker. They imagined themselves as not only advocates for dispossessed nationalities but also as the midwives of national rebirth, calling inchoate nations into existence.*[114]

Charles Gavan Duffy is the definitive example of the 'committed intercessor' in Australian Federation.[115] This Irish nationalist émigré, freshly removed to Melbourne from a deadlocked career in London, was not the first to moot the idea of Australian Federation. But he was the most tenacious in pressing it, and the boldest in vision. On account of his 'vast labours' as 'the only heart-and-soul federalist among prominent men' of the 1860s,[116] it was tolerably fair for Deakin to begin his account of the 'federal story' with Duffy. But, tellingly, in the face of frustrations of his labours – and a secured pension – Duffy returned to London in 1880 for a new political career, where he entreated Henry Parkes to leave the 'waterhole in the Lachlan' and join him at the 'tide of the Atlantic'.[117]

Duffy not only exemplifies the career nationalist; he has a double significance, for he is also an exemplar, among Federationists, of proxy nationalism; a 'false flag nationalism', whereby, in fighting under the flag of the current cause, one actually fights for another. Duffy had arrived in Australia in 1855 after foiling a charge of treason for Irish nationalist agitation. Duffy's Irish nationalism was, to be sure, not Fenianism, but the eminently constitutional cause of Home Rule, led by John Redmond, which aimed through the (unsuccessful) Government of Ireland Bill of 1893 to federalise the United Kingdom, by endowing an Irish parliament with powers over internal matters. To many Irish Australian eyes, there was an equivalence between Irish Home Rule and Australian Federation. To support one was to support the other. To fight for a federated Australia was to fight for Home Rule. Indeed, the new Commonwealth Parliament was quick to commit itself formally to Home Rule.[118] Accordingly, Federationists sometimes discovered that by identifying themselves as Home Rule sympathisers, they could suddenly transform a hesitant crowd of Irish-born into one jubilantly acclaiming the coming of the Commonwealth.[119] And not only the crowd felt this way: senior Australian Federationists committed to Home Rule included Richard Edward O'Connor (an 'ardent supporter' of Home Rule); William McMillan ('I cannot read the history of English rule in Ireland, it is too horrible'[120]); and Patrick Glynn, who helped host John Redmond's 'lively' tour of Australia in 1882-1883. Home Rule, wrote Glynn, 'means Federation'.[121]

Clearly, the federationism of Irish Australians has little Australianist root, reflecting the unrecognised truth that Irish Catholics in Australia were commonly aloof, if not cold, to Australianism. They resented their imperial oppressor; and the oppressor's far flung brood was fortunate to receive no more than their disregard.[122] They were confident they bore a culture superior to that of their oppressor and, in turn, to its scratchy mirror in the south. Corroboratingly, the Irish Australians of the Federation period made little contribution to the Australianist cultural surge.[123] As one Irish Australian observer of the period put it, 'Nationalism seems always a hackneyed, slightly ludicrous theme to a people of a different race'.[124]

The closest the Irish came to a positive attitude to Australianism is in the form of *surrogate nationalism*, where the New Country is the fulfilment of a love of the Old Country, and becomes a substitute for the Old. Cardinal Moran was certainly a proxy nationalist, but he also illustrates surrogate nationalism. In his manifesto in favour of Federation he declared, 'I love the little shamrock of my native land. That shamrock transplanted to Australia retains all its vigour and freshness, but emulating the land to which it is transferred expands its triple leaf like a giant growth'.[125] Australia as a New Ireland. Australia as a useful means to another end; there was nothing Australianist about this. On the contrary, Moran's conduct of his Australian episcopate was so utterly 'transplantational', so disregarding of any Australian context, he was a sharp point of what has been called Irish imperialism in Australia.[126]

A surrogate nationalism need not be Irish. It could be British. So not a New Ireland, but a New Britain. John Quick, perhaps even more vital to Federation than Alfred Deakin, was, in his own words, committed to 'building up a New Britain under a Southern Cross'.[127] Parkes hoped for 'a new England under these sunny skies'.[128] In accordance with his surrogate nationalism, Parkes could construe Australian Federation in terms of the central crisis of English political history. The Federation cause, he told Barton, was the same as that which their forefathers had died for: the Federation struggle would be a rematch of the 17th century contest between oaken-hearted parliamentarians and the 'vile Stuarts'. But this time his Commonwealth would win.

A defender of a nationalist interpretation of Federation may retort that the fact that the Federation movement was not a nationalist one does not imply nationalist sentiment was not fostering of Federation. Perhaps the Federation movement was *misperceived* as nationalist, and so supported by persons of nationalist sentiment. Or perhaps, for all its Empire-ist intentions, Federation was 'objectively' nationalist in its inevitable effects – unificationist and republican – and genuine nationalists realised it to be so, and so also supported it.

The difficulty with Federation being mistaken for a nationalist cause by nationalists – or its Empire-ism being seen through by a nationalist – was that nationalism as a sentiment in Australia was so weak.

There was not much national identity amongst the broader population in Australia, or even the Federation movement. True: many inhabitants had expressed an Australian identity since at least the 1830s.[129] But any Australian identity was just one of many identities (I am a worker, I am a Methodist, I am a 'government man', I am a 'cornstalk' ...), and it was a subordinate identity rather than a national one; it was not the 'ultimate' identity, the identity that is the basis of sovereignty. Thus the popular hypothesis that a 'dual identity' prevailed at the time of Federation – both Australian and British – is not wrong. The Rose and the Waratah – so delicately paired in plaster in Bruce Smith's Anglewood – expressed a genuine sentiment of dual identity. But any Australian identity was not the identity which, in nationalist ideology, would underlie the state. Australian identity at the close of the 19th century might be compared to Scottish identity in Scotland at the same time – distinctly felt, but not the basis of sovereignty. The ultimate 'identity' of almost all Australians and 'Federation fathers' – the identity would be the foundation of Sovereignty – was being British (as in Scotland). Thus Sir Henry Edward Braddon, premier of Tasmania and assiduous Federationist, declared to the Australasian Federal Convention that we are all 'Britons'. Note the simplicity of his descriptor; not 'British-Australians' 'Australian-Britons', not even 'Britishers'. Britons, plain and simple. In fact, the sense of being Britons was the basis of Federation. What unified the inhabitants of the continent was not that they were Australian but that they were British, as Parkes declared, in 1890, to the 'vociferous cheering' of Federation delegates: 'the crimson thread of kinship runs through us all. Even the native-born Australians are Britons, as much as the men born within the cities of London or Glasgow.'[130]

The Britannic sentiments of Federationists were encouraged by a seeming relaxation over the preceding generation of relations between the immigrant and native-born in NSW; a fading, at least in NSW, of the resentment of the native-born of the British-born, which was so piercingly voiced in 1867 by Geoffrey Barton at a public meeting called to express loyalty to the throne. Gone was that fissure that prompted a taking of sides; and which might lead a British-born to consider themselves an Australian.

> *I may have been an English infant, but as a man I am an Australian.*
> – Sir John Robertson, Anti-Federationist[131]

Now, it seemed, there was a confidence that the native-born really was English.

> *Although an Australian, I am at heart an Englishman.*
> – John Downer, Federationist[132]

Reinforcing the secondary character of any Australian identity was a weakness in Australian patriotism: there is not much sign of any real admiration or attachment to Australia *as it was* in the political shapers of Federation. On the contrary, among the native-born elite, a certain hauteur towards local society may be detected; an hauteur which provoked Dorothea Mackellar in 1908 to pen in protest, 'I Love a Sunburnt Country', in the home of her father, Charles Mackellar, a prominent anti-Federationist, NSW MP and personal physician to John Robertson.[133] Among immigrant Federationists there were palpable flecks of disdain,[134] disappointment, and alienation from Australia. The gold rush immigrants had been 'a tremendously British and loyal generation' and 'there was little sense among them of migrating in despair, or rejecting the old country'.[135] On the contrary, in embarking for the goldfields, the diggers, in the words of one witness, 'came not to settle but to make money and go home to old friends'.[136]

Inevitably, for many, arriving in a state of animated anticipation, the new land delivered, in Ethel Richardson's words, 'the usual disappointments'.[137] And disillusion was not restricted to diggers. Consider the 'father of federation'. To Henry Parkes, Australia was 'far more wicked than I had ever conceived it possible for any place to be'.[138] Granted, Parkes was excited at what had been done in Australia in his lifetime and, even more, by the 'great Empire of Australasia' he looked forward to.[139] He was, indeed, a man of vision. But this patriotism of Parkes was a piece of self-love; he had assimilated the country to himself. Its past of vigorous ascent was his own past; its glorious future would be his own future. He patently felt himself to be an Australian Gladstone; he would be the prime minister of a New Britain.

Corresponding to a lack of Australian patriotism was an absence of anti-British sentiment from the political elite and the great bulk of the population, despite later attempts to write a 1980s nationalism into Australia versus England sporting contests and, in particular, the violent affray at a cricket match in Sydney on 2 February 1879. That ugly affair was not, in fact, between England and Australia – it was between England and NSW, and the provocation was a ruling by a Victorian umpire. And the enmity is best construed as violence between the fans of different clubs of a 'British Empire League'. That same sense of the Australian team simply being one club of the 'Empire League' could, more happily, produce an outbreak of cheering when news broke of Australia merely beating the Surrey XI. Even the club analogy overestimates the typical sense of conflict. Thus Australia's cricketing triumph over England in Melbourne in 1897 during the Federal Convention – misrepresented by 20th century Federationists as a day of national glee – was represented at the time by cartoonists in terms of a pre-adolescent boy outpacing his bewhiskered 'Dad'. The British, their sportsmen and immigrants, were definitely 'family'.[140] They were most definitely not 'Poms', and would not be until the First World War. In 1901 a 'pommy' was a Pomeranian dog.

The national pride of most Federationists was Britain. The Federationists, with many other Australians, felt *patriotic* about Britain.[141] Quick and Garran in their massive anatomy of the

Commonwealth's Constitution exalt in the 'thrilling' victory at the Plains of Abraham in 1759 of 'our troops'.[142] The only national pride which in the 1890s could compete with a pride in Britain was a pride in Ireland. Indeed, the cause of Federation strangely coincided with a peak of Irish nationalism in Australia: just as Australians were supposedly wreathing themselves in the wattle blossom, many were sporting 'the green'. St Patrick's Day was declared a public holiday in NSW in 1900.[143] In 1899, in the midst of Federation struggle, Richard O'Connor, with the very public support of fellow Federationist, Cardinal Moran, and a fellow National Federal Party candidate, J. T. Toohey, successfully sponsored the establishment of new volunteer infantry unit in NSW, the Irish Rifles. The three favoured the unit's adoption of a green uniform as '... appealing more to the national ideas of the Irish volunteers'.[144] At the time of the 1898 Convention, O'Connor (with Glynn) was participating in the erection in Waverley Cemetery of an imposing 'centenary memorial' to the Irish Rebellion of 1798, and its hallowing by an elaborate ceremonial re-interment there of one of '98's heroes. This sort of civic sacrament, which the Irish were so committed to, is entirely missing from the Federationist agitation for a Commonwealth. Truly, NSW saw more of an effort in 1888 to celebrate the centenary of settlement in 1788, and to forge and commemorate past heroes, than anything occurring in the entire Federationist movement.[145] Even Sydney's statue of Arthur Phillip in 1897 was a long delayed initiative of Parkes's from the Centennial year. The statue was despised by the *Bulletin*, and neither Reid nor Barton attended its opening ceremony. The Women's Hospital fete engaged Barton that afternoon.

The culture clue

But the case for nationalist force behind Federation is not restricted to the discharge of an emotion directly upon political activity. Perhaps what impelled Federation were not matters of feeling – such as pride and resentment – but the emergence of new reality, regardless of whether anyone had realised it: the actual and objective emergence of an Australian nation. What would be the sign of such a reality? The enticing conception of the nation as a

Opposite: Cardinal Moran, inspecting the Irish Rifles

distinct cultural object encourages the thought that culture may provide that sign.

Might not the boom in literary authorship in Australia at the time of Federation indicate the quickening of an Australian nation? In the 1860s a total of 194 works of fiction and verse were published in Australia. In the 1870s the figure came to 325; in the 1880s, 429; and in the 1890s, 729.[146] A doubter might put this Australian literary boom of the Nineties down to 'the age' rather than 'the nation'. Federation occurred in perhaps the most intensely 'literary' age ever. Never were more people literate; never had so many politicians fancied themselves as literary.[147] The Nineties, a doubter might say, was simply a high tide effect; whereby the Antipodean literary boat simply rose with all the others. But the Nineties was not just a matter of quantity. Did not the Nineties see a creative effort that involved – not just an Australian subject matter – but a treatment of subject not found earlier, a sensibility not found elsewhere, and a concern with 'problems' not tackled in other places; which was local in immediate provenance, and which, to some degree, only local 'audiences' could 'hear'? In three familiar heads,

> The sudden birth of 'Federation' architecture.
>
> The Heidelberg School of painting.
>
> The verse, stories and novels of Lawson, Paterson, Furphy and Franklin; perhaps the purest grist for a nationalist interpretation of the Nineties. Along with the 'astonishing' *Bulletin*, which 'spoke to' so many more Australians than any journalism had before. [148]

The Nineties, therefore, may be plausibly described as culture with nationality; having sufficient localness in method, provenance and audience to demonstrate that its creators were not members of a European nation, nor members of a European nation pretending to be members of a (perhaps non-existent) Australian nation. The cultural surge of the 1890s seems proof of the existence of national community.

But the thesis that the Nineties was a sign of the reality of an Australian nation – which would have underpinned Federation – is troubled on several accounts.

Perhaps the least threat to the thesis is posed by the obviously large debts the Nineties owed to Britain. The Federation architectural style had a palpable provenance in British taste of the period and, until 1969, was known as 'Queen Anne' style, when a prominent left-nationalist critic (Bernard Smith) baptised it 'Federation style'. Lawson's uses of Dickensian models has been pressed by some critics. Others have suggested Furphy's *Such is Life* 'invites comparison with the numerous late nineteenth century European and American novels that present "scenes of provincial life"'.[149] To the same conclusion, it has been argued that mislabelling the Heidelberg School as 'Australian impressionism' has 'obscured the essential Britishness' of the movement, which 'belonged within the international movements of high toned *plein-air*-ism'.[150] And did not Streeton declare his 'instinct is English' and avow 'British supremacy'? But the booming of Empire sentiment by artists hardly suffices to make work 'essentially English'; what the nationalist account of Federation seeks is not 'nationalist art' but 'art with a nationality'. To the same conclusion, borrowing English models hardly makes a piece of literature 'essentially English': the nationalist explanation of Federation does not require art which expresses *only* nationality.

A greater menace to the nationalist account of Federation is that the flare of 'offensively Australian' literature was of barely ten years' duration – beginning in 1896 and over by the early years of the 20th century. The exactness of the coincidence of the flare with Federation could be gratifying to a nationalist – but the sudden brevity of it all is unnerving. And the quantity of activity may be misrepresented by its quality: 'the nineties, often thought prolific in valuable and representative works are really rather thin. Only two volumes of Lawson's tales, and only one volume of Paterson's verse, for instance, appeared before 1900'.[151] The Nineties, which the nationalist would revel in, was, in a word, slight. Correspondingly, the supposed bullhorn of Nineties cultural nationalism, the forthrightly Federationist *Bulletin*, was not in fact so. Its editor's 'admiration for things American ... was exceeded ... only by a love of things French';[152] its literary criticism 'represented a radical turning away from the principles of literary nationalism';[153] and the 'heroes of the stockwhip and the wattle blossom ... scarcely existed in the *Bulletin*'.[154]

And there remains a still greater menace to interpreting the Nineties as a sign of a quickening in Australian nationhood: the geography of the thing, at least in literature. For in literature the Nineties was a Sydney event, not at all a Melbourne one; and Federation was weakest in Sydney, and strongest in Melbourne. This awkwardness is only reinforced by the fact that Melbourne's literary life was vigorous, and more permeated by a 'sense of exile' than a national feeling;[155] the 'highly fashionable' Shakespeare society was the city's largest grouping, and allegedly the largest in the world; Kipling and Doyle were 'all the rage'; and some of its guardians of literature could scoff at Lawson.[156]

The location of the Nineties within NSW raises a threatening question to the entire nationalist contention of a nexus between art and nation. Allow that cultural creation is a social product; allow that it is necessarily a transaction between the artist and their society. Why should that necessary society be on a 'national' scale? Why should that society not be either sub-national (regional) or supranational (continental)? There is no reason. We are left with a question: is the Nineties best described and analysed as a regional event rather than a national one?

That the Nineties did not signify an 1890s nation does not, however, mean the Nineties does not signify at all. Henry Lawson was a folk-martyr of the 1920s, not the 1890s; but there could not be a folk-martyr of the 1920s without a bush-rapporteur of the 1890s. Here we bump against a notion far more ambitious than culture merely being a sign of national quickening: we confront the thought that culture is an active agent in national quickening; in particular, the 19th century notion that a cultural heritage (Shakespeare!) would foster nationality. The notion is, however, speculative, undeveloped in conception, and, in Australia, unsuccessful in application. Perhaps the most palpable illustration of the general thesis is an 'anthem' which articulates some nascent solidarity. The Australian nationalist would invoke the composition of *Waltzing Matilda*, first sung in 1895. But it was not sung very much; an electronic search of hundreds of newspapers between 1895 and 1901 reveals only a single report of its being sung; by a local councillor to the Governor of Queensland, Lord Lamington, on an official visit.[157] *Advance Australia Fair*? Its composition and popularity signifies local pride, but its final verse hardly suggests a nationalist one.

> *Britannia then shall surely know,*
> *Beyond wide oceans' roll,*
> *Her sons in fair Australia's land*
> *Still keep a British soul.*

But however unsuccessful the notion of culture as nation-quickening, its pursuit will lead us to the broader thesis that nations are not 'underlying', are not something which 'emerge', or are dug out, but are, famously, 'invented'. This notion allows the non-existence of an Australian 'nation' in 1900, but at the same time accommodates an aspiration to create one. Nationality, after all, was held to be a blessing; you were somewhat bereft to not have one; it was a bit like being without a constitution or a king. Thus Parkes's resolution 'to work up this material into a great nation'.[158] And not only Parkes. The phrase, 'To make a nation', issued from the mouths of Federationists with a frequency comparable to the phrase, 'to consolidate the Empire'. A critic may reply that the non-existent thing, labelled 'the Australian nation', was obscure, ill-defined, almost an empty box.[159] How can one seek to create a thing about which one has no notion? It would seem the Federationists were doomed to snark hunting. And yet, it can be countered, in turn, that an indistinct concept may still excite. It may induce the filling out of the indistinct idea, at least in thought, symbol and performance, if not reality.

'To make a nation'

It is in the Australian Natives' Association (ANA) that Federationists' sometimes perplexing encounter between a non-existent nation and a nation foreseen, the actual and the imagined, the genuine and the inauthentic, was most concretely manifested.

On its face, the ANA constitutes a decisive counter-example to all observations which marginalise, 'superficialise' and annihilate nationalism as a cause of Federation. The ANA was both a Federationist enthusiast and a patriot-nationalist – claiming the style and substance of a nationalist movement: at the very climax of its Federationist campaign, the ANA gathered its forces on 26 January 1899 to commemorate 'our foundation day', 'this red letter day in Australian history'. And its membership cannot be written off as publicity maniacs, foreign careerists in search of a cause, self-appointed would-be Founders, or exiles re-fighting old battles under new colours. Or as marginal: the five highest polling candidates in Victoria's Convention election – Turner, Quick, Deakin, Peacock and Isaacs – were all members. The ANA's ardent support of Federation is, surely, proof positive of the role of Australian nationalism in that cause.

There are three dousing responses to that contention.

The leaders of the ANA were entirely committed to the vision of a nation colony, not a nation state: the Commonwealth was to be 'a new nation in one indivisible Empire', as the ANA's Melbourne leader, William Watt, put it.

Further, the ANA's Australian patriotism was actually, in one sceptical reading, the Victorian patriotism of an organisation almost non-existent outside Victoria;[160] a compound of Victorian consciousness, the Victorian pride and Victorian chauvinism. Deakin, in presenting to one visitor a wholly Victorian outlook, illustrates consciousness.[161] Pride? The historian of Victoria's founding generation records that it was 'overweeningly proud of its achievement'.[162] The chauvinism seemed evident enough to several Federationists, who took exception to its 'spirit of exclusiveness' (Glynn), 'resolute aggrandisement' and 'galling contempt' (Reid).[163] It is betrayed in Berry's hope that in Victoria there would spring up a 'public opinion that would govern the whole of the Australian colonies'.[164] It might be detected in the martial spirit of Victoria, exemplified in her acquiring 'forts built on the latest design', 'the most modern ordnance on the market',[165] and what was, for a time, 'the most powerful warship in the southern hemisphere',[166] which, in one newspaper fantasy, managed to sink a combined Franco-Russian fleet in Port Phillip Bay. In Victoria's apparent aspiration to 'continental hegemony', Victoria seemed to be playing Prussia to NSW's Austria.

Thirdly, in a still more sceptical construal, the nationalism of the ANA was the nationalism of an imaginary Australia by imaginary Australians. Imaginary, because there was no Australia. And no Victoria either, beyond a sham Britain of the Natives' parents.[167] Victoria still bore the deep impress of the peculiar 'instant society' that characterised its origin. Explored and occupied in 15 years, and in another five bedecked with two bishops, a university, two houses of parliament, and a cargo of immigrants 'who *were* Victoria almost to the end of the century';[168] as if all packed on East India Dock and unloaded at Williamstown. 'It was possible to pretend, especially after the link by telegraph, that Victoria was almost a part of Britain'.[169] Mark the word, 'pretend'. Such a society could not be a Britain; but it struggled to be a not-Britain, too. Their parents' sham Britain induced a sham Australianism of the native-born children – a clutching for roots by the rootless, a questing of the lost to find a home. The characteristic insistence of ANA nationalism might be taken simply as a sign of its falseness; a performance to convince the unconvinced, including themselves, 'self-identifying' Australians. Other native-born Victorians at the time chose other 'self-identifications'. Thus Nicholas O'Donnell, founder of the Melbourne branch of the Gaelic League. 'Australian born and bred', and never once visiting Ireland, he invested so heavily in an Irish identity that he could 'write Irish [i.e. Gaelic] prose faultlessly'.[170] Or John Feltham Archibald, who reinvented himself as 'Jules François Archibald', of French parentage. O'Donnell chose a sham Irish identity, and Archibald a sham French one; others chose a sham Australian identity. The President of the Australian Natives' Association for many years was a New Zealander.[171]

So, rather than a manifestation of national feeling, the ANA is better understood as a purely sectional piece of self-assertion; a generational section, to be specific, reflecting the abnormal demography of 19th century Victoria. All settler societies are, at the point of origin, demographically abnormal, as there will invariably be an abnormally high proportion of single, young males. Victoria was especially abnormal as it commenced with a giant wave of immigrants – overwhelmingly males aged 20-35 –

which quickly ceased. This contrast between NSW and Victoria is brought out in Table 3.1.

Table 3.1: Immigration to NSW and Victoria
(over the decade as a percent of population at the beginning of decade)

NSW	1800-1809	1810-1819	1820-1819	1830-1839	1840-1849
	91	158	118	150	67
Victoria	1851-1860	1861-1870	1871-1880	1881-1890	1891-1900
	405	7*	-2*	13*	-10*

Note: * = net immigration.
Source: Vamplew (1987, p. 4, p. 6).

Victoria's lop-sided time profile of immigration bent its age structure. The first row of Table 3.2 indicates that, in 1861, 63 percent of adults were aged 25-44, ('the diggers'). The outsize numerousness of the diggers imparted an enlarging distortion to each age bracket they occupied as they aged over the next 50 years, like a piglet travelling down a python (Table 3.2).

The flood of diggers also embedded a second, if delayed,

Table 3.2: The distribution of Victoria's population across age brackets
(percent share of population aged 15-74)

		15-24	25-34	35-44	45-54	55-64	65-74
Level	1861	24.8	**41.7**	**21.2**	8.5	3	0.7
Change over	1871	-0.1	-15.2	**6.1**	5.4	2.6	1.2
preceding	1881	**10.4**	*-7.7*	*-9.7*	**3.1**	**2.8**	1.1
ten years	1891	*-2.1*	*9.3*	*-3.5*	-5.8	**1.1**	**1.0**
	1901	-3.6	***-3.1***	*6.7*	-0.6	-1.8	**2.4**
	1911	0.3	-2.3	*-1.5*	*5.3*	-0.3	*-1.6*

Notes: Bold = born 1817-36; italics = born 1837-1856; bold italic = born 1857-1876
Source: Vamplew (1987, pp 30-36).

distortion in Victoria's age structure, as Gold Rush parents produced, with a delay, children. This is brought out by certain cells in rows three to six of the Table, which report the share of adult population by age groups.[172] They indicate a leap in 1881 of the proportion of adults aged 15-24, that is, those born between 1857 and 1866. A second piglet was passing down the demographic tract. This 'youth bulge' produced by the sons of diggers could be expected, like any youth bulge, to cause disturbance. Hence the Kelly gang. And larrikins.[173] And plentiful smart youth participating in the constitutional ferment at the close of the 19th century. Thus the strange demography of Victoria provided one of the classic sources of upheaval: to discontented geographical margins (in NSW, Queensland and WA), it added restless youth.

The significance of Victoria's youth bulge in the latter part of the 19th century was heightened by the fact that the youth were the children of immigrants. In late 19th century Victoria, to an unusual degree, *the parent was an immigrant* and the *child was a native-born*. Thus the age-old 'father and son' generational drama was compounded with the tensions of immigrant and native-born. Victoria, in consequence, experienced a particularly intense case of 'second generation syndrome', whereby the children of immigrants strive to achieve centrality ('assimilation') and status. Their status strivings were further inflamed by the peculiar inversion of the standing of immigrant and native-born in 19th century Australia. 'Normally', the immigrant is lower in status than the native-born; but until the very end of the 19th century the reverse was the case in Victoria. Class brought a further compounding of the status abnormality. The 'smart' native-born youth who flocked to the ANA judged one part of their 'seniors' – the rough-hewn, working class portion of British immigrants – figures of fun or derision.[174]

These offended strivings of Victoria's young fostered the drive in Natives for a distinct identity. They saw their elders as old-school and, often enough, ill-educated and unsuccessful. They found their immigrant parents' Anglophilia tiresome, and their Australophobia insulting.[175] Their parents dubbed the native brood 'colonial', but the native brood would dub themselves 'Australians'.

The diagnosis of the ANA's membership as aspirational, would-be Australians is diminishing, and perhaps ungenerous. It is also speculative; perhaps no more than a hypothesis forced by the inconsistency of the apparent nationalism of the ANA with this chapter's thesis. But to say that the nationalism of the ANA is a 'sham' is not to say it was insincere. J. F. Archibald, the Victorian-born editor of the *Bulletin*, was not insincere in his lifelong fantasy that he was the son of a French Jew.[176] It was an act of believed fiction, and believed fictions, or 'myth', can be powerful, far more powerful than truth. To put the point another way: Archibald certainly was not French, but he certainly was Francophile. And the ANA may not have been Australian, but it was certainly 'Australophile'. So, like the false coin taken by all to be genuine, was it not as good as genuine? So, as a 'believed fiction', the nationalist interpretation of Federation might be validated. A vulnerability of this analogy is that it supposes there was a genuine coin to contrast with the false coin. But perhaps there was no genuine coin: no real Australians. This vulnerability, however, might be something of a let out: if there were no actual Australians to stand in for, then the president of the ANA, of New Zealand birth and upbringing, could not be said to be faking an Australian identity. But it remains the case that he and other ANA members could not be said to be Australophile if there was no such thing as Australia. These make-a-nation Federationists were engaging in a form of self-invention, upon which they chose to put the phrase, 'Australian nation'. But the one thing they managed to make was not a nation but a state.

And yet Federationists' ultimate success in constructing a state may provide a last shot in the nationalist locker: was not Federation 'objectively' nationalist, even if it was not 'subjectively' so? Did not Federationists succeed in creating a 'state-nation', the Commonwealth of Australia? And did not that state-nation – tracking the journey of earlier state-nations – ultimately become a nation state? Plausibly. And yet it could be retorted that Federationists only delayed the development of an Australian nation. They had made the not-easy task of nation-making only harder by so squarely defining the new Commonwealth in terms of the British race. In so dedicating the Commonwealth, they gave victory to Imperial Federationists; Australia would be a province of Greater Britain, a stronghold of the British Empire. From the opposite ideological corner, Laborist Federationists placed their own obstacle in the path of developing an authentic nationality by their misconceived attempt to define the Australian nation in terms of class, the working class. The only creeping introduction of nationalist symbolism in the 20th century bespeaks the consequent debility of any nation-making impulse in the new Commonwealth: Australia Day, fitfully from the 1920s, and only uniformly from 1937; the Australian flag, really only from the Second World War and the *Flags Act 1953*; a national anthem only in 1984.[177]

And to the extent the Commonwealth did exhibit a nation-making impulse the question needs to be asked: did the make-a-nation Federationists actually destroy incipient nations? A New Zealand nationality would obviously have been damaged by joining the Commonwealth; perhaps Federation did as much with Western Australia. Or Tasmania, or northern Queensland.[178] Federationists commonly expressed alarm at the six colonies condensing into their own distinct characters.[179] One lamented

> *the old tie of being British subjects and British colonists, no matter in which colony residing, is being lost, particularly in the native born, who are developing not only different physical and mental characteristics, but are also beginning to be imbued with a kind of provincial patriotism.*[180]

And so, the ultimate question: if Federation made a nation, did it make a better one than any which it stifled?

4

Was Federation status-seeking in motive?

*For there is no such thing as a democratic gentleman;
the adjective and noun are hyphenated by a drawn sword.*
– 'Tom Collins'

The weakness of nationalism in the Federationist cause might be traceable to the palpable centrality of Federationists to Australia's social web: they would not be prone to any anxious, resentful reaction to incursions of those on the fringe. But if they were confident of their centrality, Federationists were tetchy about their status. Rank and standing: these were what silently gnawed at them. As rank and standing is near the heart of political contention, Federation may be interpreted as a struggle for status.

Status anxiety

The directing elite of the Federationist cause were rich in linkages with the society they were members of. In the whole constitutional convulsion of the 1890s it would be hard to nominate a single person swept by events from obscurity to federal prominence. Correspondingly, almost every member of the Convention was a politician. Perhaps even more signal of Federationists' centrality was the prevalence of Freemasonry among them: at least 15 delegates to the Convention of 1897-98 were Freemasons[181] – sixteen, if Griffith is added; a group that numbers two future prime ministers, two future chief justices, and six premiers.

But three status traumas menaced Federationists' sense of prestige, repute and standing. Some were of convict descent;[182] many were mere native-born; all were, one way or another, colonial – the very act of immigrating was declassing. A further damage to the blood line was done by disordered Australian existence. The effective sentence to divorce of married transportees, the parentage in irregular unions among the free, together with casual bastardy, took its own toll on legitimacy; the run of secret marriages and secret divorces clouded descent further.[183]

But the greatest 'status crisis' lay in the failure to transplant the well-articulated general status system of Great Britain. The consequent levelling in the status gradient was enough to excite an itch for differentiation. 'One of the most surprising phenomena of democratic communities is their paradoxical love of titles', spoke one Federationist.[184] Not so paradoxical; on the contrary, quite predictable. Additionally agitating was the reality that, to the extent the status gradient was not levelled, it was contested. So there was not so much an agreement that all would be equal, but a disagreement over what would make them unequal. Hence the 'precedence wars' which periodically erupted throughout Australia, even, so unsuitably, on the great day of national unity, on the first day of the new century. Hence the leading spirits of 19th century Australia were beset by status insecurity, sensitivity and prickliness.[185]

Australian status anxiety was only sharpened by the burgeoning of a novel social formation in the generation after Parkes, the generation which made Federation; a formation that was, in part, a consequence of status-hunger but, for that reason, was all the more status hungry: an Australian gentlemanly class. 'We want blood, Sir, we want distinction, we want style': thus the aspiration of perhaps the earliest native-born gentleman, and early Federationist, W. B. Dalley.[186]

The Australian gentlemanly class was educated, professional, metropolitan and status-sensitive. They would be classically educated, by the grammar schools, or the universities of Sydney and Melbourne, or, sporadically, at Oxford and Cambridge; thereby both gratifying their status quest, and distinguishing them from the *arriviste*. They tended to be professionals: few members of the Australian gentlemanly class would have had property income sufficient to leave them in idle comfort as a 'true gentleman'. But what was requisite of the Australian gentleman was not that they be without occupation, but that they not be employed at the pleasure of another. The gentleman mercantile magnates – Samuel Hordern, Sir Malcolm McEacharn – were men of concerns, but obviously free of any such demeaning dependence. The remaining great preponderance of gentleman – when they were not civil servants or clerics – kept any such dependence at bay by mediating market transactions through professional relationships, being doctors, architects (surprisingly significant, thanks to the building boom), and, above all, lawyers. For all their consequent shows of disdain for dollar hunting, they were fully bourgeois in 'class' affiliation (even if not origin). Correspondingly, they were utterly urban, as permitted by the rapid growth of Australian cities, both Sydney and Melbourne roughly matching Birmingham (or Baltimore) in population by the 1890s. The new Australian gentleman would have nothing of the uncouth 'squire' figure, which (anti-Federationist) John Robertson had a good deal of. The new gentlemanly class, unlike Australia's 'old gentry', were not defined by a connection to the land. The Australian gentleman was not a sprig of some rustic locality, but a sophisticate, he felt, of a much more spacious arena.

Attentive to status, even prickly about it, the new gentlemanly class were not, for all that, lacking in morale. How could they be? In the 20 years before the First World War the Australian gentleman enjoyed a kind of golden age, a near totally forgotten era of hunts, of clubland, and of newly built mansions – Anglewood, Cliffbrook, Camelot, Goathland,[187] Norwood, Woollahra House. Their careers sparkled without underlying brilliance: the scarcity of excellence in such small societies – SA had a smaller population than the London borough of Islington – meant a glossed and burnished ability could go a long way.[188] Material circumstances were kind; NSW had not been badly hit by the 1890s bust;[189] the rate of income tax in NSW was all of 2.5 percent (1.66 percent in Victoria), and imposed only on an annual income in excess of two hundred pounds – an income which by itself, in the fond memory of one native-born gentleman cleric, 'sufficed to give a bachelor a pretty good time in those days'.[190] For the gentleman's life was cheap: a tailor-made suit sold for three 'guineas' (the gentleman's unit of account), less than $500 in 2020 prices; 'a luxurious meal in town cost 2s 6d,[191] or under $20; and a lobster bought for 1s 6d ($11). The boater-wearing classes could enjoy the days, and – to the benefit of those not obliged to rise early on six days each week – the nights were brighter, almost literally, before early-closing legislation had dimmed the streets. A single gentleman's existence was also lightened by the prospect of marriage to someone two or more decades younger than himself. Behold George Reid, bachelor, aged 46, marrying Flora Brumby, aged 24. Or John Downer, widower, 54, and Una Russell, 28; or Lyne, widower, 67, and Sarah J. Olden, 41; Joseph Carruthers, divorcé, 41, and Alice Burnett, 21; J. G. Drake, bachelor, 47, and Mary Street, 30. And J. W. Hackett, bachelor, 57, to Deborah Vernon Brockman, 18. Hackett confided in Walter James, 'This is in the strictest sense a "marriage de convenance"'.[192] And, without labouring the obvious, the degree of presumption of the male in these unions was foreign to modern notions: thus Barton could, on one occasion, change his family's residence without any prior mention of the decision to Mrs Barton, and without, it appears, noticeably ruffling the relationship.[193] But the epitomisation of the self-sufficient and indulged existence of the gentleman lay not in the family circle, but in the gentlemen's clubs of the day; not only the older (and still surviving) clubs (the Australian, the Melbourne, the Tasmanian), but also the long vanished: such as Sydney's Athenaeum, and the Reform clubs. E. H. Collis's elegiac recollections of the 1890s is a fluent testimony to the easy life enjoyed by the gentleman at the close of the 19th century, who the missorted fathers of its mid-century seemed to sire.

In these easy circumstances, a few Australian gentlemen would be able to take their social status for granted. Thus B. R. Wise was native-born, but also a descendent of a bishop, 'artists, scholars and a royal physician';[194] the son of a judge; a pupil at Rugby; a scholar at The Queen's College, Oxford; president of the Oxford Union and contemporary there of George Nathaniel Curzon and Alfred Milner; thence called to Middle Temple Bar, before returning to Australia. Or P. M. Glynn: his externals may have gleamed much dimmer than Wise's (mercantile father; Trinity College, Dublin; admission to the Irish Bar), but he was perfectly assured in the obvious truth of his own liberal social ranking. Garran's immediate connections were no shinier than Glynn's, but he believed himself to be a descendent of King Edward III, and was indubitably a relative of Thomas Jefferson, John Marshall, and various other worthies of the Old Dominion.[195]

But many Australian gentlemen could not take social status for granted. The Australian gentleman was not the real thing; or, at least, they were thought not to be the real thing; or, more to the point, they thought that others might not think them so. A sign of this insecurity is a risible volume which appeared in 1891, *A Genealogical and Heraldic History of the Colonial Gentry*, a kind of biographical register of the upwardly striving. Ten of the 54 delegates to the Australasian Federal Convention supplied their personal details, and presumably money, to be included between its covers. Another two senior Federationists, Griffith and Clark, also appear. They were evidently set on exhibiting themselves as 'colonial gentry' despite the faintness of the claims of most of them to be so. Consider the 'genealogical and heraldic history' of one Convention delegate, William Zeal, or 'Zeal of Clovelly', as the *History* records him; it amounts to nothing more than noting he was the grandson of a John Zeal, Esq., of Knowstone, Devon, who 'was a man of some position'. By the time we find Carruthers, 'whose father resided in Glasgow', we know that Burke's *Colonial Gentry* is a bit of a joke.[196] Or, more rightly, the pretensions of Carruthers and his fellow 'gentry' are a bit of a joke. But not a joke, we may be sure, to themselves. The Australian gentlemen were a bunyip gentry, the alloy of confidence and insecurity, in near equal parts.

Status soothers

The quest for status security brought forth several stratagems, some eccentric. Thus W. C. Wentworth – a classic case of status insecurity – sought to establish a hereditary electoral college to decide membership of the NSW Legislative Council. A more predictable response to the quest for status was the institution, from 1868, of knighthoods for colonials, which several leading Federationists gratefully received on the day of national unity, and several more a little later.[197] Another was the honorific style, 'The Honourable'. This prefix was carefully tended in the period; it was never granted wholesale to members of Australia's 19th century parliaments, but, significantly, from 1904 was granted to all members of the Commonwealth parliament. Correspondingly, with Royal blessing, in 1902 the Mayors of Sydney and Melbourne became Lord Mayors, surely gratifying to stalwart

Federationist's such as Sir Thomas Hughes and Sir Malcolm McEacharn, who occupied those offices. Another status salve was the appointment of colonials to the Privy Council, and later its judicial committee, including a swathe of Federationists.[198] Why stop there? Parkes, in 1874, dared to propose to Gladstone that 'occasionally' a colonial might be considered for appointment as governor.[199] And 'why should the name of colonies be retained?', asked Parkes of 'the purest and greatest of English statesmen'. Why should they not be called, 'The Empire of Australian States?'. This would all serve Parkes's earnest entreaty of Gladstone for 'a higher political status'.

Beyond titles and patronages, a more substantial solution to the status problem would lie in the constitutional character of Australia. The creation of the Federal Council of Australasia in 1885 might render a status fillip. But the Council lacked the power and prestige conferred by democratic election and, like many conciliar bodies, was a noiseless and stolid thing. The Commonwealth's creation would serve the status quest more clearly by its greater grandeur. Its creation would additionally strike at one root of the status problem: it would dispose of a key, painful, status marker: 'colonial'. And it would strike by two distinct means: a nationalist means and an imperialist means. The nationalist-separationist means of erasing the brand of 'colonial' would proceed by pooling the six colonies' strength in a single, large and supposedly reckonable and respected federation.

The imperialist means of using federation to efface Australia's degraded colonial station went in the opposite direction, and trusted in Federation to hasten Australia's full integration into a Greater Britain. Such an Imperial Federation would gratify the status quest more profoundly than an Australian Federation. Why settle for a seat on the High Court if a seat on an Imperial Court is in the offing? Many of the gentlemanly class were Imperial Federationists of a sort. And, happily, they saw no conflict in the two federations. To the imperially minded, Australian Federation was simply a stage in the progression to the greater Imperial Federation. It was this convergence of the two causes that allowed Barton to declare to a crowd, 'I want to ask you whether we regard ourselves as a portion of the English nation, or as mere hewers of wood or drawers of water'.[200] Obviously, one could be neither (or both). But Barton seemingly saw them as exclusive possibilities, and could only elect to be a member of 'the English nation', and therefore, by his own lights, in favour of the Commonwealth's creation.

By either method – 'separationist' or 'unionist' – Samuel Griffith – or is it 'Griffith of Brisbane'? – could declare on the day the Commonwealth was proclaimed that 'the status of every Australian is raised by the consummation of today'.[201]

But both the nationalist and imperialist programs for eliminating 'colonial' from the collective identity had deficiencies. The nationalist animus towards the very term was somewhat misdirected, and indirectly counterproductive; for the emergence of 'colonial' as an identity was, in truth, a seed bed for Australian identity. The term was an Australianism, arising from the presence of native-born who were not anxious to be taken for British, or even 'be' British. The term would be used by somebody *un*like Griffith – who was British-born, and concerned not to be taken for a mere colonial.[202]

And both programs for satisfying the quest for status shared a certain flaw: the new Commonwealth of Australia would be a British colony, expressly and palpably. So the nationalist could not escape the fact that the Commonwealth was a 'nation colony'. And the Imperialist could not escape the fact that the Commonwealth, being a 'self-governing colony', clearly did not constitute a province of some Greater Britain. But as far as the imperialist solution was concerned, time would deliver. And as far as a nationalist remedy was concerned, its difficulty was already partly dissolved, since the organ of the Commonwealth which most concerned core Federationists – the High Court – *did* amount to a substantial, and not far from complete, assumption of Australian equality with Britain. For whereas the Privy Council had previously been the final court of appeal, now the High Court would almost always be; and leave to appeal from the High Court to the Privy Council would only be at the Court's pleasure. Put simply, with respect to the judicature, in 1901 Australia had nearly attained 'Dominion Status', and quickly came still closer in the first decade of Federation.

And yet the creation of the High Court can be interpreted differently, to suggest a different, and less attractive, solution to the struggle for status. The High Court may be construed as an inheritor institution: it inherited the Privy Council's powers over persons, and courts, of the six colonies. Thus, unlike the system of seven legislatures which the Constitution ordained, the Commonwealth's judicature *was* expressly hierarchic. And so was the system of judicature before 1901: the one difference was that after 1901 the apex would be occupied by the High Court, instead of the Judicial Committee of the Privy Council. To generalise this thought, one might take the Commonwealth of Australia to be an inheritor institution. In this interpretation, the Commonwealth was indisputably a British colony, but its creation simply amounted to a change of governors; they would now be the Commonwealth's judges and lawyer politicians. These mayors of the palace would now rule Australia, exercising to their own satisfaction the powers formally exercised by the *rois fainéants* of Westminster.[203] Is this too extreme a characterisation to be the truth? Certainly. But too extreme to contain no truth? Not at all, as the following pages will seek to demonstrate, and even a passing reading of Deakin's detailed political commentaries of the new Commonwealth will betray.[204]

*

In the first decades of the 20th century Federationists travelling to the UK would sometimes make the disconcerting discovery that the Commonwealth of Australia had not been a complete solution to their status problem. And yet it was undoubtedly an ameliorating treatment. And so there is no surprise that Federation was, above all, a gentleman's cause. Gentlemen created it; they largely composed it; they drove it. Barton – 'a clubman in excelsis'[205] – ran much of his Federationist campaign from the Athenaeum Club. Where else? The key 1895 Premiers' Conference, which set Australia on the path to Federation, was held at the Tasmanian Club; where else?

And yet it cannot be simply affirmed, 'the gentlemanly class wanted Australian Federation, and so it happened'. They also wanted, to some degree, Imperial Federation, but that did not happen. A sufficient cause for federation remains unfound.

5

Was Federation psychological in catalyst?

*Oh! may the pray'd-for time and tide come with the
Twentieth Century of Christ!*
– Henry Parkes

If economic, nationalist and sociological explanations of Federation struggle, perhaps the search for the Commonwealth's source should shift from a social terrain to a psychological one; from an exterior environment – of markets and webs and ranks – to an interior one; of conversions and commitments, and thence to crusades. Mental interiors are stirred by a heightened state of arousal, and in the Federation decade such a heightened state was to be found. Its psychological atmosphere appears to have been not dry, but sweltering; a latent energy needed release, with obvious destabilising and event-making implications.

Séance power

To some notions Australia would be an unlikely place to find the operation of an aroused mental state. A now familiar estimate of the Australian character had been formulated by the 1890s: laconic, nonchalant, slapdash; lackadaisical in enterprise, perfunctory in religion, cursory in civic duty.[206] Passionate only about sport. Accordingly, the campaign for Federation is sometimes presented as wearisome to the public. A favoured rag is that a test cricket match between Australia and England in Melbourne in the summer of 1898 won more interest from the public than the Federal Convention's concurrent session. This particular is correct, doubtless, but also misleading.

The reality is that Federation roused the populations of NSW, Victoria and Queensland: hence the great and animated crowds in 1898 and 1899. Consider the last week of the 1898 referendum campaign in NSW. Putting aside the capstone rallies in Sydney, 6 000 heard Barton in Newcastle, and 6 to 7 000 heard Reid in the same a few days later.[207] Lesser lights drew lesser but still impressive crowds: 3 000 purportedly heard John Norton speak at the President Lincoln Hotel in Woolloomooloo.[208] Even three perfect ciphers of the Federationist cause could draw 500 people in Glebe on a cold night.[209]

Neither were the crowds of the campaign meetings of 1898 and 1899 a novelty confined to those years. In 1891 masses had thronged to hear the eloquent proconsular democrat Sir George Grey. And, in 1890, in 'a mood verging on hysteria'[210], they massed to hear Henry George – 'the Master', the 'Christ-like guiding star', 'the prophet of San Francisco', 'the successor of Mahomet, Luther, Cromwell, Kingsley and Carlyle'– to speak on 'THY KINGDOM COME' on his three month lecture tour of Australia. As the crowd-winning politician George Reid opined, 'Australians are a very enthusiastic and emotional community when they gather for the purpose of demonstration'.[211]

The size of crowds of the 1890s bespeaks the operation of 'contagion'; and that emotional infectiousness suggests in turn arousal; which itself will be intensified by crowds. There appears to have been a self-reinforcing loop of excitement, in which contagion was the closing link. Several late 19th century social theorists judged contagion to be manifest among their contemporaries. 'Suggestibility' was a coinage of the period, and some judged their society to be morbidly susceptible to forming a fused state of consciousness; thus the séance, hypnosis, and the power of oratory over audiences. These things were not lacking in Australia. The dim of the séance was well-known to Deakin and Griffith; even Dibbs tried it, and Justice William Windeyer was satisfied of the authenticity of its proceedings.[212] Hypnosis was regarded as a common marvel, a bit like electricity, and recommended to mothers for use on difficult children.[213] With the likes of Deakin, need hypnotism and oratory be distinguished? Observing journalists recollected Deakin would 'hypnotise' his audiences;[214] they 'sat back hypnotised' by his delivery.[215] Regrettably, 'in cold type', his words 'were absolutely without meaning'.[216]

But the strangest case of group communion in Australia of the

Alfred Deakin 'hypnotising' an audience

1890s had as its interfusing figure, not a mesmerist or orator, but a taciturn wife poisoner. In April 1895, George Dean, a young Sydney ferry captain, was convicted of attempting to murder his wife by means of a diet of beef tea and lemon syrup, seasoned with arsenic and strychnine. Sentenced to life imprisonment, the public quickly decided Dean was innocent, and a victim of the trial judge, Justice Windeyer. Each day 'hundreds' of letters were allegedly received by Dean's lawyers. With public excitement 'increasing day by day', protest meetings were held in local town halls, leading up to a 'monster' meeting at Sydney Town Hall to plead Dean's case. This crowning rally's organisers hoped for Parkes himself to address it. But the former premier restricted himself to a letter of encouragement: like 'all Englishmen', he said, he hesitated to spurn a court's decision, and yet he was left dissatisfied by Dean's trial. In his absence two second ranking Federationists – Mark Hammond and Ninian Melville[217] – delivered, in turn, analytic and heated speeches to the 'vast concourse of people' – rich and poor, men and women – who made up 'the greatest meeting ever held in Sydney', 'even eclipsing the gigantic reception accorded the New Zealand veteran statesman, Sir George Grey'.[218] A continual stamping of feet beckoned the meeting to begin and, when it finally did, 'the combination of nearly 10 000 ringing voices seeming almost to shake the staunch structure'.[219] Dean's lawyer, Richard Meagher, 'on rising in response to calls to address the tremendous audience, received a perfect ovation, the deafening cheers lasting some considerable time'.[220] A few weeks later, Meagher won a seat in the NSW Legislative Assembly, from its free trade incumbent, with the benefit of a 21 percent swing.[221]

That a pathology was present in the public's reaction to the Dean case is suggested by the spuriousness of the cause. Dean was guilty. He admitted his guilt to Meagher, who then confided this devastating indiscretion to his law partner, William Crick, while all the time championing Dean's innocence before a royal commission appointed to review Dean's conviction. Meagher did not succeed there in his aim 'to fasten the crime' on Dean's innocent mother-in-law. But the commission absolved Dean, and, in apparent triumph, Meagher, with an audacity suggesting mania, flourished Dean's confession to a former Chief Justice. In the wake of this remarkable admission, the Attorney-General, Jack Want, successfully prosecuted Meagher and Crick for perverting the course of justice. Meagher appealed against the conviction, retaining Barton and O'Connor as his advocates.[222] The Queen's Counsel and his learned friend secured Meagher's discharge, on the grounds that some evidence supplied to the jury was inadmissible. Barton had less success when it came to Meagher's removal from the roll of attorneys: despite Barton's 'able and eloquent' defence, Meagher was struck off. [223]

But the significance of the Dean case lies not in its strange capacity to draw in Federationists and anti-Federationists, but in so spurious a cause successfully communicating itself throughout a society, and occasioning a massed group frenzy.

The golden age ahead

If contagion closed the loop of excitement, a charge feeding the loop was the future orientation of the Australian public. Australia in this period was more interested in, more attracted by, and more emotionally attached to, the future than the past. We see this orientation in the ubiquity and popularity of the Rising Sun symbolism of the 1890s. We can see it in the novels of the day, variously set in 1988 and 1995. We see it in expostulations about the future from Federationists: the Convention's preferred statistician suggested Australia would have a population of 22.3 million by 1941. By 1988 the country would have a population of 108 million,[224] and, indeed, would be 'one of the greatest peoples on God's earth'.[225] This orientation may also be seen in the lack of status afforded the elderly by the Federation generation.[226] It is certainly seen in the contempt of Federationists for the past (the *Bulletin*), and their seeming incapacity to appreciate even its more beguiling bequests. Thus Garran's appalling statement that Sydney 'would profit by a great fire like that of London, followed by a great planner like that of Paris's Haussmann'.[227] And one may infer it from the reproaches by anti-Federationists of Federationists concerning this orientation.[228] The significance of this orientation to the turbulence of the 1890s is plain. The past is a clasp for the wistful, the regretful, the nostalgic, the one-minute silence. The future is an Aaron's Rod that would bring water from the stony present.

The future orientation of late 19th century Australia was perhaps inevitable. The society's palpable 'pastlessness' could only make it so. If many Federationists were born in Australia, how rare were the Federationists whose parents were also so born? To vary the thought: how few were the Federationist generation who knew their grandparents? The country had little behind it and plenty ahead of it. And the country's rapid progress quickly made whatever past there was both backward and irrelevant. Little wonder that the rural arcs enclosing the three oldest areas of settlement – Sydney, Hobart and Brisbane – which had lost their onetime significance, were unattracted by the Federal future. But it is also little wonder that panting for the Federal future in 1900 were places experiencing hectic growth; Corowa,[229] or Charters Towers, or Coolgardie.

On 20 July 1898, Father Long, of the Western Australian goldrush town of Kanowna, announced to the press that, the previous evening, two men had appeared at his residence, bearing something in a bag. Opening it revealed a nugget, of immense proportions, composed of almost pure gold, in the shape of an irregular crescent, and weighing 115 pounds, three times larger than the previous record fragment. The men placed this 'Sacred Nugget' in his trustworthy custody, and then left, saying no more than that they had found it near Lake Wynne, three miles from Kanowna.

Father Long's announcement created an 'immense sensation', and he undertook to appear at Donnelly's Hotel, to impart what he could about where the Nugget had been drawn from the earth. Punctually, at 2.00 pm on 1 August 1898, Father Long appeared on Donnelly's balcony, accompanied by the warden, the inspector and several sub inspectors. A crowd of 5 to 6 000 below greeted him with vociferous cheers. After a brief prologue, Long announced point-blank that the Nugget had been found 4 feet below the surface, within half a mile of the nearest lake on the Kurnalpi road. A Federationist activist reported the reaction:

> *Here a scene occurred which cannot be properly depicted in black and white. Without waiting for another word the crowd simply surged and swayed, and, disregarding any farther utterances Father Long might have been disposed to make, they simply broke loose and made one wild rush ... in the direction of Kurnalpi road. In the stampede were to be seen horses, buggies, carts, bicycles, and almost every conceivable mode of locomotion, while hundreds were to be seen frantically rushing along on 'Shanks's pony'.*[230]

It only remained for one of the worthies on the balcony – Dr S. A. Ewing, a delegate to the 'Federal Convention of Western Australia' – to call for cheers for Father Long, which were given 'with the most hearty enthusiasm'.

There is no need to expand on the disappointment of those who rushed to Kurnalpi road in eager quest of the likes of the imaginary Sacred Nugget. Or the pathetic end of Father Long, almost deranged by his hunger for notice. What is worth weighing is the unbreakable hopefulness of the animated and restless population of the goldfields – and their ardour for Federation. In the referendum of 1900, 1 154 valid votes were cast at Kanowna, making it one of the largest booths in the gold fields. 95 percent were affirmative. To the district's electors the recent past – the discovery of WA's goldfields – had been something of a fairy tale; why would they not 'believe' in the future?

But any attempt to trace an 1890s optimism about a novel future to past success strikes against the palpable fact that the 1890s in Victoria, the heart of the Federation cause, was a period of shock, smashed hopes and trial. There is something incomplete in the explanation of the hopefulness about the future in terms of the Australian past. There is also something insufficient about an aroused state – fostered by future orientation or otherwise – as explanatory of Federation. Fervent crowds were no novelty to 1890s Australia. Thirty years before, the tour of Queen Victoria's second son, Prince Alfred, had brought forth, throughout Australia, eager, excited, even riotous masses. The Australian community's 'very enthusiastic and emotional' state *en masse* was doubtless facilitating of the Federal cause, and perhaps essential. But it was not ensuring of the cause's success.

6

The 'Sliding Plane'

... events are often sent on their sliding plane of operation by the most trivial of circumstances.

– Henry Parkes

If neither economic, cultural nor psychological factors explain Federation, then perhaps it is mistaken to seek any 'underlying causes'. Perhaps it is an error to suppose political events are anchored to economic and cultural subterranea, by way of everything from rational elections to providential heroes, so that the two move in tandem with each other. Perhaps political forms do not 'ratify' the economic and cultural base. Perhaps political events are, instead, the upshot of a certain, wholly self-contained, game of skill and chance called 'politics'. In such a vision, politics is no longer 'about' anything beyond itself. Such a vision of the relation of political events to broader society is doubtless untenable in an extreme form. But is it less untrue of Federation than the 'underlying causes' interpretation?

The lack of patent movement in Australia's economic and cultural foundations weakens the anchored-to-foundations interpretation of Federation. The challenge facing any 'game of skill and chance' interpretation of Federation is to demonstrate a game-likeness in Federation's realisation. There must be a contest of individuals; each with a sense of choice in their actions; with each choice subject to rules, and unpredictability as to its consequences. A search for a game of skill and chance interpretation of Federation will close in on the contest of two contenders for power: Henry Parkes and George Reid, the master and the pretender. Both NSW patriots – NSW chauvinists, even – but each dandling Federation for the opportunity of advancing themselves; with their manoeuvring and counter-manoeuvring producing Federation as an upshot.

The *modus operandi* of the master

Federation truly begins with a vice-regal sigh at the irksomeness of administering an empire. It begins on 15 June 1889 in Government House, with a *tête à tête* between Parkes and Lord Carrington, the Governor of NSW, who 'capitivated' Parkes.[231] The Governor wistfully mused how much simpler his life would be if Australia, like Canada, was a federated entity, with a single Governor. Parkes replied that he could federate Australia; he could, indeed, do it within a year.[232] 'Then why don't you do it?' came the reply. There is no sign previous to this aristocratic goading that Parkes had any plan to act on Federation. In the general election of January 1889 Parkes had submitted his candidacy to electors with considerable loquacity, but without a word on Federation.[233] Now he would try to secure Federation within a year. To Carrington's teasing rag, Federation may be ultimately traced.

How could a trivial exchange between Governor and premier be so consequential? Because Federation was not a matter of masses, or forces, or 'something in the air'; it was, in origin, a personal contest for power and glory by a suite of politicians.

Federation came down to a contest of persons, rather than ideologies or interests, thanks to the near absence of genuine political parties in Australia. The Australian colonies had been endowed with sophisticated parliamentary structures of lawmaking. But they remained underdeveloped in terms of other political institutions. It seemed 19th century Australian society could not sustain a political organisation more complex than the 'single purpose league' – say, to abolish transportation, or reform the Legislative Council – which articulated some unanimous section of opinion in favour of some specific, immediate end. The political party – the long-term, organised collaboration of like yet divergent purposes – was beyond it. The requisite collaboration by compromise which essentially characterises the political party required a decision-making machinery, a supply of persons of arbitral authority, a broad and binding ideology, a *mystique du parti*, and a 'party patriotism' wholly absent in Australian society. Accordingly, all the 'parties' that leading Federal figures played with were personal vehicles. In the absence of genuine parties, politics was mediated by personalities, in an age which did not want for big personalities, and in a country saturated with politicians. In the absence of party discipline, politics became a tumult of individual designs; a chaos where desertion was barely distinguishable from departure.

The essentially personal nature of political contest in Australia was further abetted by a particular subversion of the constitutional structures which it did have: the pervasiveness of the politician for sale.[234] An exemplar of such political corruption was the infernal triangle formed in the NSW parliament of the 1890s by W. N. Willis, W. B. Crick, and Richard Meagher. The base of this triangle, Willis, drew his political strength from the far northwest of New South Wales, among the new wave of doomed selectors created by the 1884 *Land Act*, and its penny an acre 'homestead' selections. Willis organised these needy clients into a local electoral machine, the 'Willis push', which was 'drilled to discipline and obedience', and which secured Willis's repeated re-election, aided by their candidate's declamatory fluency. He duly delivered railways to his voters.[235] But, by contrast with the ordinary 'roads and bridges' member, Willis was also a forger of signatures, a forger of wills, a perverter of justice, as well as being strangely unlucky in the number of fires that consumed his insured properties. In parliament, Willis was in intense but unstable co-operation with his peers, William Crick and Richard Meagher, all from rural constituencies, all corrupt and, with Crick, additionally, bearing an aura of physical menace. And they all were glad to embrace certain causes oratorically. Thus Willis was vociferously pro-trade union (until Labor emerged); called for the segregation of Syrian immigrants; championed female suffrage; and campaigned for dispatch of Bushmen to the Boer War. He was also an 'enthusiastic Federationist',[236] as were Crick and Meagher by 1898. All these causes were totemic, or had a venal basis (Willis supplied the Bushmen with the horses they required), or simply gratified the ravenous hunger for notice which beset all three. Largely confined within the bounds of venality, the politics of the three remained essentially small – thus, despite their ambitions, between them they achieved only two ministerial posts. But if Crick never became premier, he very nearly did, and there is a significance in that. So, if corruption was not a directing force, it was, nevertheless, part of the context.

It might be compared to an unhealed wound of the parliamentary body politic; weakening even if not actually determining. And leaving politics even more an unmediated individual combat.

In the essentially personal contest of politics, contestants had two methods of play. The first method was the politics of particular interest, epitomised by the 'roads and bridges' members of parliament, who, however changeable in their allegiances within the chamber, were loyal to their electors in pursuit of roads, railways and bridges. The culmination of their parliamentary activity was the bargain, struck by deal cutters, which secured a 'log roll' so that each local interest, despite its rivalry with others, could obtain a majority.

The second method was the politics of the ideal, where the imperative to realise some ideal perfectly would leave any bargain no more than a passing truce in some implacable crusade; where there could be no genuine compromise, or possibility of compensation, but only victory for one side, and uncompensable defeat for the other.

The ideals of this second method of politics fell into two types. First were the ideals which united a given society; 'totemic' issues. Such issues clearly had value for the seeker of political mastery, but suffered the disadvantage that any rival could equally thrive on them. So, in 1888, for example, Parkes could press highly popular anti-Chinese legislation, but his protectionist rival, Barton, could also, with every unction, lead a public delegation to the Governor begging the same.

The second sort of ideal would not unite a given society, but instead divide it in two, to the evident advantage of whoever led the larger part produced by a division, and the disadvantage of those in the smaller. And ideals could be piled onto ideals. One type of such superadded ideal – known as the 'wedge' – did not suppress the first, but would apply a second divide with as much trenchancy as the first, with the consequence that the two segments of the electorate were now four. Wedges were plainly to the potential advantage of any politician in the smaller of the original two segments. Wedges might even prove useful to the leader of the larger of the original two ; for the leader's 'camp', now defined over two divides, might still constitute a 'plurality' of the now four sections of the electorate, while successfully hiving off rivals for leadership into a smaller segment. The danger was that an additional divide could split the majority more seriously than it split the minority; leaving, perhaps, the leader of a former majority in a minority which was not even a plurality.

Safer than the wedge was the 'sinker'; the introduction of a second ideal that pre-empted, overrode or 'trumped' the first ideal, on account of the second being prior or deeper. Such 'sinkers' were potentially to the advantage of a politician who had, for example, found himself in the smaller of the two parts of a bisected electorate.

Of these methods of politics, the politics of interest did not attract Parkes; he dismissed it as 'petty', and, doubtless, ineffective for obtaining mastery. Accordingly, he disdained the coalition – an essential technique of the politics of interest – as 'the short road chosen by short-sighted men'.[237] Parkes found more use in the second type of available politics; the politics of ideals, principle, or 'value'. Sometimes the ideals he wielded were totemic: hence the quest to be entirely convict-free in 1849, or Chinese-free forty years later. But wedging ideals were also useful. On some occasions he sought to make a wedge of trade policy – pitching a Cobdenite purity in free trade against any falling away.[238] 'What ground for agreement or accommodation', said Parkes, 'can be discovered between freedom of commercial intercourse and restriction of commercial intercourse'? Or, he added, 'between denominational and non-sectarian education?'[239] It was religion which constituted the supreme wedge for Parkes, and, from 1867, he improvised a career out of anti-Catholicism, which reached a political zenith with the *Public Instruction Act 1880*, intended to drive out of existence any school not provided by the government. But with this victory the victors – the adherents of the established churches of England and Scotland – no longer had so much use for Parkes, while the defeated Catholic party was vengeful, and Parkes lost his seat in the election of 1882, coming a dismal fifth in a list of seven candidates. Thus the politics of wedging ideals was a dangerous and experimental art. But, fortuitously for Parkes, in the mid-1880s the cause of free trade burst into prominence; to one side a litmus test of reason and impartiality; and, to the other, proof of an unwillingness to use the state to rejig the great lottery of life in favour of those who had drawn blanks. This free trade crusade provided Parkes with 'an almost dazzling Indian summer', in his great victory at the 1887 general election. And yet, early in 1889, his majority was brought crashing down by a casual blow by dissenters, and only just resurrected in the subsequent general election of March 1889. Scanning the new Assembly's 137 members on becoming premier for the fifth time, Parkes could find only one who had previously been premier – and he only for four months in total. So Parkes was the master, but his mastery was, evidently, precarious. Hence the strength and weakness of Parkes: often preeminent, but always imperilled.

His federal wand

In the wake of his modest election victory of 1889 Parkes turned to another wand, which he had several times before taken up and put down again: Federation.[240] This was hardly some epiphany. Parkes's politics of idealism was not a politics of zealotry. Ideals were devices, not devotions; they might fit the circumstance, or they might not. Timothy Coghlan, indeed, remarked of his anti-Catholic politics: 'Parkes was a man without any personal bigotry, and merely used the tools at hand … '.[241] He had picked up the federal tool before, only to put it aside. Free trade, too, he had taken up, only to toss it aside publicly in 1860, only to take it up yet again. And a year before he brandished Federation in 1889, federationism was nowhere to be seen on him. In 1888, the centenary of NSW, he indulged himself with certain grandiose-eccentric initiatives,[242] including the renaming of NSW 'Australia'. Where in this piece of NSW chauvinism is the federal spirit?[243] But Federation was a tool at hand, and Parkes in 1889 saw fit to pick it up again, casting aside, once again, his two earlier crooks. He announced he was never a 'scientific free trader'[244] and opposed Reid's 'fantastical fiscal policy'. He inspected a Catholic school, owning it 'a privilege to visit the institution and see its admirable order.'[245]

Parkes saw Federation first and foremost as operating totemically. Federation would not be used as a wedge, but as a 'sinker', something which would 'transcend' or wipe away.[246] Rhetorically based on unity, Federation had a pre-empting effect over other issues, as it amounted to the contention that any issue which could be construed as 'federal' required the settling, first, of the question of Federation. Only a federal parliament could legitimately settle the tariff question; so that question, he repeatedly pressed, should remain closed until the advent of Federation. And he would raise Federation on the universally traumatising prospect of a Chinese invasion of the Northern Territory.

Parkes first publicly flourished the federal wand in a speech in October 1889, in the NSW border town of Tenterfield, in a hall barely larger than a class room. He hung his appeal for Federation on the federalisation of Australia's defences recently recommended by Sir James Bevan Edwards, commander of the British garrison in Hong Kong. The commemorative history of Federation puts some stress on Edwards's recommendation. But his advice was little felt in the 1890s. Two weeks before the Australasian Federal Conference, Edwards wrote to Parkes with the news that a portion of the Chinese Imperial Fleet, 'consisting of two magnificent ironclads of the newest type and four very fine and very heavily armed cruisers', was anchored beneath his windows. 'Admiral Ting [the commander of China's Northern Ocean Fleet] is an old comrade of mine', Edwards told Parkes. 'I have been urging him strongly to take his fleet and show his flag in ... Australia. ... Would not this help your federation?'[247] This communication, with its contemptuous sentiments, was publicised in the NSW parliament in May 1890, and there branded, not unreasonably, as a plan of 'intimidation', even 'terrorism'.[248] In the subsequent 12 years little more was heard of Edwards, Chinese fleets, or the general problem of defence.[249]

The press paid little attention to Parkes's Tenterfield address; Lord Carrington lamented that it was 'very badly reported'.[250] The response of Victoria's politicians was further dousing: Premier Gillies pointed out that the Federal Council of Australasia was already licensed to act for 'general defence' – and was soon to do so with respect of King George Sound[251] – and he invited the pursuit of common defence by that device. But some vice-regal wire pulling induced the premiers to courteously agree to 'an informal meeting of the colonies for preliminary consultation' in Melbourne from 6 to 14 February 1890: 'The Australasian Federal Conference'.[252] This in turn resolved – innocuously it might seem – upon a 'National Australasian Convention' to 'report' on a scheme for Federation. The Convention met 12 months later – no rush – in Sydney, from 2 March to 9 April 1891, with key figures such as Griffith, Barton, Deakin, Kingston, Forrest and Clark among the delegates. The Convention 'reported'; indeed, six lawyer members supplied a fully-fledged constitution; and the Convention beckoned Australia's six parliaments to 'approve' (not 'consider') its implementation.

In the wake of the National Australasian Convention, Parkes hoped to contest the forthcoming NSW general election of 1891 on the basis of an 'Australian Unionist' party, which would include Barton among its leaders, sink the fiscal issue and realise the Convention's constitution. But Barton demurred – he was not inclined to play second fiddle. At the election of June 1891 Barton re-entered the main political arena, as an independent, lending his support in the Assembly to Parkes, now re-elected as Premier. B. R. Wise, another Federationist protégé of Parkes, also won a seat, and joined Parkes's cabinet of free trade Federationists, dominated by Smith and McMillan. Federation seemed set to be realised.

But within a few months Parkes had lost his enthusiasm for Federation. How so? Perhaps because Reid had entered the struggle against Federation, resolved, it seemed, to use Federation as a wedge rather than a sinker; in the hope Federation would not submerge the free trade cause, but instead split it, leaving Reid in what, he hoped, would be the larger fragment. But a still more significant development was the 'strange and unexpected' (Reid) advent of Labor, which swept into the NSW parliament in 1891 on the gusts of bitter industrial disputes. Labor members had little interest in Federation. 'The coalmining regulation bill', announced one of its personalities, 'is of far greater importance than any Federation fad'.[253] With nearly one-third of the seats suddenly in Labor hands, the portion of the political landscape which would sink all issues for the sake of

Federation had shrunk. Parkes was left to console himself with other imposing gestures: a resolution to give the vote to women; a grandly named Representation of the People bill. As for Federation, 'I have no wish to mention it', he stiffly declared, 'until the time comes'.[254] But, having raised this standard, he could not stop rivals flying it themselves. Barton appears now to have resorted to an 'Australian Unionist' stratagem, but with himself as the leader, and without Parkes. As a protectionist who had declared his belief in inter-colonial free trade, Barton surely would have more success in importuning free traders to join the federal cause, than Parkes ever would in enticing protectionists to join his version.

And yet Parkes was in power. Perhaps the Laborist *vs* anti-Laborist fracture could be used to wreck the structuring of politics around the free trade *vs* protectionist divide, leaving Barton as Premier, supported by Federationists drawn from anti-laborists of both free trade and protectionist ranks. In October 1891, in an action ostensibly helpful of Parkes, but in result – and perhaps in intention – provocative to Labor and its sympathisers, Barton moved to put a freeze on legislation to implement an eight-hour day. Labor support for Parkes collapsed. The chamber was now splintered into four; protectionist Laborists, protectionist anti-Laborists, free trade anti-Laborists, and free trade Laborists. Amid the ruins of his premiership, here was an opportunity for Parkes to pass on the Federal torch to a younger, more vital figure, as commemorative history supposes he did, by recommending to the Governor that Barton be appointed premier, with a remit to put the Convention's constitution to the parliament. But Parkes recommended George Dibbs, the stridently anti-Federation leader of the protectionist anti-Laborists. Dibbs's new cabinet had one surprise; Barton as Attorney-General. So Barton – Federationist and, until that moment, ardent intercolonial free trader, accepted the leadership of Dibbs – the fierce anti-Federationist and intercolonial protectionist. Dibbs rushed through a *Customs Duties Act* which raised tariffs on the rest of Australia, with the unabashed public support of Barton. 'What has become of Federation?' Parkes pointedly asked of Barton.[255] But there was an answer.

Barton and the Corowa Conference

The apparent defeat of Federation by the fiscal question saw a new subplot in the federal story emerge. Barton now sought to revive Federation by translating it into another issue. In 1892 Barton began to recast the perennial tension between town and country into a struggle between Federation versus the capital cities, especially Sydney, Brisbane and Hobart. Australian unity was thus to be founded on geographical division.

As part of the new strategy, late in 1892 Barton visited the Riverina to foster a Border Federation League. The League decided to hold a conference, over 31 July-1 August 1893, at the small Murray River township of Corowa, 240 km from Melbourne and 500 km from Sydney; on the NSW bank of the Murray, but claimed by the *Cyclopedia of Victoria* as a Victorian town. The Corowa Convention was subsequently incorporated into Federation mythology by two of its active participants, Robert Garran and John Quick, as a milestone, even a sort of turning point.

For a convention on the federation of a continent, Corowa was geographically lopsided. Both the Victorian Premier, Sir James Patterson, and Opposition Leader, Graham Berry, attended, but neither the NSW Premier nor Opposition Leader materialised. The only NSW politicians attending were the local member, Lyne, who was also Minister for Lands, and the NSW Postmaster-General, the most junior of the ten cabinet members. Neither did Parkes attend. He made a point – a rather sharp point – of visiting Corowa several weeks *after* the conference. Another person conspicuous by his absence was the League's informal patron, Edmund Barton.[256] He was, in fact, on a restorative holiday in British Columbia, visiting Banff Springs among other places. Nor did Barton depute any others to attend, as he had been requested.

For a conference on how to realise national unity, Corowa was lacking brotherly spirit. The Conference could only agree on Australia as a free trade area, and was unable to commit to the customs union which Federationists insisted on. The Conference declined to express appreciation of Barton's Australasian Federation League; there was evidently ill-feeling between the Conference and Barton. And it refused to express its appreciation of the work of delegates to the National Australasian Convention; more resentment of the non-attendance of Parkes, Barton and Dibbs, indeed, of any of NSW's seven delegates to the 1891 Convention. But one measure Corowa delegates did warmly support: Quick's on-the-spot proposal to convene a second convention, composed of persons directly elected by voters. (Was not 'Corowa' also a convention not chosen by politicians?) Unhappily, the attending politicians of NSW and Victoria had already left by the time Quick's scheme was put to vote.[257] Peacock, the most senior 'coming' Victorian at the Convention, was completely unaware of it.[258] Quick's plan was only perfunctorily reported in the press. Had not Parkes and Barton already publicly proposed a second convention, with a referendum at its conclusion?[259] Barton's Australasian Federation League dutifully examined the Quick scheme, and rejected it in favour of a scheme in which, first, conventions would be elected on a colony-by-colony basis, and, then, an Australia-wide body chosen by all legislatures would have the final say.

The Corowa Conference, then, was no 'turning point', as commemorative history would have it. Notwithstanding that the translation of the Federation cause into a crusade of the periphery versus the centre was, ultimately, essential to Federation's success, in 1893 the enlistment of the regions bore nothing. And in the twelve months following the Conference the dull state of Federationist prospects only dimmed further. In December 1893, Barton and O'Connor were forced to resign their ministries in some ignominy. The NSW election of July 1894 saw no recovery of Federation forces, despite the joint efforts of Parkes and Barton on behalf of their cardboard cut-out 'National Federal Party'.[260] In that election Parkes himself was subject to an uncomfortably strong challenge by an anti-Parkes free trader.[261] His most significant Federationist loyalist, Bruce Smith, did not stand. One of Barton's stalwarts, Sir William Manning, the President of the Australasian Federation League and Mayor of Sydney, lost his attempt to enter parliament. And Barton himself lost badly to a free trader (later a declared anti-Billite) in his own attempt to win a seat.[262] On election night Barton declared, not very modestly – but not wholly inaccurately – that his defeat 'would be received with profound lamentation by those who wished for a union of the Australasian colonies'. [263]

Correlate with Barton's electoral difficulties, free trader numbers surged in the Assembly as a whole, and Reid, the 'enemy' of Federation, now replaced Dibbs as premier. On election night, 3 August 1894, the Federation push of 1889 could be deemed dead, like parallel pushes of previous decades.[264] The Victorian election one month later only underlined this. Even an official organ of Federationists, *The Commonwealth*, lamented 'the apparent apathy on the subject of Federation displayed by People and the Press of Victoria.'[265] In September 1895 *The Commonwealth* itself announced 'the very indifferent support given to the magazine by the public compels its closure'.[266]

Federation would only have the life that Reid might choose to breathe into it.

Reid and the Quick scheme

In the early 1890s Reid had played the Federation wedge to Parkes's sinker, to the cost of Parkes, but not necessarily to the benefit of Reid. In wedging the free trade cause by the Federation divide, Reid, an anti-federation free trader, had not necessarily placed himself in the larger camp of free traders. Many free traders were Federationist, however surprising it may be given the fate of trade policy under the Commonwealth.[267] In the referendums a few years later some strongholds of free trade voted Yes strongly.[268] Already in 1891 this electoral punch of Federationist free-traders was in evidence. In the general election of that year Reid's vote in his seat of East Sydney had slumped. The seat which he had won six times at general elections – twice topping the poll, and three times coming second in the four-member seat – that year he almost lost, reduced to fourth place, surpassed by three Federationists, in what Reid publicly denounced as a concerted push by Federationists to eliminate him. Federation, it seemed, wedged the free traders more seriously than it did the protectionists. And as the new leader of the free traders after the fall of Parkes's premiership in 1891, Reid would need to unite, not divide. Already, by the close of 1891, Reid's Federation scepticism included a note of reconciliation. He was not, he wrote in the *Sydney Quarterly Magazine*, an 'implacable' adversary of Federation; to oppose a foolish marriage is not to oppose all marriages. And now, having won government in the 1894 election, any facture of free trade opinion would be a heightened matter of concern to Reid, especially since his supporters – for all their gains – remained five short of a majority in the Assembly. It appeared prudent to make peace with Federationists. This appearance was given colour by the arch-enemy's arch-enemy, Parkes, lingering in parliament a looming, baleful, vengeful presence, still presuming to free trade leadership. And now happy to deploy, as Reid first did, the issue of Federation as a wedge against a free trade government. As one free trade member protested of Parkes,

> *The hon. member had no intention but to drive home the wedge, which would cause a separation among the supporters of the [free trade] Government, for the sole purpose of letting him get into power to force to the front his one great cause ....*[269]

Several historians have presented Parkes in the last parliament of his career as a figure of scorn, pity, and laughter: a Learesque character; estranged from his son in the same chamber; feuding with Barton; proudly spurning remaining sympathisers; and, surely, grief-stricken by the 'terminal sufferings of a beloved wife'.[270] This is contrasted with the effortless mastery of George Reid. But there is too much hindsight in this contrast. 1894 was not 1899; in 1894 Reid had not won three general elections in a row as premier. In 1894 Parkes may not have seemed quite toothless.

So when Parkes moved his much heralded urgency motion on Federation in the Assembly on 13 November 1894, Reid was prepared. The premier rose to announce he and the other premiers had agreed to confer on the Quick scheme of a convention plus referendums. The scheme's appeal to Reid at a personal level is plain enough: it cut the cord of Federation with the National Australasian Convention of 1891, which Reid had spurned, but which his adversaries – Parkes, Barton, Dibbs, and McMillan – had embraced. That Parkes scorned the Quick scheme was so much the better. But the great apparent promise of Quick's scheme was that it gave something to Federationists without giving them the whole loaf, by any means; they would need to win a referendum.

Thus Reid now treated Federation not as a wedge as he did in 1891, nor as a sinker as Parkes hoped to in the same year, but as something entirely different; as a matter which could, with political benefit, be pursued by means of compromise. In terms of his own political fortune, Reid's change in strategy was fatal to him. The advances and retreats of feeling his way to a seemingly winning compromise left him seen as faithless – 'Yes-No' Reid – and thereby losing the respect of both sides.

Perhaps the greatest defect of Reid's attempt to succeed through a compromise engagement with Federation was that no engagement of any sort was actually bidden by political circumstances. In 1894 the Federal cause was out of breath and out of sorts, at a 'standstill' in one self-description.[271] Whether he realised it or not, the cause in that moment would have only the momentum which Reid chose to impart it. And Reid's growing political strength would have repelled any recovery in Bartonite strength. For if Federation split free traders more seriously than it split protectionists, it is also true that Reid's policy of an income tax, a land tax and upper house reform, split his protectionist opponents much more than it split his free trade base. In taking up these policies, Reid had achieved what Parkes could not do; a free trade-Labor compact working magnificently. In consequence Reid won a show-down early election in 1895, defeating protectionists, and seeing almost all the leading Federationists – Parkes, Barton, Wise, Smith and Copeland – out of parliament. Parkes's 'Federal Party' failed to make any electoral impression,[272] and, to Barton's great distress, Parkes himself had been brought down in an attempt to unhorse Reid in the premier's own seat of Sydney-King.[273] Then, on 29 April 1896, there came the final grim seal of victory: departing Redfern Station, without Reid, but with two Union Jacks flying, the funeral train of the 'Father of Federation', bearing The Wanderer to his place of final rest.

Yet Reid, instead of banking on his emerging political strength, chose in 1894, as leader of a minority government, in the shortest parliament in the history of NSW, to take a semi-gratuitous, prudential measure to pre-empt an attack that was never going to break, and to side-line a potential challenger at the twilight of his career. The upshot was that Reid revived an expiring Federationist cause.[274] Thus the politician who had, at the outset, sought to scatter the Federationist cavalcade was the person most singly responsible for Federation; initiating the detonations of the old constitutional order out of a wish to evade a temporary, chance, and not very hazardous political circumstance.

The Federation drama truly begins with Reid, in 1894, with his adoption of the Quick scheme. The incidents from 1889 to 1893 are no more than prologue. And if the drama begins in 1894, one might almost say, the story also there ends. For Reid had conferred the irresistible prestige of the People's Will on a new convention tasked – not with considering Federation – but with fabricating one. The carriage he set in motion might yet be overturned, but its arriving at Centennial Park, on the first day of the new century, was the likeliest.

7

Five Federationists

The next decade of time and fate,
The mighty changes manifold,
The grander growth of Rule and State,
Perchance these eyes may yet behold!
– Henry Parkes

If Federation reduces to a political tournament, attention will turn to protagonists. It is in its attention to the actors in the federal drama that Federationist history is most clearly a victor's history; designed to celebrate the winners, and to assign significance and merit to individuals according to their portion of personal triumph. Thus, traditional history ranks in importance, character and intellect Barton above Parkes, and Parkes above Reid. That squares with how much each obtained personally from the Federal cause, but a juster ranking is probably the reverse. Neither does received history acknowledge the mingling among Federationists of opportunism and idealism; of delusion and realism; of scurrility and probity. Or the degree of complementarity between these contraries, which made the cause all the more effective. Beyond missing the contrasts among the contestants, received history of Federation seems insensible to one pervading, and unattractive, resemblance between them. An eye roaming over their line-up is struck, first, not by their individuality, but by a certain likeness; by the number of Federationists displaying a 'grandiose-vindictive' personality trait.[275] Under such a classification one might include Parkes, Barton, Kingston, Deakin, Wise, Isaacs, Higgins, Symon, Smith and perhaps, also, Griffith. Among Federation late-runners one may further count several extreme specimens of the trait: Syme, Crick, Meagher and King O'Malley.[276] Compare the 'Federation Fathers' with Australian prime ministers of the generation succeeding Hughes: Bruce, Scullin, Lyons, Menzies, Curtin and Chifley. The contrast is palpable.[277] Granted, the ungrudging Reid could not be judged 'vindictive'. But, for all his ironical self-awareness, Reid was not bereft of his peers' grandiosity.

George Reid (1845–1918)

No Federation figure has experienced a greater reversal in estimation than Reid.

In the first accounts of Federation (Deakin, for example), Reid was the rogue of the drama; an opportunist interloper, superfluous to the hallowed labour of the cause; a 'shallow trickster' (Barton's phrase) whose self-aggrandising intrusions served only to make that labour more formidable.

But in later assessments Reid became almost the saviour of Federation;[278] 'more or less' a 'patriotic far-sighted statesman'.[279] By championing NSW interests, Reid reconciled the hesitant 'mother of the Australias' to Federation. Accepting he could not secure any great change in the nature of the Federation, he still managed to extract important concessions which procured the final approval of the people of NSW.

Thus Reid was, in the Old View, unprincipled, but also, mercifully, irrelevant. In the New View, Reid was relevant, and commendably heedful of his public's interest. So whereas in the Old View Reid was duplicitous and cynical, in the New he was 'realistic' and 'pragmatic'. But there remains a mixed position: Reid, was, in accord with the New View, essential to Federation; but, in accord with the Old, unprincipled. The previous chapter pressed Reid's essentiality to Federation. What remains unargued is the second premise of the mixed position: that Reid was a practical cynic; faithless, in several senses.

Estimating how faithless or faithful was Reid is hampered by his 'enigmatic' presentation;[280] a closed book, indeed, who authored notably unexpressive memoirs. A judgement is further distracted by the blatant figure he chose to cut. No politician wore more garish greasepaint on the political stage of the day, and the analyst is perplexed by this self-lampoon. Finally, and distinct from his mummery, Reid was *the most perfect actor ... that politics has produced here ... he revealed a mastery of voice control, and the lights and shades of his sentences would have done credit to any big tragedian – or comedian, for Reid was both ... Reid knew when to speak ... he knew when to roar and when to coo and when to wipe his face.*[281]

But in a search for the 'real man beneath', the seeker has, at least, the benefit that Reid had experienced plenty of formation.

Reid's biographer notes without stress that he was the son of a Presbyterian minister; the Reverend John Reid, an active but unambitious cleric, who, as the junior of Reverend Dr John Dunmore Lang, spent George's adolescent years ministering to working class congregations in the Rocks. In these two preachers there was a powerful source of judgement, doctrine and precept. Here was an outlook and style that proved to have a political power quite out of proportion to the one-tenth of the population who subscribed to Presbyterianism in 19th century Australia; [282] a style that was bellicose and doctrinal or, in secularised terms, 'ideological'. A style that in the late 19th century accounted for a suite of powerful political enthusiasms, referred to by contemporaries as 'fads', including temperance, the annexation of the New Hebrides and (in the eyes of critics) Federation.[283] But such a style hardly describes Reid.

Reid did absorb from the sermons of Lang and his well-educated father his characteristic rationalism – a sense of proposition, and of argument and implication – and Scotch utilitarianism. So he was vexed by the waste of Robertson's land laws; and he was vexed by the congestion of Sydney's narrow streets. He favoured doing away with 'regulation' for rural land; and introducing it for urban land.[284] But for all its policy content, utilitarianism is a vacant creed in terms of political society. Intended as the solvent of all other values, it was sterile in political ones. Reid's resourcelessness in political ideas is indicated by the epigram he chose to be placarded in Sydney streets on 1 January 1901, alongside those chosen by Barton, Wise, Smith, McMillan and O'Connor. Their precepts invoke 'patriotism', 'unity', 'freedom','nation', and 'race'. Reid's reads: 'May wise laws ever brighten the homes of the poor'. When it came to capturing some constitutional dimension of the essentially constitutional act of Federation, Reid could not think of anything to say.

A more significant bequest of Reid's kirk upbringing is more ironical: in the unavoidable gap between extreme ideals and reality, puritanism, historically, deposited a seedbed of satire. The two procreating spirits of satire – the fantastic and the grave – were present in extreme religion, and could operate in Reid to produce the satirical. But when the grave weakened, the simply parodic emerged; Reid, 'not picturesque, but grotesque',[285] obese but 'immaculately dressed', in a monocle, flicking repartee at the crowd in a 'high pitched' voice: the burlesque of sermon. When the impulse to the fantastic waned, the naturalistic and sober puncturer of illusion emerged; the mind of the critic, rather than creator; who argued more readily than acted, and who saw more than envisioned.[286]

Perhaps the most signal legacy of Reid's upbringing was a sympathetic education in crowds which his immersion in his father's unpolished congregations probably provided. Not quite the first foray of Reid into public life was a defence of the crowd from a headmasterly scolding by the official classes. The occasion was a cricket match between the NSW team and a visiting English XI, captained by Lord Harris, a future governor of Bombay, but, then, a former Etonian cricketer who was 'not above slyness' in his play. On a Saturday afternoon match at the Sydney Cricket Ground in February 1879, a batsman for the struggling NSW side was called out in a questionable decision by one of the two umpires. A mob invaded the ground. Harris was struck on the head. An English player 'apparently' alleged the mob's convict parentage. A melée ensued, and the match abandoned. The *Sydney Morning Herald* hung its head in shame. Among the spectators was a not entirely obscure official in the Attorney-General's Department, who chose the mass circulation *Evening News* to advance a defence. The offending umpire, Reid averred, had saluted the spectators in 'a most irritating manner'. The crowd had been moved only by 'honest indignation' at their side's raised hopes being 'suddenly strangled' by the obnoxious umpire's 'crowning blunder'. Crowds anywhere are capable of misdemeanours, and Reid closed with a reference to riotous behaviour at an Eton vs Harrow match.

George Reid, in 'self-lampoon', stretches for the camera

But the English XI was not, however, without defenders. The second umpire happened to be Edmund Barton. His own conduct had been quite unremarked in newspaper reports, but he now entered the controversy. There was no fault in the first umpire's decision, he declared. And he could not believe any 'sons of convicts' insult was thrown. [287]

The incident at the Sydney Cricket Ground brings out the contrasting sympathies of Barton and Reid. And a contrast in the constituencies they were seeking to appeal to, as both were soon to enter the NSW parliament. With a gift for popularity which the essentially unpopular Parkes lacked, Reid topped the poll for East Sydney of 1888, leaving Parkes in fifth place. Between these two Gladstonian liberals there would be no concord. In Reid's eyes, Parkes was no Antipodean Gladstone, but a vainglorious Bottom, who would play all the parts.[288] It was upon this Bottom's Dream, in the woods of Tenterfield of 1889, that Reid a year later launched a vehement assault. He expressed, 'in the strongest possible way', his fear a Federation would make its capital in 'the far bush of Australia'.

> *I do not want to see a political nest established in the centre of this continent. I do not want to see a bodyguard of lobbyists and syndicates established in the very heart of the political power of this great country, far away from the scrutiny of public opinion. Wherever this capital is to be, let it be within the reach of public scrutiny and control. Let it be in some great centre.*[289]

In the wake of the 1891 Convention, Reid was deployed as John Robertson's heavy gun at anti-Federation mass meetings. 'A national movement?' he asked. 'No! A movement confined to the great ambitious statesmen of Australia'.[290] A Federation which would fix 'the fetters of commercial slavery upon the whole of the coasts of Australia'.[291] 'I am not prepared to give up the whole loaf of freedom – I am not prepared to erect across Port Jackson barriers against the world'.[292]

But Reid's Federation fire was to falter once he had won the leadership of free traders in the NSW parliament, in November 1891. Within a month he vented the grievance that he had been misrepresented as opposing Federation in the abstract, rather than merely in the particular. 'My reward has been an attempt to brand me as "the implacable enemy" of Federation. In other words, if you oppose a bad law, you are opposed to all law'.[293] In November 1892, he announced in the Assembly what the press described as his 'conversion'. Reid declared the Age of Protection – epitomised by the fifty percent hikes of the 1890 'McKinley Tariff' act – had been vanquished by the Democrat triumph in the United States presidential election of 1892: Federation was now safe for a free trader such as himself to support. Reid further avowed the Australasian Federation League was the 'noblest organisation in the land', and became an Honorary Vice President of it. He appointed the Federationist Andrew Garran as his government's representative in the Council; Andrew's son, Robert, became Reid's private secretary. Reid conferred with Quick – who found the premier 'distinctly favourable to the cause of federation'[294] – and borrowed his schema (invention was not Reid's strong suit), and so made practical politics of a second, elected, Convention. Reid voted Yes in 1898, and in the 1899 referendum stretched every nerve to secure the conclusive approval of Federation.[295]

Reid's federal conversion was a remarkable one. Had circumstances changed? Had the proposals of Federation much changed?

Circumstances had not altered to soothe Reid's earlier anxieties about Federation. There had been a portion of importunity in Reid invoking, on 30 November 1892, the Democrat victory in the US presidential election three weeks earlier. But how much outright insincerity is less clear. Reid was not to know in 1892 that the new Democratic administration would yield only paltry reductions in the tariff, or that the abhorrent McKinley would himself win the presidential election of 1896 in an historic landslide, and rush into law the highest tariff wall yet seen in American history. But by mid-1897 Reid would have known these things, and that the salient public ground for his conversion was extinguished. Yet his conversion to Federation did not falter. Instead, his seemingly ardent free-trade principles did. At the climax of his premiership in 1899, Reid reversed his own legislation to abolish the tariff on sugar in order to win support in the chamber of the leprous Meagher.

Neither had Federationists' proposals altered significantly to meet Reid's censures of 1891. In the negotiations he endured a compromise over Commonwealth regulation on railways, and on stalemates between the House of Representatives and the Senate. On inland rivers he 'lost completely',[296] he was defeated on the maximum number of High Court judges, the election of a Senate on a State basis, and its power to reject money bills. In the judgement of his biographer, 'on nearly every important matter of principle he had failed to get his way'.[297] Here was no prudent repositioning of forces but, over the space of a handful of years, the traverse from one side of the battle ground to the other.

In Reid we are, then, looking upon one of those dazzling vaults across the political landscape, which were even more familiar in their time than ours. In the same vein, one might note the long file of politicians traversing from free trade to protection. Even Parkes now announced free trade was a 'trifling' matter and, in 1895, appeared at the Hotel Australia for the launch of the protectionist party's election campaign. Or how Reid in 1895 and 1898 could enter into an electoral pact with Labor, a party then formally committed to socialism;[298] and a few years later launch an 'anti-socialist' crusade against Labor's 'socialist tiger'.

The motor behind Reid's about-faces is obvious. By his own recollection, he knew from the age of 12 he would be prime minister by 30.[299] So what we see in Reid's trajectory is a familiar, even hackneyed, gambit of the ambitious: when quite without power, obtain notice by vocally adopting some 'firebrand' position; but when on power's threshold, tack briskly towards the midpoint.

Untethered to any cause, Reid was also disentangled from any particular human company which might have moored him to one. Reid's falseness did not have the effrontery of Barton's. Yet the bitter almond smell of personal treachery lingered about Reid. At the climactic 'Yes-No' speech at Sydney Town Hall on 25 March 1898, Reid declared he would not 'desert'. But he, in what amounted to cruel play, had had his anti-federation followers beckoned to his side, only to abandon them publicly.[300] Not a man of affections, he was a solitary; *'As always, by his resolve to make his own way'*. So, unlike Robertson, he was without his own band; but, instead, like Parkes, attended by adjutants of a troop of his own construction. The free trade caucus had made him their leader without relish; just 16 of the 35 members who attended the leadership ballot in 1891 voted for him. Want did not favour him as leader; Reid owed his elevation to the parricide of Varney Parkes, and to the machinations of Wise, later his most bitter enemy.[301]

Lacking affections, or animosities, Reid was instead a man of *attractions* and *antipathies*; and these last seem to have exerted some influence on his passage through the political straits.[302] He was, renownedly, antipathetic to Parkes. And there were obvious incongruities: the rumpled melancholy versus the well-pressed wit; a laboured dignity versus a cultivated vulgarity; the lonely and querulous versus the companionable and self-possessed; the often poetic versus the always earth-bound. The leading Federationists of the Convention were, it seems, more Reid's kind of people. He never had an ill word for Deakin, for all of Deakin's private contempt and public double-dealing. And, despite Kingston's sometimes public contempt, Reid 'liked' Kingston 'immensely'.

And Barton and Reid? Despite their intense conflict, it has been rightly observed they were not enemies, but rivals.

There were differences. Reid 'delighted in a hostile audience', whereas Barton struggled with one. Barton lacked a feeling for his listeners, while one of Reid's severest critics allowed Reid had 'an almost unerring instinct for what will touch them'.[303] Reid had the better mind: contrast the pith of Reid's speeches with the magmatic gas, legal technicalities, and sprays of irrelevance of Barton's. Barton lacked an interest in social conditions; in that respect, he was the 'antithesis' of Reid.[304]

But there were similarities. They were both youngest sons; both blue-eyed; both obese; both highly popular and essentially friendless. Both, in fact, conforming well to the 'endomorph' stereotype: rotund, convivial, self-satisfied, and lazy. Reid lacked Barton's sense of entitlement, but matched him in confidence. Both shared a sense of self–destiny. In young adulthood they became confreres on the oval and companions in the fishing boat, 'very old friends' as Barton was truthfully to declare in middle age.[305] The two entered politics about the same time; both (then) as independent free traders; both members for East Sydney; both East Sydney sort of people. They harmonised with one another; Barton had seconded Reid's nomination for East Sydney in 1880, and in 1885 Reid moved Barton's election as Speaker of the Assembly, and 'conducted him to the chair'. In 1897 Reid supported Barton as 'Leader of the Convention', disposing of his own hopes without demur. He appointed Barton to the Legislative Council in the middle of their struggle for the leadership of Federation. And, having beaten off Barton's attempt to win the seat of Sydney-King, Reid smoothed Barton's return to the Assembly by parachuting the sitting protectionist member for Hastings-Macleay into the Legislative Council. In 1898 the press bruited Barton would join Reid's ministry; it is a fact that in 1899, before the passage of the referendum, duets of the two could break out in the chamber. Not so much rivals, the two were, in truth, something of a double act.[306] As the foil may actually enhance the protagonist, Reid's temporisation braked and steadied Barton's turbulence. It was only with Federation sealed that the rivalry between Reid and Barton broke out again in the duel for the great prize of prime minister of the new Commonwealth.

It appeared Reid would outmatch Barton in the new federal politics. Dapper, humorous, unflappable, a 'character', a celebrity politician with cross-class appeal, Reid drew 'enormous crowds', 'much larger' than anything Barton managed during the 1901 campaign.[307] If Barton had the frigid honour of uncontested passage into the House of Representatives, Reid won the (federal) seat of East Sydney by a landslide, even while his own groomed successor for his old state seat of Sydney-King lost. As, in Deakin's words, 'the most influential politician in Australia prior to Federation'[308], with a 'unique' personal popularity,[309] the road would have seemed open to great office.

But circumstances overwhelmed Reid's talents. Reid's free traders won just one-third of the House of Representatives in the March 1901 election, the remainder falling into the hands of an unstable but potent accord of protectionists and Labor. The prime ministership that Reid ultimately managed to conjure out of this situation in 1904 was feeble – just eleven months long, with one former protectionist Premier of Victoria as his deputy, and another former protectionist Premier of Victoria as Treasurer. His government had been contrived by Deakin, and solely to enact compulsory arbitration, something the preceding protectionist and Labor governments had struggled, but failed, to do. In the Convention, Reid had declared it 'passes my comprehension' how the Commonwealth might aspire to legislate for the compulsory arbitration of workplace disputes,[310] yet the one significant piece of legislation his government passed was to confer such a power. Whereas once he had anathemised any notion of siting the federal capital in the 'far bush of Australia ... far away from the scrutiny of public opinion', Reid now actively endorsed siting the capital in Dalgety. Whereas he had once declared he would refuse to 'erect across Port Jackson barriers against the world', he now presided over the substantial tariffs that the *Customs Tariff Act 1902* had imposed on fodder imports from New Zealand, even while the countryside was in the blistering grip of the Federation drought, its earth 'as dry as ashes', and livestock perishing in tens of million.[311] In office Reid was left to drink from the empty cup the opportunist is often left with.

If Reid's faithlessness did him little good, did it necessarily harm NSW? Is it a bad thing for politicians to reconcile with public opinion? But Reid could not be described as accommodating to some settled state of opinion; there was no settled state of opinion. Most of the NSW public was either baffled by, or apathetic about, the prospect of an entirely new and unknowable constitutional order. A politician in this circumstance could either paint a vision for the public, or coax the public's halting choices for their personal advantage. What path Reid took is plain.[312] Abnormal politics calls for abnormal politicians. What NSW needed in 1898 was a politician of the 'terrible earnestness' of a William Charles Wentworth; it got the opportune rationalisations and temporisations of George Reid.

Edmund Barton (1849–1920)

If Reid was opaque, Barton was transparent. The obstruction faced by his analyst lies not in the man, but in his legend. No Federation figure has been so enhanced by a glazing adulteration of time and piety than Edmund Barton. The most accomplished general history of Federation goes so far as to describe Barton as 'calm, devoted, high minded', with 'no indication he wanted glory for himself'.[313] In the more restrained conventional recitation of commemorative history, Barton was the 'leader of the federation movement, and the inaugural Prime Minister of the Commonwealth'. But in a more profane telling Barton was a clubbable man with few real friends; a Queen's Counsel chronically in debt; a conservative who fathered a radical Commonwealth; an erratic politician who won the highest political office in the land; a candidate who outpolled all others in the Constitutional Convention election, but who struggled to win a seat in parliament; an office-seeker, who quickly abdicated the crowning position he had so long quested after; a preacher of national unity who, even in moments of the greatest triumph, could vent bitter maledictions on dissentients.

Barton's weaknesses are acknowledged by his biographers, at least conditionally.[314] Nevertheless, a lenience, extending almost to an official courtesy, suffuses any spotlight on him. Is he not a Federation Father? Only once the biographers of the Commonwealth's crafters are released from a kind oath of allegiance will the counsels of justice, rather than mercy, loom large in taking the measure of Edmund Barton.

*

Getting Barton's measure requires peeling away the varnish. That he was academically brilliant; that he always carried a copy of Thucydides in the Greek original; that he squired Miles Franklin on her first visit to Sydney; that he was perhaps descended from a loyalist officer in the American Revolution; that a hero of the Arctic, Sir Edward Parry, was his godfather, and Barton, in some obscure augury, was christened Edmund in honour of him: such are some of the falsehoods, fond fancies, and traditionary tales that enswathe the truth.

Barton's story truly begins, like many Australian stories, abruptly, with the appearance of his parents, William and Mary, on Sydney's shores in 1827.[315] The newly married couple had elected to enrol their fate in a tiny society of outcasts, square pegs and beachcombers, which was on the cusp of an economic adventure. It was from this last that William's employer, the Australian Agricultural Company, was ambitious to profit. But William was soon absorbed in irrational disputes with Company officers, both very high and very low. Sir Edward Parry, then the Company's manager, judged William 'insolent and insubordinate' in their brief and bitter encounter. William pitched a stone at an annoying Company menial, and was charged with assault. The charge dropped, William then sued witnesses for libel, but was left by the jury to swallow the stony fare of one farthing damages. His subsequent 'long and not very successful business career' as auctioneer and stockbroker saw him passing once through the insolvency court.[316]

By way of example or heredity, we can see in the father something of the son: the pride, the dearth of self-control, even the farthing damages.[317] But the father left a paradoxical bequest; as an evident failure, and 70 years old when Edmund was 16, to his son William must have constituted an easily displaceable father figure, with a psychologically emancipating effect: Edmund's pocket-sized world would seem even more conquerable. With a reinforcing consequence, his older brother, George, also proved easily eclipsable by Edmund as presumptive heir. A failure at the Sydney bar, George's subsequent pursuit of his literary talents was dogged by abrupt terminations of employment, and the personal turbulence of three marriages. His bookmanship did bear fruit in a first volume of a *History of New South Wales from the Records* – but in 625 pages he only managed to reach 1789; he fought furiously with the publisher, and later volumes of this labour of love were reassigned to another hand. In 1901, with his younger brother inaugurated as prime minister before tens of thousands, George was editing the *Werriwa Times and Goulburn District News*. Perhaps even in 1866, with George (temporarily) a Reader at the University and Barton an undergraduate, the true relation of the brothers may have been apparent.

From an early age Barton's apparent fitness for office impressed itself. Barton was captain of Sydney Grammar School – the mid-19th century nursery of the New South Wales elite. Approved by staff, and popular with his school fellows – they voted him 'a jolly good fellow'[318] – Barton's accomplishment in the classroom was more mixed. Contrary to the legend of scholastic brilliance fostered by Garran, Smith, Reynolds and others, Barton did not win one of three entrance scholarships to Sydney University, owing to an 'insufficiency of mathematics'. Neither did Barton win the Cooper Scholarship in classics at 'matriculation'; that was won by his school fellow, Edward Knox, later chairman of Colonial Sugar Refining.[319] But Barton was awarded, ad hoc, a £10 prize 'for superiority in Classics at the first year' at university. And in his third year he topped the class of five students in classics. But for all his eventual success in the examination room, Barton made little enduring use of the intellectual resources of the University. While his fellow Federationists were to author books on free trade, Captain Cook, irrigation, the joys of pig-sticking, volumes of poetry, lectures on Browning, quotations from Shakespeare, annotations of Milton, bibliographies of literature, annals of desert exploration, translations of Dante and Schiller, and massive treatises on constitutional law, Barton was never to write anything of the slightest weight beyond a speech or court judgement.

> As I sat in the study waiting for Mr. Barton the strange jumble of books gave me curiosity; it was strange to see solemn law folios cheek by jowl with saucy bindings of the minor poets, and Parliamentary reports snuggled beside frivolous novels.[320]

What Barton gained from his time at the indulged and self-indulgent minikin University of Sydney – just 10 students 'attending lectures' in 1868 – was another field to exercise his social sway.[321] There he was 'extremely popular' with fellow students,[322] indeed, 'perfectly adored'.[323] Varsity sport was a particular workshop of Barton's popularity. Barton was 'an ardent footballer and cricketer',[324] and a rower. And, it has been contended, a joint founder of the Rugby Union in Australia. In reflecting on his burgeoning political career, the *News* predicted, 'His connection with cricket and other manly sports is not likely soon to be forgotten by the "Old Boys".'[325]

Beyond sport, the University Union, established by his right-hand man Richard O'Connor, incited a taste in politics, and the University's Senate provided an arena where Barton could practise the political arts, long after he had graduated, and had been, in 1871, admitted to the bar.[326] A seat in the NSW Legislative Assembly reserved for University men provided a relatively easy entrée into politics proper in 1879. When that seat was abolished shortly after, an uncontested rural seat provided a still easier, and completely uncontested, entry.

In the Assembly Barton appears to have been an inactive representative of his constituents in distant Wellington.[327] But he would never practise power as the champion of some locality. Or as the tribune of some economic interest (miners, selectors, squatters). Nor as the stalwart of some political faction, let alone as the partisan of any credo. He was as free of doctrinal commitments as his less educated peers; in the space of two years he glided from free trade to protectionism with barely anyone noticing.[328] His mind was populated by simple, conventional presumptions. Women should not be able to vote; Chinese were inferior, and Indians were even worse. The inferiority of 'coloureds' seems to be one of the more enduring notions Barton had about human affairs, and one he did not trouble to articulate with the circumspection of, say, Deakin. One common prejudice he was not burdened by was anti-Catholicism, an outlook doubtless nourished by youthful friendships, with his lifetime collaborator Richard O'Connor, and with the brilliant but doomed Samuel Kelly.

Unencumbered by allegiances – he was opaquely classified as a 'government cross bencher' – and blessed with bonhomie, Barton's rapid ousting of the incumbent of the Speaker's chair is not mystifying, but, for all that, remarkable: at the age of 33, a position which, by the precedent of the House of Commons, was a reward for long service, and prepared for by the same, was Barton's as almost a parliamentary novice.[329] Perhaps encouraged by this rapid ascent, and spurred by the illusory honour of topping the poll for the seat of East Sydney in 1885,[330] he made two plunges for the premiership.[331] Both were fruitless pieces of political apple bobbing, suggesting a quantum of conceit in someone not yet 40 and without ministerial experience.

Barton's four years in the chair proved uncomfortable. As Speaker, his surface equability vanished in the face of the provocation of mischief-makers. His rulings were sometimes sophistical, sometimes high-handed. He suspended one member for the entire parliament, only for the Privy Council to nullify his draconian edict. In 1886 his alleged inconsistencies in favour of whoever had the majority provoked one of the 'most notorious episodes of disorder' of the house.[332] His speakership was now the subject of leader writers' indignation, and Parkes moved a reduction in salary.[333] For a position that was not then a gift, in effect, of the executive, but the choice of the chamber, his unseating as Speaker in a fresh parliament may have loomed, as a hostile press mooted. He resigned from the Assembly early in 1887, and Parkes, now in government, planted him in the Legislative Council. It was not the last time Barton was to change course suddenly in inauspicious circumstances, and his abrupt appointment in 1887 to a senior, more placid body does bear a resemblance to his swift exit in 1903 from the House of Representatives to the High Court.

Barton's apparent retreat to the political background was reversed in 1889 when Parkes's majority suddenly cracked into pieces, and Barton was made Attorney-General of the seven-week-long protectionist government of George Dibbs. His tenure was brief, but long enough for Barton to invoke the prerogative of the Attorney-General and 'confer on himself' silk, notwithstanding his only modest success at the bar.[334] Freed to pursue his legal profession as a Queen's Counsel, Barton's attendance at the Council was dilatory,[335] but he remained on the lookout for political opportunity. Seemingly untrue to Parkes in accepting Dibbs's appointment in 1889; he returned to Parkes's camp – evidently forgiven – once the septuagenarian had won the election of 1891. But in the wake of the subsequent collapse of Parkes's last government, Barton left Parkes a second time in order to become Attorney-General a second time under Dibbs. This characteristic shuffle of advance and retreat left him, by the close of 1893, the one dominant figure beneath Dibbs, seemingly well-positioned to succeed the beleaguered premier.

But disaster then broke over Barton's propitious position, as news surfaced that he had been retained by the Proudfoot railway contractors as their legal counsel in their claim for £1 000 000 against the Railway Commissioners. This bizarre arrangement – where the Attorney-General (paid £1 000 a year) was advising a private interest on how to best relieve the public purse of one million pounds – was exposed in parliament, and Barton was forced to resign.

The 'Proudfoot affair' bespeaks Barton's wooden hands in playing his legal career in accompaniment with his political one. His political judgement was similarly dubious in appearing as counsel for the defence of Meagher in the Dean case in 1895; or for the directors of Taranganba Gold-mining Company in 1889, the arena of perhaps the greatest gold swindle in Australian history;[336] and, above all, in 1898, for rorting the public purse so blatantly in the McSharry case. In this affair, again, a plaintiff was suing the Railway Commissioners, but this time Barton had been appointed Arbitrator. With Barton in control of the conduct of the process, his lifelong friend, O'Connor, representing the plaintiff, and his allies, Smith and Hunt, representing the Crown, here was a gift that would keep on giving. When the 13 000 pages of foolscap evidence had finally been completed, and arbitrated, Barton claimed for himself £8,266-10s, half to be paid directly from the public purse.[337] The breathtaking size of this figure may be gathered from Table 7.1.

The McSharry and Proudfoot affairs bear witness to the shamelessness of the grandiose personality.[338] The Proudfoot case additionally suggests recklessness; for the benefit of 25 guineas, Barton risked his political career. It betokens a lack of self-discipline, perhaps an itch for risk. Barton was far from the sturdy, calm figure of the studio portraiture of the day; he was a teetering one. One manifestation of his lack of psychological self-government was his chronic inability to manage his personal finances. A single week's accounts of the Barton household in July 1893 came to an extraordinary £1,070.[339] A sign of the consequences of such conduct may be a cryptic note Barton sent to

Table 7.1 Some earnings of occupations

Position	Annual income, (except where stated otherwise)
Colonial Secretary	£1 820
Barton's average earnings at the bar, 1883-1886	£841
Newspaper Editor	£500-£1 000
Railway Clerk	£210
Fireman	£134
Postmistress	£80 plus accommodation
Stockman	£41 19s 4d
C.G. Haydon's fee for the arbitration of the McSharry case (for 6 months)	£31 10s
Henry Parkes as vinedresser in 1840	£25 plus rations for 1.5
Barmaid	£12 6s
The salary drawn by Edward Braddon as Premier of Tasmania, 14 April 1894 - 12 October 1899	£0
memorandum: The median value of the estate of deceased Victorian men, 1908-9	£0

Sources: Rows 1,4,5,7 and 10; *Statistical Registers*. Row 2; Rutledge (1974); Row 3; Barton (1866, p. 19); Row 6; Richardson (1948, p. 21).; Row 8; *Worker* 9.7.98; Row 9; Martin (1980). Row 11; *Australian Dictionary of Biography*. Row 12; Rubinstein (1979).

Dibbs, advising the Premier he had conversed with their go-between, and concluding, 'I cannot say how much I thank you'.[340] More definitely known is that, late in 1899, a concerted effort was made to extricate Barton from the financial morass he was in, despite the extraordinary boon of the McSharry case. A 'Barton Testimonial Fund' discreetly established committees in NSW, South Australia and Tasmania, and privately raised at least £1 400.[341] The funds would be committed to Mrs Barton's trust, as Edmund was 'very extravagant', in the words of J. T. Walker, one of the fund's organisers. Barton's state of financial obligation to others raises the unsettling possibility of an influence of creditors over his political decisions. In the turmoil subsequent to Reid losing his majority in the NSW Assembly in 1899, it was put to Walker: 'Barton is *not* well off financially, and some of his friends (he has many) are trying to help him. They would not be so ready to do so were he to join Lyne'.[342] He did not.[343]

Barton's lack of psychological self-government was also manifested through his dogged and disastrous pursuit of unlikely legal suits; some ugly (alcohol fuelled?) nocturnal careens through the chamber as Attorney-General[344]; and in his dependence on alcohol. In one recollection, he would begin the day with a rum and milk 'eye-opener', an alcoholic's breakfast.[345] It is unclear how much this dependence interfered with his activities. If Barton was an alcoholic, he was a 'high-functioning' one. But the biographer of Atlee Hunt, Barton's private secretary, notes, 'It had been widely hinted that Barton, stupefied by the effects of alcohol, had frequently signed papers written and put before him by Hunt without knowing their contents'.[346]

Barton's mental scaffolding could reach breaking point. Thus his chronic sleeplessness.[347] Thus his murky illnesses in mid-1893, which moved him to announce in parliament he was putting aside the cause of Federation.[348] He invoked the urgent direction of his physician, Harman Tarrant. The hostile press judged this a convenient cover for his disengagement from a stalled Federation campaign. It is true that during his career Barton did episodically seek refuge in illness. And it is also true Tarrant was not simply Barton's physician; he was his campaign manager in 1891. And, in a handful of years, Tarrant had revealed himself as a sad quack.[349] But if Barton's physical crises were sometimes dubious, his mental crisis of 1893 was perfectly real. There exists a near-unhinged letter to Parkes he drafted at this period.[350] Barton complains of Parkes's 'many veiled taunts' at him in their correspondence, and growls, 'you have not lost any opportunity of publicly misrepresenting me against your better and absolute knowledge of the facts.' He put to Parkes that the premier's 'labours in the foundation of the tangible scheme of union are entirely represented by one word of its title – the noble word Commonwealth'. He charged that Parkes 'fled the field in the hour of victory'. 'Truly sir, an Attorney-General may achieve what a Prime Minister does not attempt!'.

> Sir Henry, the citizens have taken their seats in the coach which is travelling the road to union and strength. You have preferred to ride in a donkey cart with ... Mr Pulsford. A seat is still at your disposal. Sir Henry, 'all aboard!.'[351]

This ludicrous and pathetic blatancy of Barton's egotism is seen again in 1894 when, defeated in his quest to win a seat in the Legislative Assembly, he declared in public,

> he was certain that when victory was won by Australia and the federation of the colonies was an accomplished fact, on the scroll of fame his name would be inscribed; but alongside of it there would not appear the name of any other of the candidates for Randwick at that day's election.[352]

His dearth of self-control fostered a lack of self-sanction, and curdled failings into delinquency. His selfishness left him bereft of any sense of public service – he was truly 'naïve' to the notion. To the victors the spoils was his untroubled presumption. He could be audacious in misleading parliament.[353] And audacious in his insincerity,

> He wished to be connected with the creation of the Federation; but had no ambition for future office.[354]

Drawing on this talent for insincerity, Barton was something of a master of planting a slur by affecting not to. He could insinuate in parliament the slanders of John Norton against Reid, while denying his 'intention to trade innuendoes, which was, of course, the clearest way of doing so'.[355] In Barton's struggle to enter parliament in 1898 it was expected that a key meeting of Reid's would be disturbed by Bartonites, to the discredit of his candidacy. A private instruction to his electoral agents would have prevented this. Instead, Barton announced to his supporters, 'My advice to you is to give him a patient and orderly hearing and if you have any eggs to spare at home boil them and eat them'. Barton could hardly go wrong here: if his followers took him at face value, Barton was now a chivalrous opponent; and if Barton's talk of eggs actually provoked his followers to throw them, his chivalrous injunction remained on record.[356]

The Bartonian public presentation, then, is instantly recognisable: an insincerity compounded with pride, calculated little flounces of contempt, and, too often, an unmistakeable sneering tone; the voice of a diplomat dressing down a lesser power. All finished off with rotund professions of propriety in all his deeds.

An unattractive picture! Accepting it produces a puzzle as to how Barton could ever be popular. Part of the solution to this puzzle is that a hardy popularity was never his: what he had, buckled under stress. At no point in his entire political career did Barton win a contested, single-member seat at a general election. He lost both the single-member, general election contests he did undertake (Randwick in 1894 and Sydney-King in 1898). In travelling to deeply divided Queensland on the eve of the 1899 referendum, he was met in Brisbane, not by enthusiastic crowds, but by a raging mob, perfectly beyond any charm Barton was capable of.

But if Barton's popularity was not solid, it was, nevertheless, at times broad and even intense. His sentences might be hard to follow, his speech might swerve between obscurity and tedium,[357] but Barton could draw 1 500 hearers, while Varney Parkes, the son of the premier, in the same campaign could only manage 90 to 100.[358] Barton might lack a feel for an audience,[359] and, in acute contrast to Reid, his public performances were bereft of natural humour, yet he still was 'in great demand at various festive functions'.[360]

Barton had personal attractions. Women found him good looking. Men judged his appearance dignified. Garran recorded his 'finely chiselled features'. Deakin was gripped by his blue eyes. And in an age when leaders were seen in the flesh or not at all, he was 5 feet 10 inches,[361] compared to an average height of 5 feet 6 inches of recruits into the armed forces. And he was gregarious, approachable, personable, good with children. If he was grandiose in his self-conception, he was without grandness in his private presentation. This was the one strand of 'democracy' in his otherwise entirely undemocratic outlook.

And Barton had 'social sway'. More than mere confidence or presence, it was a dominance that was acknowledged and endorsed by all. Between Barton and his admirers, there was a mutually gratifying transaction; he would be the leader they sought, and they the followers he craved.

By these qualities Barton would well fulfil any totemic function of his society. He would play master of ceremonies for literary Sydney's welcome to Mark Twain in 1895; or in 1885 be very much at the front of the festive farewell to the Sudan Contingent; or, in 1886, be first speaker at the memorial service for the wreck of the *Ly-ee-Moon*; and in 1888 lead a delegation to petition the Governor for anti-Chinese legislation.

But totemic performances are, typically, only marginal to political activity. One political cause, however, was totemic in its comprehensive appeal to community: Federation. It was the context of this supposedly national crusade that occasioned the development of this merely 'emblematic' politician into a crusader, and his popularity into worship. Half a century later one observer recollected, 'His fame has waned and few people can now conceive of the fervent faith of his worshippers in the 90s'.[362] His devotees in that decade longed for a hero for the federal cause, and he filled the part in wish-fulfillment. It was a rock star–fan exchange; or, in psychoanalytic terms, the transaction of the 'ideal hungry' partisans and the mirror-hungry Barton. In their idol the crowd found the glimpse of an ideal, 'Australia's noblest son'. His propaganda machine exulted in this daffy epithet: in September 1898, during Barton's struggle to enter parliament by winning the seat of Hastings Macleay, 'every boat from Sydney' had bills styling him so.[363] While this sobriquet savours of a publicity hack's invention[364] – it is reminiscent of the phrase, 'Columbia's noblest sons' (Washington and Lincoln) which was abroad at the time – the various creation myths of this *nom de guerre* – did a rural JP hit upon it?; or a priest?[365] – are not beyond credibility. And propaganda only succeeds to the extent it resonates.

> *I met one enthusiastic Barton man. 'I'm going to vote for Barton,' he said. 'He's the finest and ablest and noblest man God ever put breath into.' 'How do you know?' 'How do I*

know, is it? Did not I hear him say so along at Frederickton [near Kempsey], and did not he make Federation?'[366]

From God inspired to something still greater! At a parliamentary caucus of 1898 called to install Barton as Opposition leader, one of his supporters declared, 'Is he not god-like?'[367] In this extraordinary remark we have the conclusive sign that by 1898 Barton had reached charismatic status in the minds of his followers.[368] It was this status that drove Barton and his disciples together at hundreds of frenzied campaign meetings. The apotheosis of this morbid relation between Barton and his followers came at the climactic rally for the Yes vote on the day before the 1898 referendum. In the middle of saluting Federationists who 'had gone through all trials', Barton halted, 'completely overcome, tears running down his cheeks'.[369] At this sight, a supporter rushed on to the stage to shake his hand; another rose from his seat to lead three vigorous cheers for Barton.[370] Recovering, he turned his sights on the legislated requirement that the Yes vote number no less than 80 000 for the Bill to be deemed approved. He declared,

> *If you find any man who, with signal treachery, voted for the proposal raising the minimum affirmative vote from 50,000 to 80,000 now opposing the bill, ... you should let that man plead before you as a criminal may plead on the gallows. Listen to what he has to say, and give him the same termination.*[371]

This appalling – and disgraceful – exhortation was never withdrawn.

The marvel is that the charismatic bond of Barton to his devotees so quickly vanished. It was, evidently, already absent from the festive commemorations of the first week of 1901.[372] During the subsequent election campaign, Barton was often irritable or bored with crowds, and sometimes they with him. He would refuse to speak until irritating interjectors had been expelled by police. At a campaign rally at the Sydney Town Hall he called an interjector an 'imported monkey'.[373] At Singleton, a Federationist stronghold, 'there was not a cheer called for at the railway station, nor at the hotel, while in the street cheers were the weakest yet given to any public man in Singleton'.[374] How so? Perhaps Barton was not, in fact, charismatic, but was simply the beneficiary of a kind of craze popularity, where the crowd is engrossed in itself as much as its subject; such popularity will surely crash. Or, if Barton was charismatic, his was a charisma without mystique – such was one price of his genial ordinariness – and that makes for fragile charisma. Perhaps the most likely hypothesis is that Barton's charisma was highly 'situational'; the transaction between worshipper and worshipped was context-dependent. The context was tagging along behind the leader in a rush to the mountain top. What happens once the summit is reached? Foley had opined of Barton a few years earlier, 'there's nothing in his case — only a blare of trumpets'. And the blare of nation-making can only happen once. The labour of legislation has a quite different timbre.

It is not a surprise that Barton was at the summit for just two years and nine months, and, aged 54, was persuaded without difficulty to surrender the prime ministership. To 'sound a trumpet ... that they may have the glory of men'; for Barton it was the glory, not power. Certainly, the stated reason, ill-health, could hardly have driven him from office: Barton lived another 17 years, all of it on the bench of the High Court, on £ 3 000 a year; £500 more than the prime minister received. There would be intermittent surges of industry. But 'in some three-quarters of ... 164 cases, Barton was content to adopt every syllable of [Chief Justice] Griffith's judgement';[375] often falling asleep, he fell largely silent, an extinct volcano. He groomed no successor, and left no disciples. He died in 1920, his passing only formally regarded and regretted.

*

In pondering Barton's course through life it helps to keep his personal inadequacy distinct from his moderate professional ability. In terms of his personality, there lay at bottom a grandiosity of self-perception, a selfishness, a sense of entitlement, shading into shamelessness; and making for an itch for recurrent 'show-off' accomplishments. The narcissist, it has been said, is constantly preparing for life's 'examinations', but with the sole purpose of excelling, and without any interest in the subject matter. Thus

Barton's 'prize winning' behaviour throughout his life; from his actual prizes, in classics, as a student, despite evincing no interest in classical languages throughout his later life. Similarly, his choice of the bar as a career, despite no real interest in the law, suggests a quest for more trials he could publicly succeed at.

For Barton, Federation would be the greatest and most glorious test of them all. Enduring this test brought out his narcissistic 'mirror hunger'; Barton was one of those who 'warmed their lives' with encounters with an adoring mass. On a smaller scale, Barton had the narcissist's talent for a passing popularity. Yet, be they crowds or individuals, his personal relations were instrumental and exploitative. Even in the flush of political triumph, Barton was unresponsive to the loyalty of those who had thrown their lot in with him politically and personally. Barton denied a 'bitterly disappointed' Frederick Holder the Treasury portfolio; and Barton refused John Downer a High Court appointment, the 'great disappointment' of Downer's life, 'devastating ... as he had been let down by a close friend'.[376] Francis Clarke, who stepped aside so that Barton might enter the NSW Assembly in 1898, later murmured that his own (apparent) generosity was unrequited. Barton did have a long and deep compact with Richard O'Connor; this might be characterised as a classic extrovert-introvert exchange, where Barton provided the dash and spark, and O'Connor furnished the steadiness and slog. Or perhaps it was, more prosaically, an occupational association; Barton was the generalissimo, and O'Connor the general, a well-known partnership style. The extant evidence suggests only one possible friendship; with Thomas Bavin, 25 years his junior, his private secretary at the time of Federation. Barton's affectionate and communicative letters to Bavin bespeak how rewarding was this association, 'so pleasant and so profitable', as Barton put it.[377] But the depth of this might be pondered. Bavin was, after all, his private secretary. 'Profitable' speaks distinctly. It might be wondered if Barton ever formed any real personal bond, beyond his birds of a feather marriage to his socialite wife, Jane Ross. And to what extent did she, like O'Connor, supply a valued compensating stability for his instability?[378] Routine is monotony to the narcissist, and he seeks relief in abrupt life changes, and reckless behaviour. Hence the stops and starts in Barton's career, his endless changes of domicile, his over-spending, over-eating and over-drinking.

It was Barton's personal failings which undermined his outward 'suitability' for public office – a fine looking, intelligent, sociable, well-connected man of good address. It was his personal inadequacies, rather than a lack of ability, that so reduced his merit as a public figure. Reid's biographer presents readers a choice about the premier's antagonist: 'Barton ... may be seen as a great statesman, or as one of those lightweights who occasionally float to the top'.[379] How the preceding pages of the present work make this determination is plain. Its verdict would find apt, in reference to Barton, a certain expostulation, written long after, protesting those 'with pleasant faces and a certain animal magnetism [who] float helium-like into the firmament of success, from plum post to plum post, without ever demonstrating extraordinary talent, original intelligence or even a noteworthy grasp of the matters at hand'.[380]

But any demotion of Australia's 'noblest son' to an upward floating lightweight poses a problem. In 1958 A. A. Phillips plausibly contended that, contrary to common presumption, the 'mediocre extrovert is conspicuously absent' from the first rank of Australian politicians.[381] So how is it that events made an exception for Barton? Perhaps the exception is traceable to the abnormal state of politics at Federation's birth. Barton was appointed prime minister without a seat in parliament, and without a parliament in existence. Perhaps the aberrant processes at Federation are to blame for Australia's first prime minister being a near trivial figure. A more speculative, and alarming, possibility is to reverse the chain of causation, and wonder if Federation might be traceable to the slightness of its leading champion. For if Barton was the necessary man – if 'No Barton, No Federation' – must not his nature have been part of the requisite he supplied? His 'maximising consensus' propensity has been proposed as the key property of that apparently requisite nature.[382] But perhaps, instead, his essentialness lies in the conjunction of his popularity with a key vulnerability of the lightweight; their manipulability. Barton's narcissism left him, in Want's words, 'a vain unstable person, puffed up by the interested flattery of other colonies'.[383]

At the heart of the movement in the other colonies were two masterful wire-pullers: Sam Griffith and Alfred Deakin. They did not always get what they wanted, or always agree with each other, or Barton. But each obtained from Barton what they most craved; the post of chief justice, and prime minister. And Barton was at the centre of those successes. But to say Griffith and Deakin manipulated Barton begs the question: why was it so rewarding to manipulate Barton? The answer lies in the thing Barton had which they lacked: popularity with the public at large. In steering him, Griffith and Deakin would follow in his draught. Barton, in brief, was the fateful Weak King of Australian politics.

Bruce Smith (1851–1937)

In Bruce Smith we encounter a different kind of Federationist than either Barton or Reid. Not a glory hunter, nor an office-seeker, but a politician with a graver, more intense aspiration. In Bruce Smith's campaign for Federation we see a questing after an ideal – a seeking after a certain commonwealth of his own mind's eye; a polity where the state would be no more than a referee of the contest of citizens for the good things of life, as classical liberalism bade. The actual Commonwealth was to prove acutely inimical to such a principle. Bruce Smith, then, stands for the sizeable segment of Australian opinion that vigorously supported the projected Federation, but found its reality obnoxious. Their disenchantment was so bitter that in seeking to explain the discrepancy between what the likes of Smith foresaw, and what they found, it is insufficient to invoke an inevitable degree of myopia. We are dealing with illusion. Smith's case illustrates the uncomfortable vicinity between vision and illusion. Behind Smith's struggle to create a Commonwealth whose reality was to repel him, we see operating the exaggerated sensibility of 'the ideal' in late 19th century culture.

*

The role assigned to Smith by the received history of Federation is devoid of ideals, but instead soaked in a ruthless calculation. He is allegedly the man who sought Federation simply as a means to neuter the insurgent labour movement, and 'remove for all time' the socialist menace.[384] That this charge is at least misleading, and perhaps simply false, is easily demonstrated. The shameful sentiment supposedly appears in Smith's 4 500 word 'Case for Federation' of 1897.[385] But the words, 'labour', 'trade union' or 'socialism' never there appear. Under the heading ,'THE END OF THE FISCAL TROUBLE', he declares 'no issue has ever served to more seriously interfere with the higher political life' than the contention between Free Trade and Protection. It resulted in the 'domination in our political institutions of a body of men ... who neither "toil or spin" for themselves, who live upon the promises of impossible things'. In a new paragraph, he continues, 'This growth upon our body politic can now be removed for all time by the proposed union of the Colonies.' This 'growth' might refer to the Labor party. But it might equally refer to politicians of the protectionist party. It might refer to the 'fiscal trouble'.

Another possible myth, however, is not so easily deflated: that as a minister confronting strikers, Smith exclaimed, 'shoot the dogs'. The source of this claim is W. N. Willis, and that is probably enough to explode the claim.[386] But a professional perjurer may sometimes state the truth, or at least part of it. If the accusation ill fits Smith's self-command, it is not incongruous with the cold glance he could give what he once described as 'the cart horses rather than the blood horses of society',[387] in such a decided contrast to the placatory mien adopted by Parkes, Reid, Lyne, and even sometimes Barton, towards the 'claims of labour'. Smith did enter the NSW political fray virtually as a refugee from bitter labour confrontations in Victoria, and his ill-reputation endured. In his attempt to enter the NSW Assembly in 1887, he was badly beaten by a former Trades Hall official risen from the carpenter's bench. On entering parliament and cabinet in 1889, Smith's meetings were besieged by roaring mobs. In one such meeting Smith,

> ... *assumed an easy attitude and a passive demeanour, and for a quarter of an hour stood silent. The uproar abated not one jot, on the contrary, it grew worse, and the more derisive it became, the more complacent was the Minister for Works.*[388]

The frankness of Smith's disregard for popularity is reminiscent of W. C. Wentworth, and Smith did have something of the 'terrible earnestness' of a Wentworth.[389] The contrast with Barton could hardly be greater. Smith was not someone whose ego fed hungrily on external 'affirmations'; his source of strength was internal, not a mirror, but the mind's eye. In the nature of an intellectual, Smith would steady himself from the knocks of the world by seeking a stronger grip on ideas. In *Liberty and Liberalism*, of 1887, he unbound himself over 683 pages in reach of a pure, unadulterated conception of liberalism. But in his conception, the subject of liberalism seems no more than the appropriate limits on state action. He had little to say about liberalism as a form of political society, in which constitutionalism and parliamentarism are central. Thus to Smith, as to many others, Federation was not so much a system of government as a blank sheet on which to depict one's wishes. And what did he wish for? In 1894, his brief front-bench career over, he recalled in *The Ideal and the Actual in Politics* that, as a youth, he had 'fondly imagined' that 'all legislators were Benthamite'. But he found 'so broad and philosophical a principle had scarcely presented itself' in the Assembly, which was not 'bearable by earnest men'.[390] To the disappointed Smith, a federal government would 'receive' broad and philosophical principles, which were painfully thwarted in Smith's present reality. His political career had stalled at the age of 40, with the fall of Parkes in 1891, and the assumption of Reid to free trade leadership: he never held ministerial office again. Smith's hopes lay in Federation.

Smith's hopes for Federation bespeak his partaking the 'ideal confidence' of his age. The historians of the 19th century – before movements were marxised, and individuals psychoanalysed – saw principles as the drivers of historical action to a degree which would today be judged as naïve. This tendency of the age reached a climax in the notion that ideas were not just the driver of history, they *were* history. The 1890s saw the very climax of the steady ascent in the English-speaking world of 'philosophical idealism'; a doctrine only at the edge of our comprehension, but which by 1900 had charmed its way into every philosophic hearth. In the Federation decade, the contention that reality amounted to no more than a certain type of experience – that the world is mind – was hegemonic.[391] The friendship between Deakin the Federationist and Josiah Royce, the eminent American philosophical idealist of the period, is a curious token of this concurrence of the two phenomena. A trim causal chain linking an esoteric philosophy with campaign crudities is unlikely; and, in any case, the reconciliatory and ordering ambience of philosophical idealism could have been politically conservative in implication. But in shrinking from mere matter, 'appearance' and 'utility', Idealism fostered certain political reveries. Specifically, it could foster an extreme political constructivism, in which the mind did not merely design, say, the House of Commons, it literally made it. For the essence of any constitutional institution – legitimacy and legality – were plausibly subjects of idealistic contentions of the world as mind: what constituted the lawful and unlawful was, undeniably, the product of some mind. Reinforcing the notion of reality as mind wrought was a kindred notion also surging in popularity around 1900: reality as will-wrought. Sustained by 'vitalist' sentiments rather than suspended from philosophic premises, the age's belief that 'man could achieve whatever forms of society he willed' was, in the judgement of some critics, 'deep'. [392]

Perhaps animated by the notion that part of the world could be constituted by an act of mind or will, Smith stood in 1897 as a candidate for the constitutional Convention. But he fell short of winning a place, receiving little more than half the vote won by William McMillan, the successful candidate who most resembled Smith in political position, if not in mental force. Several candidates did win who were surely weaker than Smith for the task of constitution crafting. The tail of NSW's delegation to the Convention was puny; in his own characterisation, 'stupid', 'unstable' and 'a nuisance'. Nevertheless, Smith embraced the Constitution which the Convention produced, stumped for it, and for his pains he was the 'recipient' on the platform of several flour bags. He reconciled himself enough with 'charlatan' Reid to win a seat in the first House of Representatives under the free trade label, and so began a long and futile political career at the federal level.

Smith was completely out of sorts with the predominant sentiment of the inaugural Commonwealth Parliament: the *Pacific Island Labourers Act* was 'emotional', and the *Immigration Restric-*

tion Act a 'legislative monstrosity and a disgrace to an age of liberalism'.[393] Barton, Smith grieved, delivered scant leadership, and he, Lyne and O'Connor were 'traitors to their own State'.[394] Smith 'recognised that if the issue [Federation] were to come again before the people it would be negatived by a large majority'.[395]

Smith was left on the backbench to ponder how much 'broad philosophical principle presented itself' in the new federal legislature. In its chamber he sometimes consoled himself that the Federation he had supported had been 'a great ideal'.[396] A few years after his forced retirement in 1919, he invoked, in *The Light of Egypt*, 'the radiant names of those great ones, who saw and judged the world through philosophic eyes'; but 'came away, wiser, but truly disillusioned'.

*

The 'problem of Bruce Smith' is to understand how he could have thrown his lot in with a cause whose success was to be so lethal to the policy principles he was committed to. One answer is to resort again to the grandiose-vindictive syndrome, so evident in Smith, and invoke how Federation would have both gratified his self-importance, while destroying the despised Reid, who had wrecked Smith's career in 1891. But the answer lies in more than just personality. A host of prominent free-traders – Andrew Garran, Pulsford, McMillan, Walker, Bevan, Symon, Glynn, the 'out and out' free trader Clark, and the zealot of all free trade zealots, Max Hirsch – committed to Federation with the confident expectation it would serve their cause.[397] The immediate source of their strange error is a lack of realism. Notwithstanding their nice calculations and tendentious premises demonstrating free trade was Federation's destiny, their political senses were deadened; that all were political failures (Glynn partly excepted) is proof enough. So why were they so unrealistic? The ailment could not be put down as a general affliction. Their most reckonable protectionist adversaries – Lyne, Copeland, Crick – breathed great gulps of cold political realism; not opportunism, but seeing how the land lay. The answer entertained here is that at this point in history, the end of the 19th century, the pervading prestige of the ideal laid several snares for semi-intellectuals in politics such as Smith, Glynn, Andrew Garran, Pulsford, Symon, Clark and

McMillan. It fostered a confidence in the power of the intellect to make events, and rotted the trite but essential contrast between idealistic and realistic.

Henry Bournes Higgins (1851–1929)

The categorisation of Henry Bournes Higgins as a Federationist may perplex. Was not the Victorian lawyer a vehement opponent of the Federation Bill? Did he not fill an expensively published volume with his tracts against the proposed Constitution, implore the Victorian public to vote No, and travel to Sydney to add his voice to a last ditch attempt to defeat it in a tight referendum race? Was not Higgins an undiscouragable and indefatigable opponent of Federation to the bitter end? Yet the same Higgins declared 'federation must come, and soon. We all want it.' And offered himself as a candidate for the Convention, won, and there successfully secured passage of clauses that would be central to the nature of the Commonwealth. And was quickly reconciled to the Commonwealth, elected to the first parliament as an (influential) member, not long after made a cabinet minister, and then a High Court judge. Higgins's trajectory with respect to Federation is the inverse of Smith's, but has the same paradoxicality.[398]

*

Like Smith, in Higgins's engagement with Federation there was no obvious quest for acclaim, nor hunt for office. Like Smith, and so many other Federationists, Higgins's mind was well-upholstered; he was learned in Greek, a student of Shakespeare, and an earnest, if not deep, reader of George's *Progress and Poverty*. But beneath the fabric the structures were not complex. His intellectual operations were simple, if sturdy; and that sometimes produced a robust simplicity, and sometimes a dismal crudity.[399] His mental style might be compared to the rationalistic Enlightenment *philosophe*: curious, but easily satisfied. Things were quite simple, really. In some ways his mind might be compared to that of David Syme, who retained Higgins to tutor his sons, and helped his early political career. Both might be described as semi-intellectuals in politics, at least in aspiration; both exercised their minds as critics; Higgins on literature (Browning, Sophocles) and Syme on science (a critique of political economy, and a Lamarckian critique of Darwinism). Both were capable of considerable crudity. Syme: 'No one will dispute that the Chinese race are inferior to the Anglo-Saxon'.[400] Higgins could and did match this sort of remark. But crudity was not a disadvantage to either. On the contrary, it helps to explain how both could be such solitary and simultaneously influential figures; one the Father of Protection, and the other the Father of Compulsory Arbitration. With respect to Federation both were ambiguous figures; initially disbelieving, but ultimately reconciled.

In accordance with this rationalistic style Higgins was exempt from the sentiments which made a popular creed of Federationism: Imperialism and Australianism. Irish birth left him aloof from the Empire, and begot no proxy or surrogate nationalism. Other lures of the Federationists cast no spell over Higgins, including the rhetoric of 'absolutely free' intercourse within Australia. He coldly appraised the prospective Commonwealth customs union: the Victorian 'importing classes', he said, 'looked forward to NSW importers being put under the same tariff restrictions as themselves under federation. The manufacturing classes expected to exploit the markets of NSW protected against the formidable competition of English and European goods'.[401]

The same rationalist susceptibility to simplicity, and a rationalist demand for obvious 'reasons', encouraged him to favour a unitary state over a federal one.

The existence of states meant that Australia would be composed of 'huge, artificial unmeaning divisions'.[402] A critic might retort that a unitary government of Australia would be far huger. And would not its own proposed borders be artificial? Or did Higgins judge that a border in Bass Strait would be artificial, but one in the Tasman Sea was not? A critic might further press that what matters is not whether borders are 'artificial', but whether those borders were wished for; whether Tasmania, for example, wished to unify with Victoria is the question. Higgins, however, opposed section 123 of the Constitution which required any revision of State borders to be approved by its electors. He, more generally, opposed any plan of a 'ridiculous' States' house. He opposed supermajorities. He favoured majoritarianism on the basis of a stark and brutal rationale:

the rule of the majority ... is not a fetish ... it is simply based on fundamental physical laws. The majority of the people are stronger than the minority, and in place of fighting it is better to yield to numbers.[403]

But if he rejected a federal structure as an end, federation was welcome as a means, a means to unification. Did not Higgins reasonably observe that federation was a unification for some purposes? Those purposes could be multiplied. Above all other purposes, he sought to empower the Commonwealth to legislate for the compulsory arbitration of workplace disputes which traversed state borders. On this object he was unswerving; it was others who swerved. 'I was beaten in Adelaide but I succeeded in Melbourne, in the face of Mr Barton's opposition, and now I find Mr Barton refers to the clause as a valuable and attractive provision'.[404] This great victory of Higgins had definite consequences for himself, and the country, still more than a century later.

But despite such successes at the Convention, Higgins looked at his work and saw that it was not good enough. Why should a future generation be bound by decisions of an earlier? Why was the Constitution so difficult to change? 'Not a word can be changed even though every member in each house would vote for change'.[405] Higgins was content with the thought that the constitution should be the property of the federal legislature. He was insensible – or perfectly well-aware? – of the truth that to make the Constitution the property of the federal legislature is to make for unification, just as to make the Constitution the property of the states is to make for confederation.[406]

Once the Convention's bill reached the public, Higgins created and led the Democratic Federal Union to fight its adoption at referendum. The bill was 'undemocratic and provincial, and ... the death knell to Democracy'.[407] George Dibbs invited him to join the No campaign in NSW in 1899, and Higgins did so, making the usual strange bed fellows of politics.

The approval of the amended Commonwealth bill in 1899 – by a gigantic majority in Victoria – produced a crisis. What to do? Higgins collaborated with conservative protectionists and young Federationists in evicting George Turner from the premiership in December 1899. But he appeared to adapt to the new reality.

Both the president (himself) and the vice-president of the Democratic Federal Union were elected to the first Commonwealth parliament. And the irony of this foe of the Commonwealth joining its ventures was to become much tauter; in 1906 he was appointed to the High Court created by the Constitution ostensibly to defend the Constitution which he had fought so hard against.

William Astley (1855–1911)

In William Astley – fraudster, mythifer of Australian history and impresario of the 'Bathurst People's Convention' of 1896 – we see the talents and vices of what was known as 'Bohemia' in rousing Federation. And how Federation, far from being some act of communion with community, was in some measure fired by alienation from that community.

*

Many of Astley's biographical particulars are obscure, and some basic inaccuracies – including his year of birth, 1855, were for years erroneously stated by profile writers. They also commonly repeated the assertion that, at the age of 21, Astley was editor of the *Richmond Guardian*; a not impossible attainment, but something unlikely and unproved, and which may be set aside as one of his fictions.[408]

The earliest occasion Astley demonstrably steps into the public eye is in 1880 as a self-described Sunday School teacher in Launceston seeking 'contributions' from the public for his labours.[409] How many citizens amiably contributed is unknown. On 9 May 1881 the *Examiner* reported Astley's arrest at a boarding house in Hobart, 'just after his return from St. David's Cathedral'; he was charged with embezzling £60. The case plodded through the courts, delayed repeatedly by Astley's avowals of illness, and his prostration, on one occasion, by 'hystero-epilepsy'.[410] He was eventually sentenced to two years imprisonment. In 1885 *The Tasmanian* records Detective O'Donnell of Geelong arresting William Astley, 'thirty-one, describing himself as a journalist ... not long come from Tasmania'. He was charged with embezzling the sum of £1 15s; the detective contended the defalcations actually totalled £400. Two years later, the *Geelong Advertiser* recorded 'a respectably-attired and gentlemanly' William Astley being charged with obtaining £10 0s 6d by false pretences.[411] Astley's intricate rationalisation of the sequence of events, combined with repayment of the sum, occasioned withdrawal of the charge.

In the late 1880s – in a natural development? – Astley advanced from fraud to what amounted to historical forgeries, in authoring densely plotted, carefully painted, convict-era dramas, under the pseudonym of Price Warung. He claimed with some flourish that his tales were based on his exhaustive historical research. Historians have exploded these pretensions.[412] They are better seen as second wind of the dubious 'Mine is a Sad Yet True Story' literature of the mid-19th century and earlier, which consisted of 'at least thirty narratives purporting to recount the experiences of convicts transported to New South Wales'.[413] Up to half of these are fictional, including, above all else, the 'Recollections of 13 years residence in Norfolk Island and Tasmania' supposedly written in 1823, but in fact 'a work of fiction actually produced about 1850 or an even later date'.[414] This would be rich meat for Warung in composing his gothic fantasia about Norfolk Island, *Tales of the Isle of Death*. He embroidered horrors (a hangman, tasked to hang 20 people, exhausting his supply of rope). He invented them: no female convict was ever branded (W, for 'whore'); no convict was ever hanged for interrupting a commandant's nap. He defamed Charles Sturt as a parade ground bully, when in truth Sturt 'earned the respect and liking of his men by his courtesy and care for their well-being'.[415] There was hanging and branding and bullying in convict society. But Astley's travesty history ignored that society's strange conglomerate of force and freedom; the potential many sidedness of any given phenomenon of it; and the unexpectedly high state of morale among convicts and ex-convicts, which so chafed Commisioner Bigge, and which was evinced by their prolific fertility. 'The early colonial period of 1788-1822 was not a time of incarceration and terror', writes the historian of convict Sydney; the Hawkesbury River, where emancipee farmers crowded, was 'for a time ... a sort of Cockaigne'.[416] Astley was a key fashioner of the 'broad arrow melodrama' which acutely misrepresented the first generation of settlement.

But Astley's tales had no merely sensational purpose. By conjuring with inversions – where criminals are victims, and law enforcers the criminals – his tales vented the rancour and pain of Bohemia of late 19th century Australia. They were the uncompromised elite of the creative world, the refuse of the commercial world, on the margin of the common junctures of the community; the pitched opposite, that is, of the philistine, prosperous and integrated population. Astley's Bohemia had its own political end. Just as the 'Mine is a Sad Yet True Story' literature was in part aimed at terminating transportation, Astley wrote with a larger political purpose of discrediting his contemporary society, by sullying its origins. Thus Astley's purpose in *Tales of the Old Regime* neatly cohered with the task of any historical evangelist of the 'state-nation', such as the Commonwealth of Australia. This task will be distinct from the ideologist of the 'nation state'. In the case of the nation state, the task is to recover, revive and even reinvent a heroic past. But the state-nation has no past – heroic or otherwise – simply a noble future which will commence with its birth. But that future may be impeded by the histories of the particularist entities that are to be dissolved into one. It would be useful, then, if that past was denigrated and scandalised; and left a pre-history, an *ancien régime*, the bad old days before the bright birth. Astley served the coming state-nation by providing a negative Australian Legend, which would fix an image of the loathsomeness of Old Sydney Town, and which was to be hotly radiated by the *Bulletin*, and re-echoed in the 20th century fiction and history of key popularisers such as J. H. M. Abbott, Brian Penton, Cyril Pearl, and Robert Hughes. In Astley's own day, these authors were anticipated by Randolph Bedford, roving writer, and poet-herald of the new Commonwealth, who adopted a still more expansive rejection of the New South Wales he was born into: her inhabitants were 'incapable of building a nation'; it was only the 'strong and discontented men' of the gold fields that accounted for its deserts of 'nationhood'.[417]

Astley's political artistry might have expired in obscurity but for Bohemia's percolation of journalism, and the less predictable *fin de siècle* frolic of Bohemia and Society with a capital S.[418] And the key intercession of J. F. Archibald. Essentially an artist bereft of talent, but who could recognise talent in others, it was Archibald who would usher Astley into publication.[419] And it was presumably Archibald who connected Astley to his boon companion of the Athenaeum Club, Edmund Barton.

The first fruit of the liaison of Astley and Barton was the self-styled 'People's Convention of Bathurst' in November 1896. This promotional event was conceived and directed by Warung, who 'shaped the Convention's structure, its central concerns, motto, even its tone'.[420] In a consultation with Barton, who was both 'manipulative and collusive'[421], Astley drafted a great collection of municipal dignitaries, dusted by an assortment of notables, including a yellow press muckraker, an emollient Cardinal, a United States consul, a son-in-law of George Higinbotham, and a son of Charles Gavan Duffy.[422] They also included Barton, O'Connor and Reid.

Was the resulting Convention a 'huge success'?[423] Or did this assemblage of 'People' do little apart from network, and congratulate the press on covering them? Certainly, the press gave the Convention extensive coverage, and that was success enough; the event has worked its way into the commemorative history of Federation. But another misfortune of money did cast a shadow over its proceedings. On 19 November 1896 Astley appeared on two charges of obtaining £15 by false pretences. But his defence by William Crick was skilled, Crick's legal fees were paid by John Norton, the plaintiff was not only a political opponent but mentally unstable, and the jury found Astley not guilty.

Astley appeared to withdraw from politics in 1897. In June of that year he attempted to extort the proprietors of Angus and Robertson over its supposed sale on its own account of books properly belonging to the Public Library. But George Robertson had previously encountered Astley, and sought a 'character reference' from a source in Melbourne.[424] A two-word telegram came in reply: 'Done time'. Robertson repulsed Warung's invitation to treat, and the bookseller was vindicated by a report of a parliamentary select committee.[425] At about the same time Astley had more success with David Scott Mitchell, successfully defrauding him of £125 for non-existent Australiana.[426]

Astley returned to politics in 1898 to direct Barton's referendum publicity. He was the media veteran to supersede the amateurish, even ludicrous, efforts of the circle of lawyers who had previously directed Federationist publicity.[427] In the election Astley took charge of producing the *Clarion Call* for the seats of Woollahra (4 000 copies), Waverley (5 000 copies) and, most importantly, Sydney-King (6 000 copies), where Barton had chosen to challenge Reid. His efforts were not rewarded in any of those seats, but they might have been more useful in Barton's subsequent and successful contest of Hastings Macleay.

With victory, Warung did not abandon Federation, but his activity took a more specifically literary turn. He penned a poem of welcome to the Earl of Hopetoun, and wrote a pamphlet urging Bathurst as the national capital. And then faded from the scene.[428] He was never a person of the front stage, but would be one of influence.

Astley represented the intersection of Bohemian alienation and political upheaval. More aggressively, a critic might infer a kindredness between the fraudulence of Astley and a falsity in the federal cause. Yet a defender could counter with figures of stainless propriety in that cause, such as Edward Dowling, president of the Australasian Federation League, teetotaller, Congregationalist churchman, advocate of worker education, and member of the Aboriginal Protection Board; whose conscientious, factual and balanced annual reports to the League remain a solace to the historian. That one publicist of the Federation movement could manifest alienation so grossly as Astley was, perhaps, no more than a piece of bad luck. But it was, undeniably, embarrassing to the Federationist movement that this talented blackguard, this 'sad rogue' (A. G. Stephens), assumed so senior a role in the campaign. Unsurprisingly, Garran urged Nettie and Vance Palmer to close their ears to ugly rumour when they were proposing to adopt Astley as an Australianist 'prophet of new day'.[429] But the Palmers got it the wrong way round. Astley faced not so much the future as the past; a mythologist rather than a prophet, the composer of an anti-history as a vent for alienation, who gratified Federationists with tales about a past of which they had so little interest or understanding.

8

Contriving the Convention

*In that Convention which prepared the way,
For the new Commonwealth to rise and rule,
In sonorous phrases gathered from the school...*
– Inglis Clark

The election of the delegates to the Federal Convention of 1897-98 by the Australian public is deemed one of the most gracious laurels of the Federation episode. The framers of the Commonwealth's constitution were not self-appointed; they were not the legates of some sovereign power, nor the emissaries of an insurgency: a ballot of all voters had chosen them. This is not only a grace, but a rarity; something almost without historical precedent.[430] And, not simply lovely, it is also crucial; in Federation histories the election of delegates in March 1897 both eluded the obfuscation of Federation by local parliaments, and bestowed a reviving energy on a fatigued movement.

That the Convention was elected was, undeniably, decisive. From that moment the project had the prestige of the people making laws, or at least drafting them. But how admirable was the act of electing Convention delegates is less clear. A systematic scrutiny of the Convention elections reveals, not the articulation of the people's choice, but its manipulation; not a representation of the people's will, but its distortion; and not the venting of popular bents, but a stoking of public restiveness. The upshot of the Convention's displacement of the local parliaments was the substitution of an assembly that was less democratic for those which were more so.

The flawed design

The slight of democratic principles might be said to begin with the Convention's remit.

The *Enabling Act* of NSW and other colonies authorising the Convention placed its delegates under a specific mandate: to frame a Federal constitution. Unlike the Convention of 1891 the delegates were not charged simply to 'report'. They were not commissioned simply to explore if an improving federal constitution could be framed. They were duty bound to frame one, regardless.[431] The presumption of the Convention was that Federation had been resolved upon. As the Federationist Symon explicitly, and correctly, declared, 'The Act presupposes that the people desire federation – that is its most happy significance'.[432] A happy presupposition for Federationists, surely. But not one democratically tested.

The ordinary tenets of democratic decision-making were further offended by the apportionment of Convention delegates between the colonies. The premiers in January 1895 had resolved that each colony would have the same number of delegates (ten), regardless of their population. The upshot was that the three least populous colonies, with 19 percent of the population, would have the same number of delegates as the three larger, with 81 percent. Tasmania's delegation – including three 'non-entities' destined to cast 'decisive votes'[433] – was as large as that of New South Wales, with eight times the population. This is an obvious violation of the common – if resistible – presumption that democracy entails 'one vote, one value'. The violation might be exonerated. Perhaps the number of delegates of each colony was a nominal matter; perhaps the delegates of the smaller colonies appreciated that any constitution would be a dead letter if it did not satisfy the voters of the larger states in referendums. But the narrowness of majorities at the Convention, and the struggles to win majorities, suggest the relativity of numbers was not a merely nominal matter.

In the event, one colony had no delegates at all: Queensland, as its legislature could not agree on the method of choosing them. The closeness of the subsequent Convention's votes – 8 percent of its divisions were decided by one vote – suggests that this absence of 10 delegates from Queensland must have been significant. Whether this absence of Queensland delegates was 'providential', as some historians have judged it,[434] or fateful, the absence was eventful, and undemocratic.

The harshest offence to democratic principles lay in the method of electing Convention delegates.

In Western Australia there was no election of delegates by voters at all; the WA parliament chose them. The delegates so chosen were also all members of the WA parliament; but whether that made WA's delegation more or less democratic is unclear. Electoral competition for membership of WA's parliament was far from intense. Nine of WA's 14 delegates to the Convention had received no votes at all in making their (uncontested) way into the WA legislature. Perhaps many were uncontested simply because no one else had a chance of winning. Forrest was one such. But if Forrest was unchallengeable in Bunbury as a local member, it was not because of his position on Federation: the electorate voted 62 percent No in the referendum of 1900. Neither was he present at the Convention on account of any general support throughout WA for his cautious sympathy for Federation: the WA electorate was polarised, and cautious sympathisers were few. Forrest chose himself.[435]

In NSW, Victoria, SA and Tasmania, the delegates were elected by the public, but by a method 'rightly considered one of the most detestable of voting systems',[436] and 'condemned by all thinking persons in the world':[437] 'block voting'. As applied to the Convention election, block voting treated each colony as a single electoral district, and required each voter to 'tick' on their ballot a number of candidates exactly equal to the number of vacancies, ten.[438] The total number of ticks received by each candidate would be reckoned, and the ten candidates with the largest number of ticks deemed elected.

In electing delegates by 'block voting', the Convention was chosen by a voting method so crudely inimical to democratic outcomes that it was already in decline elsewhere in the world by 1897, and, within a generation, it would be extinct in any genuine democracy, outside of local government. Three pathologies of block voting killed it.

Pathology 1: 'Largest wins all'. Suppose 51 percent of voters all tick a certain ten candidates, and the remaining 49 percent tick a distinct ten candidates. Then the ten winning candidates are those ticked by 51 percent; and 51 percent of the electorate wins all seats, and 49 percent win none. The problem is exacerbated by the fact that the largest of 'largest takes all' may not be very large at all. Imagine voters falling into five groups, of roughly equal size, each with a distinct set of ten candidates. Each set will get roughly 20 percent of the votes. But it is the set favoured by the largest of the voter groups (say, 21 percent of voters?) which wins all ten vacancies. This is simply a multi-candidate illustration of a familiar defect of first-past-the-post voting with a single vacancy.

Pathology 2: 'Luck wins'. Requiring N ticks may compel an elector to vote for candidates they do not know. Some votes will be random, perhaps even a majority. This defect will mar any system that requires a minimum number of votes, including 'compulsory preferential' voting familiar in Australia. But the defect is worse under the block vote, as all ticks count equally; a candidate ticked at random is not distinguished from a candidate who is enthusiastically backed. Clearly, this means a candidate might be made a winner, or loser, not by any meaningful choice, but, in effect, by a roll of the dice.

Pathology 3: 'Lowest common denominator tops the poll'. Consider Bob, who represents no one precisely, but also offends no one badly, and is, in consequence, ranked tenth by everyone. Thus Bob gets a tick from everyone: and so Bob tops the poll. But, by assumption, Bob only marginally holds the confidence of voters; perhaps his strongest recommendation is that his name is recognised. Such perverse victories may be more extensive. It may be that all voters agree in ranking Bob, Ted and Carol tenth, ninth and eighth respectively, simply on account of them being not known to offend any voter: then Bob, Ted and Carol top the poll.

The 'triumph of the lowest common denominator' is also born of the absence in block voting of any ranking of candidates. The people's 'will' is obviously blunted. And worse: as T. R. Ashworth rightly observed of the 1897 Convention election, by voters being both compelled to vote for ten candidates and being prevented from ranking them, 'many of the supporters of the defeated candidates voted for some on the successful list who just defeated their own favourites'.[439]

These pathologies of Block Voting are 'theoretical possibilities': how much did they materialise in the Convention election?

The inequitable outcome

On 26 January 1897 – very patriotic – the premiers announced NSW, Victoria, Tasmania and SA would go to the polls on the 4 and 7 March 1897. 332 000 persons voted; about one in five adults, and about four out of ten enrolled voters. Turnout was especially weak in Tasmania; only one in four of those enrolled cast a vote (see Table 8.1, Row 1). The island's press lamented 'The apathy displayed by electors during the election campaign was painfully apparent'.[440] Apart from an elite, and a few with a direct commercial interest, Federation was largely meaningless to Tasmania. But despite contributing just two percent of the total votes cast, Tasmania still supplied 20 percent of delegates.

How representative were the successful candidates of those who did vote? How much support was there for the winning candidates? The second row of Table 8.1 reveals that, in each colony, the highest polling candidate was 'ticked' by the great bulk of voters. But the second row also reveals that in each colony the least supported successful candidate did not receive an endorsement from a majority of voters. In fact, the third row indicates 16 of the 40 successful candidates received a tick from less than half the voters. But is that a large or a small degree of support?

Perhaps what the second and third row bring out is the arbitrariness of deeming the candidates with the ten largest votes elected. Why not the largest 12? Or the largest 15? To put the question another way: why not a convention of 60, or 75 delegates, instead of 50? Why is 50 a magically 'democratic' number? The decisions of the Convention would have been different if the highest polling 12 candidates in each colony had been sent to the Convention.[441]

Rows four to five of Table 8.1 report another measure of the extent to which voters had their preferences reflected in winning candidates. Of the ten candidates chosen by a given voter, a cer-

Table 8.1 Measures of support for candidates in the election of the Australasian Federal Convention

	NSW	Victoria	SA	Tasmania
Valid vote as per cent of enrolment	53.4	41.6	32.9	24.9
The proportion of voters ticking the highest polling (lowest polling) successful candidate.	70 (38)	85 (45)	60 (45)	71 (42)
Number of winning candidates ticked by fewer than half the voters.	4	2	4	6
Mean success rate of voters: votes for winning candidates as percent of votes for all candidates	52.2	59.4	52.3	52.3
Mean success rate in Assembly election. (1895 NSW, 1897 Victoria, Tasmania 1897)	60.0	61.3	na	60.0

Notes: The 'success rate' is computed on the basis of single member seats contested by more than one party. Thus SA is excluded. The computation also deems that when a party advanced two or more candidates for a single member seat, all who vote for any one of these candidates enjoy a voting success if any win.

Sources: Row 1; Rhodes 2002. Rows 2, 3 and 4; Hughes and Graham (1974) for all colonies save NSW, where *SMH* 17.3.97. Row 5; Hughes and Graham (1975), Hughes and Graham (1975a), Hughes and Graham (1976).

tain number will be elected, a number that could be as high as ten or as low as zero. Call this number 'vote successes' or, as a percent, a 'vote success rate'. We can conceive a 'mean vote success rate' – the average success rate of all voters – and this can be measured from the data. It is simply the number of 'ticks' cast for the successful candidates as a percentage of total ticks cast. In three of the four colonies the mean success rate was in the region of 50 percent, and about 60 percent in Victoria. Is this 'high' or 'low'? These success rates can be compared with the success rates in the election of the lower houses in the local parliaments: the total of votes cast for the successful party in each seat as a proportion of total votes cast. Table 8.1 indicates that in NSW, Victoria and Tasmania the success rate was higher in the local parliament than in the Convention election, if only slightly so in Victoria.

To turn more squarely to the presence of the pathologies of block voting, consider the gravest of the three potential pathologies: 'largest takes all'. In other words, the absence of significant minority opinion from winning candidates. The presence of this pathology can be detected if there were a certain number of 'position types', each of which claimed the adherence of a certain proportion of the voting public. For the question then becomes: was each position type represented in the Convention as frequently as it was in the voting public? Did the proportion of total votes received by candidates belonging to a given 'position type' match the proportion of seats won by candidates of that position type? Answering the question is made easier by the candidates' organisation of themselves into what were called 'lists', 'bunches' or 'tickets'. In SA, for example, the Australian National League recommended ten candidates, the Liberal Union ten, and Labor five. To complicate matters, some candidates were on both Liberal Union and Labor tickets. But let that be construed as its own position type, 'both Liberal Union and Labor'. We might, therefore, say that in SA there were four position types: Australian National League, Liberal Union (only), Labor (only), and both Liberal Union and Labor. So if the Australian National League receives 20 percent of the votes and wins 20 percent of the vacancies, there would be neither under-representation nor over-representation of that opinion type.

So, was the Convention election blighted by the 'largest takes all pathology'?

Victoria

There were three tickets in Victoria: the *Age* (protection), the *Argus* (free trade), and Trades Hall. The lists overlapped. To obtain a partition of candidates into mutually exclusive lists, we distinguish a list composed of those endorsed by the *Argus* only from a list composed of those endorsed by both the *Age* and the *Argus*. Similarly, a list of those only nominated by the Trades Hall is distinguished from those nominated by the Trades Hall and the *Age*.

Table 8.2: The success of tickets in the Australasian Federal Convention election

Victoria	*Argus* only	*Age* and *Argus*	*Age* and Trades Hall	*Age, Argus,* and Trades Hall	Trades Hall only	Other candidates
Proportion of Votes	24.7	9.9	41.0	8.5	4.0	12.0
Proportion of Winning Candidates	0	20	70	10	0	0

South Australia	ANL	Liberal Union only	Liberal Union and Labor	Labor only	Other candidates
Proportion of Votes	43.6	32.6	12.8	1.7	10.1
Proportion of Winning Candidates	60	40	0	0	0

NSW	Orange Lodge Only	United Protestants and Orange Lodge	United Protestant only	United Protestant and Labor	Labor only	Other candidates
Proportion of Votes	11.2	39.1	8.8	2.8	10.6	27.5
Proportion of Winning Candidates	10	70	20	0	0	0

Sources: Votes; Hughes and Graham (1974). Tickets; *Champion* 6.3.97, *SAR* 6.3.97

Table 8.2 shows Victoria clearly exhibits the 'largest takes all' pathology. Candidates endorsed by both the *Age* and Trades Hall received just 41 percent of the vote, but won 70 percent of the delegates. By contrast, none of the *Argus*-only ticket won a vacancy, notwithstanding the *Argus*-only ticket winning a quarter of all votes. A more democratic election would surely have sent to the Convention the three top polling candidates of the *Argus*-only group: Henry Wrixon, Sir Frederick Sargood and

Nicholas Fitzgerald. A variety of commentators have pressed the personal distinction of these: Wrixon was 'a fascinating mixture of radical and conservative', an 'idealist intellectual', a long-time advocate of female suffrage, a vice-chancellor and a novelist to boot;[442] Sargood had 'common sense, cool judgment and grasp of detail'; and Fitzgerald was 'was a brilliant orator with clear ideas on important political issues'.[443] But the point is not that the proceedings of the 1897 Convention would have been more impressive, sagacious, or elevated if these three had been present, but that democracy would have been better served by their presence. And, correspondingly, by the absence of the two lowest polling candidates of the *Age* and Trades Hall ticket – Berry and Higgins – and the lowest poller of the *Age* and *Argus* group, Zeal.

The results of Victoria's Convention election are usually presented as a great triumph of the *Age*. It was so; a great undemocratic triumph of the *Age*, in which its candidates won out of all proportion to the extent of their support. It was, more specifically, a great undemocratic triumph of the *Age's* proprietor, David Syme. His earliest biographer declares, 'For more than a quarter of a century he selected every Victorian Premier'.[444] He also selected every Victorian delegate to the Convention.

South Australia

South Australia had three significant lists, on the Victorian pattern; the conservative Australian National League, Kingston's Liberal Union, and Labor. In SA the distribution of victorious candidates also misrepresented the voters' support, but the misrepresentation ran in favour of the right. The League won one delegate too many, and 'Liberal Union and Labor' one too few. And so Vaiben Solomon of the ANL went to the Convention in place of Labor's David Charleston.[445]

Tasmania

The methodology of comparing list vote size with list candidate success is unhelpful in Tasmania on account of lists being so weak. Some candidates repudiated their inclusion in a list, and lists were revised at the last minute. 'Tickets as a rule were held cheap'.[446]

New South Wales

In Victoria and SA the three lists can be understood as representing positions on a left-right spectrum. In New South Wales there were also three 'lists' (of any significance) and one was Labor. But the possibility of the three assuming a conventional left-right configuration had been destroyed by a vision beheld from the Cardinal's Palace in Manly. Cardinal Moran was a man of sweep, learning and command. Federation had caught his imagination, and he acquired the notion that he would be a delegate to the Convention, attending, he affirmed, not in any official capacity but in a personal and individual one.

Moran's announcement of his candidacy 'sparked off a sectarian explosion'.[447] The Loyal Orange Lodge, at a meeting on 16 February 1897, resolved to construct a list for the benefit of 'loyal' voters by endorsing ten candidates. This seems to have disturbed the Cardinal's composure, and he gave a wandering and indiscreet interview to the *Daily Telegraph*. He called for a boycott of the 'violent' *Sydney Morning Herald*, which was 'known to be an organ of extreme Congregationalists'. He wasted breath on ironical tilts at John Haynes. He pronounced that Federation was especially desirable as the most effective means of preserving Australia from 'extreme socialism', a theme totally absent from Federationist advocacy. He declared he had 'come forward as a candidate to crush once and forever anti-Catholic bigotry'.[448]

To the Cardinal's call to conclusive battle, the more moderate Protestant clerics replied by collecting under the banner of 'United Protestants', on a platform where sat the Rev. Carruthers, brother of Joseph Carruthers (Federationist and future Premier of NSW); and the Rev. Bavin, father of Thomas Bavin (Federationist, future private secretary to Deakin and future Premier of NSW). The Rev. George McInnes declared to his brother preachers that they were rousing 'against the sworn servant of a foreign despot. This is a campaign against a man whom I hold to be no true citizen of this country, no true subject of Her Majesty the Queen, not a Briton at all ...'.[449] Having settled on their own list of ten candidates, the Rev. Carruthers then proposed – with unanimous support – that Protestant churches 'arrange that Sunday next be regarded as a day of special prayer throughout their denomination for the elections ....'. He was sure, he said, that the battle would 'be won, for the Lord of Hosts was on their side'. [450]

Whatever side the Lord of Hosts may have been on, the two Protestant tickets were successful in winning vacancies out of proportion to their voting support. All of the ten winning candidates in NSW were on either the United Protestant or Orange Lodge tickets. Candidates on both of these tickets won seven of the ten vacancies, with only forty percent of the vote. If the 'United Protestant and Orange Lodge' list had won a more commensurate five places, then Brunker and Walker would not have been successful. And with only small loss. Brunker was absent from 47 percent of divisions of the Convention, almost the worst attendance of any delegate. Walker was a patently unconvincing representative of the people's will: a Scotch-born career banker in the Bank of New South Wales, a son-in-law of an impoverished Irish aristocrat, of almost no political experience or profile, who since 1886 had had no responsibilities apart from the trusteeship of the massive fortune of the heiress daughter of his cousin.[451]

The success of the United Protestant or Orange Lodge tickets came in part at the expense of the Labor ticket, none of whose candidates was elected, despite winning one-tenth of ticks. And in part at the expense of the many candidates not on any list.[452] Winning 25 percent of all ticks, some of these non-list candidates appear to have represented a sizeable bloc of minority opinion. Although Cardinal Moran ran as an individual (unsuccessfully), and endorsed no other candidate, it appears that a 'Cardinal's bunch' did implicitly exist. The six candidates ranked 13th to 18th consisted of four Catholics, one close political ally of Irish Catholics (Copeland), and McGowen, whose name could be mistaken for Irish, even if he was a long-serving Lancastrian lay officer of the Church of England. This implicit list secured 15 percent of the vote; certainly warranting the election of Moran by democratic principles, however unhappy for all his election would doubtless have proved.

The conclusion is that Moran and Labor together merited, by ordinary democratic canons, two, maybe three, successful candidates, but in the event had none.

In the present secular age, it may be tempting to dispute the analysis above on the grounds that the grouping of candidates into Orange Lodge, Labor, etc., had, in truth, little meaning to voters; and was almost as meaningless as constructing three 'lists' on the basis of a random allocation of candidates between them. By 'the law of chance' any such pseudo-list will receive roughly one-third of all ticks, and will include roughly one-third of all successful candidates. And yet chance also permits the possibility that one pseudo-list will have a share of successful candidates somewhat disproportionate to its share of ticks. But that would not be evidence of distortion of democratic will, just a manifestation of the meaninglessness of the lists. Statistical analysis of the data, however, suggests that the Orange and Protestant lists are genuine (Appendix 2, Table A.1). In entering the polling booth to decide their constitutional future, many NSW voters went to church.

Some alternatives

Why was block voting chosen? The objectionability of block voting was well recognised. And numerous alternative voting methods were available.

Single member geographical constituencies

The United States had learned from the inevitable results of its original use of block voting for the House of Representatives, and an Act of Congress in 1842 required all the House's seats to be single-member. Australia could have usefully followed that precedent, and was beginning to do so; from 1894 NSW relied solely on single-member constituencies. This practice, applied to the Convention election, would have divided each colony into ten electoral districts, with one delegate to be elected in each. The 'largest takes all' pathology would be much reduced, as the strongest position type in one area would not be the strongest in all other areas. But for all that, it is hard to see Moran, or Labor, actually topping the poll in any seat representing as much as one-tenth of NSW's population, and so winning a place.

Plumping

To allow 'plumping' is to allow the voter to tick fewer than ten candidates, perhaps just one. This was generally allowed in multi-member parliamentary electorates in Australia. To allow it is to eliminate ignorance voting; the voter does not tick unknown candidates in order to make their vote valid. J. T. Walker – an obscure figure to the public at large – would have presumably lost if plumping was tolerated. It also reduces the lowest common denominator winner; the voter does not tick candidates known only as innocuous in order to make their vote valid.

Limited voting

Limited voting was used in the election of 40 MPs in the House of Commons between 1867 and 1880, and in local government in New York City and Boston. Under this system the maximum number of candidates a voter may tick is *smaller* than the actual number of vacancies. This reduces the largest takes all pathology. To illustrate: with three vacancies, but only two ticks permitted each voter, the more popular ticket of two rival tickets cannot win all three seats as long as the less popular ticket claims at least 40 percent of electors.[453]

Single tick voting

Each voter may tick just one candidate. Lowest common denominator candidacies get no votes. And the 'largest takes all' pathology is inhibited, as position types have a strong incentive to field tickets of a size commensurate to the size of their voter support. A position type commanding 50 percent of voters could expect to win five places if it fielded five candidates (no more) and secured a spread of ticks across the five. Standing any more candidates would only reduce their number of successful candidates. A position type which commanded just ten percent of voters could still expect to win one place if it fielded just one candidate.

Cumulative voting

Cumulative voting was used in the Cape Colony legislature until 1909, and the Illinois state legislature from 1870 to 1982. Each voter has the same number of ticks as vacancies, say ten, but may allocate more than one tick per candidate. A voter could, if they wished, allocate all ten ticks to a single candidate. This avoids 'the largest takes all' pathology. A position type with ten percent of the vote would run just one candidate, and advise its supporters to give all ten of their ticks to that candidate. A party with 50 percent support could do the same – but would not. It would win five vacancies by running just five candidates, and advise supporters to give each two ticks. Again, representation would be roughly proportionate to votes.

Proportional voting

The most sophisticated voting systems of all, the Hare-Clark system, was available to elect the Convention. It had been introduced by Tasmania's *Electoral Act 1896*, and was successfully implemented in her general election of 20 January 1897, months before the Convention election.

In the aftermath of the delegates to the Australasian Federal Convention being decided by means of block voting, Catherine Helen Spence declared that block voting 'stands condemned by all thinking people of the world, and it was an insult to the intelligence of Australia and Tasmania to impose it on us for the election of federal delegates'.[454] The choice was not, however, an insult to the perspicacity of the premiers who settled upon it. They would know that for prominent candidates single-member electorates were a good deal harder to win than the multiple-member electorates which block voting ordained. Multiple member electorates could be a walk-in; if there were two roughly balanced major parties and a third minor party, then the success of both major parties in a two-member seat was almost guaranteed. Thus Kingston had no great difficulty winning the seat of West Adelaide, with two members and three alternatives – Liberal, Labor and a minor independent. It would be hard for Kingston to lose. A single-member seat was a more challenging proposition: in 1900, Kingston lost a single vacancy contest for SA's Legislative Council, and won a second such contest a few months later by only a small margin.[455] Barton lost two of the four single vacancy contests he had fought in his career. It is not completely surprising that Barton declared at the Convention that state-wide electorates might even be used to elect the House of Representatives. Single-member electorates, he complained, 'frequently result in parliament being bereft of its best intellects in order that certain local interests be represented'.[456] Single-member electorates certainly were harder work, and the preference of politicians for multi-member electorates can be seen as an anti-competitive arrangement among career politicians to almost guarantee them seats, while squeezing out insurgents.

Another pathology of block voting may have recommended the voting method to Barton; its 'lowest common denominator tops the poll' dysfunction. 70 percent of voters gave Barton a tick in the Convention election, more than any other candidate received, a triumph his partisans revelled in. But in the light of Barton's struggles to win a single-member seat, it seems hard to believe that in *any* of the ten of the geographical electoral districts into which NSW might have been decomposed, 70 percent of voters would have ranked Barton above all other candidates, including the local interests.[457] What helped Barton top the poll was his relative inoffensiveness: his absence in 1897 from partisan politics, and his ever-moderate positioning.

*

All the candidates elected to the Convention were proudly 'representatives', in Edmund Burke's sense, and not mere 'delegates'. And this was not undemocratic. The voters chose candidates to represent them at the Convention, not to vote this particular way or that way. But the voters surely did want the candidates they chose to vote. Here appears a final offence to democracy by the Convention: so many delegates were absent from its proceedings. 19 of the fifty delegates were absent for 24 percent or more of the divisions.[458] These included nine past or future premiers or acting premiers: Carruthers, 24 percent of divisions; Berry, 24 percent; Forrest, 24 percent; Fysh, 25 percent; Solomon, 25 percent; Wise, 26 percent; Leake, an impressive 38 percent; Lyne, an arresting 49 percent; and James, an inspirational 75 percent.

Neither were these absences part of walk-outs and boycotts, which might, with some generosity, be construed as part of the 'democratic process'. Neither were they irrelevant to outcomes: given the narrowness of the majorities in the divisions, the absence of so many delegates must have affected the Convention's decisions. Close to one in twelve motions passed with a majority of just one. In 48 percent of the 150 divisions absences exceeded the winning margin. How the absentees' attendance would have

Table 8.3: The size of majorities in the divisions of the Australasian Federal Convention

Size of majority	One	Ten or less	All
Number	12	88	150
(percent of total)	(8)	(58.7)	(100)
Number exceeded by absences	12	62	72
(percent of total)	(8)	(41.3)	(48)
Median of probabilities of the presence of absentees reversing the majority	0.36	0.083	0.035
Mean of probabilities of the presence of absentees reversing the majority	0.33	0.13	0.11

Notes: Rows 3 and 4 'conservatively' assume that if the presence of absentees yields a tie, the presiding officer breaks the tie in favour of the recorded majority.

Sources: AFCP.

changed the outcome is speculative. But the probability of a full attendance reversing the recorded majority can be calculated for each division, on the assumption each absentee would have voted in the affirmative with a probability of 0.5. And the median of these probabilities may be computed (Table 8.3). Of the 62 motions which passed with a majority of ten or less, the typical probability of full attendance reversing the majority is about one in ten – not insignificant. On a significant number of motions, the identification of the outcome of the Convention with 'the will of the people' is arguable.

Absenteeism was also a bane of the 19th century parliaments. But parliaments merely legislated, they did not make constitutions. We are left wondering how many of the narrowly passed provisions of the Constitution cannot be construed, directly or indirectly, as the result of some sort of public choice, but were the unwonted upshot of the delegates' private conveniences, oversights and trials.

9

Cruelling the Constitution

Lo! We have harked to reason,
And turned from the voice of hate;
Lo we have sown in season
Seed of a mighty State.
– Robert Garran

In the standard telling, the drafting of the Constitution by the Australasian Federal Convention between March 1897 to March 1898 constituted the most arduous and testing labour of the whole federal venture; a toil not so much of construction but of navigation; the navigation of an intricate passage, by practised mariners, through often difficult and sometimes perilous waters; which almost came to wreck, but by the straining efforts of its captains made 'over the bar of provincialism', and ultimately reached the safe harbour of union.

But, in another telling, the Convention's constitutional argonauts were inexperienced in the waters they sailed, working from a sketchy acquaintance with doubtful charts, and concluding with a mistaken judgement of where they should, and did, reach.

The false lights

Few of the fifty delegates who gathered in Adelaide in March 1897 had either the experience, clear conception or belief in the federal system they were charged to frame.

How many delegates had any personal experience of a federation? Perhaps the handful of years spent in the USA thirty years before, by one of the Tasmanians, is the most any of them can claim (Charles Grant). 'None had any first-hand knowledge of American government worth calling such ... . Several had a rather superficial knowledge of American political institutions ... A large number displayed almost no knowledge of America or American government'.[459] A spectacular illustration came when the attention of Barton and his fellow delegates was drawn to the case of *Marbury vs Madison* – the foundational case of the power of constitutional review by the Supreme Court of the United States. Barton replied, 'None of us here had read the case mentioned by you of Marbury vs Madison or if seen it had been forgotten'.[460]

The delegates' unfavourable perceptions of the United States constitution would not encourage them to learn more. It was 'sadly wanting' one opined.[461] Another delegate winced at the 'commonplace and calculating men, of commercial instincts and narrow ambitions' at the Philadelphia convention.[462] The Civil War provided an awful admonition against its federal structure. One delegate brightly suggested the Civil War would have been avoided by a system of unitary government. Higgins, Deakin and John Cockburn warned that dark interests had hid under 'states' rights'; the phrase was just a 'stalking horse' for 'reactionaries', 'monarchists' and slavers. (Except, it seemed, when it came to Victoria's anti-Chinese legislation.[463]) And, in the War's aftermath, it was correctly observed, a triumphant Congress had rammed down the throats of a fallen South the 14th ('anti-discrimination') amendment.[464] Closer to their own times, American democracy, said Reid, had 'degenerated into a vast organisation of "political bossdom"' and 'party spoils';[465] 'behind the millions of votes ... there is a system of wires, held perhaps in the worst of hands, which make a mockery of the free choice of the American people'.[466] It would be 'absolutely impossible' to take the United States 'as our leading model'.[467]

To most delegates, Canada's constitutional example embodied in the *British North America Act 1867 (UK)* was superior to the American one. Mistaking the centralist appearance of the Canadian constitution for its reality, some delegates commended the Dominion as an example. Sir Simon Fraser, a Newfoundlander by birth, told fellow delegates with satisfaction, 'Names are for-

Opposite: The Australasian Federal Convention, in Sydney. John Quick is at the bottom right, holding hat and looking at the camera. Barton is seated at the table in the Prime Minister's position. Reid is sitting behind him

gotten in the Canadian Dominion. Boundaries are simply obliterated, and the people residing in Manitoba, Nova Scotia or New Brunswick have forgotten the names which marked the boundaries and are all under the same benign rule'.[468]

But, above and beyond Canada, lay the bedazzling example of Great Britain.

> **Reid**: ... *what historical model, among all the historical models, will we prefer to take as the one that must be followed more closely than all the others?*
>
> **Isaacs**: *The British.*
>
> **Reid**: *I should think so.*[469]

The United Kingdom of Great Britain and Ireland – a unitary state – was to be the shining model for Australia. Thus Reid declared, 'just as the ancient Kingdoms of England, Scotland and Ireland – countless as they seemed to be – were gradually blended into one power, so, because the Australian colonies were truly British, must they gradually grow into one'.[470] The example of the UK as unitary state did not, however, recommend itself to all delegates, on account of the ever present Irish crisis. In some minds, Ireland's unhappy situation counselled the federalisation of the UK; but only as a counsel of frustration. Unification of Great Britain and Ireland had failed, said Glynn, but we 'know', he added, separation would be 'ruinous'. Federation was the only course left. But it had 'no merit in itself'.[471]

More destructive still of an understanding of federalism was not the bald counter-example of the United Kingdom but the deceptive simulacrum of federation provided by the British Empire. In the mind of many delegates this last entity was the glory of a plural governance, and, deceivingly, by the 1890s it did have some semblance of a federal structure. The great matters of war and peace were directed from the centre, while in the parts of the Empire soon to be called the Dominions, local affairs were determined locally.[472] But this spurious semblance could not have encouraged an understanding of, or sympathy for, genuine federation. 'The Dominions' were not sovereign, but commissions of the Empire's nucleus, which made them – and sometimes unmade them – at its wish; and the governing sun of this political solar system was itself unitary, ruled by a sovereign legislature unconstrained by any constitution. The British Empire cast a false light on the nature of federalism, and gave all its admirers every encouragement to 'federal imperialism', as it insinuated the presumption of federation as an empire of loosely controlled provinces.

If delegates' acquaintance with actual federal systems was thin and unreliable, they did have more abstract accounts to draw on. Inglis Clark had supplied some studies of the legal niceties of federal states, along with some bold suggestions. Quick and Garran, and Richard Baker, had compiled descriptions of various federal constitutions. When seeking to strike deeper, the delegates relied on the commentaries on federalism of an Oxonian trio, E. A Freeman, A. V. Dicey and James Bryce. Tellingly, these are the three authorities on whom Barton relied in his one attempt at a general consideration of federation, 'The Meaning of the Federal Constitution'.[473]

Of this trio of the Convention's guides, the most engaged by federation was E. A. Freeman, Regius Professor of Modern History at Oxford. Freeman had an intense vision of historical continuity, and could freely liken the Athenian League to the constitution forged at Philadelphia. But for all his sense of the historical spectacle of federation, Freeman could not be said to advocate it. Federation was 'a compromise', a 'half way house', of a passing and contingent value. The essential premises behind these contentions were that small city states – he was thinking of the Greek polis – served political freedom well, but political order poorly; while large states – he was thinking of absolutist kingdoms – served order well, but political freedom poorly. So there existed a trade-off between political freedom and political order, and for any given society there will be some optimal point on that trade-off. Thus a federation – a combination of large states and small states – might prove the best point on the trade-off. But it was only a possibility; perhaps the optimal point was a large state with some minor municipal institutions, or, alternatively, small states connected by just a loose alliance. Further, Freeman held that with the progress of civilisation, the optimal point was shifting in favour of the large state (thinking of Great Britain?), as enlarging solidarities made order less expensive in terms of freedom. The upshot was that any optimality of federation would be a temporary one; any federation was a half-way house, on what Freeman believed was a thoroughly welcome one-way journey from the 'artificial' tie of federation towards a large unitary state.

A more sympathetic, if not more enlightening, appraisal of federalism was supplied by James Bryce, a 'close friend and devoted pupil of Freeman'.[474] Bryce's path to Oxford had been jeopardised by his refusal of its religious tests, and one biographer has found in Bryce's Presbyterianism a latent 'hostility to British monarchical and aristocratic institutions', along with an attraction to the United States, on which Scottish Presbyterianism 'had such a profound impact'.[475] Bryce's fascination with the American republic yielded his *American Commonwealth* in 1888. If the Convention had a sacred text, this was it. At the behest of Isaac Isaacs the work was requisitioned from Victoria's Public Library, laid upon the table of the Convention, and 'never criticised'.[476] But if *The American Commonwealth* is a sagacious appreciation of the American version of federalism, it is not, contrary to Deakin, 'a philosophic study of constitutional questions' of the 'very first rank'.[477] It barely provides either a useful conception of, or effective rationale for, federalism. Of Bryce's eight supposed arguments in favour of federalism, seven are arguments for a multiplicity of governments – not arguments for the same population being subject to different levels of government. These seven considerations aired by Bryce might justify the Australian landmass being occupied by six distinct governments, or 16. Or, perhaps, just one. But the delegates would find nothing in Bryce that would enjoin a federal structure.

A. V. Dicey, the sharpest in conceptions of the Convention's trio of tutors, was underwhelmed by the American commonwealth's federalism, which he first encountered with Bryce on a trip to the United States the two shared in 1870. The key premise of Dicey's jurisprudence – the sovereignty of parliament – jarred with any federation's 'sovereignty of the constitution'. His conception of parliament as a solitary sovereign power was flatly inconsistent with the federal notion of sovereignty as divided between many parliaments. It was only logical Dicey would disapprove of Canada's constitution as overly federal, and was a vehement adversary of Gladstone's attempt to federalise the United Kingdom through Home Rule for Ireland. He was, later, a champion of the union in 1707 of Scotland and England 'into one inseparable state'.[478] In the summative work of his thought, he declared 'Federalism when successful, has generally been a stage towards unitary government'.[479]

The weakness of the thinking of Freeman, Bryce and Dicey about federalism was their narrowly juristic concerns. Their predominant good was political freedom, and their predominant evil political disorder. This outlook had little to say to the problems of Australia, which had plenty of political freedom, and plenty of political order.

A brighter beam

There are cases for federalism more relevant to Australian conditions than those summoned by the three Oxonians. A defence of federalism might borrow the notion of an optimal scale of business. As there is an optimal size of a pet care business, so there is an optimal size of a steel business. And so there is an optimal extent of the 'legislative firm', reflecting the fact as that as size increases past a certain point the capability of any 'legislative firm' to achieve its proper purposes declines, relative to the resources it commands. So there should not be a single government, but many. To use this conclusion to rationalise a federal structure, one need only suppose that the optimal size differs according to function. Perhaps the optimal size of the 'legislative firm' for street cleaning is smaller than for, say, policing; then a more extensive legislature for policing than that for street cleaning is appropriate, and a local government should co-exist with non-local government. But for all this vision's commonsensical appeal, the theoretical foundation for an optimal size of government is cloudy, and the success of the concept in predicting actual federal structures is speculative. There is not the faintest evidence the delegates had any notion of it.

A surer rationalisation of the co-existence of several governments of the same population lies in the gap between the benefits which government could bring, and what it does bring; 'government failure'. It is plausible this gap is greater the more extensive government is. The more geographically extended a government (and the less easy to avoid), the more prone it is of being a tool for exploitation, either of its subjects for its own benefit, or by the interests which have privileged direction of it. Thus 'government failure' forms a ground for governments to be smaller rather than larger.

But 'government failure' by itself is only a ground for many governments, not for federal government as such. The possibility of a federal structure being advantageous begins with the co-existence of government failure with the benefits of certain government 'co-ordination' of human activity. Or, more exactly, when government failure co-exists with the different types of government co-ordination being of different territorial size. The benefits of some government co-ordination will be exhausted by a small area (a sea wall for a beach side community); others will only be exhausted by a large area (a navy). It is likely that matters where co-ordination benefits are exhausted by a small area will not provide benefits large enough to outweigh the (necessarily large) government failure costs of any territorially extensive government. Put concretely, the costs of foolishly located and exploitatively-financed sea walls will outweigh the (presumably) non-existent benefit of having a sea wall in Tasmania co-ordinated with one in Queensland. So do not make beach walls a responsibility of a central government. But where co-ordination benefits are only exhausted on a large area (a navy?), their benefits might outweigh even the (large) government failure costs of government over such a large area. Concretely, a single Australian navy might have occasioned exploitative and foolish decisions, but it still outperforms six distinctly controlled, uncoordinated navies. It may thus be best to allocate to a 'lower' level of government types of government co-ordination that are maximally useful over small areas, while reserving for larger government types of co-ordination those which are most useful over large areas.

In delegates' minds, however, the key notion that some species of government co-ordination might be most useful over a large territory, while others only over a small, was obscured by a seemingly similar but spurious principle of the allocation:

the specious saw that matters which are of 'common' concern should be subject to some central power, while matters which are of 'local' concern should belong to the local. But the limit of 'concern' is hopelessly indefinite. Tom might judge his neighbours' religion to be of his 'concern'; or their property. Restricting 'common' concerns to the actions of one that 'materially' affects any other remains hopelessly broad whenever 'Tom' is a government; for actions by government to some extent affect all and sundry. A beach wall in X doubtless, to some degree, delays, or makes more expensive, a beach wall in Y. And grander decisions in one part of the earth will surely affect, to some degree, every distant part. No government decision is a 'local concern'. The distinction between a local and a common concern – so often repeated by delegates – is a false light. It is one that obscures the benefits that may arise from a federal system, which in no way relies on such a distinction; it is one which provides a spurious rationale for massively extensive government.

Delegates were equally uncomprehending and unthinking of a feature of federal structure which was to loom large in Australia; a second legislative chamber designed as a 'states' house', where each state has the same number of senators. There are reasons – 'democratic reasons' – for a 'states' house', but the delegates had little sense that a states' house might foster mutually improving 'political exchange' between states.[480] There was, however, among delegates from the three smaller states – providing 60 percent of the total –a fierce consciousness that NSW and Victoria had two-thirds of the population. The small states consequently prized a 'federal' senate, where the two-thirds of the senate supplied by the smaller states would skew legislation in their favour relative to a unicameral parliament. But such a skew seems unlikely to make a bad federal legislature good; if the wishes of the larger states were simply exploitative – as perhaps they were – then the smaller states would do best to be wary of a federation of any kind. Given the poverty of some delegates' thinking with respect to a second chamber, it is not surprising that Barton simply contended, with a perfect dogmatism, that there must be a 'states' house' second chamber, exactly on the American pattern with equal representation of states. And it is not surprising that other delegates with an equal dogmatism repudiated any federal second chambers. Or second chambers more generally. Isaacs declared second chambers were 'an alien element in parliamentary government', [481] and Reid agreed.[482] Wise expressed the hope Federation would occasion the abolition of second chambers in all the states. In this encounter between such reverencers of 'the sacred majority' and the fears of the smaller states, who supplied six-tenths of delegates, there could be no dialectic. The upshot was that, at the Convention, the six-tenths secured one of the most powerful senates in the world.

In summary, as a principle rather than as an expedient, federalism struck no chord with many delegates. 'It has no interest in itself', wrote Glynn. To Higgins, federation was a parrot phrase, 'a mere word'.[483]

The confederal alternative

If federation was a mere 'word' to many delegates, they had, in addition, an 'expletive': confederalism. In a confederation the composing entities are bound to each other not through a 'new State', as Quick and Garran put it,[484] but by contract; the essential parallel is of a group of persons contracting. In the Australian case, the idea can be illustrated by way of an Australia-wide customs union. This did not require a federation: it could have been achieved by negotiation between the six colonies, and six enactments. But the trade agreement which one parliament can enact, a later one can repeal, as Henry Parkes rightly lamented. A confederation would contribute to enforcement of the agreement, by ordaining a court to award damages against any state violating its commitment, reflecting economic costs of the violation. To smooth 'treaty legislation' a legislative body – a Council – of all members could be established. If unanimity was required for it to legislate, there is no deviation in substance from the essential scheme. If only a majority was sufficient to impose a 'treaty', we would be moving to a system of compelled contracts (for any minority), but they would remain contracts.

So conceived, confederalism was immune to several common criticisms. It is not that the executive would be non-existent in a confederal arrangement; in fact, it would be the creation of treaty between confederal parties. It is not that taxes cannot be levied on individuals, but taxes will be invoked by treaty, and enforced by the court.

The lynch pin of this confederal vision is the enforcing court. An enormous burden is placed on it and, correspondingly, an enormous strength is required of it. The requisite strength might be met, but thereby perhaps create another evil: for with great strength comes the possibility of abuse of great strength. Alternatively, the requisite strength might be lacking. It is the spirit of confederacy that its legitimacy is lent by its components; and what is lent, may be called-in. Hence the much lamented 'weakness' of confederations.

The Federal Council of Australasia (1885-1900) was a semi-confederal body,[485] and the Federationists' case against the Council was its flimsiness. It was 'little more than a debating society' (Deakin) which 'yawns and lounges away a Christmas session in Hobart' (Barton); it was 'born lame' (Crisp), if not faintly farcical. Thus Garran cleared the board of the Council with the derisory remark, 'It passed a few acts about pearl-shell fishing and beche-de-mer fisheries'.[486] The occasion for Garran's scoffing, the *Queensland Pearl Shell and Beche-de-Mer Fisheries Regulation 1888 (FCA)* was, in truth, an exercise in labour standards; and included such stipulations as that deaths be reported, that native labourers be 'carried on ship's articles', and be paid in the presence of a shipping master. Other legislation of the Council included the *Australasian Civil Processes Act 1886 (FCA)*, which made it possible for a legal suit to be 'served' outside the colony in which it was issued, a power valuable in matters ranging from absconding debtors to divorce proceedings. The *Federal Garrisons Act 1893 (FCA)* provided a legal framework which enabled, say, South Australian soldiers to serve in Albany, or Victorian soldiers in Thursday Island. The *Australasian Naturalization Act 1897 (FCA)* established the mutual recognition by Council members of each other's naturalisations, so that a person naturalised in Queensland would be ipso facto regarded in Victoria as naturalised.

The legislation is not contemptible, and served both justice and utility. The objection to the confederalism of the Council was not its supposed lack of capability; or that it could not have effected taxation (which is misleading), or a common tariff, or common immigration policy, or a blue water navy. The real objection, to Deakin's mind and his like, is that the Council did not create a higher, greater, more magnificent state.

A higher, greater, grander state was the object of most delegates; it was what they wanted, it was what would reward them. And this explains their thin response to federation. The problem was not so much their lack of understanding of federation, but their not wanting what it offered. For the grounds for federation advanced in the pages above amount to a 'public interest rationale' of federation; a rationale which can be influential only if particular interests, with their warping effect, are not at work. Such a genuinely federal constitution could be actually wanted only when the particular interests of delegates were, somehow, unknown to them. But the interests which supported them politically were not unknown to delegates. The delegates' own crotchets they were especially alive to. For many delegates the new constitution was simply a device for securing their own pet project – the unification of rail gauges? age pensions? – or to project their wishfulness.[487] 'Federation … is to do for everybody what they most wish!'.[488] And the subject of what delegates most wished for was themselves. They would not be onlookers on what they created. Six of the NSW delegates would become members of the federal parliament, seven of the SA delegates and eight of the Victorian delegates.[489] Almost all wished to create a superior polity they could participate in. The hankering of John Downer for a grander and more suitable vista for his ambitions is palpable.

And would not the perfection of the superior, grander, greater state lie in the obliteration of any lesser one? That is, unification.[490] In the Sydney session Lyne declared, 'My ideas have converged very much in the direction of some sort of unification'.[491] A few days later Wise blandly announced to delegates, 'I do not hesitate to declare myself an advocate of and believer in unification'.[492] And if that end was presently unattainable, then Federation would be a tolerable means for progressing towards it. Was not the very first of Bryce's eight merits of federalism that it amounted to an advance towards 'national' government when unification could not be attained? [493]

Their handiwork

It cannot be said the delegates successfully defied their lack of understanding of, or sympathy with, federalism, and produced an effectively federal constitution. It is true that, for all the reediness of their federal convictions, the Constitution was nominally federalist. And yet the federal government seemed somewhat overloaded with functions. Why allocate marriage law to the Commonwealth? That the first Commonwealth *Marriage Act* came only in 1961 suggests the allocation was not urgent. Bespeaking still more a unificationist sentiment was the disastrous section 92, 'the lawyer's delight and the client's despair'.[494]

> 92. ... *trade, commerce, and intercourse among the States, whether by means of internal carriage or ocean navigation, shall be absolutely free.*

Freedom of inter-state trade was already implied by section 90, which vested in the Commonwealth the exclusive right to impose tariffs. Section 92 seems to be a celebration of the total dissolution of borders, and that is not federal joy. Appreciating that, Quick and Garran, the self-appointed curators of the new constitution, readily allowed that section 92 was not intended to unconditionally disallow the regulation of trade, commerce or intercourse at a state border. So what did it disallow? A century of jurisprudence has contended the question. So lodged within the Constitution was a 'foreign object' which has irritated, inflamed and weakened the whole, and has produced constitutional chaos. On account of that chaos, section 92 impedes the Constitution from fulfilling its fundamental purpose: to constitute 'law'. That is to say, regularity.[495]

The Convention's other offences against federalism were less matters of design and more casualties of shortsight. But they were not the less significant. The Constitution destroyed the revenue base of the states by making customs and excise an 'exclusive power' of the Commonwealth. The delegates were well aware of the problem, but their crude remedy – 75 percent of tariff revenues would be returned to the states – encouraged the Commonwealth to raise tariffs to elude the 75 'tax rate' on its revenues.[496] The one way of funding state expenditure without creating an incentive to raise tariffs would be to leave customs and tariff a 'concurrent power', so that both states and the federal government could impose tariffs on imports from overseas. But this was taboo.[497]

A less apparent, but not less significant, offence at federalism was reserving to the Commonwealth's parliament the power to initiate a referendum on revising the Constitution. Unlike article V of the US Constitution, the relevant section of the Australian Constitution (section 128) gave no right to, say, four out of six states to initiate a referendum on the Constitution. Section 128 was, then, a battery that pointed in one direction only: at the states' authority. And it was a battery discharged intensively in the first decade of the Constitution. But the impact was disappointing. Voters hesitated to approve revisions, and have so ever since, even regarding those they had every seeming warmth for, such as making terms of senators coincident with members of the House of Representatives.[498]

Historically, radical revision of the Constitution has been effected by the High Court. This 'constitutional monarch' was very casually enthroned. The Convention's Constitution said little more than that the Court shall have at least three justices. They would be appointed solely by the Executive Government of the Commonwealth, without any process specified; the consent of the parliament, or one its chambers, would not be required. No qualifications, or disqualifications, were laid down. Having an allegiance to a foreign power is not a disqualification. Neither is being 'attainted of treason'. Any justice may hold 'office of profit under the Crown' or be an 'undischarged bankrupt' or be 'convicted for an offence punishable under the law by imprisonment for one year or longer'.[499] And, of most practical importance, being a member of the cabinet that makes the decision to appoint was no disqualification. In ordinary life, selection committees are rarely licensed to appoint one of their own members. The federal cabinet is, in effect, so licensed.

The High Court was made so casually because delegates did not realise what they were making. Its most contentious occupation – constitutional review of legislation – was only occasionally struck by delegates. They were not unaware of such review; from their earliest days the laws of Australian legislatures were subject to review by local courts to ascertain if they were consistent with English law, at least insofar as that law extended to Australia. As Dicey observed, 'every court in Victoria is bound to hold void, and in fact does hold void, enactments which contravene Imperial Statute'.[500] And 'constitutional review' by Australian courts in the 19th century was not without controversy. But the battle lines were the reverse of the present day. The propriety of such review was upheld by conservatives like William Stawell, the Chief Justice of Victoria for three decades (1857-1886). By contrast, the duty and prerogative of Australian courts to scan their legislature's law for any incongruity with English statute chafed Stawell's successor as Chief Justice, George Higinbotham, a favourite of bourgeois radicals and Trades Hall alike. Thus, at the Convention, conservatives were the readiest supporters of a High Court as a guardian of the Constitution from trespass by an overweening, possibly vicious, legislature. And radicals were wary of the High Court as an overweening, possibly vicious, trespasser against the legislature. Consider this exchange in the Convention, between one of its most 'left' members and one of its most 'right' members, over the possibility of an order from the 'Supreme Court' to the parliament:

> **Isaacs**: *A mandamus against Parliament.*
>
> **Downer**: *What a shocking thing!*
>
> **Isaacs**: *Did you ever hear of such a thing!*
>
> **Downer**: *Then is the Parliament to do what it likes?*
>
> **Isaacs**: *If that is the sort of constitution you had better let us know it.*
>
> **Downer**: *I know with the liberal view of my friend, he wishes the Supreme Court to do nothing.*[501]

But the majority of delegates seem disengaged from the issue of constitutional review, perhaps comfortable in the thought that as an ordinary court could declare some by-law *ultra vires*, so a 'high' court could judge some act of parliament 'beyond its powers'. But a constitution is not a by-law. Nor is it a statute. The delegates had little appreciation that in making a federation they were making a constitution above ordinary law. Section 44 illustrates how, as Reid complained, the delegates did not appreciate that they were constitution-making, not legislating. This section enumerates disqualifications from membership of the House of Representatives or the Senate by reason of various disgraces or corrupting circumstances. This section includes the doubtless sensible prohibition of accepting an 'office of profit' under the Crown, but goes on to prohibit 'any direct or indirect pecuniary interest in any agreement with the Public Service of the Commonwealth otherwise than as a member and in common with the other members of an incorporated company consisting of more than twenty-five persons'. The decision to insert 'twenty-five persons' in a constitution is extreme, and ludicrous. Contingencies as to what constitutes a 'corrupting' indirect pecuniary relationship with government are so shifting there is little better to be done than leaving it to legislation. And that is what they thought they were doing. The constitutions of NSW and the other colonies *were* a melange of ordinary legislation: revisable by ordinary majorities in the parliament, and not subject to any judicial review.[502] All colonial constitutions had equivalent clauses to section 44; and so section 44 was added by the constitution-makers of 1897, oblivious, it seems, of the significance of it being entrenched as constitutional law, and thereby made a creature of the High Court's interpretation. The derangement of the American Constitution by the Supreme Court of the United States at points in the 19th century might have been a warning. But Bryce's *American Commonwealth* assured delegates those days were long gone.

There is one final category of failure to record, which might be tagged as 'collateral'. In attempting to fulfil their federal remit, the delegates damaged other qualities of the Constitution. Democracy was offended in the awkwardness of delegates' attempt to affix a 'strong' Senate to a Westminster system. Putting aside 'double dissolutions', the Constitution imposes a six year term on senators, regardless of any dissolutions of the House, but allows their re-election from their fifth year; with the upshot that a senator who has failed to win re-election, despite that, sits and legislates for perhaps up to 52 weeks, with an obvious offence to democracy.[503]

Most seriously, 'responsible government' – the principle that the executive stands or falls at the pleasure of the lower house – was damaged by the creation of a powerful Senate. The new Federation's elected second chamber had an eminence unmatched by any parliamentary system anywhere, and can with sufficient resolve extinguish the executive. The executive, then, has two masters. But, if there are two masters, there is no master. The delegates could have prevented latent chaos by investing responsibility in a compound of the Senate and the House of Representatives, as Baker proposed. Instead, a potential for chaos was allowed whenever the two houses were opposite in resolution over the fate of the executive. The constitutional crisis of 1975 was one distant posterity of this neglect. Hackett memorably said that either federation would be the end of responsible government, or responsible government would be the end of federation. Deakin's projection was gloomier still: 'To introduce an American Senate into a British constitution is to destroy both'.[504]

*

On 17 March 1898 the Convention came to a close. The President permitted 'that cheers should be given for the Queen, and afterwards cheers should be given for Australia'. Cheers were not given for any colony, but Glynn did point out it was St Patrick's day.

The delegates, lacking in ideas, over-dependent on book learning, and writing in the false light of unitary states, had, by default or expediency, produced a pedestrian, not very digested, and unimaginative palimpsest of pre-existing constitutions; a constitution conceived without inspiration.[505] And yet, putting aside the divided WA delegation, all delegates, with perhaps just three exceptions, approved in the large of what they had framed.[506] They dispersed to their respective colonies to commend their work. There it would encounter a much more mixed reception.

10

The Anti-Federationists

Firm alike to friend and foe,
Firm in gentleness and faith,
Firm in 'yes', and firm in 'no.'
– Henry Parkes

As victor's history will lionise the triumphant, so it will disdain and ignore the defeated. This is not only unjust but misleading. The anti-Federationist cause was well stocked with big, characterful, popular personalities with sweep, zeal and guile. They were, one might say, effective personalities without effect. And there lies the puzzle of the anti-Federationists. Were they out of joint with their times, 'behind' them, no less? Was their failure located in some crotchet of their mental make-up? Or was that traceable, not to themselves or their times, but to particular, merciless and irrational circumstance?

John Dunmore Lang (1799–1878)

In the most common telling of the Federation story, John Dunmore Lang is not behind the times, but ahead of history. He is the prophet of the Coming Event; he is the earliest public voice in Australia championing federation, some 50 years before the act was resolved upon. But Lang is thereby miscast. Lang was more a false friend than a partisan of federation. If his first words were enthusiastic, his final thoughts repudiated the federation of the Australian continent.

Lang's 'function' in Australian history was to infuse a quotient of principle, idea and political vision into the mishmash of expedience, custom and prejudice which had previously governed the colony. For that role he was well prepared by his eight years of education for the Presbyterian ministry at the University of Glasgow, during the Indian summer of Scotland's enlightenment. The premises of that movement – rationalism, individualism, materialism – became his premises. Its corollary – the value of self-direction for human growth and development – was his from early adulthood. He left Scotland for Sydney in 1822, and never ceased crossing the globe, yet it has been rightly said he 'did not travel far' intellectually. J. S. Mill described his father as the last man of the 18th century; the same might be said with even more justice of the Reverend Dr Lang. Born in 1799, in his passage through the new century he was increasingly in foreign territory philosophically.

Lang's creed, in the company of his egocentric personality, a visionary outlook and his 'heroic founder' self-image, gave him much to act upon when he arrived, in 1823, at the crude coastal outpost of Sydney. Building its first church not consecrated to the Church of England – establishing one the first schools of any aspiration (with John Robertson as the first pupil) – recruiting immigrants from Germany and France: planting and cultivating the human seed in moral and material wastelands.

Germination was a key metaphor of Lang's mind, and the essence of germination is the separation of new life from the old parent. With such a mental furnishing it is unsurprising that in the global political ferment of the late 1840s Lang should emerge as an advocate of political independence over all schemes of empire. The United States had obtained its independence long before. Ireland should obtain its independence, at least to the extent of self-government in its domestic affairs. And, to his great satisfaction, Port Phillip was on the verge of obtaining such self-government. All the Australian colonies should be independent outright of the parent society. But, Lang allowed, any single Australian colony in the conditions of the mid-19th century 'could not command the respect of the civilised world'. Lang therefore proposed a 'union or confederation' of the Australian colonies; a 'series of sovereign states bound together in a great Federation'. Beyond defence, its central authority would be concerned with foreign relations, the post office and public lands. But it would disown such unions' common prerogative of taxing imports: to Lang, one fruit of Australian federation would be the 'doing away entirely with the whole establishment of Custom Houses throughout the [United] Australian Provinces.[507] Such was the vision Lang articulated in 1850, to enthusiastic audiences.

Lang's vision of United Provinces diverged from the vision of a United Australia of later Federationists. In Lang's conception federation was entirely subordinated to independence. Australia's independence was the end, and federation was the means. To Federationists, federation was the end, and definitely not a means to independence. Lang's own conception of nationalism was also antithetical to the designs of many Federationists.[508] He conceived nationality as a kind of civic virtue, fostering co-operation and unity. But its value remained instrumental. If it was the feeling of nationality that assisted the Swiss and the Dutch in winning their independence, it was these nations' independence that produced their glories, not their nationality. Thus Lang's conception of the useful role of nationalism would be uncomfortable to the Federationists of 1901, and their goal of a 'nation colony'. If nationalism promoted independence, then they would not want nationalism. And, for that matter, if Federation stimulated nationalism, they would not want Federation.

As Australia developed, Lang's vision of federated Australia diverged still further from those of later Federationists. To Lang, in the mid-19th century, the point of Australian federation was to make Australian independence feasible in a world of rival and covetous empires. But, as the years passed, the necessity of federation for the feasibility of independence waned. By 1870, both NSW and Victoria had a population greater than the whole of Australia in 1850. At the same time, the prospective consequences of the Australia-wide federation Lang had entertained in the 1850s had darkened. Whereas the 1857 edition of *The Coming Event* had been 'respectfully inscribed' to the people of Victoria, whose new self-government Lang had championed, by 1875 he judged Victoria guilty of 'conceit and silly vanity' in demanding other colonies recognise her as the 'metropolitan colony'.[509] Victoria and her accompanying martial spirit was additionally offending; these 'veriest zealots of the British connection' are 'prepared for war: I am sorry to be obliged to confess that Sydney and the colonies of the Pacific are not.'[510] 'It is hopeless', he wrote, 'to expect an incorporating union of seven provinces at present'; 'we can no longer presume to include ... Victoria, Tasmania and South Australia, but must leave them, as God left Adam, to the freedom of his own will, with all their exploded theories of protection and the blessedness of the British connection', and 'confine the claim of Freedom and Independence to ... NSW, Queensland, Capricornia and Carpentaria'.[511]

By 1870, Lang had largely abandoned the federal scheme he had advanced in 1850. In this reversal he was out of sorts with history. Australia was not ready for federation in 1850, but by the time of his death in 1878 the forces that were to produce 1901 had already formed and aligned. Thus Lang did not represent the forces of Federation. Their protectionist project was anathema to him. He was never engaged by race. He wished Australia settled by British, but his sometime favour of restricting Chinese immigration betrayed no judgement of their 'inferiority'. Nationalism? He favoured a 'constructing nationality', but what Lang hoped that nationality would construct would disconcert and affront Federationists. Contrary to their dogmatic continental presumption, the federation which Lang envisaged would be essentially Pacific bound, ranging from the Murrumbidgee to Carpentaria; the rest of the Australian continent was gladly left by Lang 'to its own devices'.

Deakin, by the light of his own doctrines, was correct to elevate Duffy as the prophet of Federation, and to ignore Lang. He could have justly represented Lang as an opponent.

John Robertson (1816–1891)
'This accursed federation ...'[512]

In Federationist history John Robertson – premier, mountain rider, and 'great panjandrum' of the Land Question – is afforded only a parenthetical comment, as an illustration of an eccentrically intense opponent of the cause. In truth, in John Robertson Federationism confronted its most reckonable adversary. Not only in the unconditionality of his antagonism, but in the political skill and capital which he deployed in articulating it.

In Robertson Federation had, most palpably, an 'enemy'. It was not a particular form of federation that Robertson objected to; he detested anything bespeaking a federal governance, including the 'absurd' Federal Council, from which he had successfully excluded NSW. It was not just the process: he might mock the 'open your mouth and shut your eyes' trustingness of Federationists, but he would not have been mollified by their greater circumspection. He censured the presumption of Parkes to act in 1889 as if plenipotentiary of NSW – 'Who appointed Henry Parkes? Himself, I presume' – but was unreconciled by the parliament eventually authorising such an office. He rebuked the vainglory he detected in Federationists, but any proof of a genuine civic impulse would not have pacified him. Federation was a 'nonsense'.

Robertson's opposition to Federation had its roots – in abstract terms – in the offence it gave, in his own mind, to the bounds of a valid political community. To the liberal nationalist, the state properly encloses a population where there exists a measure of mutual trust, a sense of common concerns, a certain joining in the shouts and lamentations of one another; a 'brotherhood'. Robertson did not reject that doctrine – he was a nationalist of his own kind – but he rejected that the doctrine implied Australia would constitute a political community. The relations of the six colonies were more instrumental than fraternal. And circumstances were such that these instrumental relations would not be mutually beneficial. They would be exploitative: to obstruct the other, to prevent the other buying cheaply as they might, to 'plunder' the other. The neighbours of NSW 'North, South and West' were not fond; they were resolved to filch 'our most valuable territory which they have ever been eagerly straining to obtain'.[513] Robertson supposed that NSW, by contrast, did constitute a national community. It was not a 'province' – the Federationist language dismayed him – but a 'country', a usage which he, with many others, preferred; 'this great country of New South Wales ... the freest country in all the world'. He was a NSW patriot, a NSW nationalist.

But, to critical eyes, Robertson was more a NSW chauvinist than patriot: did he not support Parkes's outré proposal of 1888 to rename New South Wales 'Australia'? Was not his anti-Federationism traceable to a presumption of the pre-eminence of NSW?

She was the first of 'the Australias'; from her ribs the others were made. They were her offspring; but also ingrates, deserters, usurpers. Critics, additionally, commonly hold Robertson's cause was merely 'provincialist'; mistakenly seeing a whole in a portion, and the complete in the incomplete. And insular; underestimating the actual, inevitable and useful dependence of one part on the other. Robertson might retort that insularity would perfectly characterise his protectionist adversaries. He might have added that all nationalisms are necessarily provincial – including the Australian nationalists, who, while scorning provinciality, are under the 'impression that the sun rises over the Barrier Reef and sets behind the Leeuwin'.[514] What Robertson did do was turn the rhetorical tables by contending the Federationists were imperialists in seeking to construct an Australian empire. Not in a literal sense; not literally a state where the locus of power was confined to a geographical section. But in an effective sense, where one geographical section would always predominate over the remainder. Under any federation, NSW 'before the Dominion Parliament she would stand in whispering humbleness while her irate sisters determined. .... It was bad enough to be controlled by the great old country from which we sprang, and which had no desire to humiliate us or to plunder us'.[515] In facing Federation, NSW was threatened by a neo-imperialism far worse than the original.[516]

Robertson's sensitivity to the prospect of a new empire was plausibly heated by a previous anti-imperial experience: the struggle to achieve self-government in New South Wales. This sense of this struggle was sharper in NSW than the other colonies – Victoria, Queensland, Tasmania – where the institution of their own self-government amounted more to a relieving intervention by the Imperial government against NSW, and less something directly extracted from Westminster.[517] The (commonly) nation-defining experience of such extraction was very much part of Robertson's own personal experience of the 1850s. In the light of his own investment in that, one may sympathise with his refusal 'to surrender to any outside power whatever the liberties and privileges which we devoted our early lives to obtain for this people'.[518] Parkes could claim almost the same investment, but the investment seems to have meant more to Robertson. Robertson had a saltier attitude to the organs of Imperial government than Parkes ever did, and never shared Parkes's susceptibility towards governors. He needled the British government for 'sending rich and generous young gentlemen with lovely wives to fill our Government Houses, and thus intentionally or unintentionally influence our society in favour of protection'.[519] Indeed, the British were to blame for federation as a whole: 'The project, however stupid, ... doubtless came from England'.[520] A strain of 'nativism' evidently marked Robertson, which was necessarily absent from Parkes. Robertson left England at the age of six, his parents also emigrating, and his wife at the age of seven. Educated as the first pupil of the first school of Dr Lang, his family grew erratically to rustic wealth in the Hunter Valley frontier. To his enemies, Robertson was, all in all, an Australian barbarian: 'Born at the Rocks, taught morality by the Doctor, he killed native dogs and studied the beauties of the mother tongue, when he felt the sacred fire of patriotic ambition and was crowned at Scone [with his election to the first Assembly][521] – a politician, statesman, Minister. Now he is a prophet'.[522] Launched by the native context so disdained by the *Herald*, Robertson went on to win a seat in the NSW parliament on 24 more occasions, and to be its Premier five times. On the one occasion Robertson and Parkes stood in the same seat, Robertson won 42 percent of the vote, Parkes five percent.[523]

Thus when, within weeks of Parkes's Tenterfeld speech, Robertson – a retired widower of 73 years, secure from any charge of personal ambition, and palpably driven by indignation – commenced his charge, Federationists were not encountering a marginal, extreme figure. He was a singular and potentially formidable opponent.

Robertson plucked the right ideological notes for his audience. He was a free trader in a free trade colony. He was also squarely anti anti-Catholic – 'pandering to a set of priests' in Parkes's charge[524] – and thus on the other side of that perilous fracture which Parkes had fallen foul of. And, in a democratic age, Robertson bore the laurel of the 'extreme liberal'. He was a member of the cabinet which, a generation before, had introduced manhood suffrage; who had in 1875 declared in favour of female suffrage, and sought to make the Legislative Council elective. He was the one-time 'wild visionary'[525] – the *Sydney Morning Herald* called him a 'red republican', and he called the *Herald* a 'filthy rag' – who complemented his political democracy by the Lands Acts of 1861, which sought to convert crown land leased by few pastoralists into freeholds worked by 'industrious yeomanry'. For all these credal commitments, Robertson was also flexible enough to league with protectionists for the sake of the anti-Federationist cause. In a by-election of 1891 – the first political contest in Australia with a Federationist dimension – Robertson endorsed the successful campaign of a protectionist (but anti-Federationist) candidate against the free trade (but Federationist) candidate.[526]

Robertson's personal attributes worked to his success. In an age of oratory, he had outfought a physical disability which was especially cruel when politicians were required to hurl eloquence across the scrum. Full of deep feeling, earnest, excitable and blunt, he was also, 'with a shade of watchful distrust in his Bedouin eye',[527] 'capable of subtlety when the occasion demanded it'.[528] He was replete with the martial virtues, 'so crafty, so courageous'[529] with 'aggressive hawk-like red face, and kindly courageous eyes that looked through you and did not know how to falter or express fear'.[530] But he was also blessed with social ones: 'loyal to the last',[531] and 'generous to a fault',[532] he claimed to have no real enemies, and a bitter adversary granted only two in the Assembly. Of 'intrinsic good nature', the press could not refrain from dubbing him the 'Knight of Clovelly', always playfully, but never mockingly. A knight, but perhaps no gent, and the public thought no less of him for that. With a 'rugged candour', a 'natural gift for profanity' and an 'ability to laugh at himself',[533] 'Slapper' fathered a bevy of affectionate anecdotes, and his appeal traversed class boundaries more than any politician of comparable stature: he was returned for West Sydney ('the Rocks') eleven times, while Parkes applied his counterfeit refinement to the suffrages of East Sydney. Robertson, all in all, was rich in that recognisable charm which has proved political gold in Australia. As in Henry Lawson's salute in verse, he 'rode the crest of public adulation'.[534]

At what would prove to be Robertson's last public speaking event – opening the agricultural show at the town of Robertson, in the midst of selector territory hewn out of rainforest – he declared 'he would tell the people of New South Wales that it was his intention to again take up active politics' to fight 'this cursed federation'.[535] If he had lived two months longer, he could have re-entered the Assembly in the general election of 1891. If he had lived as long as Adye Douglas – a Premier of Tasmania, Robertson's elder and very much his counterpart – Robertson would have seen in the twentieth century.[536]

What would have been the impact of Robertson's planned frontal charge will remain unknown. But one might doubt its success; not because of his own lack of prowess but for a lack of support.

Robertson had difficulty in finding recruits in the political class for his quest. Despite the mistrust and misgivings of half of the state's voters, NSW politicians almost to a man accepted Federation in the abstract, even though not the Bill in the concrete. This acceptance reflects in part the changing nature of that political class. In 1889, Robertson had growled that the hotels, clubs and parliament 'stank of squatters'. But the aroma of power was changing. The rapid growth of the Sydney metropolis, and the concurrence of the public with the expectations of the gentleman in his golden age, made politics more than ever an advantageous occupation for professionals, in particular lawyers.[537] It need not be laboured that Federation was especially advantaging to the political careers of lawyers; or that not all lawyer-politicians were Federationists: John Want, QC, the 'destroying archangel', was Robertson's 'political son'.[538] But Want was a strange failure, who betokens a running dry of the political stream, Lang-Cowper-Robertson-Dalley, which had been a counterpoint to Parkes. It bespeaks the difficulty of that stream successfully replenishing itself from the new sources, such as G. H. Reid, who would have been that political lineage's most obvious inheritor.

Robertson's old political wellsprings were no longer flowing. The Hunter Valley was now a stronghold of Federationist sentiment. Robertson's popularity with working class voters was without fruit in this last struggle: his longtime political pastures west of George Street were not Federation's political battle ground. Absorbed by industrial disputes, working class attention was not on constitutional questions. The zone of contention lay in the Sydney suburbs, and in outlying rural regions of the colony. And there he languished. To Sydney professionals, Robertson's candour was crudity; his authenticity, uncouthness. To the boater wearers flocking to hear Barton, the graceless, 'ravingly blastiferous' Sir John was more Falstaff than Falconbridge. Style is important. To the distant rural regions, Robertson's vision of what constituted NSW weakened his patriotic cause. If the Commonwealth was a 'state-nation' – a political construction – so was NSW. The Riverina and the Clarence ('Northern Rivers'), which Robertson had striven to keep within NSW, did not want to be part of NSW.

But perhaps the key weakness in Robertson's cause was his own countrymen's lack of his pride. Or the pride of Victorians in their own colony. 'All I have in the world is in NSW, my country': so spoke L. F. Heydon, an anti-Federationist leader.[539] But how few of his fellow countrymen shared that sentiment. Why? Two externals – symbol and myth – may provide some clues. There was a dearth of symbols of Robertson's country; the 'embodiments' that might have cultivated patriotic consciousness. The very name of Robertson's country was cumbersome; he would gladly change it to 'Australia'. In 1876 Robertson had inaugurated the 'badge' of NSW, which in the 20th century became part of its flag, but its use in the 19th century seems sparse: the lion and the unicorn was the symbol of authority. The NSW ensign had informally established itself as a vernacular emblem of its society, flown by volunteer fire brigades, school cadet corps and their likes. It was almost certainly the flag that draped the Lang monument at its opening ceremony on 26 January 1891. But Federationists annexed it for their own 'accursed' cause.

Beyond symbols, it might be contended that a negative myth weighed against NSW pride – the convict stain. But any acceptance of that negative myth almost assumes the lack of pride that one seeks to explain. For the birth story of NSW was a tale of magical realism: the epic voyage of one thousand across the

John Robertson (centre) amid friends, on the last day of his life

earth; the fantastic coincidence of two ancient enemies chancing upon one another in Botany Bay; the revelation of what the gates of North and South Heads had hidden; the fascination and poignancy of the encounter of man and man separated by 40 000 years; the steel of leadership in the furnace of desperation; the Shakespearian mingling of the high and low; the weirdness of the gothic clank under an 'ardent sun', the paradox of banishment in a paradise; and of a hale new race springing up from felonry, and winning the rights of freemen; all flavoured by the intimacy of its enduring vestiges in stone and speech. This was a tale which, properly told, could have withstood the *moderne*-ism and malevolent nihilism of the *Bulletin*. It seems only for a lack of pride that this story was so fitfully told.[540] And so we are back to the question.

*

On a cool evening in the first week of May 1891, Robertson filled the chair of a meeting at Castlereagh Street 'packed from floor to ceiling' to protest Federation. After the concluding cheers, he would have – by his traditional practice – ridden 'an ancient grey-mare ... full to the teeth of statesmanship and whiskey', the seven miles home to 'Clovelly House' at Watson's Bay, the sand and pine nape of the hulking mass of South Head. A mile distant, three days later, but just a short walk from the tomb of W. C. Wentworth, a party of his long-time companions gathered around him. He declared his hope 'he would be spared a little longer to see their liberties preserved, but whatever way the battle went he would GIVE HIS LIFE'.[541] A photograph was taken; the circle dispersed; he took a pen and paper, and engaged a ferrymaster to take his letter to the *Sydney Morning Herald*. 'All we have asked', it read, 'is to be left alone with the Wentworth constitution'. Before these words were read next morning, on a near moonless night in Watson's Bay – where Captain Hunter had once made camp in anxious expectation of the *Sirius*; where George Watson of the same ship had sunk the foundations of Clovelly House; where Elizabeth Macarthur had passed her last days; under the stone and eaves raised by the quartermaster of the First Fleet's flagship – Robertson lay, stilled, in silent deliverance of his pledge.

John Henry Want (1846–1905)

In the conventional account of Federation John Want fills the role of the menacing, but thankfully undone, villain. Six feet, saturnine, with burning eyes, Want was the self-described 'arch-destroying angel' of 'the hydra headed monster' of Federation.[542] It was probably within his power to slay the monster within NSW. But, at a critical moment, he quit the field, secluded himself from the battle, and virtually hid, to the frustration of his anti-Federationist peers, the glee of his Federationist adversaries, and the bafflement of history.

*

Want had the opportunity of derailing the train of Federation before it had rolled an inch – but did not use it. As 1889 opened, Parkes was to all appearances comfortably installed in power as premier, after his great victory of 1887 gave him a majority of 42 over the protectionists. But the opposition benches included a few dissident free traders, such as Want, who denounced the premier as one of the 'greatest traitors to the free-trade party within the walls' of parliament.[543] On 9 January 1889 Want brought Parkes down in a single shot. The premier had disdained to reply to Want's charges of a corrupt appointment, so Want moved a censure motion in the government, and won. His motion may have been a lucky shot, unlooked-for by all, and achieved with the help of some dubious members seeking an aura of rectitude. For all that, at age 40, Want had the premiership in his hand. A career comparable to Parkes's beckoned.

Want was blessed with a roughshod glamour. John Henry Want, QC, was 'Jack' to the public at large; the fencer, the amateur boxing champion, the yachstsman of Sydney to Hobart adventures, and of exotic voyages to Japan. He was Jack of anecdotes; such as dodging cannon fire while navigating his beloved *Miranda* through the Heads of Port Jackson. 'Always conspicuous at the race-course',[544] Want could win the confidence of any jury, and was, in the judgement of one historian of the law, 'the greatest advocate of his own or any earlier generation in NSW'.[545] He was the big name barrister who only on special occasions would don the barristers' uniform – of frock-coat, button hole bouquet and top hat – but whose face and hands were 'always as brown and rough as a blacksmith's'.

Any premiership of Want would have the full-bodied backing of John Robertson; it would amount, in spirit, to a further round in the duel of Parkes and Robertson, the sixth premiership of Robertson. It would enjoy the support of the *Evening News*, which outsold any other Sydney daily by at least a factor of four. And with Want at its helm, it would evade the sectarian snare. Thus there was the possibility of a government of vigorous free trade credentials, with press backing and disencumbered of the baggage with which Parkes had burdened his fellow travellers. A government which would have left Parkes in impotent isolation, and not the figure who, from June 1889, would be the impressario and prophet of Federation.

For all these favourable circumstances, Want let the Governor know that he was about to sail to Japan, and he would be 'damned' if he would form a ministry.[546] The contrast with Barton, in 1887, futilely awaiting upon a call from Government House that never came, could not have been more acute. Neither did Want stand for free trade leadership when Parkes's ministry finally fell in 1891, even though Want, with many other free traders, was not happy with the prospect of Reid's leadership.

'Jack' Want, the self-described 'arch-destroying angel' of Federation

Omitted from Reid's initial ministry, he left the Assembly for the secluded political waters of the Council.

In a typically impulsive return to battle, in December 1894 Want accepted Reid's offer of the office of Attorney-General. As Want had roared for several years against federation, Reid was presumably seeking to reassure anti-Federationists, and perhaps disarm them. Want presumably saw the ministry as a means to enmesh the Federationist serpent. And yet, in January 1895, while the premiers planned the Convention, Want chose to holiday in San Francisco. In 1897 he did successfully steer through the Council, in the face of a ferocious rear guard action by Barton, a law that required the 1898 referendum to have at least 80 000 Yes votes to succeed. He led the 'anti-Billites' in their 1898 campaign for a No vote, launching it with a rally of free traders, protectionists, and Labor. And he closed it on the eve of the vote with a rally with muckraker John Norton. But with the success in his referendum of June 1898, Want again retreated. He did not treat this seeming success of anti-Billites as an opportunity to challenge Reid. He mooted re-entering the Assembly in the July 1898 election, but withdrew in favour of a free trader who, from 1899, was giving the Bill 'his unfailing practical support'.[547] And when the anti-Billites' apparent victory in the referendum of 1898 was endangered by the Premiers' Conference of January 1899, Want vanished abroad, again, this time to Egypt. He mentioned his health to journalists, but a well-disposed obituary of a few years later recorded Want was 'a picture of health' throughout his life. The press preferred to describe this journey as a 'honeymoon', as Want had recently married a self-assured, hand-shaking, 'tall, handsome, smiling' widow of 42.[548] But his marriage had taken place in November. And could not this four-month journey be delayed? Want was aware, as much as the public, that at the end of January the premiers would confer on the Bill.

The departure from Sydney Harbour on 7 January 1899 of RMS *Orotava* with Mr and Mrs Want on board was the cue for one of the more ludicrous chapters in the Federation story. The Attorney-General of NSW – the minister responsible for provision of expert advice on the Constitution – was only to learn of the premiers' decision to resubmit the Bill to a second referendum when a copy of the *Daily Graphic* had penetrated his Egyptian desert inaccessible. Want did not speed home by cable his negative reaction to these proposals (that 'would cost a fortune'), but instead consigned them to a letter to toss across the seas. And, after finally resorting to cable, rather than send it himself (the weather was 'freezing'), he entrusted the message to a friend, who unaccountably mutilated it.[549]

After these crippled communications, Want finally resigned from Reid's cabinet on 18 April 1899. But, pleading medical difficulties, he did not return to fight the June referendum on the Bill that so offended him.[550] And he was absent from the Council when anti-Billites sought to require that at least 25 percent of enrolled voters cast a vote in the 1899 referendum if it was to have any force. Want's ultimate bathetic encounter with Federation came when he agreed to be Chairman of the Reception and Entertainment Committee of the inaugural celebrations of the Commonwealth in the first week of January 1901. From the angel of destruction of Federation to its butler.

Several interpretations might be advanced of the 'unfathomable' Jack Want. In one, his apparent fury belied an elasticity of his commitments. He was, in this interpretation, as pliant as Reid to the unfolding of opportunities. But never did any opportunist make less of his opportunities, or cling tighter to lost causes. Want stuck to his fruitless fight against the Commonwealth's ambitions: in 1900 he lobbied Joseph Chamberlain to maintain appeals to the Privy Council; he protested the seating of the High Court at Melbourne; and, in 1904, pitched a pamphlet at the new Commonwealth and its Labor pivot, *Australia vs. Socialism*. He won nothing from the Commonwealth, and nothing from opposing it. So perhaps Want should, instead, be seen as the rogue bull elephant of the drama, proudly wilful in his utter unaccountability. But why, then, his long, tortuous and public justifications for his actions? So was he, instead, all political theatre? A star of the theatre of the bar; an actor of the theatre of the Treasury benches. Such theatricality need not be taken as an act of insincerity; it was a matter of playing a role – the archangel of destruction role – a role in which, to some degree, circumstance had cast him. But, then, why did he throw the role away mid-performance?

That his political affrays were highly contextualised aggressions, and need not betoken a personal enmity, suggests another possibility: was he compromised by friendship with Federationists? These included Reid and Barton. It was Want who arranged Barton's translation to the Council in 1897 – an appointment which was almost an indulgence.[551] 'This was not the ordinary course', he rightly observed. That seems to bespeak a 'sportive' attitude to politics.

The key point is that Want lacked a relish for high office. As a lawyer, he twice declined the Chief Justiceship of NSW.[552] As a politician, he destroyed Parkes in 1889 simply as retaliation for the premier's scornful language,[553] and ducked the consequent opportunity of being premier himself. This lack of ambition weakened him in the offices he did assume; for office is the currency of politics, and high office is the mint of that currency. He could not buy the second rankers who deserted him for better prospects during the referendum campaign of 1899. But even if the many had wanted to follow him, Want did not wish to lead. He was submariner rather than commodore, a solitary hunter, a sniper.

Want's aversion to leadership might be judged leniently, as a mark of a politician who was not all-consumed by politics. He was absorbed in many activities outside politics, in contrast to Reid, and in total contrast to Barton who, in his maturity, was the ultimate political animal. Want was no political animal at all. He did nothing to nurture his popularity. He never sought to please the crowd; as Attorney-General he led the case against the crowd's hero, George Dean. Neither did he cultivate the fashionable part of society: Want had married his housekeeper, and thus earned the 'cold shoulder' from 'Potts Point dames'.[554]

But less leniently, Want could be judged as an amateur amongst professionals; where 'amateur' implies neither some inner decency, nor a lack of prowess, but a lack of discipline: an 'unprofessional' attitude. As a personality Want is most impressive and appealing outside of politics. He is the least impressive, or appealing, inside it.

In having an incidental politician as their supposed deepest adversary, Federation was lucky in its opponents.

John Haynes (1850–1917)

Jack Haynes was the most consistent, long-lasting and salient parliamentary opponent of Federation in the battleground state of NSW; possibly the anti-Billites' best political asset. 'Sunny Jack' combined an impish charm with a principle of opposition to Federalism more trenchant than Want's 'Australia as it is' conservatism, and potentially more resonant than Robertson's appeal to NSW patriotism. Whereas Robertson had advanced a national critique of Federation – federation as annexation – Haynes advanced a populist critique – Federation as neither by, nor for, nor of the people, but the tool and toy of an elite who, in Haynes's formulation, hate 'the people as a power'. It is perhaps on account of his populist critique – combined with his distance from any 'saving' Labor affiliation – that makes him an awkward presence in the annals of Federation, and has left blatant, colourful, Jack the Giant Killer written out of history.

*

Circumstances encouraged a collision of Haynes and the Federationist cause. Haynes was of the Federation generation – born in 1850 – and like most of them was native–born. Unlike most of them, he was country-raised, in the Hunter Valley, Robertson country. Unlike most, he was of Irish ancestry, 'Irish in every lineament'[555] and, unlike most, raised a Catholic. But he was born into a political household – an early memory was his father placarding in the campaign for manhood suffrage in 1859 – and two of his brothers became (anti-Federationist) members of parliament. His own path to politics might have been quicker if he had, like one of his brothers, attended Sydney Grammar School and been a class mate of Edmund Barton.

Haynes first encountered Barton in the courtroom, in 1872, as a junior reporter covering the 'Parramatta River murders' for the *Evening News*. Sydney's first afternoon newspaper, it was probably the first paper in Australia priced at one penny, and a 'gigantic success', perhaps selling by the early 1890s an extraordinary 90 000 copies to a city of 400 000.[556] The *News* would not overlook the trial of a pair of multiple killers, who, on committal, 'were chased for quarter of a mile down past St. Mary's by a howling crowd of two or three thousand people'. Edmund Barton was junior counsel for their unsuccessful defence, and Haynes witnessed their hanging. 'The hinges of the same gallows', he declared (inaccurately) in 1905, 'have been worked many times since'.

In 1880 Haynes sought to apply the tone of the *News* to a new weekly magazine, *The Bulletin*, which he founded with the assistance of 'an unknown youngster', J. F. Archibald.[557] Haynes's memories, years later, of a grave digging expedition convey the atmosphere of the upstart journal:

> *Wollongong was a fine place for a fight in the early days, and no respectable skull was without its dint. ... I picked up four or five skulls, nearly all early Irish ... In the Bulletin office we put the relics to great use. The difficulty at the office was to keep our bones, many people wanting the skulls for card boxes or spittoons, and the bones for other lines. ... Sir George Dibbs had, for a tobacco bowl, the skull of [convicted murderer, Gold] Commissioner Griffin ...*[558]

Such gross revels came to a jarring halt when the owners of the Clontarf Pleasure Gardens sued the *Bulletin* for defamation. The plaintiffs were awarded only a farthing in damages but, unable to pay legal costs of £4 000, the editors were translated to the debtors' quarters of Darlinghurst gaol. Despite Haynes's defiant joviality, the prison governor's consideration, and the solicitation of George Dibbs – himself a recent denizen of the prison on account of a costs order – Haynes's thirteen weeks in Darlinghurst were an embittering experience.

> *the restless clank of leg irons' [of the lifers] ... the steady beat of sentinels' feet, and the impressive calls of the passing hours from the men on guard which came up in response from distant parts of lonely corridors ... [the] sense of strange melancholy over all. ... the iron did enter our very souls.*[559]

He charged his first wife's death to his imprisonment.

Haynes's release occasioned his first venture into public speaking: 'I believe I managed to cut the air a trifle'. Thus he was launched by journalism into politics. His final entrance into the

J. F. Archibald and 'Sunny' John Haynes, in Darlinghurst gaol

political chamber was cleared by the most picaresque journalist of the day: A. G. Taylor. The illegitimate son of a gentleman father, Taylor – 'a lanky youth, dressed in a torn coat that hung from his ears, a coloured shirt bereft of neck buttons, and a pair of pants belted with a string' – crashed into the elections of 1882, standing for the seat of Mudgee, topping the poll, and pushing John Robertson into second place. In the Assembly, in a 'well-worn cabbage tree hat', Taylor strived, with success, to keep all eyes fixed upon himself. He called attention to the inconsistency of Reid's commission as Minister of Public Instruction with a clause in the NSW constitution. The chamber's silence betokened the truth of the contention, Reid was forced to resign from parliament, and lost the subsequent by-election. When Edmund Barton, the Speaker, had ejected Taylor from the Assembly for the life of the parliament, Taylor conducted his own appeal before the Privy Council, and won. But alcoholic and doomed by disease, Taylor retreated from politics by accepting a made to measure appointment crafted by Parkes and, thereby, created a vacancy at Mudgee. Into the contest of May 1887 stepped Taylor's then 'close collaborator', John Haynes.

And so there arrived in Macquarie Street a country boy, journalist, entrepreneur, and gadfly. 'I live on justice and outspokenness', Haynes announced to the chamber.[560] This political calling was complemented by his political cosmology, which reduced to a binary antagonism between 'the people' and their rulers. He championed the new rural margins versus the old core of the 'nineteen counties'; he censured the domination of politics by 'a small class of men' who were 'people interested in the metropolis, or those situated or representing electorates in old settled districts'.[561] He was anti-whipping, anti-handcuffing, and anti-hanging. He spoke against a sentence of death in an incest case, miscarriages of justice, fraud and corruption. He accused a former minister for railways, James Fletcher, of pretending to favour the connection of Newcastle to Brisbane by rail, while privately opposing it to the benefit of his 'land jobbing'. Henry Parkes would later testify that he could not recall Fletcher growling that he would 'wring Mr. Haynes's neck', but, Sir Henry added, 'there were so many polite expressions used in the Assembly that he might not have noticed it'. Parkes did avow that 'Mr. Fletcher then deliberately rose and walked slowly, a distance of 28 or 30 feet, to where Mr. Haynes was standing, seized him by the throat, and shook him very much as a dog would shake a cat'.[562] The Taranganba gold swindle was yet to finish Fletcher's career.[563]

Haynes political cosmology gave him an easy grip on Federationism. He deemed Federation 'an artificial cause' which does not reach the people. Federation was also anti-democratic in provenance. 'Federation is a politician's cause – it never came from the people'.[564] Some Convention delegates were 'gentry who hate the people as a power'. Many delegates were lawyers; 'he was amazed at the number of lawyers now anxious to give their services to the country'. 'Every step which has been taken in this matter shows a desire on the part of the Attorney-General [Barton] to improve the position, the emoluments and the claims of the legal fraternity'.[565] And Federation, as proposed, would be anti-democratic in effect. But was it not 'the most democratic constitution in the world?'[566] Would not the Senate be directly elected? Did not any alteration to the Constitution require approval by referendum? Did not each seat of the House of Representatives necessarily represent the same number of persons? Yes, but no legislation could occur without the approval of the Senate, a chamber where a Tasmanian voter had, in effect, eight times the vote of a voter of NSW. And any constitutional amendment could be blocked by just three states, which could amount to just 19 percent of the population; the arithmetical possibility was that just 9.5 percent of the electorate could defeat an amendment which 90.5 percent favoured.

In 1897 Haynes advanced himself as a candidate for the Australasian Federal Convention, and traversed town and countryside. He came 34th out of a field of 49. In the referendums of 1898 and 1899, he campaigned for a No vote, drawing 'huge audiences wherever he went', only to see Yes win both times.[567] And, with the passage of the Bill, he supported in the inaugural Commonwealth election a newly formed Democratic Party composed of anti-Federalists. That undertaking, too, ended in heavy defeat.

The problem Haynes raises is how a 'populist' could be so unsuccessful in obtaining the popular vote. His failure was not for lack of blandishments. He was acknowledged by his opponents as a 'good platform man', and judged the best 'orator' of the anti-Billites by the press. His puckish wit still twinkles.[568] The source of Haynes's failure is more fundamental. *Political* populism was an underdeveloped sentiment in Australia in the Federation period. If populism – the perennial resentment by the margin of the centre – was distinctly felt in politics in the 1890s, any impress of *political* populism was fainter. Political populism is not simply the reverberation in politics of the frustrations of the geographical margins. It is, more specifically, a frustration at the failure of representative democracy to fulfil its purpose: to confer a centrality on all by means of equal representation of all. Political populism charges that the people's purported representatives – politicians – constitute a self-governing community, and pursue their interests at the expense of the represented. But it is hard to see much sign of political populism in the period. Individual politicians were the butt of furious charges of betraying their constituents. But politicians as a group were not. The public's passivity in the face of the McSharry case of 1898 betokens their endurance of politicians as a removed, autonomous community, with its own standards. The rural hinterland's object of ire was always 'Sydney', rather than politicians. Rural areas were accepting of the political class of the day; the era of the farmer politician was to await the First World War. In the late 19th century city barristers still had an unexpectedly good run from 'bush' voters. While Haynes fought and won his seat of Wellington four times, some years earlier the same seat had been gifted on a platter to Barton. Thus in launching himself on the bush-city divide Haynes was misinterpreting his own cause. In pitching against Federation, Haynes placed himself squarely opposite the rural margins which, out of their hostility to Sydney, were robustly Federationist.

The one sign of political populism in the 1890s was the sudden appearance of a Labor party, an attempt to bypass the traditional political class. And Haynes welcomed its advent in 1891, as a new breeze, a 'change the like of which was never known in any previous history of the country'.[569] But Haynes's individualist liberalism made Labor an impossible political vehicle for him.

Free traders were the one party that Haynes did truly represent. Unhelpfully, they were strong among the Sydneysiders and 'wool kings' he so derided. And in advancing into parliament in 1887 under the free trade banner Haynes had earned the reflexive opposition of Catholic clergy to any ally of Parkes. That vexation was the occasion of his public rejection of the Irish Catholic community into which he had been born: a clannish, crabbed and ever vigilant element of Australian society, 'a bleak moorland of perpetual resentment' in one recollection.[570] By means of the *Bulletin*, Haynes had launched himself into public life 'with tribal Irish and religious Roman Catholic backing'.[571] Now he renounced his origins – 'we did not want men coming here with the slime of bogs on their legs'.[572] Now he renounced his religion, scarified its priests and, on at least one occasion, fraternised with Orangemen at one of their tattoos. He had gone over to the enemy. Haynes's belligerent defection bespeaks an intense self-direction, as well his own personal self-construction as a warrior; a self-identification he consciously chose as another might choose to be a priest. But the consequence was that he was, and remained, abhorrent to the leaders of a sizeable segment of the community, a man whose name Cardinal Moran would spit out.

But for all of the hazards of Haynes's embrace of free traders, they were his natural political home, and the waste of his political potential is traceable to him not securing their leadership. This is suggestive of a failure in party structures. One function of parties is the selection of the most useful leadership figure of the segment of opinion they represent. In a dysfunctional party, instead of the leader being chosen as the instrument of the party, the party is the instrument of the leader. The Free Trade and Liberal Association was the much-heralded creation of the late 1880s. But as Reid established his political primacy, the Association slid into dormancy. This was painfully symbolised in 1896 by the move of the National Protection Union into the 'commodious' offices which a few years before had housed the free traders. Painters were observed 'busily engaged in wiping off the office windows' the dusty half-defaced words, Free Trade and Liberal Association, and painting in 'with brighter colour "National Protection Association".'[573] The ultimate humiliation came in 1898, when the Free Trade and Liberal Association's surviving branches dissolved themselves, so as to re-form as Reid's election campaign mouthpiece, the Federal Liberal party. The party representing, say, four-tenths of opinion in NSW had ceased to exist; the structure which would find and make a leader of this section of opinion had ceased to exist.

And yet it would be truer to say that the success of Federation made for the weakness in the Free Trade and Liberal Association, than the weakness of the Association made for the success of Federation. Perhaps half of free traders were Federationists. Thus, like all anti-Federationists, Haynes's failure lay ultimately in Federation possessing some of that chimerical quality, popularity. However disengaged were many voters, committed Federationists outnumbered committed anti-Federationists in every colony, sometimes massively. Almost all politicians were publicly pledged to some form of federation, if only in the abstract; even Haynes.[574] Federation was an idea whose time had come.

In its sudden elevation in the firmament of public opinion, Federation bore a resemblance to another constitutional idea whose time seems to have come in the 1890s: female suffrage. Like Federation, female suffrage had been mooted for a generation, supported by some and opposed by others. But by the last decade of the 19th century the debate was over, and suffragists had won. The commonplace *froideur* of feminists of the mid-Victorian period to female suffrage, such as that of Helen Spence, had thawed; Beatrice Webb kept her own opposition to female suffrage to herself when visiting Australia in 1898. Male opponents, such as Barton, Wise and Kingston, once free in expressing their opposition to what Garran called 'petticoat government', now seemed mute on the subject. The general sentiment was now in favour; it was only a matter of the legislatures registering that.

But Haynes opposed female suffrage with almost as much vehemence as he opposed Federation. To this champion of 'the people', women were not part of the people, or, at least, not part of the electorate. Politics was war, said Haynes, and war was a matter for men. Women did not belong on the battlefield, or in parliament, and female suffrage would only make a battlefield of marriage. These contentions were rooted in 'masculinist' presumptions, of which Haynes was not only conscious, but revelled in. He was, as he put it, 'a MAN'.[575] Haynes pressed the supposed implications of his masculinist outlook for female suffrage, so distant from the bent of public opinion by the opening of the 20th century, in parliamentary debates to the impatience and raillery of the Assembly.[576] And, in contrast with the nimble movement of the Assembly to the centre of public opinion – women, it decided, could now vote, but could not stand – there is something valiant in his doomed doggedness.

Haynes's one truly successful contribution to public life arose as a strange ricochet from the success of the Federation movement. The Convention of 1897-98 had, with little cause, moved to allocate 'Posts and Telegraphs' to the Commonwealth. Several delegates objected to the pointlessness of this transfer, and all Barton could say in reply was that the Commonwealth would need something to occupy itself beyond passing a tariff act. But Barton's wish prevailed, and so, on 30 March 1901, post offices passed into the hands of the Commonwealth. In consequence the NSW Postmaster-General, W. P. Crick, was shifted to a new portfolio, Lands. This occasioned perhaps Australia's greatest corruption scandal. Kickbacks in the Lands department had been burning hotly enough under the Lyne ministry, but under Crick's stewardship they exploded into an inferno, with the chief incendiaries being Crick, Willis and Meagher, and the sums received by these three coming to almost £45 000, or six million dollars in present values.[577] It was Haynes who called the alarm, and finally spurred a royal commission, which ultimately occasioned Willis's flight to South Africa and Crick's demise. But Haynes was not to see this from the benches. In 1904 he ran for the seat of Mudgee against Edwin Richards, one of the cinders of the Crick-Willis-Meagher bonfire. Richards was later to be 'closely examined' by the commission and, to 'considerable surprise', resigned from politics not long after. Richards did seem talented at winning elections by narrow margins, winning a seat by six votes in 1898 and, in 1904, defeating Haynes by 14. The parliamentary inquiry into the count, steered by Wise, produced a 'complete victory' for Richards. It found against him 'on charges of treating and bribing ... but not severe enough to justify overturning the result'.[578] And so Haynes's career was ended by 'unsevere' bribery, defeated by the corruption he fought, 'regretted even by his political opponents, who recognised his amiable temperament, generosity and fearless integrity'.[579]

Thomas Joseph Byrnes (1860–1898)

T. J. Byrnes barely appears in conventional history of Federation. But his life and death throw a strong light on how it was that Australia came to federate. It presents the possibility that the Federation of 1901 was a precarious contingency; one that would not have occurred but for an apparently robust man of 37 years dying of measles.

Byrnes traced no mazy path to office, but shot from the Kuiper Belt of social obscurity to the centre of Queensland politics. Thomas Joseph Byrnes was born in Queensland in 1860, one of the 11 children of Irish Catholic parents, who had arrived as free immigrants before the famine, to settle as homesteaders in Humpybong, on the rural fringe of Brisbane. Byrnes was native-born, but 'Irish', and, in affectionate memory, he was, as a youth, 'delighted to draw maps of Ireland',[580] animated perhaps by family lore of his forebears' role in the rebellion of 1798. More important for adult life, he was a Catholic who, according to one archiepiscopal recollection, 'never missed his Sunday Mass'. And although his family was poor, and he fatherless from age six, his talents were not left uncultivated. He won a scholarship to Brisbane Grammar School, and later an entrance 'exhibition' to the University of Melbourne in English, French and History; in his maturity he would be 'the centre of any group of literary men'.[581] Upon graduation he went 'into chambers' under another poor Irish boy made good, before building his own 'big and lucrative practice'.[582] Talent scouted by Griffith, he was appointed to the Legislative Council of Queensland in 1890 at the age of 29, and made Solicitor-General the same day. Byrnes was now a lawyer, legislator and cabinet minister, and would remain all of these for the remainder of his not very long life.

The government Byrnes had joined was a coalition of conservatives and self-described liberals who, in loose union, ranged themselves against a rump of liberal dissidents and Labor. The government's liberal wing had been led by Griffith, but his retirement to the bench in 1893 allowed Byrnes to jump from Solicitor-General to Attorney-General, and aspire to leadership. But Griffith's heir apparent tended to the ministry's 'conservative' wing. Correspondingly, his political creed applauded the development of the natural resources of his enormous colony, almost one-quarter the size of continental United States. This encouraged him to tolerate the Kanaka labour which liberals abhorred – Pacific islanders were a necessary, if temporary, expedient, and to be compared with the use of convict labour.[583] Neither did the presence of Asiatics exercise him. Had not the Japanese been very productive residents in Hawaii? He opposed the poll-tax on Chinese immigrants, and suggested instead an immigration treaty based on 'friendly relations'. Development also required exports, and he denounced Victoria's sugar beet subsidy as tainted with 'all the heresies of political economy'.[584] Development would be hampered by labour legislation and trade union militancy.[585] He responded to arson by trade union firebrands by giving police wide powers to detain for 30 days 'on suspicion', and rejected talk of conciliation: 'Are we to conciliate with brigands ? Are we to offer to compromise with incendiaries?'[586]

To Byrnes, Federation was a distraction from the pre-eminent political task: the development of Queensland. 'Our great mission', he told the Federal Council, 'is not to go and have some fantastic form of central government … Our great work is, as far as we can, to develop the resources of the country'.[587] Byrnes's hostility can be interpreted as Queensland patriotism, the pride of a Queenslander who saw nothing in Federation doing honour to Queensland. Was not Queensland the coming state? In the year of his birth, 1860, it counted 28 056 inhabitants; in the year he became premier, 1898, it had 475 000. Since 1860, its sheep had increased six-fold, and the area under crop nine-fold. It grazed more cattle than the rest of Australia, and was fitted, he said, 'to be one of the great granaries of the world'. Within a few years, its population, combined with NSW, would constitute 50 percent of Australia's. By 1941, the Convention projected, Queensland would have nearly twice the population of Victoria, and close to that of NSW. It would ultimately be the first state.

To Byrnes, Federation was a vainglorious manoeuvre of 'self-seeking politicians' with 'imperial notions';[588] which did not recognise the reality of Australia as a small power, but succumbed to 'thoughts in our mind that we are a very much larger country in the universe than we really are'. The Commonwealth would only 'vainly simulate the pretensions of another and smaller empire'.[589] An imperial Australia with an empire beyond the seas: thus the Federationists' preoccupation with French penological intentions in New Caledonia – which Byrnes dismissed as a 'bogie' – and French intentions in the New Hebrides. 'I do not think they are of any commercial value, and for strategic purposes they are no value at all'.[590] An Australian empire, which aimed at 'unification rather than federation'.[591]

Tainted in inspiration, Federation was impious in process. Its method of proceeding was anti-parliamentary, 'absolutely poisonous', 'revolutionary'. 'A new constitution is attempted to be foisted onto the colonies entirely behind the backs of ... the parliaments', who are to be 'studiously ignored'. This anti-parliamentarism will only produce chaos, and 'appeals to the masses or the people to rise up against the Federal Council' will yield 'a Frankenstein that will devour the very constitution itself'.[592]

To Byrnes's mind, the meritorious method of advancing towards any federation would be one of 'many years', 'slow gradation' and 'silent process', 'not based merely in sentiment', but on 'common interests'.[593] The Federal Council would be the 'nucleus' out of which such a federation would grow. Crucially, 'This council is a body which recognises the equality and independence of the various colonies'. The best service to federation would be to develop the Council, to exercise its functions and strengthen them.[594] In the Council's 1897 session, Byrnes presented a throng of bills: for the mutual recognition of naturalisations, the liquidation of joint stock companies, quarantine, patents, the competence of the courts of one colony to order the production of wills produced in another, and the levying of death duties according to the location of property rather than the location of the deceased. Several of these bills were met by blocks and cavils by Deakin and Turner in the Council – the Council must be seen to be ineffective, and so must be made ineffective. (This, presumably, was why Deakin, a backbencher, was a Council member in its final years. Why participate in a body he had so much contempt for?) The same session of the Council saw the stymying of Byrnes's attempts to revitalise it. He proposed the selection of delegates be democratised: 'let the Federal Council delegates be chosen at the time of the general election, let their choice be as wide as possible'. This democratisation of the Council was supported by delegates of Queensland and WA, but opposed by those of Victoria and Tasmania. An outright majority was lacking. But one Tasmanian had defected to Byrnes's cause, the Federation skeptic, Adye Douglas; and that should have produced eleven to nine in favour of election. But, for reasons unknown, WA was only represented with four delegates instead of five, and the majority fell from ten to nine. And, even more mysteriously, one of the four, Hackett – who had publicly denigrated the Council – was nowhere to be seen. And so the vote was nine to nine: Byrnes's attempt to democratise the Council had failed. This was a fateful defeat: the same Federal Council saw the premiers announce the dates of the Convention election.

Overall, Byrnes might be identified as the one Burkean in the whole Federationist episode. The great Irish parliamentarian's preference for development over invention, his recognition of the imperative to change in order to preserve – these sentiments were also Byrnes's.[595] More generally, Byrnes represented conservatism's estrangement from Federation; an estrangement which would surely have become more overt in the 20th century's first decade, as it did in his principal followers.[596]

Alternatively, Byrnes's opposition might be construed as a manifestation of the distance of Catholics from Australia's political core. This was not a distance from federation as an idea; but the Federation movement as an activity. If Federation was a certain hankering of the political class – a great knit of affinity, long association, and favour-banking – then Catholics registered marginal membership of that political class. 'The Catholic Irish … were underrepresented virtually in every public area except gaols, asylums and the Catholic Church'.[597] There had been four Catholic premiers of Victoria by the time of Federation, and one in NSW; but three had excited sectarian passions, sometimes in leading Federationists; including Parkes, Deakin, and Wise. And, in 1896, Cardinal Moran could claim of NSW, 'Of the 9 Supreme Court judges, not one is a Catholic. Of 6 District Court judges, not one is a Catholic. Of the 9 under-secretaries, not one is a Catholic'.[598] Queensland had 'a considerable number of Catholic politicians in the continuous Ministry of 1890-1903',[599] but Byrnes's failure to win the seat of South Brisbane in 1896 has been traced to sectarian tensions, and 'almost all' Catholic members of the ministry were defeated in the general election.[600] In the Australasian Federal Convention of 54 delegates only three were Catholics.[601]

Byrnes was, however, hardly an 'outsider in politics'. He was virtually a career politician, launched through the patronage of Griffith. He was perfectly assimilated into the legal political class, including its sense of entitlement, as revealed by Byrnes's lucrative benefit from the Robb arbitration case, which was reminiscent in some ways of Barton's McSharry case.[602] If Federation was, as he felt, a cause of 'self-seeking politicians',[603] he was a politician with his own ambitions.

Byrnes's display of hostility to Federation retreated on his becoming Queensland premier in April 1898.[604] If southern Queensland shared his hostility to Federation, northern Queensland by now did not. On a tour of the north, his fighting words were replaced by circumspection and diffuse professions of federalism in the abstract: 'There is federation and federation'.[605] During the NSW referendum of June 1898 an opportunity came to rock the federal boat, but he declined to take it: when Haynes claimed Byrnes would support Queensland joining the Federation on the condition that seats in the Senate would match each state's population, Byrnes helpfully wrote to Barton disavowing such a position. In the flux following NSW's election of July 1898, he accepted an invitation by Jack Want to confer with Reid in Sydney. At picnics at the National Park, Byrnes publicly declared his confidence that Queensland, Victoria and New South Wales would be at one on 99 issues out of 100. A year before he had declared he was 'pleased' that Queensland was absent from the Convention;[606] now he expressed his 'personal regret' that Queensland was not part of the Federation movement. But his 'regret did not appear to have been very poignant'.[607]

The same page of the *Sydney Morning Herald* which reported Byrnes's perhaps unpoignant regrets also recorded 'measles ... has been making itself felt very sensibly of late. ... New South Wales is being very heavily visited by the scourge which seems to select its victims with the utmost impartiality'.[608] On his return to Queensland, the *Courier* announced the premier 'is somewhat indisposed. Mr. Byrnes contracted a cold while in Sydney', making the common mistaken diagnosis of measles in its 'catarrhal stage'. On 17 September measles was announced, but there was, 'of course', no danger. Pneumonia followed. The premier was, however, still conscious, and wondered if Barton had won the Hastings Macleay by-election of 23 September.[609] He then became delirious. Drs Marks, Hardie and Maloney bled the patient. The family gathered 'in sorrowing attendance'. His spiritual adviser administered the last rites. He died ten minutes before midnight of 27 September 1898.

The significance of the case of Thomas Joseph Byrnes lies in the acute sense contingency it appears to cast over Federation.

We know what actually did happen in the wake of Byrnes's death. He was replaced by James Dickson, who 'was much happier in office, in any capacity, than out of it'.[610] From Toorak House, 'the best residence in Brisbane', Dickson soon proved acutely useful to the Federationist planning of Deakin and Griffith. Within four months, the new premier had travelled to Melbourne to attend a conference of premiers, where he agreed to put to Queensland's voters the Federation bill, very slightly amended in favour of Queensland; which he then campaigned in favour of, securing a Yes vote of 55 percent. So it was that Queensland was part of the Commonwealth proclaimed on 1 January 1901. And on that day, Dickson was made Minister for Defence, and knighted: here, indeed, was an expression of sincere thanks by Deakin and company, bestowed in liberal proportion to services rendered.

It is hard to imagine what actually did happen, with Byrnes dead, happening had he lived. One may wonder if he would have agreed to attend the January 1899 conference of premiers, having been 'pleased' to see Queensland stay out of the Convention. Perhaps he would have squared his own hostility to Federation with its more general support by insisting on another Convention, with Queensland included. Perhaps he would use the Federal Council's final meeting in that January 1899 as a stage for a different version of federation? And if Byrnes had gone to the Premiers' conference of January 1899, it is hard to see him falling in line, and agreeing to submit to referendum a constitution which Queensland had had no role in drafting, and had been only very slightly revised in the direction of Queensland's wishes. And, finally, if he did do so, it is hard to imagine No would not have won the day, with the premier so unattracted by Yes. He was Queensland's political master, 'Queensland's greatest political speechmaker', in the judgement of the unconservative Steele Rudd.[611] All in all, it is hard to see Queensland in the Commonwealth of 1901, if measles had not killed a certain 37 year old in apparent good health.[612]

Without a doubt, Byrnes's death was one Deakin's miracles.

And one can, more speculatively, stretch still further the counterfactual of a living Byrnes. Without Queensland, would John Forrest have succumbed to pressure to hold a referendum on federation in 1900? Indeed, would NSW have voted Yes in 1899?

But, going in the other direction, Byrnes's case might be used to contend the inevitability of Federation rather than its contingency; its immunity to the vagaries of human existence. Does not Byrnes's life show that the Federal Council could have an able champion and would-be saviour, but still be doomed? To the same thought, it may be observed that, during his life, the Bill won referendum majorities in four Australian colonies; and elections in NSW both confirmed Reid narrowly in government, and saw Barton returned to parliament. The drama's structure had been fully laid before his death. And, if it is hard to see Queensland in the Commonwealth in 1901 with Byrnes alive, it is not easy to see the four other colonies outside it, be he dead or alive. And 1901 was not the end of history. Federation would remain strongly favoured outside of Brisbane and Rockhampton; the hostility to Kanakas and Chinese would have continued to demand a response from Byrnes which he was reluctant to provide, but which Federation seemed to offer. How long could his own personal weight resist these forces? Byrnes, with 'luminous and expressive eyes', and 'charming manner which endeared him to a large circle of friends',[613] was, in particular, 'fast friends' with the Labor leader, Andrew Dawson.[614] Their 'unusual intimacy' might have been the foundation of an alliance that could govern an independent Queensland for a time; did not Byrnes urge that 'if there ever was a man of the people, was he not one?' But Labor was on the march, and not long satisfied with Dawson, or for the party simply to play king-maker or partner. Could an independent Queensland have provoked an irresistible Labor separationist-Federationist movement in North Queensland? Would North Queensland's own union with the Commonwealth leave a truncated South Queensland in an absurd isolation? Thus, staying separate from the Commonwealth in 1901 might only delay a union, with, perhaps, a redundant Byrnes ultimately seeking refuge in Queensland's Supreme Court?

Alternatively, one might tame the counterfactual by invoking the already foreshadowed plasticity of Byrnes in the face of Federationist strength. In the wake of their National Park conference, might not Reid and Byrnes have concluded a pact of 'natural allies', and the two former foes of Federation unite in a league of Yes-Nos? Byrnes, like Reid, could buy credibility for such a conversion with a few more concessions in the Bill; the election of Queensland senators on a regional basis unconditionally; a freeze on federal legislation on the Kanakas for ten years; a north-south transcontinental railway passing through Queensland; even Queensland administering Papua for a period. And the reward would be a Reid-Byrnes team leading the free trade party in the 1901 election, and perhaps even winning.

The upshot would still have been 'a nation for a continent' but a different commonwealth would have resulted.

11

Reading the referendums

Fair women cast sweet flowers before his feet;
From all the housetops 'kerchiefs gaily waved;
Ten thousand voices hail'd him in the street;
In blear-eyed joy the monster Rabble raved.
— Henry Parkes

The ten referendums on the draft constitution held between 1898 and 1900 constitute the climax of the contest over Federation. Proclamation of the Commonwealth on 1 January 1901 may have been the cause's Te Deum,[615] and the opening of federal parliament on 9 May have been its Hallelujah Chorus. But it was by the referendums that Federationists won the field of battle; in 1898 voters chose Yes over No by a ratio of two to one, and in 1899 by not far from three to one. Here lies, it seems, a decree of the People. Here stands a near invincible justification to any democrat of the decision to federate.

Some simple particulars of the referendums, however, mute the din of this apparent exultant shout of the populace. In each colony only a minority of those enrolled actually voted in the 1898 referendums; and in no colony did more than 20 percent of adults cast a Yes vote; the remainder absented themselves, voted No or could not vote. Even in the much better attended second round of referendums of 1899, for every seven persons who voted Yes, nine others eligible to vote either voted No or not at all. And in not one colony that year did anywhere near a majority of adults vote Yes. In the one political act which must be highly participatory to be legitimate – constitution-making – Australia's process was wanting.

Beyond the sobering facts of the low participation in the referendums, a critic may argue the referendum mechanism poorly served democratic principle. They may contend the referendum reduces the people to a merely reactive, even manipulated, agent – one with the veto, but removed from the formulation of law. A referendum sceptic may contest the meaningfulness of the assents and dissents regarding this 'most subtle and complex' bill 'to Constitute the Commonwealth of Australia'. The very existence of a coherent will of the people regarding Federation may be doubted. And 'the people', as it was implicitly defined by each referendum, might be deemed an improper whole, delivering meaningless 'larger parts', and thereby offending genuine democratic majorities. Most grossly, there is evidence that the most decisive referendum – that of 1899 in NSW – was subject to ballot fraud, encouraged by the removal of established safeguards of the vote.

The campaign

In NSW the people's choice of June 1898 began with a suspension of parliament. And a sensation, which few of the 6 000 who crammed into the Sydney Town Hall on Monday 28 March 1898 could have known Premier George Reid was about to deliver. As they cast their eyes over the ranks of the worthies who had marched onto the stage – and the 35 members of the press – they may have reflected that, since the Convention dissolved, the premier had cultivated an ambivalence towards the Bill. Accordingly, many of the members of Reid's government had joined 'the platform at the Town Hall meeting under the impression that the Premier was going to announce his opposition to the Federation Bill, and they enthusiastically applauded the parts of the Premier's speech in which the blemishes of the measure were pointed out'.[616] But the absence of John Want, the anti-Billites own champion, should have given them pause. That the Bill's champions – Barton, O'Connor and Wise – were present on the stage should have given them still more cause to hesitate. But they might have reasoned that Reid was 'nursing a hostile speech to be delivered under somewhat theatrical conditions, and thus score, as he has frequently scored before in local politics, by disappointing his enemies [Barton, O'Connor and Wise], and swinging into line with popular sentiment [that is, anti-Bill]'.[617]

But, after keeping the audience 'in a state of tension for nearly two hours', Reid 'startled' and 'nauseated' many of his listeners by making the 'staggering announcement'[618] that 'my duty to Australia demands me to record my vote in favour of the bill.' Deafening cheers erupted. Barton and O'Connor congratulated Reid on stage, and the meeting closed with Barton leading the audience in a round of three cheers for Federation. Thus the speech which Federationist mythology has successfully misrepresented as the 'Yes-No' speech.

Anti-Billites seethed at Reid's duplicity, and prepared to launch a censure motion once the parliament reconvened, bruiting the support of even 90 members in chamber's 125. Whatever the exaggeration, this must have posed some risk as, on 31 March, Reid abruptly had the parliament prorogued 'for divers urgent and weighty reasons'. This shelving of parliament won the forceful public support of Barton; it kept 'the hands of Parliament from the throats of the people',[619] a phrase which rings unpleasantly. The upshot was that Federationists may have had the advantage of an onside premier during the referendum campaign only on account of parliament being suspended.

On the same day Reid had caught his rivals unawares by proroguing parliament, Want resigned from the ministry. The battle lines were thereby clarified: Reid and Barton on one side, ranged against a more ragged line composed of free trade dissidents, the Labor Party, a former protectionist premier (Dibbs), and the current protectionist leader (Lyne). Organisationally, Yes forces were united under a Federal Association, while 'No' forces were divided between an Anti-Convention Bill League (= free trade and Labor) and a Colonists Anti-Convention Bill League (protectionist). The No organisations seemed little more than parliamentary caucuses, while the Yes groups had some rank and file, and a 'comprehensive network of local agencies'.[620] The Yes campaign's organisational weapon seemed in fine trim, while No grumbled about theirs. The No campaign was 'penniless', while the Yes campaign benefitted from funding from outside NSW.[621]

The No campaign was launched on 15 April 1898 with a Town Hall rally addressed by Want, Lyne and McGowen; an unlikely united front of free traders and protectionists, socialists and anti-socialists. The No campaign concluded even more unexpectedly. In the last days before the referendum, there suddenly swooped into the No encampment an almost unknown specimen of political life – the public speaking woman. There entered the platform of anti-Billites Rose Scott – of more than respectable birth, raised in an intellectual milieu, imbued with a Millian sensibility of freedom and utility and, at the age of 50, unmarried, childless and a leading light in the Women's Suffrage League. With 'undoubted eloquence', she spoke in an 'earnest' 'prayerful' manner against the Bill. She did claim most women were against the Bill, and charge that women would pay for men's glory, but her case went far beyond a 'woman's case'. Federation was not worth any prod it might give female suffrage, for Federation posed, she declared, 'the gravest danger which had ever threatened Australia'.[622] She was dismayed at the prospect of the people of NSW voting to extinguish her self-government. They were 'like Aladdin exchanging the magic and precious flame of freedom for the shoddy legal political lamp of a Federation which is being hawked around to the cry of new lamps for old'. The rewards Federationists held out for this trade had no savour. 'The cry was for unity, but it was forgotten that many crimes were committed in that name'.[623] The promise of 'ranking among nations' held no allure. 'National glory consisted not in the glorification of kings and politicians, nor in bloated expenditure of territory or public buildings'. She traced the public's willingness to treat with Federation to a flagging of their spirit of freedom. Like Aesop's frogs petitioning Jupiter for a king, she said, 'they are asking heaven to give them a constitution under which they will be governed instead of governing themselves'.[624] And this she traced to 'the freedom of the Australian people' having been 'too easily gained, and, therefore, too lightly prized'.[625]

Freedom weeps
Wrong rules the land, and waiting justice sleeps.[626]

Scott's sincerity, philosophic texture, and palpable elevation, made her to Federationists both a necessary target and a delicate one. So they assumed a cold courtesy, before proceeding to correct her. She had slighted the importance of Australia's military preparedness: had she not heard the news of the French add-

Rose Scott: 'The people are being sold for 25 pieces of silver instead of 30'

ing to their fortifications in Noumea? She hoped to insert in the Constitution something like the Hare-Clark system for electing the Senate; but this was 'an absurd demand, and one which any intelligent man can see should not be tolerated for a moment'.[627]

The Yes campaign climaxed in a fervid and singular rally two days before the referendum. There was, in contrast to the universal practice of the campaign, just one speaker: Edmund Barton. And the crowning moment was no piece of eloquence, but the presentation to Barton of a NSW Ensign – recently repackaged as the 'Federal Flag'[628] – which had been especially sewn by Federationist ladies. This is an unexpected transaction. National flags are not commonly 'presented', outside of funerals or memorialisations; they are flown – almost always with a proud preeminence over all else, receiving, for example, the salute of even a head of state.[629] It is tributes which are presented, in expression of gratitude or submission.

> *Send unto us a king that will rule over us and keep us in order.*[630]

The results' significance and insignificance

The Table 11.1 reports some contours of the Yes victory in the four referendums held on 2 and 3 June 1898. In all colonies the majority voted Yes; narrowly in NSW, and overpoweringly in the other colonies. Could such an outcome be doubted as an expression of the will of the people?

Table 11.1 The results of the 1898 referendums

		Yes majority	Yes	No	Valid Vote	Abstention	Enrolment
NSW		5 367	71 595	66 228	137 823	168 221	306 878
as percent of	vote	3.9	51.9	48.1	100.0	122.1	222.7
	roll	1.7	23.3	21.6	44.9	54.8	100
	adults	0.8	10.2	9.5	19.7	24	43.8
Victoria		78 421	100 520	22 099	122 619	128 933	252 560
as percent of	vote	64.0	82.0	18.0	100.0	105.1	206
	roll	31.1	39.8	8.8	48.6	51.1	100
	adults	12.1	15.5	3.4	18.9	19.9	39
SA		19 480	36800	17320	54120	81551	136387
as percent of	vote	36.0	68.0	32.0	100.0	150.7	252
	roll	14.3	27.0	12.7	39.7	59.8	100
	adults	10.5	19.8	9.3	29.1	43.9	73.4
Tasmania		9 772	12 572	2 800	15 372	15 979	31 613
as percent of	vote	63.6	81.8	18.2	100.0	103.9	205.7
	roll	30.9	39.8	8.9	48.6	50.5	100
	adults	11.3	14.6	3.2	17.8	18.5	36.7

Sources: Rows 1, 2 and 3 for each colony; Rhodes (2002). Row 4 for each colony; 'adults' is defined as persons 21 and over, and measured by the 1901 census.

Ad hoc and *ex post*?

At the time of the referendums the practice of referring a political decision directly to voters suffered a tainted provenance on account of the 'plebiscite' having played usher to the autocracies of Napoleon Bonaparte and Louis Napoleon. These older Napoleonic 'plebiscites' were faulted as ad hoc and ex post. In 1851 Louis Napoleon had seized power by coup d'etat and, three weeks after the event, he had this action put to a plebiscite: it was ex post. Further, Napoleonic plebiscite was not an element of the systematic machinery of law-making, but was resorted to, when the occasion was judged favourable by established power, as a means to a specific end of that power: it was ad hoc.

Were the Federation referendums free of the two besetting faults of plebiscites? There was something plainly 'for this' (ad hoc) about the schema of referendums of 1898; it was instituted to circumvent the parliaments which could be predicted to submerge any federation Bill. It was not that the scheme's devisor, John Quick, had any general preference for law-making by referendum over parliament; on the contrary, he judged it an 'extraordinary' limitation on parliament that the final Constitution would require that any changes in state borders be approved by referendum. Rather, it was the local parliaments' decision over Federation that he faulted. Thus the referendums of 1898 were born of political utility, not from some principled attraction to the 'immediately' democratic referendum.[631]

But no critic can claim the referendums of 1898 were, literally, ex post; they were not instituted to sanction a federation that had already been effected. But in another sense they were ex post: the proposed constitution had already been crafted, and was presented to voters on a take it or leave it basis. It was, declared Federationists, Yes or No, now or never, take it or leave it. Voters were not given any option to return the Bill to the Convention – the Convention had been dissolved, not prorogued. If voters had had that option then the process would have been more heedful of the truth that democracy is not simply the people approving laws: it is the people making them.

Putting aside adhocness and expostness, the referendums could also be criticised as amounting to a manipulated choice, on account of constraining the people's choice by admitting just two alternatives: Australian Federation or the status quo. Other options were omitted, such as imperial federation. To the Imperial Federationist the ultimate goal was an Australia fully integrated into a Greater Britain dappling the globe, and represented in the supreme councils of this Greater Britain, where would be directed the foreign affairs, defence and (perhaps) commercial policy of the whole Empire. To imperial enthusiasts, Australian Federation was simply 'a great step', in Smith's words, to Imperial Federation; simply 'a stage of growth in the Empire', as Wise put it. These enthusiasts were augmented by more temperate advocates of Imperial Federation, such as Parkes and Deakin.[632] With such influential patrons, it might be asked, given a majority of voters preferred Australian Federation to the status quo, might a majority also have preferred Imperial Federation to Australian?

Does the will of the people exist?

But there is another, and completely different, sting in the possibility that a majority might have voted for Imperial Federation, if given the choice. For it is possible that if granted a further choice still between Imperial Federation and the status quo, the status quo might be preferred by the majority. The upshot would be that for any of the three constitutional forms that might be adopted – Imperial Federation, Australian Federation or the status quo – a majority would always agree upon one of the remaining two forms as superior.

An awkward conjuncture! Such a prospect of interminable constitutional turmoil is easily rationalised as the outcome of the presence of three rival outlooks. Imperial Federationists, we know, hold Imperial Federation to be superior to Australian Federation, and Australian Federation to be better than the status quo. But we may imagine a second opinion type, the 'Continentalist', who judged Australian Federation as better than the status quo, and the status quo as better than Imperial Federation. Such continentalists encompassed Labor republicans, Irish conservatives with little sentimental tie to the British Empire (such as O'Connor) and those, like Reid, who, despite every sentimental attachment to Empire, dismissed Imperial Federation as an arrant waste of political capital.

Finally, one may imagine competing with Imperial Federationists and continentalist a third strand of opinion, 'localists'. To localists the status quo was best of all; but if the 'six Australia's' were to join some larger structure, then Imperial Federation would be a better way of doing that than Australian Federation. The epitome of localists was L. F. Heydon, Legislative Councillor, a minister for justice under Robertson, and president of the protectionist Land and Industrial Alliance, who led an anti-Federationist 'bunch' at the convention election in NSW, receiving one tick from eleven percent of voters. A NSW patriot, he did not rank Imperial Federation highest, but, as a rejoinder to plans of Australian Federation, he declared, 'I say, let us have unification of the British race'.[633] Under the same mind-set may be included Byrnes: 'I am part of a bigger nation than Australasia – I am part of the British Empire. That is nation enough for my aspirations'.[634]

Table 11.2 Imperial Federation, Australian Federation and the status quo ranked by three outlooks

Ranking	'Imperialist'	'Continentalist'	'Localist'
1st	I	F	S
2nd	F	S	I
3rd	S	I	F

Table 11.2 summarises how these three outlooks would rank the three constitutional alternatives.

It is easy to see that, as long as each of the three outlooks claims less than fifty percent of the voters, then the key result mooted above is obtained: none of the three options would beat both the others in a head-to-head referendum. So in a referendum pitting F against S, F would win, as a coalition of 'Imperialists' and 'Continentalists' produce a majority in favour of F (roughly what actually happened). But, in a further referendum, pitting I against F, I would win, as a coalition of 'localists' and 'Imperialists' produce a majority for I. But, in a further referendum, pitting S against I, S wins, as a coalition of 'Continentalists' and 'Localists' brings us back to S.

This is an example of what is known as 'the paradox of voting'. A 'voting paradox', but a majoritarian's dilemma. For the paradox constitutes a standing crisis to any 'will of the people' interpretation of democracy. Which of the three constitutional alternatives can claim to be 'the people's will'? None can. There is no will of the people. Any referendum can only award a spurious triumph to the non-existent will.

Is the paradox of voting more than a logical possibility, a scholar's fancy, an academic toy? Weighing in favour of possibility's reality is that the illustration does not rely on any of the three opinion types being numerically significant; only that none of the three claims a majority of voters.[635] What the existence of the paradox does require is that each of the options be judged worse by one of the opinion types, and judged the better by another. This can result from the existence of two different dimensions of value. Consider the valuation of the 'great state'. Some will be attracted by the grandeur, strength and capability of such a state. Others will be repelled by its grandiosity, aggression and incompetence. Presumably, Imperial Federation will serve any attraction to the great state the most, and to the status quo the least. Australian Federation serves up a middling quantity of what the believer in the great state admires, and what the disbeliever abhors. The key consequence is that, while the status quo may well be one person's worst choice (the devotee of the great state) and Imperial Federation might be another person's worst choice (the great state's detractor), Australian Federation will not be judged the worst (or best) by any opinion type; thus the precondition for the paradox is not observed.

But ponder the effects of introducing a second dimension of value: an esteem of Britishness, or 'Britannicism'. Introducing Britannicism as a value destroys the middle of the road character of Australian Federation, as it delivers not only less Britannicism than Imperial Federation (obviously) but probably also less than the status quo. It is now possible that Australian Federation will be judged the worst case by some (the ardent Britannicist), and the best case by others (the ardent anti-Britannicist). Now it is possible each of the three alternatives is judged the worst by some, and the best by others. The paradox has re-emerged as a possibility, and, perhaps, in these terms, as a reality in late 19th century Australia. Insofar as the paradox was a reality, the democratic sanction the referendums apparently provided Federation was spurious.

The ambiguity of 'the people'

Any reference to 'the majority' begs a question: the majority of what? What is the population of which the larger part constitutes 'a majority'? In geographical terms, what are the boundaries which enclose the population of which the larger part is 'a majority'? To the democrat the boundaries should not be taken as given, but are those which best serve democracy. Inasmuch as democracy is about maximising assent, those boundaries are those that best serve the maximisation of assent. No boundaries can ever perfectly serve that pursuit of assent, since for any boundaries there will always exist some voters (namely the minority) whose votes will be disregarded by the acceptance of the majority's wish. But some boundaries serve that pursuit better than others. Some boundaries will make larger the number of votes heeded, net of the number of votes disregarded. Consider a referendum on some measure conducted in an area of M geographical regions. It is not difficult to see that the total excess of the heeded votes over the ignored votes in that area will be maximised by letting the majority have its way on a region by region basis: so for each of the M regions, the measure applies if a majority in a given region voted Yes, and not if a majority in that given region voted No. In other words, the principle of 'self-determination'.[636]

How would the principle of self-determination work in the NSW referendum of 1898? In 65 electoral districts, overwhelmingly located in the Riverina and the Northern Rivers, the majority voted Yes. They would join the Commonwealth under this principle. In 59 districts, almost the entirety of the remainder of NSW, the majority voted No, and they would not join. But, regrettably for the principle of self-determination, the 65 Yes voting districts also included 16 metropolitan Sydney electorates, and the principle of self-determination would entail the absurd and obnoxious division of Sydney.

But there are other procedures which, while not amounting to self-determination by electorate, nevertheless give more heed to the wishes of a minority than a simple majoritarianism. Imagine identifying the largest contiguous subset of seats in which the position which is the minority position in the overall vote constitutes, within the subset, a (bare) majority. And then let that

Table 11.3 The results of the 1898 referendums in terms of electorates

		Electorates with a Yes majority	Electorates with a No majority	Largest aggregation of electorates in which No is a majority
NSW	number	65	59	118
	Yes percent	61.2	42.1	
	No percent	38.8	57.9	
Victoria	number	84	0	0
	Yes percent	84.0	na	
	No percent	16	na	
SA	number	25	2	6
	Yes percent	70.1	39.5	
	No percent	29.9	60.5	
Tasmania	number	25	4	8
	Yes percent	81.5	42.1	
	No percent	18.5	57.9	

Source: Rhodes (2002).

position rule within that subset of seats; while the remainder of seats abide by the majority in that remainder, which is also the majority position in the overall vote. This schema may be called 'minority-regarding majoritarianism'.[637] And in terms of net assent maximisation, it is no worse than deferring to the simple majority over the entire area: the number of persons whose judgement is heeded, net of those disregarded, is the same as the simple majority principle.[638]

What results would this minority-regarding principle produce when applied to the referendums of 1898 in NSW, Victoria, SA and Tasmania? Since every seat voted Yes in Victoria, minority-regarding majoritarianism, self-determination, and the simple majority all yield the same result. In SA only four seats voted No;

and minority-regarding majoritarianism yields a certain enclave of six seats in Adelaide.[639] In Tasmania, a similar sized enclave in its rural south is produced by minority-regarding majoritarianism.[640] Presumably neither of these enclaves would be viable polities.

In NSW the implication of the results of the 1898 referendum is profoundly different from the other colonies. The largest set of seats in which No retains a majority is 118, amounting to the entirety of NSW, save for seven seats in the Riverina (see Map 1 below).[641] The 'minority-regarding' response to the 1898 referendum, then, amounts to almost all of NSW staying out of the Commonwealth, while the heart of the Riverina joins it, either as a state in its own right, or perhaps by incorporation into Victoria, as some of the Riverina press advocated in the referendum's wake.[642] Federationists would have been maddened, and the Victorians at the centre of that movement would have found only cold consolation in a greater Victoria federally conjoined to SA, Tasmania and perhaps WA. But other Victorians may have been gratified: the plans of Syme for the annexation of the Riverina, not dead even then, would be happily realised.[643]

Map 1: 1898 NSW Referendum

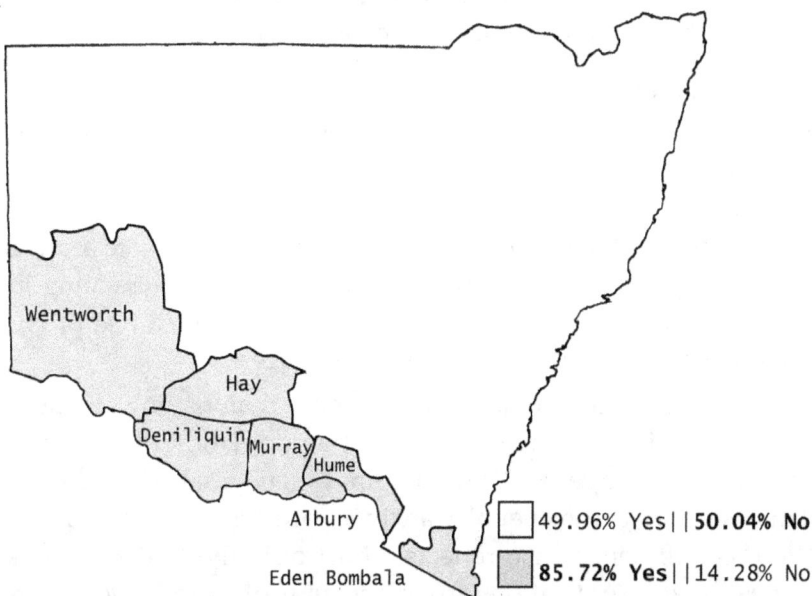

Although the secession of the Riverina into the Commonwealth, and the remainder of NSW staying outside, would have been no less respectful of democracy than a heeding of the majority in NSW overall, it would barely have been more respectful. A secession of the Riverina core – defined by the seven seats – would have left a truncated NSW divided between almost equally sized Yes and No. Some remedy for that painful equality would be the addition to the secession of several Yes seats physically contiguous to the Riverina,[644] which would have reduced the extent of the disregard of Yes in the remainder of NSW. And if Queensland had joined the Commonwealth, a secession in the south of NSW could have been complemented by a secession on the north of the Yes voting seats of Clarence, Grafton, Tenterfield, Richmond, Lismore, Ballina and Tweed. That would have provided 'No' in the remainder of NSW with a majority of 3.8 percent, essentially equal to the majority of Yes overall in NSW, which Barton noisily declared warranted NSW as a whole joining the Commonwealth. Even more to the point, the heeded majority (the No majority of truncated NSW plus the Yes majority of secession NSW) would come to 13 533 votes, or 9.8 percent of the total vote, compared to the No majority in NSW overall of just 5 367 votes.

The truest spirit of democracy in encountering the result of the 1898 referendum would have counselled partition of NSW.

Of the people?

If democracy is about maximising assent, then a readiness to obtain the 'right boundaries' is far from democracy's only requisite. Democracy requires that everyone's assent and dissent be equally counted: everyone has a vote, and an equal vote at that. Serving that requisite, by the 1890s property tests for voting in lower houses had been virtually eliminated, to create approximately manhood (and, in SA, adult) suffrage.

But an ideal democracy requires more than having an equal vote; it requires an equality across the population of a general capability to shape political outcomes – an equal *effective* vote. This necessitates an equal franchise, but also requires more. 'Political affluence' also reflects a host of individual attributes – wealth, zeal, education, articulacy as well as more social attributes, such as connections, and solidarity. An equality of political affluence, so broadly understood, is chimerical. But it remains reasonable to enquire if political affluence – wealth, zeal, etc. – was negatively or positively correlated with support for Federation; and to infer whether a truer democracy – one with a greater equality of 'political affluence' – would have produced, more or less, support for Federation. The question is hard to investigate. Historically, wealth was correlated with political affluence. In the 20th century this correlation was counterbalanced by labour and socialist parties making use of trade unions as a vehicle of collective action, to which other parties had only scattered replies. But trade unions remained shaky entities in the late 19th century, and by the time of the referendums, the representatives of manual labour had barely entered any ministry, or any upper house.

So we may take wealth as an indicator of political affluence. This suggests inequality in political affluence remained biasing in favour of Federation, as what data there is suggests persons of 'industrial occupation' tilted sharply against it.[645] That the Federal cause received less support from manual labour is easily observed in Victoria. No Victorian electorate recorded a majority for No in 1898; only five of 81 recorded fewer than two Yes votes for every No. Of these five, one was a border district, and the other four were Collingwood, Emerald Hill ['South Melbourne'], Melbourne West [Footscray] and Port Melbourne. As one non-Labor Billite groused, 'The Trades Hall Council, and the majority of the Labor leadership, Trenwith excepted, were for its rejection'.[646] The eleven electorates of the 'city' of Sydney tell the same story. Its social geography was organised around the north-south axis provided by George Street.

> ... *George Street ... was in fact a real dividing line in terms of both status and function ... Visually, the social differences between east and west were unmistakeable. Well-heeled people who worked in the shops and business houses along George and York Streets probably seldom ventured further westward, but if they did, they would have soon found themselves, if not in a different world, at least in one considerably meaner and dirtier than their own. ...*[647]

Billy Trenwith, labour orator. A Federationist exception among Labor leaders

To the west of George Street lay four electorates, and to the east, seven.⁶⁴⁸ In 1898 all four to the west recorded a majority of No votes; six of the seven to the east recorded Yes.⁶⁴⁹

A still brighter light is thrown on working class coldness to Federation in 1898 by SA census data, which reports occupation (and other variables) by electorate, and therefore allows the quantification by statistical analysis of the impact of 'industrial occupation' on an electorate's Yes vote (Appendix 2, Table A.3⁶⁵⁰). Taken at face value, the data suggest that a one percent increase in the share of the population in an industrial occupation reduces the Yes vote by almost 1.5 percent.[651] The heavy vote of manual workers against Yes is awkward for any 'the people' characterisation of the movement.

But some adults of 1890s Australia could not vote at all. The major element of unfinished business in that respect was that in only three of the seven referendums – those in SA and WA – could women vote. How their enfranchisement in the other colonies might have affected the result is an interesting question, but there is no evidence in SA of a purely gender effect.[652]

The greatest menace to the democratic force of the referendums is not that some did not have the vote, but that many had it, but did not vote.

The problem of abstention

Federation history has long recognised the weakness of the turn-out. In none of the referendums of 1898 and 1899 did a majority of those enrolled vote Yes; that is, in no referendum did the majority exceed the abstention. In no referendum of 1898 did a majority of those enrolled cast a vote one way or another. In no referendum did even a third of those eligible to enrol vote Yes.[653]

But if absenteeism is a palpable challenge to the significance of the referendums, the weight of the challenge is not obvious.

Not voting may arise from indifference. Presumably, such voters may be justly dropped from the calculus of assent and dissent, notwithstanding their unconcern tarnishing the glory of the victor. On the other hand, not voting may arise from the effective cost of voting (say, the distance from the polling booth) being unusually high. This amounts to disenfranchisement by an illegitimate criterion, and such abstentions cannot be disregarded.

Not voting may also arise from the voter not understanding the proposal being put: either what is being proposed, or the arguments for or against. How many voters could understand a Bill which was 'most subtle and complex',[654] in parts 'mysterious',[655] and even 'frankly unintelligible'?[656] Some who did not understand would have voted No, on a 'better the devil you know is better than the devil you don't' principle. Their judgement is recorded in the tally of votes. But some who did not understand would have not voted at all. They were the 'no opinion' people, who were obviously not counted in either the Yeses or the Noes. But should they be? Have they not excused themselves as disqualified to judge? But the problem of the lack of knowledge is not so easily left behind. For some voters 'did not know' but, regrettably, did not know they did not know; and, ignorant of their ignorance, *did* have an opinion, and did vote.

And this portion was not small. Perhaps this portion was very large. Perhaps *nobody* could claim to understand all parts of the draft Constitution. For in the subsequent generation, and century, parts of the Constitution proved remarkably mutable in the High Court's interpretation. Who could have foreseen the range of judicial decisions, even in its first twenty years? Thus the Court's accommodation in 1908 of the Commonwealth's circumvention of the mandate of section 94 to distribute to the states all surplus revenue of the Commonwealth.[657] Or the Jumbunna decision of the same year, in which the Chief Justice extended the potential reference of compulsory arbitration beyond 'production and manufacturing' to just about any paid activity.[658] Or the Court's effective invalidation, in 1915, of section 101, which had unequivocally mandated the creation of an Inter-State Commission. [659] Or the Court's extraordinary, if not perverse, decision of 1920,[660] that section 92 did not apply to Commonwealth legislation, 'leaving the Commonwealth free to impose any embargo it desired on interstate transport', thereby causing 'untold losses' to WA, by licensing the Commonwealth to forbid 'either goods or passengers to travel by ocean-going steamers' to WA. [661]

The conclusion: nobody in 1898 knew what the Constitution meant; and nobody knew what it 'probably' meant either. And how can anyone approve, or disapprove, what they do not understand, even if they think they do? The referendums, in this line of criticism, were as meaningless a choice as choosing from a menu in a foreign language you do not know (even if you think you do).

A Federationist may defend the meaningfulness of the balance of Yeses and Noes on the grounds that voters were not expressing a (necessarily irrational) favour or disfavour of a Bill they could not understand: they were expressing a view of the desirability or undesirability of Federation in general terms. They were treating the referendum as an indicative plebiscite on the broad idea. But the referendums were not indicative plebiscites on a broad idea. What was being approved, or not, was an intricate and lengthy statute. But perhaps, it might be countered, voters *were* actually voting to express a response to the general notion of Federation, and not out of a blindness to the reality that it was the Bill which was at stake, but out of a rational realisation that the probability of any referendum being decided by their single vote is (effectively) zero. Realising this, a voter voted not in order to make a difference to the result – their vote will never make a difference to the result – but for the sake of expressing their feelings. Voting Yes became a means of shouting 'three cheers for Federation'. So the question becomes: did the emotional basis of such 'making a statement' voting bias the vote towards Yes? A No vote might also be expressing emotion. We are left wondering whether Yes or No had the greater emotional resonance. The No camp repeatedly charged that the support for Federation was a matter of sentiment; a matter of being 'blinded', in Rose Scott's words, 'by the tinsel glory of a false sentiment'.[662]

There remains, finally, abstention arising from a rejection of the legitimacy of deciding the issue by a referendum. Such a position repudiates the referendum being held at all, and cannot be disregarded in inferring the degree of assent indicated by a referendum result. But how to count these?

Perhaps the only way non-voting can be said to be democratically weighed in any democratic calculus is to let the people decide how it should so weigh. They might require a certain minimum number of votes be cast in order for a measure to succeed, regardless of any majority. Equivalently, the people might require that a certain minimum number need to vote Yes. Tasmania's legislature settled on a minimum Yes of 6 000, or about 19 percent of the roll; Victoria 50 000, about 20 percent of the roll. NSW also had a minimum of 50 000 Yes votes, until a 'fiercely independent' member of its Assembly, Harry Levien, proposed that, for the referendum to succeed, a majority of those enrolled must vote. This would at least guarantee that a majority of voters approved of taking the question to referendum. In legislation, his proposal would be implemented by requiring Yes votes to number at least 80 000; or about 26 percent of the enrolment. The Legislative Assembly approved the proposal by 53 to 28.[663]

But on 2 June 1898 the number of Yes votes in NSW fell 8 000 short of 80 000.

The upshot was that in NSW the 1898 referendum, in law, failed. This was a brutal shock to Federationists. Barton 'regarded the matter 'as a forgone conclusion before the days of the referendum. ... It was Lombard Street to a Chinese orange that the bill would go through with at least 10,000 votes to spare'.[664] Barton's reactions were defiant to the point of 'denial'; he described the Yes majority as amounting to 7.5 percent of the vote (it was 3.9 percent); he pledged himself to 'fight to repeal' retrospectively the 80 000 minimum Yes vote requirement;[665] and he urged Turner not to deal with Reid. But these were empty words as long as Reid retained a majority in the Assembly. The next solution was to defeat Reid at the polls, and make Barton premier.

The 1898 NSW election

An election in NSW was called for 27 July 1898, and was fought over who would bring NSW into Federation: Reid or Barton? Both leaders had voted Yes; both agreed on key desirable revisions. Both their party vehicles claimed Federation: Reid's candidates were now styled the 'Liberal Federal Association'; and Barton's the 'National Federal Party'. Organised politics in NSW was thus 'united in doctrine but divided by personality'. The election was a struggle for who would 'lead' Federation; and so who would be prime minister.

On election night Reid's following in the Assembly was reduced by a dozen, although free traders of all stripes combined with Labor still amounted to a majority. This result can hardly be interpreted as a choice of Barton's leadership, especially as he and his circle did so poorly. To 'some astonishment' McMillan lost his seat of Burwood.[666] Of five senior National Federal candidates who were launched to wrest seats from sitting opponents – Wise, Smith, Manning, O'Connor, and Barton – four lost. Wise did wrench a seat from an anti-Billite incumbent by five votes. Smith failed badly in his quest to win back his old seat of Glebe from an anti-Billite. Manning lost his challenge in Woollahra against an anti-Billite of 1898. O'Connor decisively lost his joust against Chris Watson, the future Labor leader, another anti-Billite.[667]

But the greatest and most spectacular defeat was Barton's. He had chosen to go head-to-head with Reid in the seat of Sydney-King, in what amounted to a quasi-presidential contest over who would lead Federation, perhaps the most democratic event in the entire Federation episode.

On Reid's side were the working class and the publicans; including Larry Foley, the much lionised larrikin pugilist of the past, now proprietor of 'Foley's Hotel', and sometime purveyor of his pat political wisdom to the *Evening News*.

> Look here. I'll tell you what George Reid's done; ...Things are getting better. Ask any mechanic, he'll tell you that. The working classes know what they're about, make no mistake. Of course, Barton will get a lot of votes; but Reid needn't address another meeting, and he'd beat him by 100.[668]

But Barton would have the support of civil servants, who regarded the seat of King as 'peculiarly their own', and who were angered by Reid's civil service retrenchments – annual leave reduced from three to two weeks, and abolition of long service leave. So the premier could not be complacent. In 1895 Parkes had won a swing of four percent away from Reid in contesting Sydney-King at the general election, reducing Reid to 56 percent of the vote. And while the *Sydney Morning Herald* had opposed Parkes's candidacy, it supported Barton's now. In the Convention election Barton had received 10 percent more votes in Sydney-King than had Reid. Further, the seat of Sydney-King had voted 55 percent Yes in the 1898 referendum, the highest Yes proportion of any urban seat. And the only other candidate was a certain patent medicine vendor by the name, oddly enough, of R. W. Reid.[669] The Bartonites were confident, their supporters rampant, and Reid's meetings severely disturbed.

But Barton lost, taking only 46 percent of the vote.

In the face of Barton's prospective exile from parliament, there stepped forward Francis Clarke, his virtual neighbour in Carabella Street, Kirribilli, and the member for Hastings Macleay.[670] The seat consisted of a pair of river valley enclaves 400 km north of Sydney, each with a port at their river mouths, and a sprinkle of selectors along their lonely river banks. Clarke now obligingly

vacated the seat for Barton. Less obligingly, Reid decided not to leave the Hastings Macleay by-election of 23 September 1898 uncontested, and had one of his closest lieutenants, Sydney Smith, stand. Reid was taking a long shot. In 1894 protectionists had won Hastings Macleay by a country mile, and, more narrowly, in the 1895 general election, Reid's electoral high tide. Free traders did not trouble to contest the seat in 1898. Further, the free trade candidate of 1894 and 1895 was, in the words of the *Herald*, 'a staunch supporter' of Barton in June's referendum, and would stump for Barton in the by-election. Finally, Hastings Macleay had voted 65 per cent Yes in the 1898 referendum, putting it in the top quintile of Yes voting seats. True: the very likelihood of Barton winning would make any defeat a crisis for Barton; this would be a lure for Reid to enter. For all that, to contest Barton's probable victory amounted to probably granting Barton a showpiece of his strength. In the event, the Hastings Macleay by-election brought out how overstretched was Reid.

The ten-day campaign began on Tuesday 13 September, when the *Pelican* delivered a top-hatted Barton to the boaters and bowlers of 200 welcomers on the wharves of Kempsey. That evening Barton delivered a two-hour speech to an excited audience, in 'good form' as even his critics allowed, a performance capped by the Reverend Kelly's platform declaration that Barton had been sent by God Almighty.[671] But before Barton had travelled as far as Port Macquarie, on the southern edge of the electorate, Reid made the shock announcement that he would make a lightning trip to 'The Hastings and the Macleay'. But lightning travelled ponderously to the district, given the lack of even a railway link from Sydney. Reid arrived by day steamer at Port Macquarie at 3.30 pm on the Saturday, with an engagement to speak at Kempsey at 8 pm. He 'expressed regret' to the crowd of Port Macquarie greeters that he could not stay longer, and set off, in a buggy and four horses, to race north to Kempsey. On the road his single vehicle passed Barton's cavalcade of 25 vehicles travelling south to Port Macquarie. A little beyond this unlooked-for encounter, Reid's horses bolted, downhill, towards the bridgeless Wilson River, and apparent disaster. At a providentially opportune moment,

Opposite: On the hustings, September 1898. Barton and Reid battle for the prize of Sydney-King.

Reid gave a 'tremendous tug' on the reins, and the buggy hit a bank, sending Reid and the driver flying. Reid 'looked up to see, as I thought, the wheel coming on top of me, as the buggy overturned'. But he was spared.[672] A shaken Reid eventually arrived in Kempsey, 45 minutes late, to speak to a rally which was infiltrated, and vigorously disrupted, by Barton supporters.

At the end of this unpleasant conclusion to a gruelling day, Clarke approached Reid by way of a peace offering: 'I never saw a man look more tired and exhausted'.[673] The next morning, Reid took off again, without cavalcade or well-wishers, on a 270 km coach trip back to Newcastle. While Reid was departing, Barton's reinforcements from Sydney were joining him in the south, in particular the free trade candidate of previous contests, W. H. Vivian, who was 'proving a tower of strength'. But the most significant assistance arrived in the form of the Protectionist rabble rouser, William Crick. He was cleverly scheduled to speak in Kempsey simultaneously with Smith, and won 900 auditors – 200 hundred more than Barton's biggest meeting there – forcing Smith, pathetically, to reschedule. Forty years later, Francis Clarke recalled that Billy Crick also relieved the rigours of the campaign for Barton, by intercepting his leader on the road to Kempsey, and providing an impromptu *al fresco* champagne refreshment. It was all a pleasant preface for Barton's easy victory, winning 59 percent, as he harvested a slump of the free trade vote in its traditional local stronghold, Kempsey.[674] Reid's hasty and ill-provided sortie had failed.

But other memories of Barton's Hastings Macleay campaign were not happy. In 1938 Clarke recorded, 'There is something which I feel ought to be said. I ask myself this question now. Would you resign your seat under similar circumstances and conditions? My answer to that is decidedly No!'. On the campaign trail, he explained, an interjector hissed, 'Traitor'. 'I felt as though I had been shot dead'.[675]

The 1899 referendums

By the last week of September 1898, Reid may have felt cornered by events. His plan – to have the Bill approved by the referendum[676] – had gone awry. And yet Yes had achieved a majority of the votes; so simply abandoning the cause was untenable. A promising solution had been brewing: bring Queensland into the Federation, while excluding the small states for the time being, and thereby make NSW more central to federation, and so reconcile her to it. But not long after the Queensland premier's August rencontre with Reid, Byrnes had died, eliminating the possibility. Reid's one remaining manoeuvre was to seek mollifying concessions from the directors of the Federation campaign. But this option was contested territory. Barton had already proposed significantly amending the Bill: by locating the capital within NSW; ending the automatic disbursement of 75 percent of tariff revenues to the states; and allowing a joint sitting of parliament to legislate with only a simple majority.[677] And with his triumph at Hastings Macleay, Barton was the new Leader of the Opposition displacing the anti-Federationist, Lyne.

As leader, Barton sought to exploit the seeming greater popularity of Federation than protection by supressing the free trade *vs* protection fracture, to the great anger of the protectionist wing of his cause.[678] For his part, Reid was content to push back, by pressing the free trade *vs* protection fracture as much as ever,[679] and rule NSW with the old free trade and Labor accord. A sign of the rallied free trade-ism was an entente between Reid and Haynes, leader of the free traders' bitter-ender anti-Federationists. Early in November, Reid accompanied Haynes on a visit to his electorate, Wellington; in October Reid was best man at Haynes's wedding. But this entente suddenly passed. Did the versatile Reid judge more benefit might be obtained by bending in the opposite direction? Reid abruptly cancelled the scheduled reductions in tariffs ordained by his *Customs Act* of 1895. Free traders growled. 'From this time forward I can guarantee to give the Premier a very rosy time', declared Haynes.[680] On the other side of the chamber, protectionist leaders were left to ponder this attempt of Reid 'to get the taxes and the men too!', as Barton put it. Might it be prudent to not risk the success of Reid's effort, and confer on him some stake in the federation dynamic? He would be granted a meeting with the premiers, and they would offer him something.

And so, in the last days of January 1899, the six premiers converged on Melbourne. As a kind of prologue, the ANA organised a ceremonial banquet to commemorate 26th January, 'this great national holiday'; and all the premiers attended, and spoke, save Reid. Thus national unity. Deakin declared to the banqueters that the watchword of the Premiers' conference should be, 'No Concessions'.[681] Beyond the concessions mooted by Barton months before, the premiers agreed the boundaries of a state would require a referendum of its inhabitants to be changed. And the Commonwealth capital would be within NSW, but at least 100 miles distant from Sydney, and the location would not be named in the Constitution as Reid had wanted.[682] These modifications were settled by the premiers in private conclave: no observers were admitted; no record of debate kept; and, above all, contrary to Dickson's mooting, there would be no second convention. The people were not gathered to make laws: they were now simply beckoned to approve them.

Between April and September 1899 referendums were held in all colonies save WA on the Bill as revised by premiers in Melbourne, which included some significant concessions to NSW, and a single, almost nominal, one to Queensland.[683]

The Table 11.4 indicates that Queensland voted 56 percent in favour. But nowhere in Australia was the ambiguity in defining the bounds of 'the people' evoked more painfully by a referendum than in Queensland. As Table 11.5 reports, in Queensland 36 seats voted Yes, but 25 No.

Even more harshly than in NSW, Queensland was geographically split, in terms of a No voting 'South' and a Yes voting 'North'. This split cannot be resolved into occupational terms. Unlike SA, industrial occupation contributes nothing to the statistical prediction of the No or Yes vote. Geography was everything in Queensland. 23 of the 25 seats with a No majority were in Brisbane and its environs.[684] The nearest seat to Brisbane that gave a Yes majority was Warwick, 150 km distant.[685] Support for Federation was a revolt against the capital.

The application of the principle of self-determination, it seems, would create a Brisbane city-state. But what Brisbane wished most of all was to be capital of an independent Queensland, not an enclave. And doubtless what the rest of Queensland wanted was a Commonwealth which included Brisbane. The application of a 'minority accommodating majoritarianism' – find

Table 11.4: The results of the 1899 referendums

		Majority	Yes	No	Valid vote	Absention	Enrolment
NSW		24 679	107 420	82 741	190 161	116 146	307 473
percent	of vote	13.0	56.5	43.5	100	61.1	161.7
	of roll	8.0	34.9	26.8	61.9	37.8	100
	of adults	3.5	15.3	11.8	27.1	16.6	43.9
Victoria		142 848	152 653	9 805	162 458	123 548	287 331
percent	of vote	87.9	94.0	6.0	100	76.0	176.9
	of roll	49.7	53.1	3.4	56.5	43.0	100
	of adults	22.1	23.6	1.5	25.1	19.1	44.3
Queensland		9 132	42 590	33 458	76 048	30 717	107 113
percent	of vote	12.0	56.0	44.0	100	40.4	140.8
	of roll	8.5	39.8	31.2	71	28.7	100
	of adults	3.5	16.3	12.8	29.0	11.7	40.9
SA		49 347	66 550	17 158	83 663	57 982	155 254
percent	of vote	59.0	79.5	20.5	100	69.3	182.3
	of roll	32.3	43.6	11.2	54.8	38.0	100
	of adults	26.6	35.8	9.2	45.0	31.2	82.1
Tasmania		13 323	14 167	844	15 011	19 255	34 528
percent	of vote	88.8	94.4	5.6	100	128.3	230
	of roll	38.6	41.0	2.4	43.5	55.8	100
	of adults	15.4	16.4	1.0	17.4	22.3	40.0

Sources: as in Table 11.1.

the largest area in which the minority position in Queensland as a whole constitutes a majority, and let that position prevail there – would divide the state in two. Mackay and everything northwards, and everything west of Cape York, voting 60.2 percent Yes. And the remaining south-east corner of Queensland, by construction, with a small majority for No. How much such a partition would have served democracy is dogged by uncertainties surrounding whether 'North and West Queensland' would have wished to be part of the Commonwealth which lacked 'South-East Queensland'; and whether 'South-East Queensland' would wish to be outside the Commonwealth without 'North and West Queensland'.

Table 11.5 : The results of the 1899 referendums in terms of electorates

		Electorates with a Yes majority	Electorates with a No majority	Largest aggregation of electorates in which No is majority
NSW	number	79	46	91
percent	Yes	63.6	45.3	
	No	36.4	54.7	
Victoria	number	84	0	0
percent	Yes	94.0	na	
	No	16.0	na	
Queensland	number	36	25	51
percent	Yes	74.2	36.6	
	No	25.8	63.4	
SA	number	27	0	0
percent	Yes	79.5	na	
	No	20.5	na	
Tasmania	number	29	0	0
percent	Yes	94.4	na	
	No	5.6	na	

Sources: as in Table 11.4.

In the four other colonies, each of which had had a referendum in 1898, the outcome in 1899 was in summary terms the same: Yes won a majority. The difference is that there was a significant swing to Yes in all four, and it is these swings which need to be 'read'.

Victoria, SA and Tasmania saw a roughly 10 percentage point swing to Yes relative to 1898. The upshot was that in SA almost

80 percent of valid votes were cast for Yes, and an extraordinary 94 percent in both Tasmania and Victoria. Every electorate of these three cast a majority for Yes.

Since the revised Constitution contained some non-trivial concessions to NSW – the capital would not now be in Melbourne nor Ballarat – this increase in support in Victoria is a puzzle. It may reflect a loss of all hope by Victoria's No voters. Or it may be tied up with the substantial increase in turnout; by about one-third in Victoria. Yes voters came out to vote. Did the frustration of Yes voters with the 1898 referendums bring them back to the ballot box in 1899 with determination? But the concessions which cost Victoria the capital surely also guaranteed victory. Perhaps assurance more than anxiety was the root of the massive Yes vote in Victoria. Victory is raucous; defeat is wordless: perhaps turning out to vote Yes was something of a victory yell.

Understanding the swing to Yes in SA is helped by the existence of census data on each seat's social characteristics. The sharp swing to Yes in SA in 1899 can be wholly traced to the reconciliation of blue collar workers with the Bill (see Appendix 2, Table A.4). Analysis of occupational data indicates the negative impact of industrial occupation on the Yes vote, which was so sizeable in 1898, completely disappeared in 1899. But why? A clue to part of the answer may lie in participation. The number of valid votes cast leapt by 55 percent in 1899. Part of the explanation lies in SA's 1899 referendum being held on the same day as a general election. This drew voters to the polls. A significant proportion of those who voted for the Assembly, 91 289 in all, evidently had no interest in the referendum; only 83 663 valid votes were cast for the referendum. Further, 11.5 percent of referendum votes which were cast were informal, compared to 0.5 percent in 1898, and newspapers reported 'the vast number of informal papers' 'strewn about the Town Hall floor'. In summary, many new faces appeared at the booth in the 1899 referendum in order to vote for the House of Assembly and, as a postscript, cast a vote for Yes. More specifically, the new faces were overwhelmingly blue collar, who appeared in order to vote for their hero, Kingston, in the Assembly and, as an afterthought, cast a vote for Yes, their hero's cause.

Certainly, the increase in participation seems wholly explicable in terms of an increase of blue collar participation. Statistical analysis of the data suggests that, in 1899, 100 persons of industrial occupation yielded 51 votes (either Yes or No), but 95 (Yes or No) in 1899 (Appendix 2, Table A.4). No other occupation indicates any such increase. The census data suggests 100 persons of industrial occupation yielded 19 Yes votes in 1898 but 73 Yes votes in 1899. And a 100 persons of industrial occupation yielded 32 No votes in 1898 and 22 in 1899. This is not so much a switch from one side to the other, as a decision to vote rather than not to vote. The suggestion of these particulars is that the working class Yes voters tended to be less committed than working class No voters, and in need of an incentive – such as an opportunity to vote in a general election – to go to the booth. The strength of feeling is not weighed in the electoral ballot.

The swing to Yes in NSW was about five percent. The real question is why the swing was not larger. The Yes campaign was efficiently organised by Atlee Hunt through the newly-forged United Federal Executive – bringing together the Australian Federal League, the Federal Association, the Free Trade and Liberal Association and the Protectionist Union – with a full-time Organising Committee, meeting at 4.00 pm each day, and busy with 'telephonic communications' and typed communiqués. And the Yes campaign was united. It concluded the night before the referendum, at the Town Hall, with Barton and Reid appearing on the same stage, as the principal speakers. O'Connor assured the audience that a Commonwealth over which the 'flag of Great Britain waved' could never fail; and, as Drake unfurled the self-described federal flag, the near 9 000 pipes of the Town Hall organ plunged into 'Rule Britannia'.

The No campaign in NSW was depleted and divided. Meeting places were 'generally closed to anti-billites'.[686] Want was puzzlingly absent throughout 1899 campaign.[687] And their cause had been deserted by some former political supporters who had absorbed a palpable lesson of the 1898 election. 54 of the candidates in the 1895 election had voiced their opposition to the Bill, and had recontested the same seats in the 1898 election. These candidates experienced in 1898 a mean swing against them of 2.7 percent, a modest decline given that so many had their natural constituency split by the federation issue. But of the 49 who had won seats in 1895, eight lost in 1898.[688] In a first-past-the-post system, free trade anti-Billites were squeezed between free trade pro-Bill candidates and National Federalists. And they lacked the funding from Victoria and elsewhere being arranged by Deakin.[689] For all that, the toll was a sobering one for anti-Billites. A number of adaptable politicians had since that election forsaken the anti-Billite cause for Yes. E. D. Millen, the key organiser of the Anti-Convention Bill League campaign of 1898, defected, and was now preparing for what would be a long federal career; along with other former luminaries of the League (James Ashton, John Neild), including three of Reid's cabinet who had in 1898 opposed the Bill, but were soon to be to be in Federal parliament (Joseph Cook, Sydney Smith, and A. J. Gould). The leadership of the persisting No cause was split, between Haynes (free traders),[690] MacLaurin (protectionists), and Lyne, cutting his own path.

In 1899 the most vociferous No voice sounded from the margins. Labor advanced 'vigorous and well-organised efforts to defeat the [revised] Bill',[691] and 17 of the 19 members of parliament 'worked strongly for no'.[692] Rose Scott was now bolstered by trade union and Labor-linked suffragists such as Belle Golding.[693] The splash Scott made in 1898 had evidently moved Federationists to devise their own reply: the Women's Federal League. Its President was Lady Harris, the Mayoress of Sydney, and it vice-presidents were 'Mrs Barton, Mrs See, Mrs Reid, Mrs Wise, Mrs Bruce Smith and Mrs Meeks', the last being the wife of the President of the Sydney Chamber of Commerce. It was, evidently, a wives' committee, and it must have been a tempting target to the Suffrage League. The inaugural meeting of the Federal League in the Town Hall had not long progressed before a 'determined-looking woman, with a foreign accent' rose to challenge any member of the Federal League to a public debate with Rose Scott or Belle Golding. The taunt was noisily repudiated, and Lady Harris jumped up to announce, 'Every woman who isn't a federalist can leave the room'.[694]

On 20 June 1899 Yes won 56.5 percent of the vote in NSW; a solid margin, five Yeses for every four Noes.[695] And yet the strength of the No vote is remarkable given the circumstances. The press was strongly Federationist; 189 newspapers advocating Yes, and only 18 No.[696] The Australasian Federation League could contentedly remark of the Sydney dailies, 'the *Herald*, the *Evening News*, and the *Australian Star* all did splendid work'.[697] But despite the intense media support for Yes, despite both Premier and Opposition Leader strenuously campaigning for Yes, and despite both free trade and protectionist parties actively committing to Yes, 43.5 percent of voters still voted No. Sydney actually recorded a (narrow) No majority, 50.3 percent.[698] And the strength of the No vote was not merely a matter of inertia. In 104 of 125 electorates the number of Noes cast actually increased. The total number of No votes increased by 25 percent. The pattern of the 1899 NSW vote is not consistent with a simple shift in sympathy towards Federation of all voters, which would have produced a decline in the number of No votes, as was seen in 1899 in SA, Victoria and Tasmania.

How to interpret the surge in both Yes and No votes in NSW in 1899? It might be traced, innocuously, to a decline in the difficulty of voting, as that would bring out both more Yes and more No voters. And certainly the difficulty in voting was reduced by the efforts of Reid to reduce the number of checks on voting integrity. There might, equally, have been an increased benefit in voting, reflecting an increase in the decisiveness of the vote. A Yes result would make Federation unstoppable, while No would have made it impossible. So it was a life and death battle. Another source of an increased benefit in voting may be that in 1899, unlike 1898, there was no minimum vote requirement for Yes to hurdle. The minimum of 1898 may have discouraged both voting No and voting Yes; No voters perhaps thinking they did not 'need' to vote; and Yes voters perhaps thinking there would be 'no point' in voting. In April 1899 the Legislative Council did debate requiring a Yes vote of at least 25 percent of enrolment for the second referendum to be deemed successful; in other words, requiring a majority of those enrolled to vote, one way or another, for the referendum to pass. But a few days earlier Reid had appointed twelve Councillors in one swoop, and all twelve voted against the motion, to defeat it by 30 votes to 23. The consequent absence of any minimum vote hurdle in 1899 might have encouraged participation from both sides.

But increased incentives to participate do not capture the increase in the percentage share of Yes in 1899. The NSW result is best interpreted as polarisation – both the Yeses and the Noes more fervid – combined with a shift of the largely indifferent voter to Yes. The premiers' amendments of the Convention's Bill were placatory to NSW, and must have enticed at least a few of those previously indifferent. But about the unchanged essence of the Bill feelings sharpened: those who liked it, liked it still more, and those who disliked it, disliked it still more. It was that accentuation of feeling that allowed for the No vote to increase its percentage share in 25 seats. But those who did not care about the Convention Bill in 1898, were now sufficiently roused to vote Yes.

Hence the renewed heave for union left NSW no more united – perhaps even more divided. If the overall Yes majority of NSW was, in 1898, wholly attributable to the Riverina, in 1899 it was now attributable to a much larger area. But the core of NSW still constituted a No majority (see Map 2). If the periphery of NSW swung harder still to Yes, central regions stuck with No, including the Southern Tablelands, where two seats – Boorowa and

Map 2: 1899 NSW Referendum

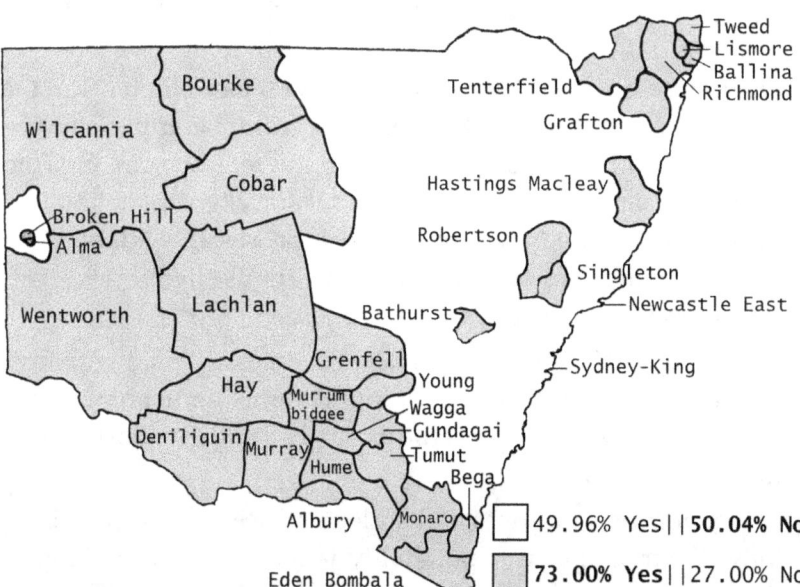

Queanbeyan – recorded increases in their No majority, despite being represented by cabinet-ranking members of the National Federal Party.[699] Whatever Federationists were doing, it was not working with these regions. On referendum night, the *Queanbeyan Age* recorded one anonymous poet enquiring,

> *Why sell so cheap which is so dear*
> *My native land, good night.*[700]

The problem of electoral fraud

The sharpest menace to the significance of the Federation referendums would be some blight on the integrity of their processes.

Fraud was a curse of 19th century elections in NSW and elsewhere.[701] Legislation and regulation did seek to stay classic abuses; thus the *Parliamentary Elections Act 1893 (NSW)* required a voter identity card ('an Elector's Right') to be presented upon voting. But safeguards were reduced for the NSW referendum of 1898, and still further for 1899. There were – remarkably – no scrutineers at either referendum. And, in 1899, 'in numerous places in Sydney the electoral office was kept open until late at night for the purpose of issuing rights to any persons who chose to apply for them'.[702] A renewed space was given to several classic abuses.

Ineligible voting. Tom may not have been eligible for the Right in the first place, but obtains one from a complaisant 'assistant registrar' casually recruited for the referendum. Or Tom may have been eligible in the past, but forfeited that eligibility by residing outside NSW, and yet still possesses a Right. Rolls would normally provide some check on Tom's eligibility to vote, but in 1899 rolls were, in effect, not in use.[703]

Multiple voting. Tom votes several times in his own name. Tom may have several Elector's Rights in his name; having applied for a replacement on reporting (truthfully or not) that he had lost the original.

Personation. Tom uses Ted's Electoral Right to vote.[704] Pungently illustrative of this possibility is that Willis, according to one contemporary, had accumulated 200 voting rights.[705]

Roll packing. The practice of organising the enrolment of ineligible or fictitious voters *en masse*.

Box stuffing. Grossest of all, this is the invention of votes by polling booth officials. Helpful to that purpose, officials were issued ballots in excess of voters. The checking off of each voter on the district roll was not in 1899 any great bar to officials filling out these excess ballots as they wished; these ballots could be ascribed to voters enrolled in another electoral district.[706] But would not the presence of scrutineers prevent such offences? In NSW, unlike the other colonies, there were no scrutineers at the count of the referendums.[707] Australia had won renown by introducing the Secret Ballot. The Reid government in 1898 and 1899 provided a new innovation previously undiscovered by democracies: the secret count.

There was, then, a more than ordinary opportunity for ballot fraud. Did it happen?

Consider the important centre of Hillgrove, and its neighbouring village, Metz, in the seat of Armidale. 'The Anti-Billites plumed themselves of having captured' these booths.[708] Yet, in the event, both recorded 78 percent Yes in 1898; 'aberrant' not only to (partisan) expectation, but to the 46 percent Yes recorded in the remainder of the electorate of Armidale. The one explanation proffered is that a 'remarkable change' took place on account of a visit by Barton and J. T. Walker. But the suggestion that these could conjure up such a remarkable shift is speculative at best – did a visit by Barton work such miracles anywhere else? Fraud is a competitive hypothesis. Doubts harden in the light of the fact that in the 1899 referendum Hillgrove's Yes vote fell to 53 percent; a shift of 25 percentage points, while the rest of the colony was recording an overall swing to Yes.

The particulars of some other seats invite wonder. In two seats valid votes exceeded enrolment: in Sydney-Lang by 28 percent, and in Sydney-King by 131 percent. The only way to reconcile this feat with a legitimate vote is to invoke absentee voting. But why should there be an explosion of absentee voting in these two seats? There was absentee voting in the 1898 referendum, but in that year both seats recorded valid votes much smaller than their rolls. What had changed between 1899 and 1898? The regulations. Unlike 1898, any person who voted absentee in 1899 was not recorded as doing so. If you had a second Right in 1899 it would now be undetectable if used to vote, a second time, outside your electorate. But to vote outside your electorate you need to travel outside your electorate, and Sydney-King, the city's 'central business district', would have been a convenient place to which to travel. So too, for many, was Sydney-Lang. And yet both seats saw in 1899 only a small increase in the Yes vote as a share. So, if the massive increase in votes in 1899 was spurious, the No cause must have been giving almost as good as it got.

In no other seats did voting exceed enrolment, but some still recorded remarkable leaps in electoral participation. Consider the seven seats in NSW with the highest share of Yes in 1899, all Riverina border seats. The last column of Table 11.6 records the vote in 1899 relative to the average vote in the elections of 1895, 1898 and 1901.

In Wentworth, Eden Bombala and Albury the vote in 1899 was unremarkable in size. So, it might be said, there was nothing in the Murray water that engendered an urge to vote in referendums. Additionally, they indicate there was nothing in being an ardently Yes electorate that provoked an onrush on the polling

Table 11.6: Total vote in Riverina electorates, 1895-1901

	Average of general elections, 1895, 1898 and 1901	Referendum vote, 1899	Referendum vote, 1899, as a percent of average of general elections
Wentworth	887	953	107.4
Hay	951	1 365	143.8
Eden Bombala	1 340	1 342	100.2
Hume	1 161	1 555	133.9
Albury	1 634	1 780	108.9
Deniliquin	1 296	1 677	138.7
Murray	1 325	2 448	184.8
memorandum: NSW	172 770	190 161	110.1

Sources: Column 1; Green (2007). Column 2; Rhodes (2002).

Notes. In Hume the by-election of 21 April 1901 has been substituted for the (uncontested) general election of 22 June 1901.

booth. In Hay, Hume and Deniliquin the vote was substantially higher than in the general elections, which will raise an eyebrow. But it is the turnout in Murray which is a singularity. And its abormality is confirmed by statistical tests (Appendix 2, Table A.5). This is *prima facie* evidence of substantial ballot fraud in this seat.[709] Statistical analysis also concludes that no seats outside the Riverina exhibited an abnormal turnout, save for Newcastle East (where an above average swing to Yes was recorded), and Sydney-Gipps (another above swing to Yes).

The apparent fraud in Murray may not have been restricted to Yes votes. Although extremely small in absolute terms, the No vote experienced one of the largest percentage increases in NSW relative to 1898. There may have been an underhand war of fraud within Murray, as in Sydney-Lang and Sydney-King, but with Yes forces here easily getting the best of it.

So what was 'Murray'? It was Corowa. Thus the germ of Federation democracy proved to be the crown of its corruption.

*

A defender of the Federation referendums may observe with justice that the problems with democratic processes are not restricted to referendums. Almost any democratic choice may be manipulated; in every democratic process the potential absence of a 'will of the people' lurks; in every election abstention deflates the significance of outcomes; in any democracy a universal legal franchise is undercut by the existence of the 'politically affluent'. Ballot fraud, too, large or small, constantly pollutes.

But the referendums of 1898 and 1899 were especially vulnerable to the ever-present defects of democratic processes on account of their special character; the decisions being made were asymmetric, in a way ordinary democratic decisions are not. A law one parliament passes, a later parliament may repeal.[710] No remedying symmetry prevails in the referendums on the Bill. The Federation was to be 'indissoluble': the people of Queensland of 1899 could vote themselves into Federation, but the people of Queensland of 1999 could not vote themselves out.[711] So, instead of the votes of electors of 1898 being compared to the votes of a normal election, they might better be compared to a hypothetical referendum to close the electoral rolls once and for all, and confine the franchise henceforth to those who presently have it. Would such a referendum be 'democratic'? Or, alternatively, they might be compared to holding a referendum on altering the Constitution so that it could no longer be altered by referendum. Would such a referendum be 'democratic'?

In constitution-making we are, indeed, proposing the rule of the dead. Five million Queenslanders can ponder what was taken from them, and left to them, by 4 567 voting Yes rather than No in 1899. And taken from them, often enough, for acutely particular and passing material motives. The most careful student of the Queensland referendum has concluded that 'places to which Premier Dickson promised railways voted for the Bill'.[712] Such voting according to particular and passing material motives will occur in any democratic process. But when the subject of the vote is a one-way constitutional journey, the offence against democracy by the one-way passage is galling.

The Federationists were perfectly untroubled by the one-way journey. Indeed, they were insistent on it. The most noisily 'democratic' of them all – Charles Kingston, who had drafted the Enabling Acts – had originally proposed that every sentence of the Constitution be subsequently revisable only by a two-thirds majority of electors.[713] Some Federationists, it seemed, were resolved to rule from the grave.

12

The Finale

To Herald in the Round of Happy Days
– Henry Parkes

With the referendums won by Federationists, the remainder of the Federation story is something of a denouement. For all that, the 20 months prior to the election of the Commonwealth's first parliament is rich in incident and revelation; extending, in the standard telling, from a vast, national *fête champêtre*, to an oafish attempt to snatch the Federal coronet from its guardians. In truth, the events of the Federation finale are grosser, more revealing and more dissonant than in the stock narration. They range from an expense account scandal, to the ousting of Reid and Barton from their leadership positions within weeks of their referendum victory; and amount to a march past of incongruities: of Federation leaders upended in their year of triumph; of a man without a seat made prime minister; of a new nation racing to fight the old country's imperial wars; of champions of 'greater self-government' scheming for a dubious governor to dismiss an elected premier; and a diplomatic deadlock in London solved under the shade of palm fronds in George Street, Brisbane.

The fox at bay

On 16 August 1899 the Legislative Council of NSW deliberated the crowning wreath of the Federationists' victory in the referendums of 1899: an Address to Her Majesty in which Her Majesty's most dutiful and loyal subjects expressed their prayer that Her Majesty may be pleased to submit to the Imperial Parliament the Bill to establish an Australian Commonwealth. The anti-Billites of the Council proposed that the Bill be amended so that, if the permanent location of the capital had not been established within four years, the new parliament would alternate in sitting between Sydney and Melbourne. This precisely even-handed proposal – advocated years before by both Reid and Deakin – was defeated by a vote of 20 to 16, and with the essential aid of ten of the twelve members of Council whom Reid had hastily appointed in April of that year. On 17 August the anti-Billites in the Council moved that if a majority of the electors of NSW expressed their wish to secede from the Commonwealth, the Queen should 'give due consideration' to this wish. This last modest attempt of preserving the possibility of leaving the 'indissoluble' Federation was also defeated. Finally, the Council approved the Address, on a vote 24 to 21, again with the essential assistance of ten of Reid's 12. With this act of self-immolation the decision to federate may be deemed consummated.

With the conclusive legislative endorsement of Federation in August 1899 the precarious and abnormal political equilibrium which had ruled NSW since January 1899 now dissolved. Since the beginning of that year Reid's free traders had ruled in implicit coalition with Barton's protectionists, for the purposes of securing Federation. In Reid's words, 'this House was elected unmistakably as a federal parliament by the people of this country, under the leadership of the hon. member for Hastings-Macleay [Barton], on the other side of the House, and of myself upon this side of the House'. Or, as the *Muswellbrook Chronicle* put it, 'Mr Barton's chief anxiety has been to keep the Government in power till the Federal addresses were passed'.[714]

The Reid government of 1899 was not, then, as so commonly reckoned, a free trade minority government, sustained in office by a compact with Labor. Reid's government had been repudiated by five free trade MPs led by John Haynes, irreconcilably opposed to the amended Bill, and now bent on destroying Reid.[715] Shorn of this Haynes group, Reid, even with Labor support, commanded no more than 60 or 61 of the chamber of 125.[716]

Thus between January and August of 1899 Barton's protectionists and Reid's free traders – between them holding nearly 100 seats – sustained power, and ruled over the rump comprising the Labor group, Haynes's clutch of anti-Billite free traders, and a sprinkle of protectionists. NSW, then, had a parliament without a genuine functioning Opposition; to critics a deplorable state of affairs rarely met in a parliamentary system in preceding centuries. One party ruled, the 'Federation Party'.

But with Federation effectively accomplished in August 1899 the coalition of federationists that ruled New South Wales lost its raison d'être. The moment the Council passed the Bill, the Reid government was a minority government, facing a hostile majority. Reid's free traders did not have a majority, and neither did Reid's free traders plus Labor. But the protectionists had no majority on their own account. A majority could, however, be constituted, of protectionists plus Labor, claiming 69 to 70 of the chamber's 125 seats. But any protectionist–Labor compact was impossible as long as Barton was leader. Lyne, however, was not offensive to Labor, as long as Lyne could make some concession on protection. And with Federation now just a matter of time, Lyne became willing to do so. Lyne assured Labor that NSW's free trade policy would be untouched under his premiership. With these words Lyne pronounced sentence on Barton, and Wise and Crick set about arranging the execution.[717] On 23 Au-

Reid in 1917, with children, and Mrs Florence Reid, one-time Vice-President of the Women's Federal League

gust 1899 Barton announced his essentially forced resignation as Leader of the Opposition, and Lyne replaced him.[718] It was Reid who was now in an untenable position; Haynes was 'jubilant at the turn of events', and within a few hours the demolition of Reid's premiership began.[719]

The pretext – the required detonator – for Reid's destruction was found in the misconduct of John Neild, the member for Paddington, divorce reformer, Lieutenant-Colonel of St George's English Rifles, and Grand Master of the Loyal Orange Institution of New South Wales. Voluble, vehement, poetical and, to Labor, absurd. None of these attributes, however, made him unuseful to Reid, to whose cause Neild had transferred in 1899, having earlier campaigned against the Bill. The day after the Council had dispatched the Address to Her Majesty, the *Star* reported that parliamentary estimates included a payment of £350 to Neild for his preparation, at Reid's request, of a report on old age pensions, despite the House having 'no intention whatever to pay him one farthing towards his expenses'. The protectionist *Star* added,

> It will take a good deal of explaining to account for the expenditure of that £350. The country by this time has had quite enough of the Reidian euphemism, the artless habit of calling the same thing by two different names; as, for instance, "deficit" "surplus," and so on.[720]

Labor moved Neild's seat be declared vacant. In response, Reid unguardedly volunteered that, apart from expenses, he had arranged a second payment to Neild of £250, out of 'recognition' for the report. Haynes seized on this disclosure to shift the target from Neild to Reid.

> **Haynes**: *The right hon. gentleman said distinctly that he was surprised at the volume, the value, and the character of the report of the hon. member.*
>
> **Reid**: *Hear, hear!*
>
> **Haynes**: *And that he thought such labour should not go unrequited.*
>
> **Reid**: *Hear, hear! That is what the amount of £250 to be submitted to Parliament is for.*

> **Haynes**: *I think that statement by the right hon. gentleman justified my statement that on those terms the Premier could buy this House in detail. ... the Premier himself must answer for this in the course of a few days.*
>
> **Reid**: *Hear, hear! That is what makes it pleasant to the hon. member!*
>
> **Haynes**: *Exactly. The hon. member never committed a bigger blunder in his life than he has committed on this occasion.*

Reid had publicly acknowledged his authorship of an act which was construable as the subornment of a member of parliament. He could only lamely declare, 'If I made a blunder in this matter I think my hon. friend will admit, in fairness to me, that during my five years of office I have been singularly free from blunders of that kind'.[721]

Initially, the Reid party professed confidence he could withstand any no confidence vote. The ousted Barton had around ten personal adherents; why would they wish to make Lyne premier? But Barton's adherents judged Reid's premiership a more reckonable threat to the 'noblest son' than Lyne's. Reid's hunt for Bartonite support yielded only the soiled Meagher. The declaration of Labor for Lyne as premier underlined Reid's ruin. On Tuesday 29 August 1899 Lyne foreshadowed moving a motion of no confidence in Reid the next day. With the Assembly due to gather at 4.00 pm, Reid, in desperation or effrontery, presented himself at 2.45 pm at Government House. 'Would I please', Beauchamp later recalled Reid requesting, 'sign a document in his pocket which would prorogue the House?' Reid took the Governor's refusal 'very well'.

The debate over the no confidence motion was a hunt where prey could devise no escape. For five days parliamentary kangaroo dogs trailed their quarry; and their target, reinvigorated by its extremity, lacerated with freezing contempt. But what Reid called 'the party of revenge' – 'headed by the hon. gentleman at the head of the legitimate Opposition [Lyne], and the hon. member for Wellington, at the head of the Red Indian Brigade' [Haynes] – had the greater strength.[722] Three hundred persons applied to fill the narrow public gallery for the final vote. A crush of spectators filled the halls, lobbies and galleries to absorb the climax. A few minutes after midnight on Friday 8 September 1899 the chamber divided, the motion of no confidence succeeded, 75 to 41; the most fateful premiership of NSW – and Australia – was extinguished.

In the ten weeks following Reid's demise, four more Federationist governments fell. In Tasmania, on 6 October, Stafford Bird, 'one of the few public men to resolutely to oppose Federation',[723] moved a motion of no confidence in Premier Braddon, and won 18 votes to 17. On 22 November a revolt of seven MPs from Queensland's south-east corner, including four anti-Federationists,[724] forced the removal of Dickson. In South Australia on 28 November a Federation sceptic successfully sponsored a no confidence motion in Kingston, winning, 26 to 25.[725] Finally, in Victoria, on 30 November, Turner was defeated, 47 to 36, by a challenge led by the staunch anti-Billite Allan McLean, and supported by Higgins. In the space of eight days, three of the premiers of the 'secret' conference of 1899 had lost office; and in the space of three months, five of the six had.

Unsurprisingly, one politician of the period declared Federation was 'the downfall of nearly all the ministries in the States'.[726] But the causation is indirect. None of the motions that felled these premiers concerned Federation – that question had been settled. Some prominent Federationist MPs supported these motions. In SA, Tasmania and Queensland the unseated premiers were succeeded by Federationists. For all that, four of the five motions were advanced by anti-Federationists or anti-Billites (NSW, Victoria, SA, Tasmania). In riding Federation as an issue, Federationists won office as long as Federation was the issue; but in doing so they damaged their 'normal' sources of support; and when it was no longer an issue, found their support shrunken and insufficient. Federation burnt up part of the political capital of all parties, save Labor.

The Bill in London

With the successful passage of Addresses to the Queen, the fate of the Constitution shifted to London where, in April and May 1900, the Bill's patrons were to wrangle over its clauses with the Secretary of State for the Colonies, Joseph Chamberlain.

The telling of this encounter has been strongly coloured by Deakin's self-serving *Federal Story*. In his account, three 'very Sir Galahads' – Deakin, Kingston and Barton – cross the seas on a quest for the Constitution – and engage in a contest of wit and endurance with the wily pasha of St James Park. Successfully, of course, and the trio return home with the 'sacred lamp' unprofaned.

The truth is there was no contest in London between Australian patriots and English imperialists, but a battle which pitched parts of Australia against each other. The truth is there was no victory of the Federationist three over Chamberlain, but a face-saving compromise. The truth is that the Federationist three and Chamberlain were agreed on the desirable course of action; to get the Bill through the Imperial Parliament without delay, and with WA included. Instead of demonstrating a simple and dignified resolution in the face of the imperial power, the three manifested imposition, arrogation, and a virtual usurpation of the prerogatives of the Australian governments on whose behalf they had been deputed to act.

An account of 'London' begins with a question: why did the larger states trouble to dispatch anyone to London?[727] The Bill doubtless required explication, and negotiation on detail, but that could be managed by the colonies' agents-general in London, just as Tasmania used its agent-general, Philip Fysh. These agents-general comprised senior and experienced politicians, including a former premier (Cockburn), a former acting premier (Horace Tozer), Barton's most senior loyalist (Copeland), and, for Victoria, Sir Andrew Clarke, who did, in fact, complete the management of the Bill after Deakin's departure for Australia.[728]

The case of Barton, Deakin and Kingston to be 'entitled' to be Federal emissaries was not formidable. By the plain (and crude) criterion of precedence, they did not signify; two of them were without a seat in parliament, and none held executive office. Weighing in the other direction, Barton, Deakin, and Kingston had won election to the Convention. But so had 37 others.[729] It is true that Kingston (very narrowly) and Barton (clearly) had topped their colony's Convention poll; but in that election Deakin received fewer votes than Quick, or Turner, who in Victoria received a significantly higher percentage of the vote than Barton did in NSW. Barton had been Leader of the Convention, but the Bill considered in London was not that produced by the Convention. Its draft had been significantly amended in the premiers' conference of 1899, which had been chaired by Turner, and which none of the three had attended. Above all, Barton lacked the greatest legitimation of any such commission: having been so commissioned by parliament. In 1853 the NSW Legislative Council had, in a vote of 23 to 2, dispatched James Macarthur and W. C. Wentworth to London to 'combat' objections by British legislators to the proposed NSW constitution.[730] Parliament gave no approval for Barton's journey in 1900; it was the gift of Lyne. The motive for this gift was presumably political: Barton's exit from the Assembly would certainly convenience Lyne. Lyne's vanquished rival might have made the London commission a condition of his stepping down with grace from Leadership of the Opposition in September 1899.[731]

The motives of the three in travelling to London are obvious enough. The gratification of walking through the pages of history in the capital of the world's greatest empire needs no elaboration. Less salient is the financial incentive. In Deakin's judgement, one of Barton's motives was the expectation of 'a handsome retaining fee'.[732] Barton did receive such a fee, or 'allowance', of £1 000, as did Kingston and Deakin.

What needs emphasis is the motive of Joseph Chamberlain and the Salisbury government in so attentively hosting the visit of these three. Any facilitation of the Bill would be a subordinate motive: they were not blind to the active presence of the agents-general in London. Chamberlain's leading motive was to overwhelm with flattering attention the persons they believed, and wished, would be the pre-eminent ruling figures of the new Commonwealth. Thus the intense round of luncheons, banquets and 'innumerable dinner invitations'; the honorary doctorates from Oxford and Cambridge; the extended hospitality of dowagers, marquises and lords; the hosted visits to Warwick and Windsor Castles. It was the Victorian equivalent of the Duchess of Kent dancing the foxtrot with Kwame Nkrumah during Ghana's independence celebrations. The people of the Commonwealth of

Australia whom the Colonial Office could and would deal with would be duchessed.

The Colonial Office and the trio had every reason to anticipate a harmonious *rencontre*. Had not the Colonial Conference of 1897 resolved to 'gather under a federal union' all colonies of the Empire which were geographically contiguous?[733] Had not Chamberlain 'often declared [Australian Federation and South African Union] the pre-condition of Imperial Federation'?[734] Chamberlain's biographer records 'from the day he took charge of the department he hoped to see the movement for Australian unity crowned with success during his term of office'.[735] The introduction of the Bill into the House of Commons on 14 May 1900 'was one of high days of all his career'.[736]

Neither would there be a lack of mutual understanding between Chamberlain and the most reckonable of the three heralds, Alfred Deakin; the two were almost counterparts. Religiously heterodox bourgeoisie from provincial towns; the same early anti-Irish political position; the same passage from free trade to protection; the same dissenter/non-conformist commitment to 'free, compulsory and secular' education; the same attraction to Imperial Federation.[737] Chamberlain 'did not care a straw for office or position', but ultimately 'cared for power': precisely Deakin's outlook.[738] This disregard for the 'dignified' elements of politics might be one reason why both would, in their careers, hear the cry of 'Judas!' being shrieked at them from the chamber.

Despite the common aims and political style of Deakin and Chamberlain, the delegates and the Colonial Secretary came to an impasse. The standoff was over the rights to appeal judgements of the High Court to the Judicial Committee of the Privy Council. Chamberlain wished to revise the Bill to give more space to such appeals, while the delegates wished to leave them restricted. The ambit claims and bluffs of the protagonists cast a haze over their actual dispositions. But to all appearances, there was an elasticity in Chamberlain's stance,[739] and a rigidity in the delegates', which was manifested in a phrase the press used to describe their position: 'the bill, the whole bill and nothing but the bill'.

The obduracy of the three might be praised as a fidelity to the

Bill, but it was inconsistent with its undergirding premises. To insist on the 'bill, the whole bill, and nothing but the bill' reduced the Imperial Parliament to a notary, 'merely to register the decree of an Australian referendum'.[740] This would amount to a repudiation of Australia's colonial status – and however gratifying that would be to an Australian nationalist, Federationists never repudiated the essential subordination of Australia. Neither was any such repudiation desired, aimed at, or even pretended to by Federationists. And if there was to be such repudiation, it would presumably be declared in Australia before manifested in action in London. And if it was so declared in Australia, why go to London at all?

The roots of the delegates' obduracy were psychological.

It is hard to conceive of a warrior-chieftain like Kingston actually negotiating, as distinct from palavering with a confederate, hurling terms at a supplicant foe, or, for that matter, withdrawing in the face of a superior force. By contrast, Deakin had acted as negotiator, deal-cutter and king-maker throughout his career. But the context of the occasion in London bore a latent presumption that was disabling of this facility: a superiority-inferiority relationship between himself, the backbencher, and Joseph Chamberlain, the Secretary of State for Colonies. And this presumption was unendurable to Deakin. He was a man who had, in 1887, publicly and successfully told off a prime minister of Great Britain, at least in his own self-satisfied recollection. In 1900 the trauma of a seemingly inevitable insinuation of subordination froze Deakin into an unbending posture. So 'London' was not about appeals from the High Court to the Privy Council at all; it was about obliterating any shadow of such an insinuation.

This insinuation would not be traumatising to Barton. But the article of the dispute – legal appeals to the Privy Council – was the occasion of Barton's disappointment, and even humiliation, in 1886, when his own appeal to the judicial subcommittee of the Council – in the hope of confirming the validity of one of his rulings as Speaker of the NSW Assembly – was rejected. In 1890 Barton lost another appeal to the Privy Council – this time concerning his attempt to overturn a NSW Court of Appeal's decision against himself and in favour of the Bank of New South Wales, leaving him with nothing but the burden of the Bank's costs of a five-year legal battle.⁷⁴¹ This personal history would not nurture a sympathetic predisposition towards the Privy Council; the disappointments of 1886 and 1890 were plausibly some of the seeds of his Federationism, and his concern to displace the Council by a High Court.

Neither was the obduracy of delegates a matter of constancy to the instructions of those who delegated them. There were no instructions to speak of. In any case, the delegates saw their own wishes as superior to the wishes of the premiers. Deakin, shortly after the events, described the three as 'representatives', rather than 'delegates'; the three exhorted the premiers to 'submit' (Deakin's word) their proposals to Deakin before putting them to Chamberlain. The trio was surely behind Chamberlain's telegram of 5 April 1900 asking the premiers to empower the delegates to accept amendments; in other words, to transform them from delegates into plenipotentiaries. Deakin freely records in his memoir that Lyne 'openly condemned them for arrogance'.⁷⁴²

The obduracy of delegates was not grounded in some consensus dispensation of Australia in favour of a 'the bill and nothing but the bill'. Commercial interests were strongly in favour of preserving appeals to the Privy Council. Deakin would dismiss these as 'people of wealth'. But it was the NSW Labor leader, James McGowen, who, in the middle of the controversy, declared:

> I thoroughly believe in the full power of appeal to the Privy Council being retained. ... The Privy Council is a splendid Court, and it costs us nothing to run. ... I know of cases where poor men have been parties in suits taken to the Privy Council, and although they were not represented at the beginning of appeals owing to a lack of means, the Privy Council has awarded them verdicts because they have had right on their sides.⁷⁴³

Joining McGowen on the 'right' of the labour movement was Rosa on 'the left'.⁷⁴⁴ The legal profession was divided. The Chief Justices of NSW, Victoria, Queensland, SA, WA and Tasmania supported appeals to the Privy Council.⁷⁴⁵ Had not the *Judicial Committee Amendment Act 1895 (UK)* placed five of the ten Chief Justices of the 'dominion' colonies on the Privy Council's judiciary committee? And yet the barristers who led the Federation movement tended to favour the truncation of appeals. So in baulking at that truncation, Chamberlain had exposed a deep fracture of opinion in Australia. The premiers of Queensland, Western Australia, and Tasmania were in favour of revising the Bill to accommodate appeals.[746] But the premier of SA was vehemently against such revision, while the premiers of Victoria and NSW were privately supportive, but publicly against.[747] The Federationist movement was badly split on the issue, as it was in the Convention; but with the difference that some Federationists – Carruthers, Walker – now found themselves in the same cause as anti-Federationists – Dibbs and MacLaurin.

There could, then, be no victory, or loss, for 'Australia' or Federationists in this encounter, only a victory of one section of Australian opinion over another section of Australian opinion. At best, a compromise.[748]

The compromise which dissolved the impasse was formulated by Griffith, Chief Justice of Queensland, who enjoyed Chamberlain's obvious and public confidence, and who, privately, damned the behaviour of Barton and Kingston as 'monstrous'.[749] Griffith reformulated the clause at issue in a manner that increased the discretionary power of the High Court, and thereby appeased all, or at least gave hope to all, or at least saved face for all.[750] Here is an irony: in Brisbane was devised what the emissaries in London could not. In the NSW Assembly, a future prime minister, Chris Watson, stressed the futility of the trio's venture:

> *I believe that had no delegates gone at all precisely the same result would have been arrived at by communicating with the various governments of Australia. This much is noticeable: that for the compromise which is being arrived at, and which, I think, is a reasonable one, the credit is given to ... Sir Samuel Griffith and not Mr. Barton. Not to any of the delegates who went to London.* [751]

Barton's former rival for the seat of Randwick, David Storey, pronounced in the Assembly,

> *The proper way to have dealt with that great question would*

> have been for the colonial governments to have cabled direct instructions to their agents-general … . Had that been done, it would have saved this colony the humiliation of what has been going on in London … .[752]

What 'humiliation' was Storey referring to? To a ludicrous and bathetic cadenza to the trio's expedition. Barton had been more than amply financed for his excursion to London. His allowance of £1 000 was the same as that allowed Deakin, half of which the sober Deakin restored to the public purse upon his return. In addition, Barton was paid his 'saloon class' (that is, first class) passage, with that of Mrs Barton, amounting to £125. To appreciate the size of these sums, values need to be expressed in current terms. The £125 is equivalent to not quite $20 000 worth of goods and services in 2020, and £1 000 equivalent to about $157 000. Even these still underestimate the significance of this 'fee'. In 1901 the average annual earnings of a government employee was a little under £60 per annum.[753] Thus Barton was paid for ten weeks' occupation what the average government sector worker would earn in 19 years.

Remarkably, in spite of its liberality, Barton managed to exhaust his allowance while still in London. He consequently was 'stranded' there, as Lyne put it, and sought another £500. One may marvel at how, in the space of 10 weeks, he could spend the equivalent of $157 000. One paper slyly suggested that Mrs Barton's wardrobe might be part of the answer; she had been arresting Sydney society in 'electric blue' and the like for decades, but she was now to be presented to the Queen. More plausibly, the allowance might have been drained, not by expenses, but by the demands of his creditors.[754] Perhaps it might not have been exhausted at all if Barton had departed England once the House of Commons had confirmed its confidence in the Griffith compromise, on 24 May. But six weeks after the announcement of the agreement he was still lingering, enjoying the hospitality of his patrons. Not until after 7 July did he board ship for the voyage home, from Marseille.

Barton returned home not much financially poorer, and certainly politically richer, bearing an invisible gift from the Colonial Office; the massive prestige of being treated by Britain's ruling circles as the worthy, presumptive head of the new Commonwealth. Thus was Australian democracy deformed by Federation in the context of empire.

Tommy Cornstalk goes to war

While the clause regarding appeals to the Privy Council was being fought over in England, there suddenly broke some wildly happy news: the siege by Boer forces of a beleaguered British contingent at Mafeking had been lifted. Church bells began to

Bushmen's Contingent farewelled to South Africa, Melbourne

peal; bonfires were lit; torchbearers paraded; a coal hulk set aflame, and William McGonagall composed a commemorative verse. Kingston declared that Australia 'was prepared to spend its last penny and last man in maintaining' the British Empire.[755]

Across the other side of the world, a British visitor to Australia dryly noted 'a display of "mafficking"' even more excessive than in the mother country'.[756] At the 'relief of Mafeking' there brimmed over in Australia an excitement that had been bubbling furiously since her several governments had decided, late in 1899, to contribute military forces to the Boer War. The British visitor:

> *Men of all ranks and occupations vied with each other for the distinction of being selected for active service. ... The soldiers found themselves the object almost of fetish worship. Finally, the 'send-off' was made an opportunity for the wildest demonstrations, in which young and old alike gave themselves up to an unrestrained excitement.*[757]

Here is a distinct difficulty for any nationalist interpretation of the Federation episode: how is it that the Australian public raced to the war just as it was flying to Federation? Nationalism in a colony is not consonant with the colony's ardent embrace of the cause of the imperial power. But as far as the war's many Federationist supporters were concerned, it was a matter of upholding Britain's imperial due. This would be a war by the British Empire, for the British Empire.[758] 'The Empire right or wrong' declared Barton.[759] 'Let it be treason', thundered Walter Murdoch, Deakin's first biographer, 'to even hint' at the Empire's dismemberment. In the same January 1901 issue of *United Australia* he sang, 'Because, on the bones of the English the English Flag is stayed'. And William Watt, the favourite of the ANA – the redoubt of apparently 'national' Federationists – recited to his fellow parliamentarians, 'The Bushman's Question':

> *Why am I going to War?*
> *Son, ... You in this bright daughter-state of England born and bred,*
> *Are kin with the noble Englishmen of yore.*
> *Fitzwalter, Drake and Hampden are but elder brethren dead,*
> *And that is why you are going to War.*

The simultaneous embrace of the Boer War and Federation is easily explained if both crusades are interpreted as species of pan-Britainism. Both the War and Federation amounted to a rallying of Greater Britons; both were culminating expressions of a sense of British commonality. Did not Parkes invoke the Crimson Thread as the foundation of Federation? Did not Barton in parliamentary debate declare that, 'if any justification was needed', it was that the Britons in the Transvaal are of 'the same blood'? Put simply, Australian Federationists, in this thesis, were also Imperial Federationists.[760] Accordingly, centres of Federal sentiment in Australia seem not to have been surpassed by any others in triumphing over British success in the War. 'Perhaps the most glorious evening in Charters Towers's history was Mafeking night'.[761] In Corowa, 'the fire bell, the church bell and everything else that sounded like a bell was continuously rung.'[762] In Ballarat, 'vying with all comers to be the most loyal city in the Empire',[763] the 'continuous wet weather could not damp the ardour of the rejoicing citizens'.[764] The most Federationist state also erected 58 percent of Australia's Boer War memorials. Victoria's most conspicuous anti-Billite was her most conspicuous opponent of the War, Higgins, who lost his seat in Victoria's parliament because of his opposition. The most determined adversaries of NSW involvement in the War (Haynes, Hughes, Holman), were also the most determined adversaries of Federation. It can never be known, but one may wonder if Byrnes, the anti-Billite premier of Queensland, would have embraced the War – especially after his unfortunate spat with Chamberlain during the Diamond Jubilee.[765] By contrast, Dickson, his Federationist successor as Premier of Queensland, was the first of all the premiers to offer forces.

The irony about the correlation between War and Federation is that it corroded the most palpable justification for Federation; defence. For it was the pre-federalised forces of Australia that creditably acquitted the challenge of Australia's first war; it was state military units which contributed 80 percent of Australian forces in the Boer War, suffered all of the combat deaths, and won all of the decorations.[766] This irony is doubled in the case of one state, where the Boer War possibly made Federation still easier.

Western Australia at the gates of the Commonwealth

In Perth the news of the Relief of Mafeking was received about 10 am on 19 May 1900.

> Men, women, and children seemed to spring from nowhere and anywhere. ... Government offices were discharged of their living contents in a few moments. Above the din of bells and whistles arose the excited cries and applause from several thousand throats, varied with the singing of 'God Save the Queen', 'Rule Britannia', 'The Soldiers of the Queen', and other patriotic songs ... Government House grounds, which were thrown open to the public, were ablaze with illuminations, and every window of the vice-regal residence was lighted up. ... Dozens of fire balloons soared aloft, their aerial movements being watched by a perfect sea of upturned faces. ... Shortly before 10 o'clock, the Mayor and councillors, with the Headquarters Band, headed an immense procession to Government House, ... and so excited had the crowd become by this time, that a large portion of them resolved themselves into something that approached a disorganised, disorderly rabble ... the.... police vainly endeavoured to resist the encroachments of the crowd ..., and His Excellency was nearly pushed off the chair several times.[767]

The doors were locked, and His Excellency cautioned the crowd, 'They must not forget they were Englishmen'. Upon the doors being later re-opened, it was 'found that the Premier (Sir John Forrest) had been seeking admission, but without success'.[768] Here lies something of a parable of Forrest and Federation.

The Bill being debated in London announced in its first sentence, 'the people of New South Wales, Victoria, South Australia, Queensland, and Tasmania, humbly relying on the blessing of Almighty God, have agreed to unite in one indissoluble Federal Commonwealth'. Western Australia was omitted, and seemed to face a closing door. And by her own action, or lack of it.

Forrest, for his part, was a Federationist. He had publicly advocated Federation even before Parkes's Tenterfield speech.[769]

He had led WA's delegation to the Convention; had attended its proceedings more assiduously than the oddly truant Federationist zealots in WA's delegation; and had voted for what the Convention approved more frequently than, say, Deakin. He had wrung out of the Convention section 95, which would phase out WA's tariffs over five years instead of abolishing them immediately. But, for all such sops, the majority of Forrest's ministry was emphatically and publicly opposed to the Bill which the Convention produced. So were six of WA's ten delegates to the Convention.[770] Only two of his 30 followers in the Assembly, said Forrest, supported the Bill.

Forrest would wait for something more agreeable to the ministry, and parliament, to materialise. And he did so with the support of the parliament. The leadership of the Opposition – George Leake and Walter James – who were vehement in supporting the Bill, were badly defeated in the Legislative Assembly, 24 votes to 10, when they attempted to dislodge Forrest as premier, in the wake of the Yes victory in NSW.

But Forrest's waiting game did not prove fruitful. 'Federal leaders in other colonies were bombarded with telegrams and letters from Leake and James imploring them not to make any concessions to Forrest or even enter into discussion with them on the subject'.[771] Deakin was glad to acquiesce. 'Forrest has appealed again to the eastern colonies', Deakin advised James, 'and has received an absolute refusal to treat with him so that the situation you desired has been created'.[772] And Forrest could not simply outlast Deakin. The goldfields were chafing for Federation.

Exhausted of manoeuvres, and caught between the pressure for action and the pressure for inaction, Forrest sponsored a compromise: the Bill was to be accepted *in toto,* save for WA Senators to be elected, as in Queensland, by region rather than on a state-wide vote; a commitment in the Bill to the transcontinental railway; WA's tariff to be fully preserved for five years; and WA to set its own railway charges for five years. To Federationists the concessions were abhorrent. Neither were Federationists willing to pitch to voters both the Convention Bill and this amended version. On 30 November 1899, a majority of Billites and Anti-Billites on the Council rejected putting to referendum both the

Convention Bill and the amended Bill.[773] Forrest then sought to have a modification implemented in London. Despite the efforts of Leake with politicians east, 'Forrest ... knew from his private correspondence with them that several of the Premiers would agree to the Western Australian amendment if Chamberlain asked them to do so ...'.[774] But Deakin en route to London had conferred with Federationists in Albany – then the constituency of Leake – and absorbed (or already concurred with) their resolutions, and he advised Chamberlain to tell WA there would be no revision. Thus Chamberlain, by a telegram of 27 April, 'pointed out the advantages of Federation' to Forrest, reminding him that section 95 – the half a loaf on tariffs which Forrest had fought hard for – would be lost if Western Australia did not join as 'an Original State'. At this 'instigation' of the Colonial Secretary, Forrest summoned parliament to enact a referendum, tellingly entitled, 'An Act to make provision for the Acceptance and Enactment of the Federal Constitution of Australia'. So it was that WA's attempt to obtain better terms expired in the Colonial Office, at the urging of Deakin and his confreres.

'Many things in the scheme', declared Forrest publicly of the Constitution, 'had been carried out, as it were, at the point of the bayonet'.[775] Not at its point literally. But what is salient in this whole affair is the adamancy of Federationists to have their own way; at the cost not only to the ideals of unity, but regardless of the offence they gave to constitutional and personal propriety. Thus James and Leake were quite happy to deal in bad faith, even with those who followed them in good faith, such as the goldfields miners in the matter of 'Separation'.

The goldfields' old campaign for separation was steered into a demand for a new colony, 'Auralia', which would join the Commonwealth. On St Patrick's Day 1900, a petition (secretly) drafted by Glynn,[776] with 28 000 signatures, ceremoniously began its journey to London in quest of that end. Federationists at large were hostile to granting this wish: if it came to pass, the rest of WA would surely be lost to the Commonwealth. But they seemed confident separation would not come to pass in the wake of a defeat of the Bill; and additionally confident that their adversaries in WA would worry it might. So separation was a useful, if bogus, threat, to sponsor. Thus James told Barton that separation was a legal impossibility, but 'because our object would be obtained' if Federationists 'declared themselves' for it, Barton should 'beat up the separation movement'.[777] Similarly, Leake described separation as a 'bogey' to Barton, but saw a benefit in having the 'bogey' ventilated, and pressed Barton to do so. Chamberlain displayed a similar bad faith. He had no sympa-

The WA goldfields' Separation for Federation petition unfurled. W. R. Burton (top right) was dismissed as Assistant Registrar for Kalgoorlie on account of ballot irregularities in the 1900 referendum

thy for separation. But when WA's agent-general requested Chamberlain to clarify his position, the Colonial Secretary met the request with what was meant to be taken as an ominous evasion.[778]

The usefulness of separation was also deemed worth constitutional grossness. Leake took the extraordinary step of proposing to Deakin that the Governor of Victoria persuade the Governor of WA – the dubious Sir Gerard Smith, whom the Colonial Office would very soon force into resignation[779] – to dismiss Forrest; the premier of an elected government, with 29 of 44 seats in the Assembly, and a majority in the Council. This would have been a dismissal that would put all other dismissals in the following century in the shade.

That Federationists deemed these crude offences at propriety worth their price begs the question: why did Federationists begrudge any concessions however slight?[780] Why refuse five years of complete tariff preservation, when the Constitution already conceded to WA partial preservation for five years?[781] Why begrudge exempting WA from the Inter-State Commission; when WA railway pricing could hardly be of concern to the east? Why begrudge granting geographical Senate constituencies to WA, when the Constitution already permitted them in Queensland? Indeed, why would a *Western Australian* resent these? Why were Western Australia's Federationists so fervid for their state not to receive any concessions?

Presumably Leake envisioned himself as the premier who would see in Federation. To that end, Forrest must be allowed no victory, and should be framed as a failure. For Deakin's part, his inflexibility was rooted in his characteristic quest for mastery. WA was different from Queensland: Dickson had done as he was bidden. Forrest had not. Now he must stoop.[782] This quest for mastery moved Deakin to persuade Chamberlain to advise Forrest that WA would receive no concessions: Forrest must take it or leave it.[783] But why did Forrest 'take it'? One answer is evident: Forrest wanted Federation, and would not dump the Bill on account of imperfections. But, more importantly, he could not dump it.

Federationists were a formidable force in WA. They were so on account of an unlikely compact of two groups. On the one side, youngish, well-born, town professionals; thus Leake and James, both lawyers, both members for Perth localities, and 40 and 33 years of age, respectively, at the Convention. On other side were the densely populated and restive goldfields. In normal politics there would be little overlap, but in 1900 there would be a *mariage de convenance;* a brittle one, as events were quickly to prove after Federation, but ardent for the moment. There came, additionally, invigorating financial support from the east. Thus Deakin's plain entreaty to his comrades in struggle in the west: 'Tell me also what sum you would require from us to enable you to carry on the campaign efficiently but of course as economically as possible'[784]. But Deakin's financial tonics would not have made any noticeable difference. WA's vote in favour of Federation was almost 70 percent.

In the gold fields a dazing 95 percent voted Yes.

As in NSW, a haze of dubiety enfolds the exact dimensions of the vote. As in NSW, expedients ostensibly intended to enlarge participation had occasioned multiple voting and roll-packing. The root of this misconduct was the introduction of the 'voter's certificate' for the referendum. Voters not on the roll could apply to a (casually recruited) 'assistant registrar' for a certificate that would entitle them to vote. No proof of the applicant's eligibility was asked for, beyond their own affirmation. In addition, rolls for certificates were only kept for a given polling booth; permitting multiple certificates for the same person to be issued. Nothing stopped an assistant registrar from signing off on a stack of applications, and giving them to the Federal League activist to complete, legitimately or illegitimately. Nothing stopped an assistant registrar from filling out applications with details of wholly fictitious persons.

Table 12.1: The results of the WA referendum

		Majority	Yes	No	Total	Abstentions	Enrolment
		25 109	44 800	19 691	64 491	24 563	89 592
percent	of vote	38.9	69.5	30.5	100	38.5	138.9
	of roll	28.0	50.0	22.00	72	27.4	100
	of adults	20.0	39.2	17.2	56.4	21.5	78.3

Source: Rhodes (2002).

There is circumstantial as well as direct evidence for the exploitation of these frailties in process. The number of certificates issued for several seats are in outlandishly round numbers,[785] betokening an anarchy in their issue. That the electoral roll contracted by 20 percent (from 89 138 to 70 021) in the nine months from the referendum to the first Federal election suggests a good number of aerial enrolments. The member for North East Coolgardie, aligned with the Opposition, and the member for Yilgarn, aligned with the Ministry, charged extensive voting abuses.[786] One assistant registrar in Kalgoorlie – who was a member of the executive of the Separation for Federation League – could offer no defence regarding the accusations against him, and was dismissed. [787]

But ballot fraud could hardly have altered the result in WA.[788] The majority of Yes over No was massive, 25 000, or about 28 percent of the total vote. The goldfields' enrolment amounted to over 30 000: even if 20 percent of the goldfields' vote was fraudulent, only a moderate dent on the majority would be made.

The failing in accenting the massive Yes majority lies not in any lack of its essential authenticity, but in that the majority obscures that WA was badly split. 18 of her 44 Assembly seats voted No. 66.5 percent of votes in those electorates were cast for No.[789] The 24 seats which could be aggregated to yield a bare No majority, amounted to everything south of Geraldton and west of Albany, save the centre of Perth and Albany.[790] This division reflects the fact that the gold discoveries had introduced into WA a society acutely anomalous to the remainder.

The greater question is whether the goldfields should have had any say in the fate of WA as a whole. The right to vote on constitutional issues, as distinct from ordinary law, surely has a price greater than mere residence; and that price is allegiance. The right to vote on ordinary law, by contrast, is no more than a strengthening of the important but mundane protection-obedience exchange; whereby the government demands of a subject their obedience in return for their protection, and the subject demands the protection of the government in return for their obedience. Constitution-making is a much deeper transaction, based on what might be called an allegiance-citizenship exchange; whereby allegiance is the price of the rights of citizenship, above all the right to participate in constitutional formation. The government requires allegiance in return for that right to participate, and the citizen demands the right to participate in return for their allegiance. It is palpable that no miners had anything approaching the devotion, faithfulness or loyalty to WA which might come under the head of 'allegiance'. To these visitors, WA, like Victoria half a century before, was simply the object of their venal hopes, to be discarded whenever it proved disappointing.[791] In this logic, the only constitutional development in which they would be entitled to participate in would be their own secession.

But the miners who poured into the goldfields during the previous six years did have the right to determine constitutional issues. And WA can ponder the constitutional legacy of the miners of 1900, no more than 6 923 in number, and their peculiar 'social ecology': simultaneously individualistic and collectivist; credulous and crafty; demanding and expectant; an ecology that has produced tumult throughout Australian history.

The Hopetoun incident

With Western Australia now gathered in, all that remained was to anticipate the pleasures.

With the help of coded telegrams and covert consultations masked by Federation celebrations, Deakin and Barton busied themselves in November with selecting the first ministry, and publicising it (anonymously). Since no parliament or Commonwealth existed, their choices of ministers were highly 'previous'.[792] But they had every cause for confidence that events would confirm their decisions. Was not Kingston putting it about that Chamberlain had personally told him, 'Barton would be prime minister'?[793] Had not Barton's 'friend at Downing St', John Anderson – the principal Clerk of the Colonial Office, and secretary of the colonial conferences – clearly intimated a preference for Barton as prime minister? Had not Anderson, extraordinarily, supplied Barton with the draft Instructions of the first Governor-General?[794] And was not the man who, as Governor-General, would actually make the choice of prime minister an additional grounds for confidence? The seventh Earl of Hopetoun's conduct as Governor in Victoria in 1889 had been reassuring. And between Barton and Hopetoun there had sprouted a birds of a feather friendship. Those personal attributes of Hopetoun which so disturbed his term in office – the emotionality in speech; the grandiosity of life style; the towering pride, so oddly conjoined with a good natured condescension – these were Barton's, magnified. Did not Hopetoun describe Barton as 'one of the family'?[795]

But a few days before Proclamation, Deakin's designs re-

William Lyne (right) conferring with a Victorian legislator

ceived a ghastly jolt from the man in whom they placed so much hope: Hopetoun had invited the despised Lyne, premier of NSW, to form the first ministry of the new Commonwealth. Deakin grieved to Barton, 'Even our defeat by a neck in NSW in 1898 was not as bad as this'.[796] In shock and dismay, Deakin made frantic efforts to organise a boycott of Lyne by the prominent Federationists.[797] Not all co-operated, but these were sternly dealt with.[798] And with Syme's support finally secured, Lyne was left with refusals of almost all to serve him. With good grace, Lyne conceded to the Governor-General, and the world at large, that he was unable to form a cabinet, and Barton was commissioned as prime minister early on Christmas Day 1900.[799]

The affair of Barton's appointment is known as the Hopetoun Blunder. 'Blunder' is the brand that Deakin affixed to it in *The Federal Story*. There was no blunder. Or, if there was, it was Hopetoun's yielding to the impositions of Deakin and his confreres.

The key point about the 'Hopetoun Incident' is that prior to the Federal election no one had a good claim on the executive positions that Hopetoun sought to fill. The only good claim on any executive position is to have the confidence of the House of Representatives. But until the Commonwealth's first election, on 29-30 March 1901, there was no House of Representatives to have, or not have, the confidence of. In the absence of a good claim, resort might be made to figures who retained the confidence of state parliaments. Barton was not a member of a parliament.[800] O'Connor was not one either, and, in fact, had never been elected to one. Deakin and Kingston were backbenchers. Turner was, since November 1900, premier of Victoria once again, the second largest state. Lyne was premier of the largest.

But, in the absence of any good claim, the best proceeding would be not to award a ministry to any claimant until after the inaugural election. This was how the transition to self-government was managed in Western Australia in 1890. The governor declined to appoint any ministers until after the election of the first parliament: 'how … can I possibly select any Ministry until the country has done its part, and furnished me with a Parliament from which to make my selection?'.[801] And if it was felt that executive dispatch required a minister, entrust it to a simple custodian of the office, a political neuter, such as the longest serving clerk of the parliaments, a senior public servant, the 'father' of the six state houses, or a judge. They would bear a title indicating they were not a prime minister in the ordinary sense; they would be 'Inaugural Minister' or, even better, 'Minister of All Portfolios', for they would be the sole minister. There was no call for all the conjuring up on 1 January 1901 of five costume jewellery ministries (a Minister of Defence without an army, a Postmaster-General without a post office): the one and only required duty of the ministry was the issue of writs for the general election.

It is no accident that provisions for a neutered 'Inaugural Minister' did not appear in the Constitution, despite the protest of Paddy Glynn at the illegitimacy of a prime minister being appointed without a parliament.[802] The precious diadem was not to be in anyone's hands but the circle around Barton. To him, above all, the emblems of office were the point of it all. Deakin did not care about them as such. But he was interested in power, and the bearing of emblems of office would be a useful advantage in the first election campaign. Deakin could, with understandable self-satisfaction, enter in his diary: '1900 – defeated Lyne and placed Barton in Power'.[803] Thus the 'greater self-government' of Federation.

A day to misremember

It is universally acknowledged that any *nouveau régime* is in want of a 'Day', to epitomise its advent, to honour its creation, and to serve as a legitimating myth. The Royal Assent to the Bill, on 9 July 1900, might have been the kernel of such a day. But, inimical to the purposes of myth, this news was met with complete indifference in Australia. The *Freeman's Journal* grumbled,

> As a matter of cold, hard fact, there was no celebration of any sort. A rise of a farthing a pound in the butter market would have stirred the great heart of this patriotic community much more violently than did the fateful message: 'Federation at last'.[804]

Instead, the great exclamation mark in the Federation story would be the Proclamation of the Commonwealth in Sydney on the very first day of the new century – and its festal sequence:

first a procession through the city, then the Proclamation in Centennial Park and, finally, a gala banquet in the Town Hall.

Historians have not omitted to notice some of the missed notes. Thus the squabble over who would conduct prayers to bless the new era of Australian unity; which ended in the Catholic clergy's boycott of the official proceeding. Or the state governors' boycott of the same ceremonies, produced by the dispute over the rights of state governors to communicate directly with the sovereign. Or Zeal storming out of the evening Banquet on not being seated at the 'top table'.[805] Or Griffith's speech there being quite drowned by the garrulity of the banqueters.[806]

Historians have, however, ignored Barton's appalling and petulant declaration from the Centennial Park dais to the gathered throng below: 'A strenuous appeal has been made to the 80 000 who voted against the Bill. I make no appeal'[807]. In victory, ignobility.

And historians have embraced the mythology of the huge crowd that supposedly attended the Proclamation. The most authoritative historian of Federation states that 'well over one hundred thousand people did come, perhaps two hundred thousand'.[808] La Nauze flatly states there was 'an audience of a quarter of a million'.[809] Patrick Glynn's biographer does not brook at a figure of half-a-million.[810] This embrace of claims of extraordinary attendance is in accord with an affirmative history of federation; a massive crowd legitimates the proceeding, and adds an air of drama to an otherwise prosy event.

So, what is the truth?

The answer begins by asking, which 'crowd' are we are interested in? There were many crowds in Sydney that first day of the new century.[811] The Lyne government had strained to make 1 January a 'gala occasion'. To foster a festive atmosphere it had packed the surrounding period with public holidays:

> Monday, December 31
>
> Tuesday, January 1
>
> Wednesday, January 2, a half
>
> Thursday, January 3
>
> Friday, January 4, a half
>
> Monday, January 7, a half

And Sydney would be a fête of entertainments. On the day to remember itself, one could visit the Zoo, the aquariums, the 'Cyclorama' [a 360 degree panorama], the 'biograph' [cinema], and circus performances 'both in the afternoon and evening', including 'Professor Godfrey's Wonderful Troupe of Trained Animals'. Harbour trips were advertised to raffish Manly, Watson's Bay, and Clontarf, as well as to the more hale Lane Cove River. At Moore Park the Indian Contingent could be surveyed for 6d; and the Sydney Cricket Ground promised 'sensational motor races', and a cycling carnival starring the English and Australian bicycling champions. At the Town Hall the Sydney Philharmonic performed Handel's *Messiah*, at the direction of the Lyne government. Matinees were provided at the Lyceum and Her Majesty's, with all the theatres open in the evening. And the Tattersall's Club held its annual race meeting at Randwick racecourse. By special arrangement, trams would run until 2.00 am.

Those crowding into Randwick racecourse were not honouring Federation. It was the crowd in Centennial Park whose size counts. The contemporary claims of that size are not to be taken literally; they are impressive round numbers, pulled out of the air by journalists, certainly unacquainted with the sight of a crowd in the region of 100 000 and more. The crowd which gathered to hear Barton in the climactic rally just prior to the 1898 referendum, in fervid expectation of victory, was estimated by Federationists to be between four and five thousand in size. An attendance of 14 000 at the Sydney Cricket Ground for a test match was deemed good; and on the afternoon of Saturday 14 December 1901, a supposedly 'world record' crowd of 36 000 to 38 000 gathered under 'perfect' weather for the test match against England.[812]

That these events, at the extreme edge of popularity, received an attendance so massively less than the hundreds of thousands claimed for Centennial Park subvert the credibility of the claim.[813] Neither is there objective evidence for later investigators to support, or controvert, the claim. No tickets were issued to the mass of spectators; no seating was provided them. There is not the information on public transport usage which is sometimes used to weigh crowd estimates.[814] There were no aerial photos to permit head counting; the extant photos are truncated, and untimed. The truth is nobody has any clear notion what the crowd in Centennial Park numbered, and good history would drop any reference to a number. A defender of received history might return that the actual number is unimportant: the crowd was unusually large, and evidently impressive to all observers, and that is sufficient to show that Sydney greeted Federation with animation. But the size of a crowd is not proof of animation; a crowd may be large and bored. Did a 'vast crowd' at Centennial Park display 'unbound enthusiasm'?[815] One well-expressed eye-witness recorded an 'entire absence of enthusiasm' at the Park:

> *the same stolid silence, held the vast majority of those present. A few pressmen now and again tried to raise a feeble cheer, and the shout of the knot of tired men made the general silence more obvious, more impressive. The school children ... tried manfully to act as a claquer, to stir the wooden mass to life, to enthusiasm. These heroic little hearts, ... lifted up their voices again and again, at the word of command, to cheer everybody, anybody— ... in vain. The sharp trebles of the children aroused no mass of sound from the great assemblage. A tired almost sulky silence still held the Park. At half-past 2 it was all over, and the crowd listlessly melted away.*[816]

The opening round

The final piece of the finale might be deemed the contest for the control of the Commonwealth's first parliament.

The campaign for the election of the first Commonwealth Parliament began on 17 January 1901, when Barton arrived in the Federationist stronghold of Maitland, flanked by his fellow ministers and protectionists – Deakin, Kingston and Lyne. Escorted to the Town Hall by a half-squadron of the NSW Lancers, Barton at 7.30 pm delivered his manifesto before a 'densely packed' auditorium. Any further influx of Kanakas would be prohibited; but no hint was given of the deportation that proved to be in store for this 'murderous hordes of savages', as the new Commonwealth Postmaster-General had described them.[817] The parliament would confer on the Commonwealth one power which Barton had opposed at the Convention – the compulsory arbitration of workplace disputes – but, he said, 'I trust the occasion will seldom arise for this to be brought into operation'.[818] The most particular position he raised – female suffrage – also revealed his discomfort with the currents he was sailing. Barton had previously publicly expressed his opposition to women having the vote. In now retreating from this former position he was not wholly yielding: women would have the vote, but not the right to stand for parliament. This mix of concession and intransigence was presumably not very gratifying to women supporters of female suffrage. Could this be one reason why women were excluded from attending the speech, and the town placarded during the day publicising this fact? Well could E. J. Ward of the National Council of Women demand to know in the next day's paper, why this gratuitous insult to women? Barton's policy launch may have been the last public meeting in Australia, of any significance, where women were excluded.

Barton also announced at Maitland his intention to establish a tariff, rationalised as an imperative of revenue raising. This rationalisation was at best misleading and at worst false.[819] But Barton had long thrown his lot in with protectionists, and Barton's only rival for power was the Free Trade and Liberal Association of Australia. The very thing that Parkes and Smith said would unburden the country of the tariff dispute – Federation – succeeded in splitting the country in two in the first months of Federation, with the leading newspapers carefully allocating each candidate either a 'P' or an 'F'. Did not Deakin say that Federation 'is a foremost party question'?[820]

If the candidates were divided over trade, one power of the new Commonwealth evoked complete agreement. While its powers over defence, banking, workplace relations, and age pensions aroused almost no interest, on how to use the immigration power candidates expressed a vigorous unison, be they Protectionist, Free Trade, Labor, Socialist Labor, or Democratic League.

> *Of course, I believe in a white Australia.*
> – **Pulsford**, Australian Free Trade and Liberal[821]
>
> *Chinese should be either poll-axed or poll-taxed in such a manner as would make the country too hot for them.*
> – **Ronald**, Labor[822]
>
> *He had fought for a white Australia all his political life .... The mischief in the past had been the absence of a Federal authority to crush out this evil. Let them prevent the contamination of our shores ...*
> – **Kingston**, protectionist[823]

Can even a single candidate be found who actually expressed a rejection of White Australia?

As the Reverend Ronald's exhortation makes plain, White Australia was not limited simply to forbidding immigration, but extended to compelling emigration. Point 5 of Barton's campaign association, styling themselves for the election the Australian Liberal Party, read:

> 5. A White Australia. The Kanaka must go, and with him the Chinaman. Such a consummation must not be brought about by revolutionary means, but gradually, though surely, we must get rid of them

On the campaign trail in Bundaberg, Barton sympathetically, if cautiously, received a delegation of 'white workers who to their humiliation were brought into contact with these aliens'. He was more confident when greeted there with banners reading, 'Australia's noblest son Edmund Barton has unfurled the flag of a white Australia'.[824]

For all the vehemence of candidates, none of the matters mooted for legislation seemed to capture much public interest, at least outside of NSW. In each state the turnout in the inaugural Commonwealth election was lower than every immediately following State election, and five of the six immediately preceding (Table 12.2).

The turnout in WA was spectacularly low. Having voted to enter the Commonwealth with such apparent zeal just nine months before, only a little more than one in three on the roll

Table 12.2: Turnout at Commonwealth 1901 election vs state elections circa 1901

(valid votes as percent of enrolment)

	NSW	Victoria	Queensland	SA	WA	Tasmania
Commonwealth 1901	67.1	58.5	60.0	39.8	36.6	45.6
First state election after Federation	72.0	65.3	77.0	63.0	45.1	57.3
Last state election before Federation	60.0	62.1	77.4	62.9	51.1	63.1

Notes: Contested single member seats are the basis of the calculation, excepting Tasmania, where multi-member seats are included. Invalid votes included in SA, WA and Tasmania.

Source: Hughes and Graham (1968).

Table 12.3: Voter turnout at the national level circa 1900

(valid votes as percent of enrolment)

Country	Year	Percent
Japan	1902	87.6
New Zealand	1905	83.2
Canada	1900	81.4
Belgium	1900	78.0
France	1902	76.1
Germany	1903	75.7
United Kingdom	1900	75.1
USA	1900	73.8
Netherlands	1901	63.9
Australia	1901	56.7
Italy	1900	56.5
Denmark	1901	55.7
Norway	1900	55.2
Switzerland	1902	53.6
Sweden	1902	47.1

Sources: Australia; Australian Politics and Elections Archive 1856-2018. https://elections.ewa.edu.au. UK; Rallings and Thrasher (2000). All others; Mackie and Rose (1991).

saw benefit in voting now. For Australia as a whole, for every five who voted, four on the roll did not trouble to; a low turnout by international standards, and much lower than New Zealand, UK, Canada or the USA (Table 12.3).

Some electors on the roll could not vote at all, for five House of Representatives cabinet ministers stood unopposed, including Barton. This would be the last electoral contest of his life. Barton thereby concluded his political career, never having once won a contested single-member electorate at a general election.[825] Such was the record of the first prime minister of a Commonwealth founded for greater self-government.

But most candidates did face contests in standing in the inaugural Parliament, and most seats won in rough proportion to the shares of the popular vote. In the House of Representatives protectionists won 31 of the 75 seats. So with the fitful support of 14 Labor members, Barton could form a government.

It was in the Senate that democratic failure occurred. It was elected on the same 'block voting' system as the Convention election, and the same 'largest takes all' distortion as occurred in the Convention election, most grossly in NSW. The Australian Free Trade and Liberal Association won 83 percent of senators with just 47 percent of the vote. A democratic failure, the Senate proved a refuge for democratic failures. The electorally unappetising O'Connor found a seat there in 1901, as did the perfectly unelectable Pulsford, and one complete stranger to parliamentary politics, J. T. Walker. A vast invalid vote further marred the Senate election in NSW; 17.5 percent of ballots were declared so, as voters struggled with the replacement of the 'striking in' system by the 'striking out' system. A less demanding voting system would surely have given a place to the eighth-placed John Norton over the sixth-placed Pulsford. In Queensland block voting was also distorting, with Labor winning 50 percent of the seats with 29 percent of the vote. And again the electorally insipid were rewarded; thus the Senate victory of Drake – a place-hunting freak of transitional politics, who was to receive only 4.7 percent of the vote six years later when he stood for Brisbane North. In WA six neophytes were elected, with an average length of residence in WA of just six years. They included four free traders, none of whom lasted longer than a single Senate term, but one who was the elder son of a baronet.[826]

Australia's Senate had been expressly intended as a democratic house, in a satisfying contrast to the US Senate as it was then chosen, and in gratifying contrast to the upper houses of the Australian states, which were either appointed or, when elected, notoriously uncontested and subject to property qualifications. But the Senate was to have more of the flavour of an inheritor institution than a new start. In the four largest states, half of the senators were former MLCs. In the two states with appointed Legislative Councils (NSW and Queensland), half the senators were former MLCs.[827] The Senate, evidently, replicated the function of the states' upper houses, as a politician's refuge from the voter. As it has done ever since.

13

The birth of a state

> *While foams the wild democracy all round,*
> *And the new Empire rises arm'd and crown'd!*
> *Yet oh, how little all which men call great*
> *Has bless'd men's homes, or form'd a happy state!*
> – Henry Parkes

Where did Federationists venture with the great political craft they had launched? When, six weeks after the election, its company first gathered to be invested in their offices, some well-wishers suspected this new ship of state would simply be left to ornament home waters. But her captains proved more restless. They aspired to dissolve barriers between Australia's inhabitants; to fashion, from a 'fabric of freedom', enlarged 'powers of self-government'; and to 'make a nation' which would be one of 'the greatest Powers of the world' (Parkes). A critic would return that they inflamed the country's divides, eroded its democracy, offended its justice, debilitated its defences, profited some of its parts at the expense of the whole, and did not so much make a nation as much as make a state. A rich and confident state; a not very necessary, illiberal and aggrandising one.

Some true colours

On 9 May 1901 twelve thousand people crammed into Melbourne's Exhibition Building to observe the inauguration of the first Commonwealth parliament by the Duke and Duchess of Cornwall and York. At the conclusion of proceedings, the Duchess pressed a button 'which would be the signal for the Union Jack to be raised in every school throughout Australia'.[828] This ceremony had been conceived by Sir Frederick Sargood, a freshly elected Senator for Victoria who had for several years been championing the flying of the Jack in Victoria's schools, with the support

of Alexander Peacock, now Premier, and his education minister.[829] This last, who had advocated Federation on the ground that it would provide a 'national life in place of a provincial one', would require before the end of 1901 that the Union Jack be saluted in all state schools on significant occasions.[830] A symbol of the victory over provincialism was, evidently, to hoist the Union Jack. Truly, the Union Jack was the banner of the new Commonwealth and its creators, from the terrible dignity of it draping Deakin's coffin, to the pathos of Glynn in his dotage drifting about the streets of Adelaide grasping it between his hands.[831]

The introduction of a distinctive flag for the Commonwealth was not an initiative of the 'Fathers', but a response to a request for one by the Colonial Office.[832] To meet this wish, Barton's cabinet announced a public competition for the design of the flag, to be 'adjudicated' by a 'board of experts'. They settled upon a Union Jack 'on a blue or red ground … A six pointed star immediately under the Union Jack'. As the *Age* correctly observed, this design was, 'practically, the Victorian flag, with a six pointed star added'.[833] Announced by the *Age* as 'The SELECTION OF THE VICTORIAN ENSIGN', the judges' decision could be predicted to cause some dissension in cabinet. Fortunately for Barton's equanimity, any flag required the approval of the Colonial Office. This gave the opportunity for cabinet to submit two flags for the final decision by the Office: first, the competition winner; and, secondly, the 'Federation Flag', that is, the New South Wales Ensign, appropriated by the Federation League during the campaigns of 1898 and 1899, as, in Barton's words, 'the handsome, bold, striking … flag of United Australia'. So it was that Australian Unity was to be served by the choice between the Victorian Ensign with a star added ('Design A'), and the NSW Ensign, perhaps very slightly altered ('Design B'). The Colonial Office chose Design A. 'We are not concerned', it declared, 'with Design "B" which represents the Australian Flag without any authority. … Lord Derby in his Circular Despatch of the 21st March 1884 asked that the use of this flag might be stopped'.[834] So the NSW Ensign, ostentatiously brandished for 18 months at so many Federationist gatherings in New South Wales, was now dispatched into vestigial obscurity.

Opposite: A nation is born? The Union Jack is hoisted at Fort St School, Sydney, and schools across Australia, on 9 May 1901

The NSW Ensign flown by volunteer fire fighters

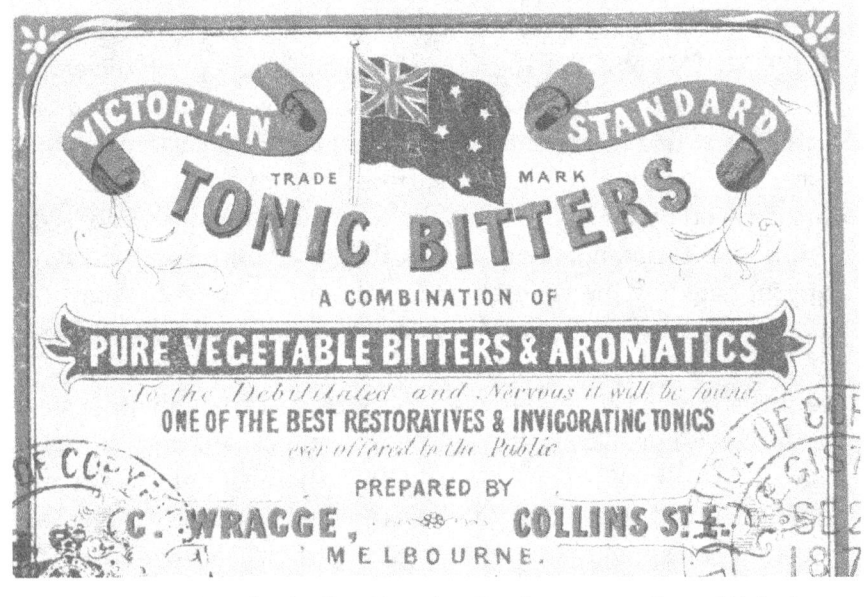

Victoria's Standard. The Victorian Ensign was well established by the 1870s

The Australia of 1901 would have two flags, bespeaking the realities of its double state: the Union Jack for the ultimate state, and a federalised Victorian flag for the proximate state.

Installed in Melbourne

If the capital of the ultimate state was London, where would be the capital of the proximate state? Section 125 of the Constitution prescribed that the Commonwealth's capital ('seat of government') be located within NSW, but with the proviso that, until the Seat's location was decided, the parliament would meet in Melbourne. In accord with the section's proviso, Barton had the Commonwealth parliament installed in the 'monumental interiors' of the building of the Parliament of Victoria, a familiar haunt of Deakin and Turner. And, in apparent accord with the section's substance, a *Seat of Government Act* was passed in August 1904; one of the briefest and baldest Acts of the Commonwealth. Composed of just three substantive sentences, the key provision reads:

> *It is hereby determined that the Seat of Government of the Commonwealth shall be within seventeen miles of Dalgety, in the State of New South Wales.*

The decision, Reid advised the NSW premier, was 'mandatory, final and binding'.[835] But how to reconcile this bald decree with the evident content of MPs to relax indefinitely in Melbourne comfort? Presumably because the choice of Dalgety would quell any impetus to vacate Melbourne. Buckley's Crossing, renamed Dalgety in light of its links with the pastoral company, was a tiny village located on the Snowy River, at an elevation of 760 metres, without a railway connection, which could only be constructed at 'immense cost'.[836] The official investigators reported the site was 'very rough', and largely 'treeless', although they were assured that 'hardier trees' could manage to grow. The same investigators conceded the site was 'somewhat exposed', as 'high winds prevail at certain seasons'.[837] One Federation advocate attempted a dip in the Snowy River, only to find 'the water cut and pained limbs and bodies as if it was boiling'.[838] The Dalgety Progress Association did not add much support by holding out their town as an excellent prospect for a 'future sanatorium ... especially for consumptives'. But the Act was purely rhetorical – no action was mandated. It was, additionally, a piece of play acting. One journalist who accompanied MPs on tours of rival sites noted a 'remarkable' 'lack of interest shown by the Federal Parliamentarians with the Capital site project'.[839] It was not 'remarkable' if there was no intention of ever realising a capital within NSW. The pretence of fixing the Seat in the drab, frigid, ungiving hills of Dalgety was a means of keeping the parliament in Melbourne indefinitely.

The choice of Dalgety in order to elude the behest of section 125 was not motivated simply by considerations of the ease of parliamentarians, but also, in part, by a presumption of Victoria's hegemony in the new Commonwealth, exhibited most blatantly by Deakin. For what was quickly established in Melbourne was not just a legislature but a 'capital'. The Constitution said nothing about the location of the organs of government apart from parliament; administration, the courts, the armed forces. And, taking advantage of that silence, Reid in campaigning for a Yes vote in 1899 had declared the temporary seat of 'government' – as distinct from parliament – would *not* be in Melbourne.[840] With seemingly similar bad faith, Barton in the election campaign of 1901 had publicly toyed with the possibility of administration actually remaining in Sydney. But the apparatus of government was quickly established in Melbourne, and was to long stay. The Army's headquarters remained there until 1945, most of the civil service until the 1960s, and the High Court's Principal Registry until 1973. And the location of the capital in Melbourne signified more than simply the location of those branches. To be in Melbourne was to be under the censuring scrutiny of the Melbourne press, and to be reflected to the rest of Australia through their lens. Few papers outside of Victoria were represented in Melbourne,[841] and the *Age* and the *Argus* had 'immeasurable advantages over newspapers from other states'.[842] And that press had intimate relations with parts of the parliament: Deakin was a long-time leader writer for the *Age*, and Quick was a past chief of the *Age*'s parliamentary staff. The parliament's location in Melbourne was also to the great advantage of her non-parliamentary residents. Living in Melbourne 'afforded daily direct access to Federal ministers' for Victorian figures in agriculture, industry, and trade unions.[843] Location brought power.

On the march

The shift in the precedence of Sydney and Melbourne was more than just the jostle of two cities to wield the power's sceptre: it also embodied a qualitative shift between two phases of the Federation episode. This may be simply described as the 'before 1901' phase, and the 'after 1901' phase. They may also be characterised as an instance of a commonly seen transition between two different phases of political upheaval: 'the march on the capital' versus 'the capital on the march'.[844] In both of these 'marches' the underlying motor is 'the people'. But the 'march on the capital' phase is 'populist': mass in its style and methods, hostile to extant authority in its immediate objects, yet traditionalist in rhetorical accent. The 'capital on the march phase' is 'nationalist'; it is elitist in style, and statist in its objects, and radical in form and substance. These two marches can be interpreted as the first and second phases of a revolutionary transition from an old equilibrium to a new. The first phase consists of an insurgency by mass methods overwhelming an existing power centre. The second amounts to a digging in exercise, with those formerly at the margins now at the centre and in control, fastening their insecure hold by warring against both the remnant of the dislodged power centre, and still more marginal groups. In terms of the American revolution, '1776' can be seen as a march on the capital (New York), and populist; and '1787' as the capital on the march (Washington, DC), and nationalist. In this reading, the furious contest between Federalists (that is, nationalists) and anti-Federalists (that is, populists) over the Philadelphia constitution is simply testimony to the strength of American populism in resisting the second phase of the transition.[845]

The passage in Australia from the last decade of the 19th century to the first decade of the 20th can be interpreted as the succession of a populist 'march on the capital' by a nationalist 'capital on the march'. If the Federation cause in the years before 1901 was indisputably elite in its leadership, it was 'populist' in its electoral energy. If it was a quest for status by the elite, it was also a quest for centrality by the periphery, in NSW, Queensland, WA and Tasmania, which smouldered at the local capital and the centralisation it imposed. The heat spots of the Federation movement was the small town, so often the heartland of populist sentiment: Ballarat, Bathurst, Charters Towers.[846] And the capital marched on was Sydney.

From 1901 Melbourne was 'the capital on the march', embodying a state, acting on the people's behalf, but conducting its war on remnant polities and despised minorities, in significant part not through mass methods – the referendums of the first phase – but through corridor machinations, court appointments, and audiences with governors-general. In this period Sydney, the old capital, was discarded; a place where Deakin as prime minister was 'rarely seen and still more rarely heard',[847] when it was not actively lambasted by Deakin's ministers for its not forgotten disloyalty to the Federationist cause.

The phenomenon of two successive marches may also be detected in the strange change of trains which Australian literature took at the crossing of the 19th and 20th centuries. The Nineties – Lawson, Furphy, Franklin and the *Bulletin* – were obviously and distinctly populist in strain. The subject matter and style were of the people; its writers, and even more the readers, often had limited education and rural background; they were children 'of the mighty bush'.[848] But come the new century a change takes place, which can be seen as a nationalist phase displacing the populist. It is a period of relatively well-educated urbanites formulating manifestos in favour of national art, recasting 1890s figures as nationalists, expressing a concern about the dangers of foreign infection of local art (by, say, modernism), encouraging the artist to assume a formative social role – 'men who will bind us together in an indissoluble bond' and, above all, urging the state to act to nurture national art.[849] The artist was to be a public, even semi-political, figure. In sympathy, the new literati themselves are active in political parties; a prime minister might attend one of their opening nights, they might sometimes stand for parliament, or even be appointed to a Legislative Council. The leading illustrations of such heralds are Vance Palmer, Louis Esson and Bernard O'Dowd. A more tigerish example is the novelist Randolph Bedford. Old enough to have mixed it with the bohemians of the Nineties, Bedford quickly emerged in the 20th century as a devotee of the cult of strength and purity, his Lindsayesque version of bohemia, characterised by a loathing of those on the margins which is foreign to a true Bohemia. A poetical apostle of the new Commonwealth, Bedford in the 20th century became a publicist for the continental Australia Felix, extolling its wonders, and urging with a vehemence its racial purity and the expulsion of 'filthy aliens'.[850] Not surprisingly, if not inevitably, his white Australianism had extended by the end of his life in 1941 to venting on 'picture-dealing Jews ... selling at high prices daubs without form-sense, colour sense or sanity'.[851]

Bedford's fate does beg the query of how beneficial for art was this new role of the artist. The earliest manifesto of 'Australian National Art' in the new century declared, 'What we require in our present development is not so much cultured writers but ardent nationalists'.[852] And perhaps that is what Australia got. The first decades of the 20th century – the nationalist phase in this interpretation – is commonly judged by critics as barren in significant literary accomplishment in Australia.[853] The older talents faltered and ran dry; and the new ones were second or third raters. So, to put directly the question that hovers: were these first decades artistically barren because a nationalist ethos prevailed? Any answer must be speculative, but may draw on this judgement by one Lawson specialist of the author's 'long and painful' decline. '1901', says this critic, 'may reasonably be considered the year in which Lawson's submergence became clear'.[854] He ventures to trace the decline to Lawson's assumption, in this period, of 'the role of the Australian folk voice'. Did not the new Commonwealth atmosphere assign him that role?

The Commonwealth empire state

In the 'capital on the march' phase, the concrete capital is not necessarily fixed in location. And if Melbourne's claim to be capital was part and parcel of Deakin's understanding of Federation as the establishment of Victoria as Australia's hegemon, the claim was undermined by the logic of the *Commonwealth of Australia Constitution Act*. This created a supreme state, the Commonwealth, effectively autonomous to any component part, and in consequence indifferent to the presumptions of any part. It is on account of that logic that, for all the evasion of the *Seat of*

Government Act 1904, for all the *Bulletin's* 'ceaseless and virulent campaign' in favour of Dalgety,[855] and despite all of Deakin's cabinet (save Lyne) voting in favour of Dalgety in all nine consecutive ballots in the House of Representatives, the parliament in 1908 resolved to establish the capital, *de novo*, in Canberra.

The laying of the foundation stone of Canberra on 12 March 1913 symbolises a new dimension of the Commonwealth, of far more enduring significance than the passing pre-eminence of Melbourne: the inauguration of the Commonwealth empire state. And Canberra would be its nourishing germ.

The Constitution directed that a federal territory be created to house the Commonwealth's permanent seat of government. Inglis Clark had proposed a size of at least 100 square miles, and the Constitution concurred; a liberal size, but not gratuitously large, and comparable to the District of Columbia's 68 square miles. With Federation, King O'Malley proposed 1 000 square miles; the *Bulletin* wanted 5 000 square miles, an area considerably larger than the area of Lebanon. Drake, Deakin's Attorney-General, had proposed 50 000 square miles.[856] In the event Deakin, as prime minister, sought 900 square miles; and this was eventually obtained by the consent of the NSW government, although not by referendum, in crude violation of the spirit of section 123.[857] In the creation of the Federal Capital Territory there was at work, undeniably, the impulse to create a new state, the Commonwealth empire state; not as the precipitate of a solution of six political substances, but as an autonomous regent power, with its own 'possessions'; a rapidly expanding territorial entity, the 'great Australian Empire' envisioned by Parkes.

The most significant acquisition by the new 'Australian Empire' was the Northern Territory which, from the first, the Commonwealth was hankering after, incited by the ANA, David Syme's urgent injunctions to 'colonise' the Territory federally, and the rhapsodies of the Reverend Llewelyn Bevan. It was eventually acquired from SA in 1911, again without a referendum, again in breach of the spirit of section 123. The Commonwealth's acquisition of the Northern Territory served no very clear federal purpose, but the purpose of the SA government was plain enough: to disburden the expense of administering the bankrupt

Territory onto the taxpayers of other states.[858] That the Commonwealth did accede to this intention speaks of its impulse of aggrandisement, and search for 'possessions', which the NT was now reduced to.[859] The NT had been an integral political part of SA. It had been represented in the SA parliament, and, in 1899, the member for the Territory had very briefly been premier. Now it was not to send a member to any parliament, and not to have even an advisory 'legislative council', but an Administrator; along with a chief justice – a son of the Reverend Bevan – seeking abolition of trial by jury in the Territory. It was to be ruled by the Minister for External Affairs, and that choice of ministry was logical enough. By Commonwealth legislation 95 percent of her population were ineligible to vote and, if they departed Australia, liable to be refused entry at her ports on their return.[860] Here was a foreign possession of the Commonwealth; to be held tight, but a foreign possession all the same. The Territory's trade unionists did have the advantage of a Labor government banning non-white labour on the docks, increasing wage rates to 25 percent above state levels, and arranging agricultural labour be paid a miraculous £4 per week.[861] Unfortunately, this made requisite an 'extraordinary' degree of productivity if hired labour was to be a commercial proposition.[862] The Territory did have the compensation of the Commonwealth's resolve to spend money, and willingness to lose it. Undeterred by SA's experience in spending £3 931 045 on the Territory to little effect, the Commonwealth offered blocks of 150 to 300 acres to settlers on the Daly and Batchelor rivers. Regrettably, Hunt was to find in 1915 that of 200 blocks surveyed for a township in Daly, only two had been sold, and those for 3s 9d each. He added 'experience on the Government Farm at Batchelor has been most disheartening'.[863] By 1920 'the farms at Daly and Batchelor had been converted into Aboriginal compounds and most of the settlers had left the territory'.[864] By the middle of the 1920s, 'the only evidence of the great resolve to settle the north with white people had been the great increase in public servants … Darwin was not a happy town'.[865] The first decade of Commonwealth rule ended in 1918 in colonial rebellion, and the dispatch of HMAS *Encounter* to secure the extrication of the Administrator from Port Darwin back to Melbourne safety.

The Commonwealth's spirit of aggrandisement would not confine itself to the Australian landmass. In Deakin's words, 'We intend to be masters of the Pacific, by and by'.[866] The most spectacular step to mastery was the transfer of control of Papua from Great Britain to Australia. From 1907 Papua was administered by Hubert Murray, an unsuccessful member of the Sydney Bar, commanding officer of the Irish Rifles, and protégé of O'Connor and Barton. Murray proved to be the most potent and enduring of 'Barton's kindergarten' – the bright young men, such as Garran, Hunt, Bavin and Robert Broinowski – who were scattered across the Commonwealth, like so many *intendants*, to busily inspect, investigate, assess, and, sometimes, to spy.[867] And, as in Murray's case, to rule, as 'Milner's kindergarten' aspired to rule South Africa.[868]

This spirit of expansion of the Commonwealth was not too proud to strain for morsels. The same spirit drove the acquisition in 1913 of Jervis Bay from NSW (again without referendum), and of Norfolk Island. The case of Jervis Bay was simply the itching after a port, a thing which every power must want. The case of Norfolk Island is more revealing of the particular nature of the Commonwealth. 46 years before the Commonwealth's proclamation, the convict settlement at Norfolk Island had been evacuated, and the island detached from Van Diemen's Land, and established as a distinct crown colony. Its new purpose was to provide a new home for the descendants of the mutineers of HMS *Bounty*. Accordingly, in May 1856, *Morayshire* deposited 196 of the posterity of Fletcher Christian, Mathew Quintal and John Adams on the island, where they were left largely to their own devices. Each year, on Boxing Day, all adults – male and female – would elect one of their number as chief magistrate. The Governor of Norfolk Island was simply one and the same person as the Governor of NSW, and for forty years his external authority had an only intermittent presence on the island. Such an anomalous, functionless and promiseless colony would not long escape the exacting scrutiny of Joseph Chamberlain, Secretary of State for Colonies from 1895. The obvious solution was to discharge responsibility for this pointless curio upon New South Wales. Accordingly, Reid installed an 'administrator'; but legally the island remained a British crown colony, as Reid declined any suggestion of NSW annexing it. Reid's resistance is unexplained – why have the responsibility and not the power? – but it is a fact that Barton had become involved. The source of this unlikely engagement was the new concern of the NSW Department of Lands, then in the hands of Joseph Carruthers, for the state of land title on the island. The Islanders commonly believed that their forty years labour in using and preserving the buildings and fields abandoned by the British gave them some title.[869] Barton, retained by Lands to provide a legal opinion, disabused the islanders of these rude notions. They had title only to what they had been formally granted, and evictions followed. More yet lay in store. In 1902 Chamberlain was 'delighted' by Deakin's positive response to his hint that the new Commonwealth acquire Norfolk Island. Regrettably, the evictions had embittered some of the population, and Atlee Hunt, visiting the island on one of his far-flung inspections, related reports of 'strong statements' of the islanders' 'antipathy to the suggested transfer to the Commonwealth'.[870] He was, however, glad to add that he himself found no justification or sign of such sentiments and, in 1913, the *Norfolk Island Act* was passed. There would be no annual council of islanders; they were to elect no representatives of any kind. The law of the land was to be the ordinance of the minister, answerable only to a resolution of parliament. Executive power was soon vested in an 'administrator' appointed by the Minister for External Affairs; and a Lands department official, and friend of Hunt, was chosen to fill the post.[871] The story of Norfolk Island not only exemplifies the acquisitiveness and arrogance of the Commonwealth, it also gives a glimpse as to its nature: it was an inheritor state of the British Empire. Norfolk Island had been a colony of Great Britain; it was now to be a colony of the Commonwealth Empire State.

And the former colonies, now states? The distinction between 'territories' and 'states' did not weigh heavily on the new Commonwealth. Its every presumption was that the states now stood in the same relation to the Commonwealth that they had previously stood as colonies with respect to Great Britain. 'The rights of the self-government of the States have been fondly supposed to be safeguarded by the Constitution', preened Deakin.[872] But Deakin knew better: 'the States, instead of rivalling those of the

American Union, may easily sink into a status inferior to that possessed by the Canadian Provinces'.[873] Deakin stopped short of comparing them with colonies. But in every concrete sense, the Colonial Office and Governor-General took the Commonwealth as the legatee of the Imperial government's former dominion with respect to the states.[874] Certainly, the Colonial Office was valuable in making colonies of the states. 'Deakin was increasingly willing to take up cudgels on behalf of the Commonwealth, partly no doubt because he could rely on the support of the Secretary of State'[875] and the 'fundamentally centralist attitude to the Australian Federation' of the Colonial Office.[876] One may wonder if it was the presumption of an imperial legatee, admixed with a venal motive, which sustained Deakin's and Lyne's refusal to pay Victoria's income tax on their parliamentary salaries.[877] It must be of the same presumption that the High Court found an 'implied immunity' against such taxation, and so granted Deakin and Lyne their extraordinary resolve to create in the new Commonwealth 'a privileged class of citizen' exempt from state income tax.[878]

In some respects the Constitution did undoubtedly grant the Commonwealth the status of legatee of the Imperial power, and the High Court itself is illustrative. A truer sense of federation as a division of powers would – following the US example – have created a court of appeal regarding federal law, but not made the same body a court of appeal to state law as well. That the High Court of Australia is a court of appeal to state law, as well as federal, has nothing to do with federation; it has everything to do with the fact that the High Court was the inheritor of the Judicial Committee of the Privy Council, which, on account of the British Empire not being a federal structure, was the ultimate court of appeal for every court in the Empire.[879] Correspondingly, the Griffith High Court was hardly free of an impulse to Commonwealth supremacy, in obvious violation of the federal spirit of the Constitution.

It was the High Court, as much as prime minister Deakin, which was the object of Carruthers's protest against 'federal tyrants' during his term as premier of NSW (1904-1907). He was joining the earlier example of Robert Philp, the premier of

Queensland from 1899. Prior to 1901 Philp had been 'one of the most persuasive and passionate advocates of Federation' on the grounds that 'all we will be doing under federation will be to extend our power of self-government'.[880] He soon discovered the flavour of the extended self-government when Barton refused to acknowledge him at a Premiers' Conference. By 1902, he favoured secession.[881]

The premiers' indignation was part of a piece with a widespread buyers' remorse in the aftermath of Federation. 'Several people have told me lately that if the Commonwealth was put to the vote in the States tomorrow, there would not be a single vote in favour of it ... The people say they have been entirely deceived.' Thus the wife of a future Governor-General in 1902.[882] Neither were such sentiments confined to the familiars of governors' wives.

> [He] deplores the Australian Federation; but when questioned admits the necessity of defence, posts, telegraphs and railways – he thinks it should be limited there. Australia is far too big for one government.[883]

Thus the précis, in 1910, of the views of Adrian Knox, prominent constitutional lawyer and, from 1919, Chief Justice of the High Court.[884]

The decline in parliamentarism

Although consciously territorial, the new Commonwealth was, more essentially, an assemblage of salient institutions; a parliament, a High Court, the army, and the post office. All were closely fashioned on their predecessors. All were inferior to them, if not dysfunctional.

The nerve centre of the new state was the parliament, inaugurated with a peal of voices. But the Commonwealth parliament faltered in reproducing the system of government it was intended to, at the expense of Australian democracy.

'Parliamentarism' is parliament as an efficient and potent machine for accommodating the wishes of electors. Its mechanism is a counterpoise of opposing forces; where the legislature creates the executive, and yet the executive may dissolve the legislature. The component parts of this machine are neither hostile interests, nor miniature epitomes of society of no characterising interest, but communities, each with a distinct, but not inescapably antagonistic, interest. This machine is powered by speech; neither discussion nor declamation, but verbal jousts, of 'debates', 'question time', and committee hearings.

Parliamentarism had reached the zenith of its vigour in mid-Victorian UK, and in that hey-day had been exported with little damage to the Australasian colonies. But parliamentarism is a delicate and unstable system. The balance between the executive and the legislative chamber is precarious, and prone to sliding towards a system whereby the executive preponderates over the chamber, and legislates by 'parliamentary plebiscite' at general elections; or, in the other direction, sliding towards the chamber preponderating over the executive, and 'executing' at the instruction of its majority. From the late 19th century parliamentarism began to falter in the parent society, and the first cracks of its demise in Australia sounded before the 20th century. The executive, critics protested, was becoming no more than a committee of the chamber,[885] and any enhanced accountability of the executive was coming sadly at the cost of its capability, to the detriment of meeting the wants of electors. But the creation of the Commonwealth parliament tipped the balance in the opposite direction: the mechanism of parliamentary counterpoise was subverted by the executive subordinating the legislature. And the enhanced capability of the executive came at the cost of its accountability, also to the detriment of meeting the wants of electors.

A mark of an unsubordinated legislature is the independence of parliamentary officers from the executive. But from the moment of its commencement, the executive controlled all officers of the Commonwealth parliament,[886] in sharp contrast with the precedent of the NSW and Victorian parliaments.[887] Perhaps the greatest manifestation of the legislature's independence of the executive was the office of Speaker, simultaneously the governor and servant of the House, who, custom ordained, was completely autonomous from the executive. Thus, prior to 1901, Speakers of the NSW Assembly gave a casting vote to the government of the day on 45 occasions, and on 35 to the opposition.[888] The first appointment of any Speaker would be a matter of parliamentary contest, with their reappointment subsequent to an election, and perhaps a new government, taken for granted.[889] But from the first days of the Commonwealth the Speakership was a cabinet appointment.[890] And with the confrontation between Deakin and Fisher in 1909 over the appointment as Speaker of Carty Salmon, an unpopular and incapable Deakin loyalist, the office became simply a partisan one, the Speaker's casting vote henceforth always given to the executive, barring only the rarest, and dubious, occasions. The culpability of the Commonwealth for the ruin of the impartiality of the office of Speaker might be questioned, on the grounds that a partisan Speakership had already established itself in New Zealand in the 1890s.[891] But a critic of the Commonwealth may reply, in turn, that the Australian parliaments of the 1890s had not done as New Zealand had done. It was the Commonwealth that did so. It would be more germane to observe that the ruin of the bipartisan Speakership occurred in NSW at about the same time as in the Commonwealth; and there, as with the Commonwealth, its end coincided with the emergence of a disciplined party system. But the establishment of the Commonwealth and the emergence of a party system are not necessarily independent.

The early Commonwealth saw the rise of parliamentary parties; representation within the parliament of parties replacing representation of numerous component communities. Parties had already tentatively emerged from the late 1880s, but they were more devices for identifying the position of individual candidates than devices for acting in concert in parliament. Accordingly, in the Reid government of 1894-99, even a minister could cross the floor.[892] Prior to Federation, Labor had trialled party discipline in parliament, not always successfully. But in 1902 'The Pledge' was introduced for all federal Labor candidates; [893] and state candidates followed suit. Finally, with the 'fusion' of protectionist and free trade parties, crossing the floor became a rarity. The House of Representatives was now a house of parties.[894]

The rise of parties may be traceable in part to a renewed tyranny of distance in the wake of Federation. The House of Representatives had only 75 electoral districts. The number of electoral districts NSW had in the House of Representatives was about one-fifth of the number of seats in its Assembly; in Queensland the proportion was about one-seventh, and one-ninth in WA. These huge Commonwealth seats could hardly constitute a community. Extreme distances entailed by the 'continent for a nation' also damaged parliamentarism by discouraging attendance; George Reid, the Leader of the Opposition, was present in only 83 of the 222 sitting days of the first session of the new parliament.[895] The Commonwealth parliament remains, by international standards, one that meets infrequently. Distance additionally weakened the functioning of the Governor-General in the parliamentary mechanism. The intimate, even pervasive, presence of the Governors in their respective colonies in the 19th century could not be replicated – save for Victorians – by a Governor-General (usually) domiciled in Melbourne. The position of later Governors-General in Canberra could only be much worse.[896]

Labor ascendant

The extensive, sometimes vast, seats of the Commonwealth's parliament might be one source of the rapid emergence of the first of the modern parties, the Labor party.

By 1901 Labor had been winning seats for a decade, but without any upward trend in its support. Within a decade of Federation, the Labor party moved from the cross-benches to being the largest single party, forming three Commonwealth governments, and, by the outbreak of the First World War, supplying governments in five of the six states.

That Labor so soon won for itself the 'fiery Cross of Union'[897] obviously had deep implications for the tenor of Australian politics and policy. Federation may have been responsible for Labor's sudden ascent, by three separate channels.

Labor may have benefitted from the depersonalisation of electoral contests consequent upon the large electorates and distant government of the new Commonwealth. As one self-described 'young Australian zealot' reflected decades later on pre-federation Australia, 'Individuals were more prominent and more subject to criticism than they were when the outlook became national'.[898] This depersonalisation assisted Labor by two channels.

Table 13.1: Labor members of lower houses of Australian parliaments
(percent of total)

year	percent	year	percent
1891	12.6	1901	17.7
1892	12.6	1902	18.7
1893	17.7	1903	21.2
1894	13.4	1904	29.5
1895	12.1	1905	30.0
1896	13.6	1906	31.9
1897	14.5	1907	29.8
1898	13.8	1908	35.2
1899	13.8	1909	36.6
1900	14.0	1910	45.5
		1911	48.1

Source: Hughes and Graham (1968).

Non-Labor voters voted more on the candidate as an individual – while Labor voters voted according to whether the candidate was Labor or not; the upshot being non-Labor voters would vote less in the face of depersonalisation. Or perhaps, in the face of depersonalisation, both Labor and non-Labor voters now voted more according to 'creed' (party); but Labor had a far more effective branding of their creed. The number of non-Labor parties, and their changes of name,[899] their executives' lack of control over pre-selections, their ephemeral character; all left any non-Labor party label faint.

The Labor upsurge might instead be traceable to an inflammation of sectarian tensions by the federation process. Cardinal Moran's entry into the race for the Convention in 1898 had exacerbated these strains. They became dismally apparent in the discord over prayers at the inauguration ceremony of the Commonwealth. And in the bizarre divorce case of a few months before Proclamation, *Coningham vs Coningham*, which turned on the Cardinal's favourite, Monsignor O'Haran, allegedly having sex with a Mrs Coningham in the Cardinal's Hall of St Mary's Cathedral, and which drew out rival religionists and attendant politicians into warfare.[900] These clashes were of apiece with 'tribal' tensions mounting in any colony as the imperial power recedes; the significance of any one group's primacy over the others enlarges and, with the raised stakes, a spiral of countermeasures ensues. And so it was in Australia that the former devotees of the cause of national unity now took their stand on one side or the other of the sectarian divide. Symbolically enough, in 1905 in the village of Federal – voting 90 percent Yes in 1899 – a meeting of Orangemen met to commemorate the lifting of the siege of Derry in 1689, and hear the Reverend MacAulay declare that a 'militant spirit' was necessary in 'preventing Roman encroachment'.[901] For its part, the *Bulletin* now recast its militant protectionism in anti-Catholic terms, and made the unexpected discovery that, 'So far as Australasia is concerned, free trade and Catholicism have in the main gone together'.[902]

Political forces now moved to harness this new heat. In the 1890s political actors had been little aligned to religious fractures. Reid, as premier, avoided the anti-Catholic stance of Parkes, and adopted as his successor in the seat of Sydney-King a scion of the Hughes family; the protectionist party in NSW, for all its Irish support, chose protestants for its leaders; the Labor party was not yet strongly flavoured by Irish descent, but was dense with English and Scottish immigrants. In 1896 Reid had travelled to the Bathurst People's Convention in a special carriage, together with Cardinal Moran, who had announced he wished to journey to Federation 'hand in hand with Protestant fellow citizens'. But in 1903, in another railway carriage, travelling to Melbourne, Reid was overheard, by Francis Clarke, grousing he had never received support from Roman Catholics.[903] Bigotry, Clarke lamented, 'had broken loose in the peaceful garden of New South Wales'. Or, as a free trade MP put it more tersely, from 1901 'the fight was to be between the Orange and the Green'.[904] In this fight, the Orange could only be free trade, and the Green only Labor. The traditional Catholic political vehicle, the protectionists, no longer possessed that issue at state level, and at Federal level their cause was soon won, and so was defunct.

Perhaps the greatest stimulus to the growth of Labor lay in the Commonwealth's novel remedy for workplace disputes: the compulsory arbitration of disputes by quasi-legal tribunals, where court orders regarding wages and conditions would supposedly supplant business and unions 'fighting it out' through strikes and lock outs. Thanks to Higgins's efforts in the Convention, the Constitution hopefully accommodated this remedy, and the *Commonwealth Conciliation and Arbitration Act* of 1904 sought to implement it. A Court of Conciliation and Arbitration was established to resolve work place disputes; and, in 1907, Higgins was appointed as President of the Court, and its sole judge. As only 'registered' unions had a right to be heard by the Court, the Act gave an enormous stimulus to the formation of unions.[905] And thereby the Labor party. So it might be said the Labor party was precipitated in the main by trade unions; which were precipitated by the Arbitration Act; which, in turn, was precipitated by Federation.[906] Thus Federation may be why Australia experienced a majority Labor government 'a generation early', in 1910. The first majority Labour government in the UK took office in 1945, and in 1935 in New Zealand. More fundamentally, in the US and the UK, it was only in the inter-war period that class-based politics displaced religion and regional factors. But in Australia it did so before 1914. As Bryce noted, in Australia 'Party coincides with Class'.[907]

But any laying of compulsory arbitration at the feet of Federation is troubled by the fact that similar systems had already been established in SA (1894) and NSW (1901). And yet the NSW legislation cannot be construed as independent in origins from Federation; it was passed in the wake of the legitimation afforded compulsory arbitration by the *Constitution of the Commonwealth of Australia Act*. Neither was the NSW legislation unconnected to a surging Labor party federally. The state acts, additionally, were milder in several respects.[908] A greater difficulty in attributing compulsory arbitration to Federation is posed by New Zealand's legislation for compulsory arbitration in 1895, well before the Commonwealth.[909] This suggests that common forces in Australasia produced compulsory arbitration. But New Zealand's chronological priority does not prove this contention. Every appearance is that the Commonwealth's Act gave enormous stimulus to compulsory arbitration which the states alone, or New Zealand, would not have delivered.

Industrial discord

How successful was compulsory arbitration in establishing the 'New Province of Law and Order' it aimed for? The *Commonwealth Conciliation and Arbitration Act* dealt in severe and summary terms with strikes and lockouts.

> *No person or organization shall, on account of any industrial dispute, do anything in the nature of a lock-out or strike.*
>
> *Penalty: One thousand pounds.*
>
> – Commonwealth Conciliation and Arbitration Act, section 6(1).

But the state of workplace peace in the subsequent decade was hardly consonant with either the Act's aims or its intimidating provisions. In 1912 Brisbane experienced a general strike 'which almost paralysed a city, and was one of the few such strikes the world has known',[910] and which saw the killing of a strike breaker.[911] This industrial strife in Australia in the years before the First World War was, however, paralleled by a wave of mass strikes in England. What would be most telling as to the effect of the 'new province of law and order' is a systematic 'before and after the Act' comparison of Australia with another country. Canada might be the best possible comparator, and data does exist to sustain a comparison across time.[912]

Table 13.2: Number of strikes in Canada and Australia, 1860-1959

Period	Number		Number per annum per million of inhabitants	
	Canada	Australia	Canada	Australia
1860-1900	1 212	676	275	261
1913-1938	3 588	8 617	381	1 447
1939-1959	4 535	21 388	331	2 585

Sources: 1860-1900; Quinlan and Gardner (1995, p. 181). Canada, 1913-1959; International Institute of Social History, https://datasets.iisg.amsterdam/file.xhtml?fileId=3435&version=1.0. Australia, 1913-1959; Vamplew (1967, p. 165).

Food supplies under guard during the Brisbane General Strike of 1912

Table 13.2 does not require close scrutiny to distil its message. Australia's 'New Province of Law and Order' appears to have been a formula for strife. And this is not against expectation; it is no great paradox to suppose that to outlaw the threat of strikes and lockouts is to outlaw the devices which keep the workplace peace; for it is the threat of a strike/lockout that induces each side to settle. The Act, then, removed the peacemaker; and did not foster truce as much as entrench an adversary posture; and exacerbate the 'intense' 'class bitterness' that so struck foreigners observing Australia in that period: a relatively classless society with a class struggle.[913] The counterproductive Act, additionally, had a 'long career as a wrecker of governments'.[914] Finally, the obligation of the Act to resolve any dispute by an 'award' of the Court constituted the tap root of the great forest of judicial legislation for wage rates, hours and conditions that quickly grew.

The purity of the race

The resolution to secure by judicial legislation a higher price of manual labour was complemented by a resolution to remove by legislation any supply of labour that might reduce it. Thus the new parliament quickly passed, without a division, the *Pacific Is-*

land Labourers Act 1901 – harsh, arbitrary, and illiberal legislation – which voided all agreements of Kanaka labourers with employers,[915] and ordained the deportation of almost every Kanaka by 31 December 1906.[916] Deportation had not been foreshadowed before 1901, even though Ewing had declared in Federationist literature that 'the deportation back to Africa ... appears to be the only one feasible plan' for America's 'negro problem'.[917] In response to the Act, a Pacific Islander Association was formed by 'a well-educated Melanesian', Antonius Tui Tonga, who had lived in Australia since the age of four, and was currently a boarding house owner.[918] The Association petitioned the King. This 'desperate and pathetic' appeal asked no more than that a portion of uncultivated land in Queensland be set aside, as a kind of Kanaka reservation.[919] Such a reservation, the petitioners promised, would ensure that Kanakas could not compete with whites. Deakin advised Chamberlain that the petition was just a front for planters. Chamberlain accordingly instructed British authorities to cooperate with the deportations of Kanakas to the Solomon Islands and the New Hebrides, where 'neither property, nor rights, nor welcome awaited them'.[920] The Association then appealed to the High Court. But this was a recourse of desperation: two of the Court's three Justices had been members of the cabinet which had devised and championed the legislation, and the appeal was refused. With this travesty of justice, the deportation of the Kanakas was sealed.

The logic of deportation of the Kanakas suggested that the Commonwealth should be used to prevent other 'coloureds' from entering Australia in the first place. Had not Parkes declared 'a uniform law regulating the introduction of aliens of inferior races' the 'great work of federal action'?[921] Did he not make the prevention of their influx a plank of the program of his National Federal Party? In accord with that sentiment, Barton announced, before the Commonwealth was one year old, that

> He hoped Australia would have a handsome New Year's gift in the shape of ... the Immigration Restriction Act, thus realizing the dream of a white Australia.[922]

And so it did. Barton's legislative gift prohibited the admission of any arrival who 'fails to write out at dictation and sign in the presence of the officer' a passage of fifty words in length in a European language directed by the officer. Despite the apparent rigour of this provision, its efficacy did rely on 'the officer' using the test in ways which would secure its intended, if unstated, purpose. And the new Commonwealth was concerned that her officers were not always doing so. In 1909, Atlee Hunt, secretary of the Department of External affairs since 1901, was dispatched to Western Australia to investigate apparent laxity in implementation of the test there.[923] In that year Leoncio de Garra, a Philippine who had worked for six years in the state's pearling industry, was subjected to the test in English, and had passed. Procedure in this untoward situation required a test in a second language be applied. But the officer, who knew only English, asked de Garra to simply paint a water colour with the words, 'Advance Australia'.[924] De Garra was the last 'coloured' person ever to pass Australia's dictation test. Its operation after its polishing by Hunt is illustrated by the testing in 1916 of three hundred Maltese arrivals in Dutch, and their subsequent deportation to New Caledonia.[925]

An amendment to the *Immigration Restriction Act* in 1905 ensured that even former (and wholly legal) residents of Australia were, in effect, banned from re-entering if they were Chinese.[926] And not only Chinese. In 1907 immigration officials brought to Deakin's attention certain Australian-born persons who, apparently having served in Australian armed forces in South Africa, were now seeking to return to Australia. They were aboriginal. Deakin confirmed the refusal of their entry into Australia.[927]

But had not the states already advanced similar legislative bars to the immigration of 'persons belonging to any coloured race'? 1888 had seen a round of anti-Chinese acts, and several colonies in the 1890s extended them to all natives of Asia and Africa. But the advocates of the Immigration Restriction Act did not see themselves as simply replicating the older pre-Federation acts; Deakin judged the Commonwealth's law-making on this matter as 'more severe than anything to be found in the State Acts'.[928] Certainly, the dictation tests of the three states which had introduced them in the 1890s did not match the rigour of the Commonwealth's.[929] And this rigour, the advocates of Commonwealth legislation believed, was not accidental; they were confident the states could never have achieved what they achieved. As Ewing told the House, 'I always told my constituents in the north ... that we should never get a white Australia until it was washed white by a Federal Parliament'.[930] And was not the Commonwealth a united and doughty voice?

> **Higgins**: *I wish to place upon record the distinct and almost unanimous expression of opinion that Australia must be kept for the white races.*
>
> **Forrest**: *The Imperial Government refused assent to the New South Wales Bill on account of the colour line.*
>
> **Higgins**: *It is one thing to refuse New South Wales, and another thing to refuse Australia, when the desire of Australia is voiced by the Federal Parliament.*[931]

Underlining the responsibility of the Commonwealth, New Zealand's act of 1899 – parallel to that of NSW – was not superseded in the opening years of the new century by any act with a rigour comparable to the Commonwealth's.[932]

The visionaries of White Australia would not leave its means of achievement confined to immigration policy. In 1902 Higgins successfully sought to have Australian Aboriginals removed from the Commonwealth electoral roll. 'It is utterly inappropriate to grant the franchise to the aborigines, or ask them to exercise an intelligent vote', he told the House of Representatives.[933] In the spirit of aiding his honourable and learned friend, Braddon ventured, 'if there was anything to make the granting of the franchise to women more absurd, it would be giving the innumerable gins of some of the aboriginals the right to vote (Laughter)'.[934] Hugh Mahon, the Labor member for Coolgardie, volunteered, 'I am free to admit that there is perhaps no lower type of humanity on this planet than the aboriginal of Western Australia', but suggested it would be less stigmatising to impose a literacy test. But scruples about stigmatisation were waved away. The leaders of the protectionist, free trade and Labor parties joined the majority in the House in effectively prohibiting Aboriginals from voting in Commonwealth elections.[935] This was a clear break with pre-Federation Australia. The only state which had any statutory restriction on voting by Aboriginals was Western Australia.⁹³⁶ Aboriginals voted for the Assemblies of NSW, Queensland and SA before 1901,⁹³⁷ and sometimes stood as candidates. Some Aboriginals voted in the 1899 referendum.⁹³⁸ When, in 1891, Parkes was confronted with a move to deprive Aboriginals of the vote, he repulsed it as 'barbarous'.⁹³⁹

The proximate cause of the disenfranchisement of Aboriginals lay in the Labor party. Two years earlier Dawson had sought the exclusion of Aboriginals from voting in Queensland's referendum of 1899. In 1901 it was Labor's leader, Chris Watson, who broached limitations on Aboriginal voting rights in the House of Representatives, and thereby cued Higgins's motion. Labor groused that the 'aboriginal vote' had lost them the seat of Barwon in the NSW election of 1898.⁹⁴⁰ But calculations of electoral advantage seem a weak explanation of Higgins's stridency. His concern was that an Aboriginal vote would be 'forced' on Victoria, but Victoria's 294 adult Aborigines could hardly weigh in its electoral balances. To Higgins the notion of an Aboriginal vote was simply 'ridiculous'. And this distempered rationalism evidently resonated with the majority setting about framing from scratch a franchise bill for a newborn state.⁹⁴¹

Higgins did not restrict the application of his premises to Australia, but extended them to South Africa, under 'the shadow', he said, of 'the black difficulty'. 'The problem of the Kaffirs is very grave indeed'.⁹⁴² Evidently sharing Higgins's interest and concern with South Africa, the House, in 1904, vented a protest against the importation of Chinese labour into the Transvaal. The racial obsession in Australia in the first decade of the Commonwealth had reached such a pitch that the *Sydney Morning Herald* could announce, 'The question of a white South Africa is in many respects similar to that of a white Australia, ... in a sense our battle is being fought in South Africa'.⁹⁴³ Such sentiments underpinned in part the fraternal greetings of the Commonwealth to the Union of South Africa upon its formation in 1910; and Fisher's official visit to the Union that year, along with the visits of Higgins and Watson. Had not 17 sections of the South African Constitution been copied word for word from the Australian Constitution?⁹⁴⁴ These dignified connections had been preceded by the *South African Preference Act* of 1906, which granted significant trade concessions to South Africa; 25 percent on some items. These were the first such concessions Australia gave any country.

There could be tariff concessions only because the Commonwealth had erected tariff barriers. One of the much-heralded purposes of the Commonwealth was to rid the country of much resented customs barriers at state borders; their removal would be 'a central symbolic act of federation',[945] even if the tariffs on interstate trade were, generally, minor. But if the Constitution had grandly resolved intercourse within Australia to be 'absolutely free', it was silent on any barrier between Australia and the rest of the world. And the erection of such a barrier would constitute the completion of a complementary triad of White Australia, compulsory arbitration and protection, each plausibly serving, separately and jointly, the average wage earner in import-competing industries. And so the *Customs Tariff Act* of 1902.

In instituting a tariff the Commonwealth was also granting manufacturers in Victoria and NSW their long sought, great aim; the sequestering NSW from overseas suppliers, to the benefit of manufacturers in Victoria and NSW, and the cost of the smaller states.[946] The simplest measure of the size of this barrier – and the end of free trade in NSW – is supplied by the comparison of the size of the tariff acts of NSW with that of the Commonwealth. The schedule of NSW *Customs Duties Act 1895* was 1.5 pages in length. The schedule of the *Customs Tariff Act 1902* was 38 pages long, and that of 1908, 68 pages. Such was the 'very light Customs duty' which Barton held out to Sydney audiences a few days before the 1898 referendum.[947]

The High Court

An Australian customs union might have come to pass without Federation. Protectionist momentum in NSW might have forced a customs union on Victoria as a *quid pro quo* for access to NSW. But the Federation customs union was more than a bargain congealed in legislation; that trade between the states be untariffed was inscribed in the Constitution, and enforceable by a High Court.

The High Court had been envisaged as the loftiest culmination of the Australian union, and the Convention welcomed it. Of its establishment, Barton rightly suggested there would not be 'more than one or two dissentients' to it among delegates, and Griffith was soon drafting the Bill to implement the Constitution's licence to establish a supreme court with a widely presumed power of constitutional review. But by the time the High Court was instituted, in August 1903, Barton's government was taking on water. In the House of Representatives it was badly beaten on legislation; Kingston had recently resigned his cabinet post in a dudgeon; and Reid had resigned his electorate of East Sydney in order to force a by-election in September 1903, and thereby a popularity contest. Winning 83 percent of the vote against a Labor protectionist, Reid then flourished the threat of standing in Barton's own seat, Hunter, at the rapidly approaching general election of 1903; a seat which free traders would, in fact, win easily. Toughing it out for long was not Barton's forte. But he held the card of the prime ministership, and Deakin would have destroyed the government to simply challenge Barton. A deal – it seems – was done. It seems plausible that Barton agreed to cede the prime ministership if Deakin, as the lynchpin of cabinet, would support him for a High Court position. The Governor-General scrupled at appointing Barton as Chief Justice,[948] and Deakin had evidently secured some détente with Griffith. So Griffith would be the Chief Justice, and Barton an ordinary justice. O'Connor's appointment as the third justice would be a sweetener.

The appointments to the first bench of the High Court must test even the driest historians' resolve to simply relate how it came to pass. Perhaps the least of its offences against propriety is the thin preparation of the majority of appointees. A suitable grounding to judge in a senior court would be having presided in one of the ample number of lower courts in Australia and abroad. Griffith was the Chief Justice of Queensland. But O'Connor's experience was limited to having acted as a Justice in the NSW Supreme Court for five months. And Barton could claim no more than being a circuit judge for a few months in Broken Hill and Grafton.[949] The chief justices of NSW, Victoria, SA and WA were passed over for appointment. As was Inglis Clark, the senior member of the Supreme Court of Tasmania, legal scholar of federalism, and author of the freshly published, *Studies in Australian Constitutional Law*.[950]

Regardless of preparation, the spectacle of Barton crafting a vacancy, and then, in effect, appointing himself to it, is queasy making. But the greatest objection to the filling of the first bench of the High Court is its offence against any vision of liberal constitutionality. Such a vision will include a court of constitutional review. But the touchstone of that review would be the consensus consent of the citizenry. A consensus is required in the legitimate choice of the court of recourse in some dispute over a private contract; likewise, the legitimate construction of a court of constitutional review betokens a consensus on the appointment of its justices. Such a consensus would not admit the appointment of partisan politicians sitting in judgement on the constitutionality of laws they had made, or opposed. It would not admit appointments be made by the grace and favour of the executive, without even, perhaps, a majority in the legislature.

Despite the travesty of procedure in the appointments to the Court, there was little opposition. Was there, in fact, a consensus? Most newspapers of the day were supportive, as they were of the Federation project.[951] But hegemony is not consensus. And neither is popularity: that Barton, Griffith and O'Connor were, after all, located near the midpoint of political opinion does not signify. What is noteworthy is the lack of protest even from Barton's sometime political enemies. Carruthers, once a brunt of Bartonian contempt, and soon a Premier of NSW badly aggrieved by the Griffith Court, was, in 1903, all placid praise. Perhaps Carruthers was disarmed by the appearance of the three to come straight from the core of the Australasian Federal Convention. Such an appearance may be objectively measured. Given the record of divisions of the Convention, one may compute for each delegate 'a net balance of concurrence' with any other delegate. To illustrate: Barton voted the same way as Abbott 86 times, and voted differently 25 times; so Barton may be said to have had a 'net balance of concurrence with Abbott' of 61 (and *vice versa*). One may further imagine a hypothetical delegate, called Majority, who voted with the majority on every division. A net balance of concurrence of each delegate with 'Majority' may be computed.

Table 13.3 reports the net balance of concurrence of each delegate with 'Majority', and reveals that no delegates voted more with Majority than Barton and O'Connor. The apparent centrality of Barton is underlined by pursuing the analysis of Convention divisions. The data can be used to position each delegate across a political spectrum. Consider the pair of delegates with the most negative net balance of concurrence with each other – Deakin and Douglas. They might be deemed the opposite ends of a 'left–right' spectrum. Every other delegate can be ordered on that spectrum by assigning to each a number equal to their net balance of concurrence with Deakin minus their net balance of concurrence with Douglas. Barton by this measure receives a score of minus 8, and, out of 45 delegates, is 'located' 24 places to the left of Douglas, and 20 places to the right of Deakin.[952] It appears that Barton was in the 'centre' of the Convention, distanced roughly equally from both Deakin and Douglas.[953]

So there was a plausible air of representativeness about the three first appointments. In the event, the Griffith Court did not hold very tightly to the average delegate's conception of the Constitution, and made unexpected discoveries in the matter of 'implied immunities'. A former junior of Griffith later admiringly declared that the Chief Justice 'was always clever enough to twist the law to enable him to give the verdict where the moral rather than the actual legal right lay'.[954] But at least the appointees of 1903 could have been reasonably expected to be central to the spirit of the Convention that fashioned the Constitution.

The same could not be said of the appointments of Isaac Isaacs and H. B. Higgins to the Court in 1906. Table 13.3 indicates that Isaacs is on the far 'left' wing of the spectrum of delegates. Of the 45 delegates, only Deakin had a more extreme spectrum value. With 45 delegates spanning the spectrum, Higgins is just five places from Deakin. The distance of Higgins and Isaacs from the centre of the spectrum was reflected in their vocal judgement of what the delegates produced. It is a piercing irony that these two, appointed to secure the Constitution, held it in such low esteem. At the completion of the Convention, Isaacs, as Attorney-General of Victoria, publicly declared that 'the value of the constitution was not yet clear', containing features that were 'doubtful', 'unsatisfying' and

Table 13.3: Convention delegates' voting proclivities with one another

Delegate	Balance of concurrence with majority	Agreement score with majority	Spectrum location value	Absences from divisions, percent of total
Barton	76	0.76	-8	4
O'Connor	71	0.74	-2	3
Abbott	61	0.77	-7	23
Zeal	60	0.75	-22	19
Brown	56	0.71	-79	12
Fysh	56	0.75	-30	25
Lewis	56	0.72	-39	16
Symon	55	0.71	-64	13
Walker	54	0.68	-26	3
Downer	52	0.71	-96	16
Howe	52	0.69	-32	8
McMillan	49	0.70	-57	19
Solomon	48	0.71	-49	25
Forrest	47	0.68	-21	24
Hackett	47	0.73	16	33
Leake	45	0.74	-51	38
Moore	45	0.72	-75	33
Lee	44	0.70	-88	28
Fraser	42	0.70	-44	22
Henry	41	0.71	-32	35
Wise	39	0.68	19	26
Clarke	35	0.69	-34	39
Reid	33	0.64	61	21
Braddon	31	0.62	-85	14
Dobson	30	0.60	-115	2
Douglas	29	0.61	-189	10
Glynn	29	0.60	-29	2
Gordon	27	0.61	-14	18
Hassell	27	0.66	-52	43
Brunker	19	0.62	53	47
Carruthers	19	0.58	22	24
Grant	19	0.57	-97	12
Holder	18	0.56	32	7

Trenwith	16	0.56	84	15
Turner	16	0.56	112	8
Quick	15	0.55	119	5
Higgins	14	0.55	105	8
Peacock	14	0.55	117	9
Deakin	13	0.55	193	7
Cockburn	8	0.53	-4	1
Kingston	8	0.53	64	1
Lyne	4	0.53	45	49
James	3	0.54	0	75
Berry	-6	0.47	92	24

Notes. Baker is excluded, along with delegates who did not participate in all three sessions. 'Agreement score' = votes with the majority as a proportion of total divisions voted in.

Sources. AFCP.

'extremely disappointing', and he could not recommend a Yes vote.[955] Isaacs did, however, ultimately reconcile to Yes. Higgins, in contrast, throughout the referendums of 1898 and 1899 remained vehemently opposed to the Constitution which he was later appointed to safeguard. Higgins's single sharpest objection to the Bill was that the guardian of the Constitution would be a jailor of the people's will.

> In America and Australia, Parliament (and the people) are kept within the prison walls of the Constitution, and the High Court keeps the key.[956]

Who from 1906 held the key? The unificationist revolution which these, with their new attitudes, worked, after Griffith's retirement, need not be expanded upon, beyond recording that their 'radically new approach to constitutional interpretation ... effectively reversed the intentions of the framers of the Constitution'.[957] The intentions of most of 'the framers' were reversed, but not those of these two delegates. Did not Isaacs declare to his fellow-framers, 'The states, as states, according to my view have no place in the Federation'?[958]

The Post Office

The institution of a Commonwealth Post Office was part of the self-conscious process of state-creation. Less grand than the High Court, less stirring than the army, the Post Office was nevertheless not only dignified, but also easily the most useful activity of the new government to most inhabitants. And, exploiting this significance, Federationists had promised a 'penny post' with the advent of the Commonwealth. Barton's publicity had declared, 'We will probably see a penny rate throughout Australia in the first Federal year'.[959]

Barton's bright promises regarding postal services were not realised. In its centralisation, bureaucratisation, submergence of the economic criterion, and official racism, the Commonwealth Post Office proved an unhappy epitome of the Federation.

One root of the Commonwealth Post Office's difficulties lay in its fundamental redundancy. Prior to 1901 the six postal services of Australia, with their 7 100 offices, performed their task with every show of approximate efficiency. Forrest and Holder protested the 'absurdity' of Barton's wish to transfer the posts, telephones and telegraphs to the Commonwealth, but unsuccessfully.[960] With Federation a Central Office was affixed atop of the existing six, captained by a Director-General with complete authority over six deputy directors – one for each state – each of which, in turn, oversaw seven branches within each state. 'The organisation' of this Commonwealth Post Office, purred one Deputy Director, 'is complete in every detail'.[961]

A second root of difficulties was that the new post office constituted a political recreation field. The Post Office was simply a department of the government. And the Postmaster-General, a cabinet minister. The first fourteen years saw twelve different Postmasters-General. And what did they do in their brief stay? The Post Office was easily the most significant point of contact of the Commonwealth with the public, and it consequently constituted a habitat for 'showcase syndrome', and symbolic policy formulation. For example, the Post Office was assigned the task of fostering national sentiment by conquering distance. And so the charge of sending telegrams inter-state was cut variously by 100, 200 and 300 percent. The slashing below cost of inter-state cables was doubtless welcome to politicians, newspaper proprietors and larger businesses, but would mean little to the ordinary person, who was left waiting more than a decade for Barton's much touted 'penny post'. And with a grand new object in their hands, there was inevitably a politicisation of its particulars of management.

> *According to Mr. Outtrim, the deputy Postmaster-General, the political influence which was got rid of under the Victorian Public Service Act has sprung into active life under the Commonwealth Postmaster General. ... Officers suffering under grievances—public servants are seldom otherwise occupied than in pondering over their grievances (why they had not received promotion, why increments are so long in coming, etc.)—now ignore the head of the department, when he is unsympathetic, and induce members of Parliament to interview the Minister on their behalf.* [962]

With four of the Postmasters-General appointed by Labor, and staff unions multiplying, there followed higher wages for the lowest ranks, and relaxation of discipline. In Queensland provision was made for 374.5 special holidays for staff – various showdays, races and carnivals. Not all who laboured would have welcomed all changes promoted by Labor; as these changes included the use of competitive exams as a barrier to entry from the General to the Clerical division; the institution of a compulsory retiring age of 65, and the 1901 *Post and Telegraph Act*'s ban on the use non-white labour by any mail contractor. But they reduced the general supply of labour, and increased its price. For all that, 'embarrassing feuds' between Labor Postmasters-General and unions persisted.[963]

The upshot was that the Post Office was beleaguered from all sides; with 'constant complaints' about service, a decline in maintenance below pre-Federation levels, disconsolate postmasters, disgruntled unions, and irate customers. Complaints to the Post Office were not welcome;[964] it charged 2/6d (about $20) even to lodge a complaint about a registered letter that had not been received. As Rose Scott put it, 'if we complain, we are fined'.

The Post Office's unpopularity forced Deakin, with Labor support, to call a royal commission. Its report in 1910 was 'one of the most condemning documents in Australian administrative history'.[965] A few years later the other side of politics commissioned a report into the Post Office by Robert Anderson, a timber merchant and future deputy quartermaster of the AIF. The *Report on the Business Management of the Post Master General's Department of the Commonwealth of Australia* makes for a fascinating exposé of the diseases of bureaucracy. Anderson faulted Central Office for 'indiscriminate issue of instructions' (about 1 600 a year), including a certain 'C.M 750/13', which directed how a hole is to be made to receive a pole. 'An examination of them makes one wonder why 90 percent of them were ever issued at all'.[966] He is further exasperated by the Post Office's commitment to 'a system of infinite correspondence' where all communications are to be done by paper. 'Report writing has become almost a disease' and 'this "itch of writing" extends from the oldest hands to the latest joined'. He instanced a dispute between two telephone officers comprising 539 pages.

But by now the world was at war, and reform of the Post Office was not at the forefront of ministers' minds.

The armed forces

In the armed forces the new Commonwealth possessed the most imposing symbol and tool of a state. And in the consolidation of the existing armed forces into a single Commonwealth weapon of war there lay the most palpable justification of federation: a stronger defence. Yet the most damning case against 1901 lies in the damage this consolidation caused. This consolidation was more harmful than the creation of a Commonwealth Post Office or the High Court. The High Court did not interfere with the operation of the lower courts. And the Commonwealth only intensified pre-existing centralisation and bureaucratisation of state Post Offices. But the armed forces, prior to 1901, were not a bureaucracy; they amounted to a collage of decentralised, independent, competitive, often community-based units: a 'volunteer democracy'.[967] It was on the basis of this 'utilitarian citizens organisation'[968] that Australia forces fought the Boer War, and won three Victoria Crosses. It was this military collage that the Commonwealth assumed control of on 31 March 1901.

The inaugural Commonwealth government squarely rejected the greatest opportunity this control afforded to improve defence: the establishment of an Australian navy, furnished with capital ships of a cost which would daunt any single state, but would be manageable by the six together. Barton, along with his Minister for Defence, John Forrest, and the man who would be key defence minister of the decade, Thomas Ewing, emphatically repudiated such a project. Instead the Royal Navy would be paid to continue to station some of its ships in Australia as an 'Australian Squadron'. Barton further conceded the Royal Navy its well-known wish to be able to redeploy the 'Australian Squadron' north of the equator whenever the Admiralty thought fit, in place of the stipulation of the 1887 agreement that any such redeployment require the consent of Australian governments. Thus the deeper self-government of Federationists.[969] The birth of an Australian navy awaited the advent of the premiership of Deakin, and the Royal Navy's exhortation to the Dominions to create their own navies, under Admiralty control, naturally. And so it was, on the outbreak of the First World War, a newly created Royal Australian Navy went to sea with modern destroyers, light cruisers, and, at the importuning recommendation of 'Jackie' Fisher, a less clearly useful but newly launched battle-cruiser, HMAS *Australia*; all an unsought and unlooked for benefit of Federation.

But if the Commonwealth ultimately produced a navy, it quickly brought its army to a state of semi-ruin.

The land forces of Australia that the Commonwealth inherited in March 1901 were in six parts, each something of a mosaic laid down by voluntarism and localism. Voluntary rifle units had been raised by universities and the civil service, alongside Irish Rifles and Scottish rifles, army nurses, and artillery (partly paid). There were doubtless a lack of 'coordination benefits'. The 'federalisation' since 1891 was a least a partial remedy, and had resulted before 1901 in a movement towards uniform equipment, the stationing of forces on an Australia-wide basis, and the integration of certain units into Australia-wide ones. With the advent of control, the Commonwealth could have pressed the 'federalisation' of forces. But all these fruits of 'federalisation' before 1901 had necessarily proceeded by negotiation. And to negotiate when you can command is not a natural posture for anyone. So it is not surprising that the Commonwealth chose to affix atop the six land forces a Headquarters, furnished with a miniature general staff, and presided over by a British officer, Sir Edward Hutton, who the Canadians had sacked as their forces' commander only shortly before,[970] but whom the Commonwealth judged worth an ample salary of £2 500 pa.[971] It is not surprising that this planners' unit recoiled at the medley of units, uniforms and pay rates – not to mention the division into permanent, paid part-time, and unpaid part-time (volunteer) units – and went about imposing uniformity and branching hierarchies. There followed a decade of resented amalgamations of units, of forced conversions from infantry and cavalry to light horse, of imposed new uniforms, and the requirement for even the long-experienced to sit examinations.

That the commanders of the new army were high-handed needs little emphasis. It probably does require notice that these doyens of efficiency produced an inefficient and chaotic administration. It was a decade of 'almost constant change', in which the army was 'fundamentally re-organised twice', under eleven ministers in ten years. 'The paperwork was endless', as one not unsympathetic history puts it.[972] It will not surprise that planners underappreciated non-rationalistic motivations; that, for example, colourful uniforms were an incitement to both volunteer and support – so much so that some of the old, more colourful uniforms were granted a (temporary) reprieve, to the disgruntlement of the Defence minister, Thomas Ewing.[973] Nor will it surprise that planners' attempts to invent tradition were less successful than those of local units.[974] Or that the braided cords imposed by planners were not popular. What might need more emphasis is that the planners' own rationality failed: that khaki was not, for example, a useful colour for artillery.

The army voted with its feet. A third of NSW's artillery resigned in protest.[975] In February 1904 parades in Tasmania were heavily boycotted, and Hutton 'subjected the few soldiers before him to a passionate speech about how British soldiers were motivated by loyalty [and] he would ... identify and punish those absent'.[976]

Opposite: En garde – boy trainees at Pulteney Street School for Boys, Adelaide

But it was in the volunteer (that is, unpaid) units that morale was 'destroyed'.[977] Unit after unit 'fought furiously' to retain their independence, or their infantry status, but were 'forced to submit' to amalgamation, conversion or abolition.[978] Numbers fell from 11 361 on 1 March 1901 to 5 094 by the end of 1909. Symbolic of the disdain and neglect of the voluntary soldiers was their treatment by Lord Kitchener on his investigative tour. At the capping field exercise of this tour, 'the Volunteers' only glimpse of Kitchener came when they were marching back from the Heads after the sun had set and he passed them in a car'.[979]

The wilting morale was only a cue for pushing further with the same approach. If young men did not wish to volunteer, then compel them. The political upshot was that Deakin's Defence minister, Ewing, with the indispensable assistance of his private secretary, Legge, set about planning to make compulsion an integral aspect of Australian defence. Legge's scheme of mass compulsory military training passed back and forth between Deakin and Labor with minor variations, and was implemented in the *Defence Act*, proclaimed on 13 December 1909. Every male between the age of 14 and 25 was required to undertake military training every year.[980] There was no allowance for conscientious objection.

Compulsory Military Training, unlike White Australia, Compulsory Arbitration, and Protection, constituted a radical break with everything that came before 1901. It would have been inconceivable in 1901 that within twelve years military police would be 'very busy' in Melbourne, searching 'shop after shop and office after office' for 15 year olds who had not turned out for parade.[981] A search by military historians for appeals for compulsion before 1901 yield only Kingston, Henry Taylor, and Legge.[982] Defence in all states prior to Federation was entirely based on voluntarism and localism, with widespread satisfaction.

Neither was compulsory military training an echo of international currents. In the first decade of the 20th century the English-speaking world moved towards the centralisation and professionalisation of armies. But the creation of the National Guard in the USA in 1903, and the Territorial Army in the UK in 1907, was entirely based on voluntarism. New Zealand also introduced compulsory military training by legislation in 1909. But teachers, doctors, Post Office employees, railway workers, and prison and hospital wardens were exempt. And New Zealand's 'junior cadets' were abolished almost as soon as they were instituted. Kitchener, in his report on Australian defences, did support compulsory military training, but 'he only developed and applied what was put before him'.[983] What Australia saw was an amplification of overseas practice, not an echo.

All organised opinion was in favour of compulsory military training. Across the party system consensus was complete: Deakin of the protectionists, Cook of the free traders, and Labor, stretching from its right wing (Billy Hughes) to its left wing (William Maloney): they all approved. In the churches, the arch enemies Cardinal Moran and Reverend Dr W.M. Dill Macky were united in their support. Most of the press was in favour; Syme 'strenuously advocated a system of universal compulsory military service'.[984] As did, predictably, the Australian Natives' Association.

Given the consensus in favour of compulsory military training, the total absence of it before Federation and, finally, the new Commonwealth outpacing any international currents to the same effect, compulsory military training might be considered the culminating manifestation of the Commonwealth.

But to assert compulsory military training epitomised the Commonwealth is not quite to say it was a consequence of the Commonwealth. Was it? The feasibility of compulsory military training was somewhat enhanced by a single Australian army. Evasion, by removing to another part of Australia, was now curtailed. But to enhance political feasibility is not at the same time to enhance political advantageousness. A still more direct culpability of the Commonwealth is that compulsory military training gratified the grandiosity that was so essential to the Commonwealth. Australian Federation would provide a new grand Australian arena; in Parkes's words, an 'Australian Empire' which would 'rank with the nations'. It was this grandiose conception of Federation which allowed Ewing and Deakin to conjure with visions of armies of 214 000,[985] sometimes 300 000. Even 800

000 was mentioned. Such dreams are undreamable if you have the population of County Durham.[986] Even with the Commonwealth's four millions, to 'rank with the nations' would remain a challenge. It was the consequent stretching to realise this vision which fostered the authoritarian and drastic measure of compulsory military training.

To stretch for grandeur is not to reach greatness. Compulsory military training was wasteful of the defence budget; being widely conceded as costly, despite adult trainees receiving only half the basic wage. It was harsh in operation. Evasion was significant, but enforcement determined. The minimum fine for failing to attend training was £5, a bit under $700 in present values. The Fisher Labor government, additionally, introduced massive fines for parents who 'prevented' their sons from participating in compulsory military training.[987] A military police force was specifically established to apprehend 14 to 18 year olds evading training. There were 27 749 prosecutions in the three years to June 1914.[988] Detention could await those who did not pay fines: military prisons to house such were established in 1912. Official records indicate 5 732 had actually been imprisoned by mid-1914.[989] And parents were sometimes imprisoned. Arthur Linley Henzell was convicted for 'having wilfully contravened the Defence Act by failing to register' his 13 year old son.

> *The Defendant*: *I will not pay one farthing, and I have not any furniture, so you know the alternative.*
>
> *The S.M*: *Fined 10/- with £1 costs.*
>
> *The Defendant* (defiantly): *I will pay nothing.*
>
> *The S.M.*: *In default of payment and distress, 14 days imprisonment.*[990]

A spirited, indignant minority was provoked into existence. In 1912 an Australian Freedom League was established in Adelaide. Quaker in its auspices, the League included the perfectly establishment, Federationist figure, J. W. Macarthur-Onslow: a great-grandson of John Macarthur, Cambridge graduate, lieutenant-colonel in the NSW Lancers, a National Federation candidate in 1898, then an aide-de-camp of Hutton during the Boer War, and from 1907 an Independent Liberal member for Waverley in the NSW Assembly. An avid opponent of compulsory military training, in 1912 he was elected President of the NSW branch of the Freedom League. The League spanned conventional divides, and claimed (unbelievably?) 55 000 members.[991]

But to say compulsory military training was grandiose in conception, wasteful in execution, draconian in enforcement, and detested by a minority is not to say it was ineffective. But it was ineffective. Cadets were sometimes 'totally incompetent'; 'ignorant of the rudiments of drill, or, worse, so badly trained that they had to expend great efforts in eradicating faults that were the result of poor initial training'.[992] And so it was the AIF of 1914 was 'lacking in basic military skills', and that the first contingent which left Australia for Gallipoli was 'essentially untrained'.[993]

The ending

On 25 April 1915, Sergeant Ted Larkin, the Labor member for Willoughby, was killed by machine gun fire at Pine Ridge, Gallipoli. In the subsequent by-election John Haynes, ever the warrior, stood as an independent on a platform of pursuing the war with vehemence, and won easily, in a large turnout. To Haynes the people had always been a latent force, a thing silently brewing, a storm slowly gathering on the horizon – now in war, the storm had broken; and now the Australian people, 14 years after Federation, emerged, defined as a host in arms. If the war granted Haynes the anti-Federationist one last hurrah, it equally seemed to leave behind certain heirs apparent of Federation – such as Deakin's seeming successor, William Watt – his rigid imperialism isolating him in opposition to the Dominion status which Australia now sought. Other apparent heirs the war had simply and brutally judged unfit, including Deakin's favourite soldier, and commander of the AIF, James Legge, sent home to Australia early in 1917.

Beyond achieving what Federation did not achieve, the War seems to have spent, fulfilled, redirected or extinguished the impulses behind the federal cause. The pointless onslaught at Gallipoli can be seen as a cathartic expression of the same restless idealism so animating of the federal struggle. Behold a grandson of Peter Lalor, Captain Joseph Lalor, rushing the Turk;[994] or the heavy toll of 'old boys' of Sydney and Melbourne Grammar schools. But with these military tests endured, and the nation proved in blood, Australia seemed to have her fill of glory and 'ranking with the nations'. With the end of the War, the new Commonwealth's symbols of might have lost their old prideful excitement and, on 12 April 1924, HMAS *Australia* was scuttled off Port Jackson, an apparently unregretted fee for the 'maintenance of the general peace' which the Washington Naval Agreement on disarmament would surely bring.

The Federation quest for status might also seem completed by the War, in 1917, with the transition of John Forrest into Baron Forrest of Bunbury. So one could be born in Bunbury and yet die a baron. More prosaically, the revision in Britain's constitutional arrangements and practices in the 1920s vanquished, in formal terms, the inferior status that so provoked Federationists.

Other impulses behind Federation were not so much fulfilled as redirected. Rural alienation – for generations resentfully glaring at Sydney, Brisbane, Perth and sometimes Melbourne – now directed its glower towards the Commonwealth, so enlarged and enabled by the War. This alienation now sought relief in a Country Party, or even a new state, rather than in a Commonwealth. Correspondingly, the smaller states no longer invested their hopes in a Commonwealth, but vented their frustrations in self-assertion.[995] Thus in WA, in 1933, former enthusiasts for Federation, most notably Walter James, pleaded with her inhabitants to vote in favour of Secession.[996] And Leopold Broinowski, Barton's private secretary in 1899 and Federationist campaigner in his own right, became in the 1920s a candidate for Tasmania First.

If some impulses for Federation were redirected, others might be extinguished, including the diffuse sense of homelessness of Irish Catholics, which had often responded to Federation. On the face of it, the dislocating apartness of the Irish might appear more pronounced than ever in the wake of the events of 1916. Certainly, some of the older Irish-born were polarised; some driven to republicanism, others into loyalism. But for the younger generation of Australian-born of Irish descent, the military experience of the First World War was a great integrator. Thus

Captain Lalor. And Sergeant Larkins. Or the two soldiering sons of Labor radical and republican 'martyr', Hugh Mahon.[997] Or a nephew of Ned Kelly, raised by Ned's mother, who enlisted in the AIF, and died in the desperate defence of Lagnicourt.[998] And, for Australians at large, 1916 destroyed the vision of Home Rule Ireland, which had been so animating of the Federationist vision. The subsequent agony of Ireland was dismaying, while a frankly republicanising Free State could not be a model for Australia.

Federation was decided 15 years before the outbreak of the First World War, but, on account of the exhaustion, displacement or extinction during the War of the impulses behind the decision, the Federation episode might, with the outbreak of war, be deemed completed.

14

A Codicil

> But who shall change our destinies ... ?
> – Henry Parkes

A better understanding of this work might be gained from a flight of fancy; an imaginary account of 'the 4th of August 1914' in Australia if 'the 1st of January 1901' had not taken place.

> *On Tuesday the Prime Minister of the Council of the Australian Federation called a meeting of Premiers and deputies in Hobart. The Council which, under British pressure, had in 1910 succeeded the old Federal Council of Australasia, was to confer with the Federation's Naval Minister, Alfred Deakin, on the mobilisation of the Royal Australian Marine Corps. The Corps, established as a particular project of the Minister, had only recently survived a challenge to its legality, on the grounds that the cavalry units raised by the enthusiastic minister did not constitute the 'naval force' permitted under the Australian Federation Act. But Lord Griffith, presiding over the new Australasian Division of the Imperial Court, ruled that the Corps was constitutional, as long as the cavalry was 'trained for marine operations'. As for Australia's land forces, they remained the responsibility of the 'states' (as the colonies were now styled), and it was the task of the Premiers to mobilise the infantry. This task seemed a personal pleasure to Billy Hughes, who had only recently led a Labor-Free Trade coalition to replace the Lyne government in NSW, which had long reigned ever since George Reid had been killed in a buggy accident during the Hastings-Macleay by-election of 1898. Hughes could barely keep himself away from rallies to recruit the all-volunteer forces, even though recruiting was not difficult. In Queensland even a group of Kanakas, eager for the*

adventure, had volunteered. The Queensland Premier, T. J. Byrnes, declared that such a corps might be valuable in providing logistical support for the troops, especially in the matter of unloading railway cars. The Premier's concrete allusion proved unfortunate, as it quickly provoked a strike by the Railway Union, demanding inclusion of a whites-only labour clause, of the sort their fellow unionists had been (unsuccessfully) striving for in the Post Office. A Board of Conciliation found a formula that would keep Kanakas off the railways on this occasion, without conceding the general point. The Board's rulings had no sanction beyond public opinion, but every recommendation of their past efficacy, and the union called a return to work. Thus in the days of August, Australia's forces were gathered, fortified by the resolution of her parliaments in favour of placing troops at the disposal of the Imperial Government for the defence of any part of the Empire. A discordant note was heard when a government motion to place all members of permanent forces in the hands of the Empire – and not just those who volunteered – was defeated by the casting vote of the Speaker, John Quick. But a more perfect unity was found in the resolution of the Premiers and Council of 23 August 1914 to suspend all tariffs on inter-state trade for the duration of hostilities. The Australian Protectionist League assured the Age that manufacturers would not flinch at this patriotic sacrifice, but added that the matter would need to be re-examined once shipping had been restored to normalcy. The same resolutions used provisions of the Federation Act to vest in the Council all legislative powers over tariffs on imports from overseas as well. Whether the Premiers realised that this transfer would prove permanent seems unlikely ...

Airing this fantasy may clarify the contentions of the preceding pages. They have not argued that a closer political integration of Australia should never have happened. Rather, that it might have happened later with better effect. It is not that federation is wrong, but that the Federation of 1901 was premature and botched. Alternative histories were possible; better histories were possible.

New Zealand underlines the contingency of the Commonwealth as it was proclaimed in 1901, and has remained. The *Commonwealth of Australia Constitution Act* treated New Zealand as a potential state. Accordingly, in 1901, Barton granted long interviews to an official party of New Zealanders dispatched to investigate the new Commonwealth. Other Federationists, including Reid, believed that New Zealand would join in a 'comparatively short time'.[999] This expectation kept the Australasian Federation League alive for a decade after 1901.[1000] (Would not New Zealand have every incentive to be within the Commonwealth's tariff wall?) Weighing against such expectations were long-held and widespread doubts in New Zealand. And yet some interest appears to have been kindled in 1899 by the Bill's approval in NSW, the colony New Zealand was closest to. Federation Leagues were now formed. One British visitor ventured that public opinion in New Zealand at this time was 'keenly alive' to Federation.[1001] Perhaps opinion was evenly split between favourable, unfavourable and uncertain.[1002] The matter seemed to rest in the hands of Richard Seddon, 'King Dick', the prime minister since 1893, and then in the midst of the longest premiership New Zealand has experienced. Joining the Commonwealth presented an attractive opportunity to Seddon. He would be an easily recognisable quantity to Australians; in their eyes another Lyne, tinctured with some Parkes and Kingston. And he knew them. British-born, Seddon had emigrated first to Australia, shifting to New Zealand after some years in Victoria's goldfields. He made extensive return visits to Australia, including attending the Premiers' Conference of 1897. He would have instantly assimilated if he had returned permanently to Australia by way of an Australasian federal politics, and was a more reckonable politician than any Australian rival. But there was a risk. In New Zealand, 'King Dick' was king; how would fortune treat him in a Commonwealth of Australasia? So he dandled with the matter. He instructed his agent-general to petition Chamberlain to amend the Bill to include an 'open-door' clause for New Zealand, to permit appeals from New Zealand courts to the High Court, and to formally facilitate a trans-Tasman defence force. But Chamberlain was not amenable. The New Zealand public's interest in the Commonwealth crested about 1900, and slumped. New

Zealand's 'Federation moment' passed. But there was such a moment. Federation was a passing wave that lifted all boats. It did not quite lift New Zealand onto to the shoreline, but could have, with decided consequences.

Western Australia illustrates in a different way the contingency of the Commonwealth. The possibility of WA staying outside was not fanciful. Forrest could have outlasted goldfields' pressure by grounding a disengagement from Federation on the Commonwealth's refusal to grant WA tariffs for a full five years; its rejection of the election of Senators on a geographical basis (and not allocating, say, two or three of the six senators to the goldfields); and its reluctance to fund a railway from Kalgoorlie to Esperance. Reinforcing the possibility, the goldfields' wealth and population began to slide after 1901. Successful resistance of the goldfields' ebbing sway may have underwritten itself. For outside the Commonwealth, WA would have been able to give free rein to its rapid economic and social development, rather than endure as the ill-cast, minor character of a drama written by others. Come the 1930s, Western Australia, instead of feeling acutely disaffected from the Commonwealth, might have been willing to enter, and able to do so, on more suitable terms.

The envisioning of such counterfactuals to the Federation of 1901 might be depreciated on the grounds that they are fertile only in regrets and not at all in utility. For even if such counterfactual speculations were actual possibilities, they were only actually possible in a now unreachable past. They are roads not taken, which were once open, but are now definitely closed. We cannot get 'there' from 'here'; Australia is stuck with a Constitution and a six-state Commonwealth; and the now annihilated possibilities of the past provide no guide to present day action.

But it may in turn be retorted that the value of contemplating counterfactuals lies, not in the recovery of some overlooked path of action, but in illuminating the enduring nature of Australian society. Such is the underlying intention of the present work. To venture a summary of its claims: the Federation episode illustrates the mechanicality of Australian commitment to democracy, the weakness of national feeling, the slightness of ideas in its public counsel, the political ascendancy of the professions, and the pre-eminence, contrary to mythology, not of the utilitarian, but of the ritualistic, the legalistic, and the bureaucratic. Finally, the persistence and prevalence of the historical myth of the Federation, the particular butt of the present work, is illustrative of the grooved character of Australia's intellectual life.

This critique of Australian political society countenanced by this history of Federation, may be refused, and in several ways.

It may be deemed untrue. Or it may be deemed not so much untrue as misrepresenting. Thus what has been referred to as 'ritual', 'legalism' and 'bureaucracy' may be accepted as both fostering of, and fostered by, Federation, but the pejorative with which these words obviously are loaded needs to be repudiated. This is essentially the position of the old nationalist left, the pre-1970 left, who exalted in the creation of the Commonwealth, and to whom what has been here dubbed 'legalism' was justice, 'bureaucracy' rationality, and 'ritual' propriety.

An alternative rejection of the critique may accept the pejorative nature of legalism, bureaucracy and ritualism – accept these as banes of Australia's society – but deny that Federation is tied up with them in any important way. This is essentially the position of what may be dubbed 'Commonwealth conservatives'; those largely acquiescent in the Federation myth, but who, more particularly, hold that the Constitution was conceived with barely a blemish, and was only later defiled, and largely ruined. They uphold the original Constitution of 1901 with its undoubtedly formal federal remit; they deplore the sequence of High Court decisions which over the decades – from the Engineers' case to the Tasmanian Dams case – have destroyed that remit. But an incoherence troubles their position: if the original Constitution was irreproachable, why could it not sustain the federalism it was charged to sustain? Was not the destruction of federalism largely a consequence of operation of the Constitution? Did not the Constitution, by so loosely licensing a court of constitutional review, place in sovereign eminence the visions and vagaries of a handful of lawyers?

A third rejection of this work's critique of the nature of Federation denies not its truth, but its utility. This rejection would be favoured by 'conservatives of myth', who stress, above all else, the existence and subscription to some myth of an institution as essential to that institution. The myth of 1901, as the incarnation story of the Commonwealth, is, in their view, more valuable on account of its cohesive effect, than any legalism, etc., it may have fostered. To their minds, then, the present work is just another act of cultural destruction; a destruction of part of society's store of the myth which furnishes the reason which rationalism cannot. Thus the fact that the Australian flag, contrary to endlessly repeated Federationist legend, was not chosen by a public competition, but by the Colonial Office, does not matter: it is the flag Australian armies, fleets and squadrons have fought under, and is now received as the country's symbol, and subverting it would only subvert the country.

Such a conservative defence of the myth of the Commonwealth, is, however, vulnerable to the contention that if an institution is dying, then the utility of that institution's myth is also dying. Indeed, if the myth itself is dying, so must its utility. Both the institution and the myth of 1901 are dying. The institution and its myth was the Australian 'nation-state', and the myth is now painfully beleaguered. Internally, an 'anti-myth' of a 'counter nation' is in dire antagonism, and prolific in its own counter mythology.[1003] Perhaps even more fatal to the myth of the Australian nation-state is the rejection by many of any 'nation' of any kind at all, and its displacement by a vision of a borderless world, composed of a salmagundi of various identities, with no state but a world state.

But, however moribund the nation-state may be, there must remain some force in the liberal vision of the distinct, discrete, non-universal state; a vision which would have in one house all who can, at least, do business with one another, perhaps even make music with each other, and which for that end will discard interior walls, and yet, for that very same end, will maintain some exterior walls. Perhaps the nub of the matter is that this vision is no longer served by the myth of the nation. In brief, the nation-state no longer serves the liberal state. The inevitable 'monism' of any nation's historical mythology always sat awkwardly with the pluralism of liberal society: with the intensification of that pluralism, the requisite ideological contortion now seems unendurable. And the geographical dimension of the myth of the nation also now seems unhelpful to the liberal state. The myth of nation always went to battle under a certain geographical bewitchment. The nation must have a luminous geographical identity. A continent for a nation! Anything without that sweep was a 'province'. For centuries that bewitchment was useful in creating conglomerate state structures. But now that spell seems enfeebled, as the moribundity of hopes for a 'European nationality' underlines. In the wake of that failure, and of like continental nationalities, the future of the liberal state may perhaps lie, not in the restoration of 'Britain', or 'England', or 'Scotland', with their defunct or false mythologies, but in still smaller entities, of more utilitarian foundation, and less invested in embracive myth.

On the debris of the nation-state – itself erected on the rubble of 'the province' – perhaps the polis will re-emerge.

Appendix 1

Some biographical thumbnails

(Age at 2 March 1891, place of birth, position on Federation, position on free trade)
'Delegate' = delegate at the Australasian Federal Convention

Abbott, Joseph (49, NSW, Federationist, protectionist). NSW Speaker, Delegate, confrére of Barton, and sometime denizen of his house.

Archibald, J.F. (35, Victoria, Fed, prot). Magician of the *Bulletin*, 'full of resentments [and] ... personal charm', 'mercurial, intellectually arrogant' 'intensely human personality', with an 'incendiary mind' (Conor Macleod).

Astley, William (35, England, Fed). Author, swindler, impresario of the Bathurst People's Convention, Barton's media manager in 1898.

Baker, Richard (49, SA, Fed, f t). SA Speaker. Delegate, who perhaps thought harder about federation than any other, but as Chairman of Committees was almost totally silent.

Barton, Edmund (42, NSW, Fed, prot). NSW Speaker and Attorney-General; Delegate; Prime Minister. Reigned over, but did not always rule, the Federationist cause.

Barton, George (54, NSW, Fed?). Wayward, literary elder brother of the prime ministerial Barton. Disenchanted Federationist *avant la lettre*.

Bavin, Thomas (16, New Zealand, Fed, prot). Private secretary to Barton and Deakin, later Premier of NSW. The legal class politician *par example*. Perhaps Barton's truest protégé.

Beauchamp, Seventh Earl (19, England, Fed). Governor of NSW, diarist and, later, exile from polite society. 'Liked bohemian company' (Bedford).

Bedford, Randolph (22, NSW, Fed, prot). Literary apostle of the Commonwealth; 'large, aggressive, loud-voiced, moustached' (Macleod).

Braddon, Edward (61, England, Fed). Premier of Tasmania and Delegate; 'an adventurer not overburdened with conscience' (J.B. Walker); 'a bit of a rogue' (Roe). He gave his name to the 'Braddon blot' of the Constitution, that required 75 percent of tariff revenue be returned to the states.

Brunker, James (58, NSW, Fed?, free trader). Delegate. A Parkesite unenthralled by federation.

Bryce, James (52, Ireland, Fed). To the British, their interpreter of the 'American Commonwealth'. But to Australia, the most senior of her 'committed intercessors'.

Byrnes, T.J. (30, Queensland, ~Fed, f t) Queensland Premier. The great 'what if' of the federal epoch; 'one of the most enigmatic personalities in Queensland's history' (Gill).

Carrington, Charles (47, England, Fed). Liberal politician and land owner, appointed by Gladstone to be Governor of NSW, 1885-1890.

Carruthers, Joseph (34, NSW, Fed, f t). Premier of NSW and Delegate; 'a peppery little man' (La Nauze) of 'untiring energy' (Percival Serle). Beauchamp suspected his deafness was 'often feigned'.

Chamberlain, Joseph (54, England, Fed, prot*)*. Colonial Secretary from 1895, 'he seemed increasingly desperate to set the agenda, but repeatedly blundered' (C. A. Wood).

Clark, Andrew Inglis (43, Tasmania, Fed, f t). Attorney-General and justice of Supreme Court of Tasmania; 'eloquent, impressive and dignified ... doctrinaire politician ... wanting in practical ability' (J.B. Walker).

Coghlan, Timothy (35, NSW, ~Fed). NSW Statistician and Reid advisor. Closest thing to a mandarin before Federation.

Copeland, Henry (51, England, Fed, prot). Barton lieutenant. Ballarat digger. A plain talking man of the people. 'He will light his pipe, and tell you slowly and deliberately, with that strong Yorkshire accent of his, what he thinks' (*AE*).

Crick, William (29, NSW, Fed?, prot). A corrupt NSW Lands minister from 'the backblocks outside Dubbo' (O'Sullivan); a 'conservative dressed in the garments of democracy' with an 'unbridled ambition and craving for public notice' (Willis).

Dalley, W.B. (deceased, NSW, Fed, f t). Native-born of convict parents; a Sydney College educated dandy; led NSW delegation to 1883 Intercolonial Convention, from which sprang the Federal Council of Australasia.

Dawson, Andrew (27, Queensland, Fed, f t). Orphanage-raised, momentary Labor Premier of Queensland. Watson's minister for defence.

Deakin, Alfred (34, Victoria, Fed, prot). Spiritualist, journalist, barrister, Delegate, Prime Minister, and the ultimate director of the Federation cause. A 'clever sort of fellow' (John Morley); 'a lover of life, of metaphysics, and of power' (Royce). Humane in thought, sometimes brutal in deed.

Dibbs, George (56, NSW, ~Fed, prot). NSW Premier and businessman. A 'plain, blunt man of simple manners' (P. Serle); 'no believer in federation but a firm believer in office' (A.B. Piddington).

Dickson, James (58, England, Fed, f t). A Queensland Premier. ' ... believes in Federation no more than I do, and yet for the sake of carrying out Federation while he is the premier, he stands at the head of it'(McIlwraith). Wore a 'large, oval and highly polished gold stud which scintillated like an Evening Star' (Bernays).

Douglas, Adye (75, England, Fed?, f t). An 'aged and virile' former premier of Tasmania, 'not without enemies' (P. Serle). Delegate.

Drake, James (40, England, Fed, prot). ' ... one of the most divisive and controversial Queensland politicians of his era', with 'highly flexible principles' (Megarrity).

Duffy, Charles Gavan (74, Ireland, Fed, prot?). Irish nationalist journalist, briefly premier of Victoria, and 'committed intercessor'.

Ewing, Thomas (34, NSW, Fed, prot). Deakin's minister for defence. An adroit 'roads and bridges' MP, who also practised the politics of (ugly) ideals.

Garran, Andrew (65, England, Fed, f t). Editor of the *Sydney Morning Herald*, and Reid minister in NSW. Fervent free trader, fervent federationist. Friend of Edward Thomson, and father of Robert Garran.

Garran, Robert (24, NSW, Fed). Private secretary to Reid.

Later Convention draftsman and publicist. Sincere and 'natural' Federationist.

Gillies, Duncan (57, Scotland, ~Fed). Premier of Victoria. Ballarat digger. His 'large square jaw, firm and rather thin lips, suggested the massive strength of character of a man who had cut his way with nothing but a miner's pick'(*Newsletter*).

Glynn, Patrick (35, Ireland, Fed, f t). Literary lawyer and Delegate. A minor actor in Federation, but an important observer. President of the Adelaide chapter of the Irish National Federation.

Griffith, Samuel (45, Wales, Fed). Chief Justice of the Supreme Court of Queensland, and later the High Court of Australia; 'an acute and subtle lawyer, an adept at the little intricacies of bill crafting' (A.G. Stephens); 'a very skilful tactician in all political movements' (A.D. Graham); 'could not be described as a popular' but 'had perfect faith in himself' (P. Serle).

Hackett, John Winthrop (43, Ireland, Fed). Forrest's deputy; 'a power behind the scenes' (Crowley); close ally of Deakin and Barton.

Haynes, John (40, NSW, ~Fed, f t). An 'infectiously humorous' maverick politician (Miles Franklin); 'the city's popular press was his true and natural habitat' (S. Lawson). A great unexploited political talent of the day.

Holder, Frederick (40, SA, Fed, f t). Treasurer and Premier of SA, later Speaker of House of Representatives. Methodist preacher.

Hughes, Thomas (27, NSW, Fed, f t). Reid's private secretary in 1899, Federationist and 'leading Roman' (Beauchamp).

Hughes, William (28, England, ~Fed, f t). NSW Labor MP. Natural born fighter.

Hume Cook, James (24, New Zealand, Fed, prot). President of the Australian Natives Association, later Deakin's whip. Fluent and facile. Protectionist true believer.

Hunt, Atlee (26, Queensland, Fed). '… a disciple of Barton, who had worked strenuously in Federation campaigns' (J.A. La Nauze). A driven, chain smoking, bureaucrat.

Isaacs, Isaac (35, Victoria, Fed?, prot?). Attorney-General in Turner government and later Chief Justice of the High Court.

'Ultra democrat' (Glynn). Sharpest legal mind in Convention. Vain, obstinate and unpopular.

Kingston, Charles (40, SA, Fed, prot). Premier of SA, later Commonwealth Minister for Trade and Customs. 'A bully with a short fuse . . . who excited extremes of passion' (Glass).

Lang, John Dunmore (deceased, Scotland, Fed?, f t). The first public advocate of Australian federation. Later favoured its indefinite postponement.

Leake, George (34, WA, Fed, f t). Delegate, WA Opposition Leader, and later Premier. An 'immensely popular' politician (P. Serle), of the 'old settlers' elite.

Legge, James (27, England, Fed). Soldier bureaucrat unsuited to soldiering. Hand picked by Deakin for military eminence.

Lyne, William (46, Tasmania, ~Fed, prot). Delegate and premier of NSW. 'A singular mixture of good nature and wiliness' (Reid). Opposed federation until the cause was won.

McGowen, James (35, England, Fed, prot). NSW Labor leader, later Premier. A Sunday School superintendent of 32 years; 'a man of essentially moderate views' (Coghlan).

McIlwraith, Thomas (46, Scotland, ~Fed). Premier of Queensland. 'One of the few Australian merchants who excelled in the political arena' (Reid).

Mackay, James (31, NSW, Fed, prot). Lyne minister, novelist and soldier. Convinced of the 'utter incapacity of the average Australian volunteer officer', he did 'excellent staff work' for the Commander-in-Chief of British army during the Boer War.

MacLaurin, Normand (55, Scotland, ~Fed, prot). Led the protectionist anti-Billites in 1899. 'A clever Scotchman' (Beauchamp) who traversed business and professional worlds.

McLean, Allan (51, Scotland, ~Fed, prot). Anti-Billite, Premier of Victoria in the rural interest.

McMillan, William (40, Ireland, Fed, f t). A Treasurer of Parkes. Delegate. 'Dully, prosy, preachy and much too long' (Carrington).

Macrossan, John (56, Ireland, Fed). The epitome of the north Queensland separationist as Federationist.

Maloney, William (36, Victoria, ~Fed, prot). Senior in Higgins's anti-Federationist Democratic League. Deakin called him a 'creature'; he tossed a glass of water in Deakin's face. 'Bore himself with a cloak and dagger air of a hero of melodrama' (Norman Lindsay).

Meagher, Richard (25, NSW, Fed?, prot). NSW MP. Rogue. Candidate for Protectionist, Labor and Nationalist parties.

Moran, Patrick (60, Ireland, Fed). Cardinal and Archbishop of Sydney. 'Liked and intensely disliked, he moved in the highest political circles ...' (Ayres).

O'Connor, Richard (39, NSW, Fed, prot). Barton's 'chief of staff' (McMinn), later Senator and then justice of the High Court. Conservative and Home Ruler. 'Always wise and helpful' (Hunt); 'a man who gradually became popular (G. Haines).

Norton, John (33, England, Fed??, prot). Editor of *Truth* and NSW MP. Unattractive enigma.

Parkes, Henry (75, England, Fed, f t). Premier of NSW. 'A renegade Chartist' (J.D. Fitzgerald), who observed 'the ceremony of high life ... a prince could sit at his table' (*Review of Reviews*)'; 'vain and temperamental' and 'too conscious of his superiority'.

Parkes, Varney (31, NSW, Fed?, f t). Henry's one adult son. Opposed the Bill in 1898. Appointed Postmaster-General by Reid. Supported the Bill in 1899.

Peacock, Alexander (29, England, Fed, prot). Delegate, later premier of Victoria. Highly popular; 'fervent apostle of protection' (F.W. Eggleston). At the Convention 'He frequently said 'Hear, Hear''' (La Nauze).

Pulsford, Edward (46, England, Fed, f t). Politically deaf and blind publicist and organiser for free trade and federation. Defeated in April 1891 in the earliest electoral confrontation over federation: the *Star* claimed six came to hear him speak.

Quick, John (38, England, Fed, prot). Unsuccessful Victorian parliamentarian who coined the scheme to elect the Australian Federal Convention. Delegate. More legal academic than politician. Estranged from Deakin.

Reid, George (46, Scotland, Fed, f t). NSW premier and, later, prime minister. 'He looked like an Opera Bouffe theatrical' (J.T.

Walker). 'His aspect was grotesque but his manner admirable' (Beauchamp).'It never occurred to people to follow him – they came crowding around him' (Jose); 'Reid was the man with hundreds of friends but no friendship' (Piddington).

Robertson, John (74, England, ~Fed, f t). Five-time premier of NSW. A NSW patriot. A previous generation's captain, stranded by the departing tides of time.

Ronald, J.B. (29, Scotland, Fed). Labor MP in Commonwealth parliament. Turbulent priest. A clerical 'sensation of the 90s', who drank too much and feuded too much. Repudiated by the Presbyterian church, but not by his political allies.

Rosa, Samuel (25, England, ~Fed). Journalist leader of left agitation in NSW against Federation. Wrote *Olive Spence, The Australian Ceasar*, in which 'Olive Spence' (=William Spence) leads a socialist rebellion against a plutocratic Federal government commanded by 'Israel Smith' (= Bruce Smith).

Sargood, Frederick (56, England, Fed, f t). The merchant prince of Melbourne. A politician of judgements rather than creed; save for beliefs in Federation and Empire.

Scott, Rose (43, NSW, ~Fed, f t). Women's movement leader of 'intellect and heart'. Salon hostess; Reid, Barton, Wise, Lyne, Holman, Hughes, and Haynes all partook.

Seddon, Richard (45, England, Fed?, prot). New Zealand Prime Minister. 'There have been few more remarkable figures of our time than this popular dictator, who gained and kept power without education and without eloquence' (Bryce).

See, John (45, England, Fed, prot). Protectionist, and NSW Premier following Lyne; 'a self made man of good heart but a most pushing and disagreeable manner' (Beauchamp).

Smith, Bruce (39, England, Fed, f t). A Treasurer of Parkes. In labourist history, an ogre of the federation drama. Epitomised the illusions of free trade idealists about Federation.

Storey, David (34, Ireland, ~Fed, f t). NSW MP who defeated Barton for the seat of Randwick in 1894. Perhaps NSW's last 'merchant in politics'. Believed Federation would damage NSW for 'centuries'.

Syme, David (63, Scotland, Fed??, prot). Owner of the *Age*, he 'could hate as few men can ... loved power as few men have ever loved it' (Pratt).

Symon, Josiah (44, Scotland, Fed, f t). Unsuccessful SA parliamentarian but 'formidable forensic barrister' (Bannon). Delegate. Iron willed, behind the scenes player, encumbered by his crotchets.

Taylor, Adolphus George (33, NSW, ~Fed?, prot). Provocateur, nationalist anti-Billite, who got much the best of his parliamentary jousts with Reid and Barton. 'He could discern the weakness of his contemporaries, he could not cure his own' (W.B. Melville).

Trenwith, William (Billy) (44, Tasmania, Fed, prot). Delegate. The sole representative of Labor at the Convention. Often wore a silk top hat. 'Commanding intellect' (Eggleston).

Turner, George (39, Victoria, Fed, prot). Premier of Victoria, 1894-99, 1899-1901. Delegate. 'A pertinacious and combative little man, especially when he is on the winning side' (John Anderson).

Walker, J.T. (48, Scotland, Fed, f t). Delegate, later Senator. A free trade Bartonite. Rose without trace. And left without any.

Want, John (44, NSW, ~Fed, f t). NSW Attorney-General. The pantomime villain in commemorative history of Federation. More truly, a man of action out of place in professional politics.

Watt, William (29, Victoria, Fed, prot). Victorian MP. Point man of the Australian Natives Association's federationist campaign. Heir apparent of Deakin.

Willis, William (32, NSW, Fed, prot). NSW MP, newspaper proprietor, rogue, 'remarkable personality' (W.B. Melville).

Wise, Bernhard (33, NSW, Fed, 'freetectionist'). Attorney-General of Parkes and Delegate. 'A rising young man who somehow had never risen ... A most agreeable companion' (Beauchamp), with 'clear musical voice' (*Age*) and 'attractive manner' (Quick), but with 'inveterate personal and political enemies' (W.B. Melville). 'A most unstable politician' (Carruthers), rightly distrusted by all; 'a sort of Australian Randolph Churchill' (*Review of Reviews*).

Wrixon, Henry (51, Ireland, Fed). Defeated by a hair by Higgins in the Convention election. 'Lucid in his arrangement, clear in argument, practical in debate' (J.B. Walker).

Appendix 2

Some statistical relationships

Constant terms are included in all regressions, but not reported.
95 percent confidence levels in brackets.
* = significantly different from zero at the 5 percent level.
** = significantly different from zero at the 1 percent level.

Table A.1: Explaining candidate support in the election of NSW delegates to the Australasian Federal Convention

dependent variable: candidate vote

Loyal Orange Lodge ticket, dummy	United Protestant ticket, dummy	Labor ticket, dummy	R^2	N
31616	33534	-219	0.84	49
(21 464	(23 636	(-8 229		
41 770)	43 433)	7 900)		
**	**			

Table A.2: Explaining the Yes Vote in the NSW referenda by means of party support at 1898 general election

dependent variable: Yes as percent of vote, by electorate

Year	Federal Liberal (=Reid), percent of vote	National Federal (=Barton), percent of vote	R^2	N
1898	-0.01	0.34	0.15	80
	(-0.31	(0.05		
	0.29)	0.63)		
		*		
1899	0.10	0.31	0.09	80
	(-0.18	(0.04		
	0.38)	0.59)		
		*		

Table A. 3 Explaining the Yes vote in South Australia's referendums

dependent variable: Yes as percent of vote, by electorate

Period	Industrial occupation, per cent of all occupied persons	Industrial occupation: 1899 dummy	English birthplace, per cent of all adults	Constant, 1899 dummy	R^2	N
1898	-1.49 (-0.93 -2.07) **		-0.76 (-0.18 -1.33) *		0.74	26
1898 and 1899	-1.57 (-1.1 -2.05) **	1.57 (0.95 2.20) **	-0.59 (-0.23 -0.94) **	-10.0 (-1.4 -18.6) *	0.72	52

Notes: Industrial Occupation = manufacturing, building, construction, 'indefinite industrial occupation', and transport and communication. Northern Territory dropped.

Sources: SA 1901 Census and Rhodes (2002).

Table A.4: Explaining the Yeses and Noes in South Australia's referendums

dependent variable: number of Yes votes (No votes), by electorate

	Industrial occupation, number of persons	Industrial occupation, 1899 slope dummy	Constant, 1899 shift dummy	R^2	N
Yes	0.19 (0.02 0.36) *	0.54 (0.30 0.78) **	74.7 (-511 660)	0.71	52
No	0.32 (0.27 0.37) **	-0.10 (-0.2 -0.17) **	158 (-16.9 335)	0.83	52

Notes: Northern Territory dropped.

Table A.5: Explaining turnout in the NSW referendum of 1899

dependent variable: total vote, by electorate

Average of total vote in the 1895, 1898 and 1901 general elections	Murray, dummy	Albury, Eden Bombala and Wentworth, dummy.	Hay, Hume and Deniliquin, dummy	Newcastle East, dummy	Sydney-Gipps, dummy.	R^2	N
0.89 (0.75 1.03) **	1143 (690 1598) **	88 (-177 353)	437 (169 706) **			0.61	123
0.89 (0.76 1.01) **	1151 (725 1577) **		444 (192 696) **	526 (101 951) *	734 (308 1159) **	0.66	123

Appendix 3

Authors and sources of introductory quotations

Chapter 2, Parkes quoted in Moore (1902, p. 56).

Chapter 3, 'My Native Land', Parkes (1889).

Chapter 4, Furphy (1990 [1903], p. 205).

Chapter 5, 'The Twentieth Century', Parkes (1895).

Chapter 6, Parkes (1890, p.137).

Chapter 7, 'Seventy', Parkes (1885).

Chapter 8, Untitled poem, A.I. Clark, Ely (2001).

Chapter 9, 'A Commonwealth Hymn', Robert Garran in Francis (1973).

Chapter 10, 'The Strong Man', Parkes (1885).

Chapter 11, 'The Patriot', Parkes (1885).

Chapter, 12 'One People, One Destiny', Parkes (1895).

Chapter 13 'Bismarck', Parkes (1885)

Chapter 14 'Gone!', Parkes (1885).

Abbreviations

Debates

AFC: Official record of debates of the Australasian Federal Convention

CPD: Commonwealth Parliamentary Debates

FCA: Federal Council of Australasia: official record of debates.

NSWPD: New South Wales Parliamentary Debates

QPD: Queensland Parliamentary Debates

Proceedings

AFCP: Proceedings of the Australasian Federal Convention

PC: Proceedings of a conference between the Secretary of State for the Colonies and the premiers of the self-governing colonies, at the Colonial Office, London, June and July 1897

P&T: Proceedings and Debates of the Postal and Telegraph Conference.

Newspapers and periodicals

AB&WE: *Albury Banner and Wodonga Express*

AC: *Armidale Chronicle*

ACJ: *The Articled Clerks Journal*

AE: *The Armidale Express and New England General Advertiser*

AF: *Australian Federalist*

AO: *Adelaide Observer*

AS: *Australian Star*

AT&CJ: *Australian Town and Country Journal*

BA: *Bendigo Advertiser*

BC: *Brisbane Courier*

BI: *Bendigo Independent*

BS: *Bendigo Star*

C&RE: *Clarence and Richmond Examiner*

CA: *The Cumberland Argus and Fruitgrowers Advocate*

CM: *Cumberland Mercury*

CoFP: *Corowa Free Press*
CP: *Catholic Press*
CuFP: *Cumberland Free Press*
DT: *Daily Telegraph*
EN: *Evening News*
GE: *Goulburn Evening Penny Post*
GI: *Gundagai Independent*
KH: *Kanowna Herald*
KM: *Kalgoorlie Miner*
LC: *Law Chronicle*
LD: *Labor Daily*
LE: *Launceston Examiner*
MB: *Morning Bulletin*
MC: *Muswellbrook Chronicle*
MD: *Maitland Daily*
MM: *Maitland Mercury*
MaM: *Mackay Mercury*
NA: *National Advocate*
NMG: *North Melbourne Gazette*
NMH: *Newcastle Morning Herald and Miners' Advocate*
NS: *Northern Star*
OC: *Our Country*
QA: *Queanbeyan Age*
RRH: *Richmond River Herald and Northern Districts Advertiser*
SA: *Singleton Argus*
SAR: *South Australian Register*
SM: *Sydney Mail and New South Wales Advertiser*
SMH: *Sydney Morning Herald*
ST: *Sunday Times*
TC: *Toowoomba Chronicle*
TDT: *Tasmanian Daily Telegraph*
TN: *Tasmanian News*
WA: *Western Australian*

WC: *Western Champion*
WM: *Western Mail*
W&RG: *Windsor and Richmond Gazette*
WWA: *Wagga Wagga Advertiser*

Manuscripts

BD: Beauchamp diary, Mitchell Library
BEP: Edmund Barton papers, Mitchell Library
BEPNLA: Edmund Barton papers, National Library of Australia
BGP: George Barton papers, Mitchell Library
CFP: Francis Clarke papers, Mitchell Library
CJP: Joseph Carruthers Papers, Mitchell Library.
DAP: Alfred Deakin papers, National Library of Australia
DGP: George Dibbs papers, Mitchell Library
GD: P.M. Glynn dairy, National Library of Australia
HCP: Hume Cook papers, National Library of Australia
HP: H.B. Higgins papers, National Library of Australia
JP: Walter James Papers, Mitchell Library
MP: McMillan Papers, Mitchell Library
NFLP: National Federation League papers, Mitchell Library
OP: O'Connor Papers, Mitchell Library
PHC: Henry Parkes correspondence, Mitchell Library
SAGP: A.G. Stephens papers, Mitchell Library
SJP: Josiah Symon papers, National Library of Australia
SRP: Rose Scott papers, Mitchell Library
WP: J.T. Walker papers, Mitchell Library

Select bibliography

Abbott, J. H. M. 1905. *An Outlander in England: Being Some Impressions of an Australian Abroad*, London: Methuen.

Abbott, J. H. M. 1944. *Out of the Past*, Sydney: Currawong.

Abjorensen, N. 2015. *The Manner of Their Going: Prime Ministerial Exits from Lyne to Abbott*, Melbourne: Australian Scholarly Publishing.

Affleck, William 1916. *Reminiscences of William Affleck from Infancy to Present Date*, Sydney: R. Dey, Son and Co.

Anderson, Robert McC. 1915. *Report on the Business Management of the Postmaster-General's Department of the Commonwealth of Australia*, Melbourne: (Government Printer) Albert J. Mullett.

Andrews, B. G. 1976. *Price Warung (William Astley)*, Boston: Twayne Publishers.

Aroney, Nicholas 2009. *The Constitution of a Federal Commonwealth*, Cambridge: Cambridge University Press.

Ashworth, Thomas Ramsden and H. P. C. Ashworth 1900. *Proportional Representation Applied to Party Government*, Melbourne: G. Robertson.

Australian Association of Cultural Freedom 1963. *Seminar on New Interpretations of Australian History*, held on 25th August, 1963: Sydney.

Australian Government 2020. 'GARRAN, Robert Randolph', http://legalopinions.ags.gov.au/opinionauthor/garran-robert-randolph?page=5.

Ayres, Philip 2007. *Prince of the Church: Patrick Francis Moran, 1830-1911*, Melbourne: Miegunyah Press.

Bakker, Peter and Thomas J. Rogers 2019. 'Dismantling a myth of the south African war: Bushmen, Aboriginal trackers, and public debate, 1899-1902', *Journal of Australian Colonial History*, 21, 151-168.

Bannon, John 1994. *The Crucial Colony: South Australia's Role in Reviving Federation, 1891 to 1897*, Canberra: Federalism Research Centre.

Bannon, John 1998. 'The gathering of tribunes and oligarchs: delegates to the Australasian Federal Convention, 1897-98', *Canberra Historical Journal*, 41, 2-14.

Bannon, J. C. 2009. *Supreme Federalist. The Political Life of Sir John Downer*: Wakefield Press.

Barker, A. W. 1982. *Dear Robertson. Letters to an Australian Publisher*, Sydney: Angus and Robertson.

Barnard, Alan 1962. 'Pastoralists in the Legislative Assembly of New South Wales', *The Simple Fleece: Studies in the Australian Wool Industry*, Alan Barnard ed., Melbourne, Victoria: Melbourne University Press.

Barrett, John 1979. *Falling In: Australians and 'Boy Conscription', 1911-1915*, Sydney: Hale & Iremonger.

Barton, G. B. 1866. *The Poets and Prose Writers of New South Wales*, Sydney: Gibbs, Shallard and co.

Barton, G. B. 1901. 'The troubles of Australian federation', *The Imperial and Asiatic Quarterly Review and Oriental and Colonial Record*, 11.

Basson, Lauren L. 2005. 'Fit for annexation but unfit to vote? Debating Hawaiian suffrage qualification at the turn of the century', *Social Science History*, 29(4), 575-598.

Bate, Weston 1978. *Lucky City: The First Generation at Ballarat, 1851-1901*, Carlton South, Victoria: Melbourne University Press.

Bavin, Thomas 1941. *Sir Henry Parkes: His Life and Work*, Sydney: Angus and Robertson.

Bedford, Randolph 1944. *Naught to Thirty-three*, Sydney: Currawong.

Bedford, Randolph 2007. *The Circled Continent*, Peter J. Bridge, Gail Dreezens and Chris Holyday, eds, Victoria Park, WA: Hesperian Press.

Bennett, J. M. 1969. *A History of the New South Wales Bar*, Sydney: Law Book Company.

Bennett, J. M. 1972. 'Sir Julian Salomons: fifth Chief Justice of New South Wales', *Journal of the Royal Australian Historical Society*, 58(2), 101-111.

Bennett, J. M. 2004. *Sir William Stawell: Second Chief Justice of Victoria 1857-1886*, Annandale, NSW: Federation Press.

Bennett, J. M. 2007. *George Higinbotham: Third Chief Justice of Victoria 1886-1892*, Annandale, NSW: Federation Press.

Bergh, George van den 1956. *Unity in Diversity: A Systematic Critical Analysis of all Electoral Systems*, London: Batsford.

Bernays, Charles Arrowsmith 1919. *Queensland Politics During Sixty Years (1859-1919)*, Brisbane: Government Printer.

Berryman, Jim 2016. 'Nationalism, Britishness and the "souring" of Australian national art', *Journal of Imperial and Commonwealth History*, 44(4), 573-591.

Bevan, Walter 1912. *Opinion of the Solicitor-general Regarding the Claim of the Government of Victoria to the Territory (Known as the Riverina) Lying Between the Murray and Murrumbidgee Rivers*, Sydney: New South Wales Solicitor-General's Department.

Birrell, Robert 2001. *Federation: the Secret Story*, Potts Point, NSW: Duffy & Snellgrove.

Blacket, Wilfred 1927. *May it Please Your Honour: Lawyers and Law Courts of the Olden Times in New South Wales*, Sydney: Cornstalk Publishing Company.

Blackwell, Leslie 1970. *Death Cell at Darlinghurst*, London: Hutchinson of Australia.

Bolton, G. C. 1970 [1963]. *A Thousand Miles Away: A History of North Queensland to 1920*, Canberra: Jacaranda ANU Press.

Bolton, Geoffrey 2000. *Edmund Barton*, St Leonards, NSW: Allen & Unwin.

Bolton, Geoffrey and Duncan Waterson 1999. 'Queensland', *The Centenary Companion to Australian Federation*, Helen Irving, ed., Cambridge, UK: Cambridge University Press.

Botsman, Peter 2000. *The Great Constitutional Swindle: A Citizen's View of the Australian Constitution*, Sydney: Pluto Press.

Boucher, David and Andrew Vincent 2000. *British Idealism and Political Theory*, Edinburgh: Edinburgh University Press.

Boyce, F. B. 1934. *Fourscore Years and Seven: The Memoirs of Archdeacon Boyce*, Sydney: Angus & Robertson.

Breward, Ian 2001. 'The Presbyterian churches and Federation', *Proceedings of the Uniting Church Historical Society*, 8(1), 60-68.

Broinowski, Richard P. 2001. *A Witness to History: The Life and Times of Robert Arthur Broinowski*, Carlton, Victoria: Melbourne University Press.

Brooks, David 2004. *On Paradise Drive: How We Live Now (And Always Have) in the Future Tense*, New York: Simon & Schuster.

Brosnan, Peter 1982. 'Australian net internal migration 1881-1911', *Australia New Zealand Journal of Sociology*, 18(3), 441-448.

Bryan, Harrison 1954. 'John Murtagh Macrossan and the Genesis of the White Australia Policy', *Journal. Historical Society of Queensland*, 5(2), 885-906.

Bryce, James 1889. *The American Commonwealth*, London: Macmillan.

Bryce, James 1905. *Constitutions*, New York: Oxford University Press.

Bryce, James 1921. *Modern Democracies*, London: Macmillan.

Bullen, Frank Thomas 1907. *Advance Australasia: A Day-to-day Record of a Recent Visit to Australasia*, London: Hodder and Stoughton.

Burgmann, Verity 1980. *Revolutionaries and Racists: Australian Socialism and the Problem of Racism, 1887-1917*, PhD thesis, Australian National University.

Burke, Bernard 1891-5. *A Genealogical and Heraldic History of the Colonial Gentry*, Melbourne: E.A. Petherick.

Burton, Brian Keith 1973. *Flow Gently Past: The Story of the Corowa District*, Corowa, NSW: Corowa Shire Council.

Burton, Tony 2008. 'John Bingle's notebooks and Australia's original ensign', *Crux Australis. The Journal of Flags Australia*, 21(2), 73-90.

Byrnes, T. J. 1897. *The Resources of Queensland*, London: Waterlow and Sons.

Cahill, A. E. 2001. 'Catholics and Australian Federation', *Journal of the Australian Catholic Historical Society*, 22, 9-30.

Caiden, G.E. 1965. *Career Service. An Introduction to the History of Personnel Administration in the Commonwealth Public Service 1901-1961*, Melbourne: Melbourne University Press.

Cambridge, Ada 1903. *Thirty Years in Australia*, London: Methuen.

Campbell, T. W. 1999. *George Richard Dibbs: Politician, Premier, Patriot, Paradox*, Braddon, ACT.

Cantrell, Leon 1976. 'A.G. Stephens, *The Bulletin*, and the 1890s', *Bards, Bohemians and Bookmen. Essays in Australian Literature*, Leon Cantrell, ed., St Lucia, Queensland: University of Queensland Press.

Carment, David 1977. 'The making of an Australian liberal: the political education of Littleton Groom, 1867-1905', *Journal of the Royal Australian Historical Society*, 62(4), 232-50.

Carney, Gerard 2013. 'The story behind the land boundaries of the Australian states – a legal and historical overview', Public Lecture Series of the High Court of Australia.

Carrington, Charles Robert Wynn-Carrington 1889-1890. *Sir Henry Parkes' Federation Scheme 1889-1890: Extracts from Lord Carrington's Diary*, Sydney.

Carruthers, J. H. 2005. *A Lifetime in Conservative Politics: Political Memoirs of Sir Joseph*, Sydney, NSW: University of New South Wales Press.

Cave-Browne-Cave, W. C. 1897. *Australian Federation: Notes of the Views, etc., expressed at the National Convention of 1891*, Melbourne: Government Printer.

Cawood, Ian 2016. 'Joseph Chamberlain: his reputation and legacy', *Joseph Chamberlain: International Statesman, National Leader, Local Icon*, I. Cawood and C. Upton, eds, N.Y.: Palgrave Macmillan.

Clifford, Eamonn, Antony Green and David Clune, eds, 2006. *The Electoral Atlas of New South Wales 1856-2006*, Bathurst, NSW: Department of Lands.

Clune, David and Gareth Griffith 2006. *Decision and Deliberation: the Parliament of New South Wales 1856-2003*, Sydney: Federation Press.

Cockerill, George 1943. *Scribblers and Statesmen*, Melbourne: J.R. Stevens.

Coghlan, T.A. and T.T. Ewing 1903. *The Progress of Australasia in the Nineteenth Century*, Toronto: Linscott.

Colebatch, Hal 1951. 'The Federation campaign', *Journal and Proceedings of the Western Australian Historical Society*, 4(3), 1951, 4-30.

Coleman, William 2017. 'The Social and Economic Determinants of Voting "Yes" in South Australia's Federation Referenda', CEPR Discussion Papers 700, Centre for Economic Policy Research, Australian National University.

Coleman, William 2018. 'Six problems in the biography of Alfred Deakin', *Agenda: a Journal of Policy Analysis and Reform*, 25(1), 79-92.

Coleman, William 2020. 'Federation without affirmation: A sketch of a revisionist program of research into "1901"', *Agenda: A Journal of Policy Analysis and Reform*, 27(1), 87-104.

Coleman, William 2020a. 'The Impact of the "Braddon Blot" on Australia's Tariff Structure, 1901-1910: A Leviathanic Analysis', CEH Discussion Papers 2020-10, Centre for Economic History, Australian National University.

Coleman, William 2020b. 'The Revenue Maximising Tariff Rate: A Theoretical Model Applied to 1890s Victoria', CEH Discussion Papers 2020-07, Centre for Economic History, Australian National University.

Coleman, William 2020c. 'Which States Gained, and Which States Lost, from Australia's Federation Customs Union of 1902? The Answers of a Theoretical Schema, with an Empirical Check', CEH Discussion Papers 2020-08, Centre for Economic History, Australian National University.

Collis, E. H. 1948. *Lost Years: A Backward Glance at Australian Life and Manners*, Sydney: Angus & Robertson.

Commonwealth Bureau of Census and Statistics 1911. *Official Year Book of the Commonwealth of Australia Containing Authoritative Statistics for the Period 1901-1910, (1911)*, Melbourne: McCarron, Bird and Co.

Conlon, Anne 1969. '"Mine is a sad yet true story": convict narratives 1881-1850', *Journal of the Royal Australian Historical Society*, 55(1), 43-70.

Corfield, W. H. 1921. *Reminiscences of Queensland, 1862-1899*, Brisbane: A.H. Frater.

Corris, Peter 1973. *Passage, Port and Plantation: a History of Solomon Islands Labour Migration, 1870-1914*, Carlton, Victoria: Melbourne University Press.

Coulthard-Clark, C. D. 1984. 'From Eureka to Gallipoli. Captain Joseph Peter Lalor', *Defence Force Journal*, 44, 44–48.

Coulthard-Clark, C. D. 1988. *No Australian Need Apply: the Troubled Career of Lieutenant-General Gordon Legge*, Sydney: Allen & Unwin.

Cramp, K. R. 1937. 'Some aspects of the life and career of Sir Henry Parkes, *Journal of the Royal Historical Society of Australia*, 23(3), 205-220.

Cramp, K. R and George Mackaness 1938. *A History of the United Grand Lodge of Ancient, Free and Accepted Masons of New South Wales*, Sydney: Angus & Robertson.

Crisp, L. F. 1949. *The Parliamentary Government of the Commonwealth of Australia*, Adelaide: Longmans, Green.

Crisp, L. F. 1978 [1955]. *The Australian Federal Labour Party, 1901-1951*, Sydney: Hale & Iremonger.

Crisp, L.F. 1990. *Federation Fathers*, J. Hart, ed., Melbourne: Melbourne University Press.

Crosby, Travis L. 2011. *Joseph Chamberlain: A Most Radical Imperialist*, New York: I.B. Tauris.

Cross, Jack 2011. *Great Central State: The Foundation of the Northern Territory*, Kent Town, SA: Wakefield Press.

Crowley, F. K. 1960. 'A vice-regal defendant', *Australian Historical Studies*, 9(34), 117-130.

Crowley, F. K. 1997. 'Forrest and the federal constitution: centenary reflections', *Early Days: Journal of the Royal Western Australian Historical Society*, 11(3), 285-303.

Cunneen, Christopher 1973. *The Role of the Governor-General in Australia 1901-1927*, PhD thesis, Australian National University.

Dalgety Progress Committee 190-. *An Unique Site for the Federal City*, New South Wales.

Davison, Graeme 1995. '"Our youth is spent and our backs are bent": the origins of Australian ageism', *Australian Cultural History*, 14, 40-62.

Davison, Graeme, John Hirst and Stuart Macintyre, eds, 2001. *The Oxford Companion to Australian History*, South Melbourne: Oxford University Press.

Deakin, Alfred 1899. *Speeches on Australian Federation by the Premiers of Victoria, South Australia, Queensland, Tasmania, and Western Australia*, Alfred Deakin and T. Brassey, eds, Melbourne: G. Robertson and Co.

Deakin, Alfred 1944. *The Federal Story. The Inner History of the Federal Cause*, Melbourne: Robertson & Mullens.

Deakin, Alfred 1968. *Federated Australia: Selections from Letters to the Morning Post 1900-1910*, J. A. La Nauze, ed., Carlton, Victoria: Melbourne University Press.

Deniehy, Daniel Henry 1860. *How I became Attorney-General of New Barataria: An Experiment in Treating Facts in the Forms of Fiction*, Sydney: Edward Greville.

Dicey, Albert Venn 1886. *England's Case Against Home Rule*, London: J. Murray.

Dicey, Albert Venn 1915. *An Introduction to the Study of the Law of the Constitution*, 8th ed., London: Macmillan.

Dicey, Albert Venn and Robert S. Rait 1920. *Thoughts on the Union Between England & Scotland*, London: Macmillan.

Donovan, P.F. 1984. *At the Other End of Australia. The Commonwealth and the Northern Territory 1911-1978*, St Lucia, Queensland: University of Queensland Press.

Drake, James G. 1896. *Federation: Imperial or Democratic*, Brisbane: Benjamin Woodcock.

Driehuis, Raymond 2000. 'Joseph Furphy and some American friends: temper, democratic; bias, offensively self-reliant', *Antipodes*, 14(2), 129-35.

Earnshaw, Beverley 2000. *One Flag, One Hope, One Destiny: Sir Joseph Carruthers and Australian Federation*, Kogarah, NSW: Kogarah Historical Society.

Ely, Richard (ed.) 2001. *A Living Force: Andrew Inglis Clark and the Ideal of the Commonwealth*, Hobart: Centre for Tasmanian Historical Studies, University of Tasmania.

Evatt, H. V. 1945. *Australian Labour Leader: The Story of W. A. Hol-*

man and the Labour Movement, 3rd ed., Sydney: Angus and Robertson.

Fahey, John, 2018. *Australia's First Spies: The Remarkable Story of Australia's Intelligence Operations, 1901-1945*, Crows Nest, NSW: Allen & Unwin.

Ferry, John and Bruce Pennay 2000. *New South Wales Railways and Federation*, Sydney: State Rail Authority of New South Wales Rail Estate Heritage.

Fitzgerald, John D. 1922. *The Rise of the Australian Labor Party*, Sydney : Worker Print.

Fitzgerald, Shirley 1987. *Rising Damp. Sydney 1870-1890*, Melbourne: Oxford University Press.

Fitzpatrick, Brian, 1941. *The British Empire in Australia: An Economic History 1834-1939*, Melbourne: Melbourne University Press in association with Oxford University Press.

Fitzpatrick, J. C. L. 1909. *When We Were Boys Together: Reminiscences of the Hawkesbury District*, Windsor, NSW: Campbell.

Fletcher, John Percy and John Francis Hills 1919. *Conscription Under Camouflage: An Account of Compulsory Military Training in Australasia Down to the Outbreak of the Great War*, Glenelg, SA: J.F. Hills.

Ford, Patrick 1966. *Cardinal Moran and the ALP*, Carlton, Victoria: Melbourne University Press.

Foster, Leonie 1986. *High Hopes: The Men and Motives of the Australian Round Table*, Melbourne: Melbourne University Press.

Francis, N. G. 1977. 'Sir Robert Garran: a man of many parts', *Canberra Historical Journal*, 4, 37-51.

Franki, George 2001. 'A World War I Link with Ned Kelly', *Sabretache*, 42, 39-40.

Franklin, Miles, 2004 [1902]. *My Brilliant Career ; My Career Goes Bung*, NSW: HarperCollins.

Fraser, Malcolm A. C. 1904. *Seventh Census of Western Australia*, Perth: Government Printer.

Fredman, L.E. 1989. 'Australian and American History: Contrasts and Comparisons', *Antipodes*, 3(2), 125-128.

Freeman, Edward Augustus 1893. *History of Federal Government in Greece and Italy*, J.B. Bury ed., London: Macmillan.

Freudenberg, Graham 2009. 'William Lygon, Earl Beauchamp', *The Governors of New South Wales 1788-2010*, David Clune and Ken Turner, eds, Annandale, NSW: The Federation Press, 381-395.

Fricke, Graham L. 1986. *Judges of the High Court*, Melbourne: Hutchinson of Australia.

Furphy, Joseph 1990 [1903]. *Such is Life*, Sydney: Angus and Robertson.

Gale, John 1907, *The Federal Capital – Dalgety or Canberra? Which?* Queanbeyan.

Galloway, William Johnson 1899. *Advanced Australia: A Short Account of Australia on the Eve of Federation*, London: Methuen.

Ganter, Mary 1998. *Australian Coastal Shipping: the Vital Link*, Canberra: Department of Defence.

Garis, Brian de 1999. 'Western Australia', *The Centenary Companion to Australian Federation*, Helen Irving ed., Cambridge, UK: Cambridge University Press.

Garran, Robert 1933. 'Australia', *The Cambridge History of the British Empire*, volume 7, J. Holland Rose, A.P. Newton, E.A. Benians, eds, Cambridge: Cambridge University Press.

Garran, Robert Randolph 1958. *Prosper the Commonwealth*, Sydney: Angus and Robertson.

Garvin, J. L. 1932. *The Life of Joseph Chamberlain*, London: Macmillan.

Gibbney, H. J. 1967. 'Sturt, Charles (1795–1869)', *Australian Dictionary of Biography*, 2, Melbourne: Melbourne University Press.

Gill, Rosemary Howard 1975. *The Career and the Legend of Thomas Joseph Byrnes (1860-1898)*, BA thesis, St Lucia, University of Queensland.

Gill, Rosemary Howard 1979. 'Thomas Joseph Byrnes. The Man and the Legend', *Queensland Political Portraits, 1859-1952*, Murphy, D. J. and R. B. Joyce, eds, St Lucia, Queensland: University of Queensland Press.

Glass, Margaret 1997. *Charles Cameron Kingston: Federation Father*, Melbourne: Melbourne University Press.

Glynn, P. McMahon 1890. *Federalism: Its Principle and Application*, Adelaide: W. K. Thomas & Co.

Glynn, P. McMahon 1974. *Patrick McMahon Glynn, Letters to his Family (1874-1927)*, G.G. O'Collins ed., Melbourne: Polding Press.

Golder, Hilary 1985. *Divorce in 19th Century New South Wales*, NSW: New South Wales University Press.

Gordon, Donald Craigie 1965. *The Dominion Partnership in Imperial Defense, 1870-1914*, Baltimore: Johns Hopkins Press.

Gorman, Zachary 2016. 'A contested contest: George Reid's election to the leadership of the New South Wales free trade party', *Journal of Australian Colonial History*, 18, 182-197.

Gorman, Zachary 2020. 'Birthplace of a nation? Why Sydney voted no to Federation', *Agenda: A Journal of Policy Analysis and Reform*, 27(1), 125-148.

Graham, Austin Douglas 1939. *The Life of the Right Honourable Sir Samuel Walker Griffith*, Brisbane: The Law Book Co. of Australasia.

Green, Antony 2007. 'New South Wales Election Results 1856-2007', https://www.parliament.nsw.gov.au/electionresults18562007/HomePage.htm

Green, F. C. 1965. 'The battle of the site of the federal capital', *Papers and Proceedings of the Tasmanian Historical Research Association*, 13, 10-18.

Green, Frank C. 1969. *Servant of the House*, Melbourne: Heinemann.

Griffith, Samuel 1899. *Australian Federation and the Draft Commonwealth Bill*, Brisbane: Government Printer.

Grimshaw, Patricia 2002. 'Federation as a turning point in Australian history', *Australian Historical Studies*, 33(118), 25-41.

Grover, Montague 1993. *Hold Page One: Memoirs of Monty Grover, Editor*, edited and introduced by Michael Cannon, Main Ridge, Victoria: Loch Haven.

Gurner, John Augustus 1930. *Life's Panorama: Being Recollections and Reminiscences of Things Seen, Things Heard, Things Read*, Melbourne: Lothian Publishing.

Haines, Gregory 1976. *Lay Catholics and the Education Question in Nineteenth Century New South Wales: The Shaping of a Decision*, Sydney: Catholic Theological Faculty.

Hall, A. R. 1963. 'Some long-term effects of the kinked age distribution of the population of Australia 1861-1961', *Economic Record*, 39, 43-52.

Hamer, D. A. 1977. *The Politics of Electoral Pressure: A Study in the History of Victorian Reform Agitations*, Hassocks, England: Harvester Press.

Hamer, David 1993. 'Richard John Seddon', *New Zealand Dictionary of Biography*, Wellington: Allen and Unwin.

Hammond, Mark J. 1988. *Remembered with Pride*, Sydney: Cambaroora Star Publications.

Harding, Justin 2000. 'Boots and all: the Benjamin Kitt affair: Queensland's constitutional crisis, 1888', *Journal of the Royal Historical Society of Queensland*, 17(5), 228-240.

Harvie, Christopher 2004. 'Bryce, James, Viscount Bryce (1838–1922)', *Oxford Dictionary of National Biography*, H. C. G. Matthew and Brian Harrison, eds, 8, Oxford: Oxford University Press.

Hawker, Geoffrey 1971. *The Parliament of New South Wales, 1856-1965*, Ultimo, NSW: Government Printer.

Headon, David 1998. 'Resurrecting the federal ideal: Mr Astley goes to Bathurst', *Papers on Parliament*, 32.

Headon, David and John Williams, eds, 2000. *Makers of Miracles. The Cast of the Federation Story*, Carlton: Melbourne University Press.

Hergenhan, L. T. 1980. 'Convict legends, Australian legends: Price Warung and the Palmers', *Australian Literary Studies*, 9(3), 337-345.

Higgins, H. B. 1900. *Essays and Addresses on the Australian Commonwealth Bill*, Melbourne: Atlas Press.

Higgins, H. B. 1910. *Some Recent Constitutions*, Sydney, NSW: Balmain Citizens' Cultural Association.

Hirst, John 2000. *The Sentimental Nation. The Making of the Australian Commonwealth*, Melbourne: Oxford University Press.

Holt, James 1980. 'Compulsory arbitration in New Zealand, 1894-1901', *New Zealand Journal of History*, 14(2), 179-200.

Howard, Colin 1978. *Australia's Constitution*, Ringwood, Victoria: Penguin.

Hughes, Colin A. and B. D. Graham 1968. *A Handbook of Australian Government and Politics 1890-1964*, Canberra: Australian National University Press.

Hughes, Colin A. and B. D. Graham 1974. *Voting for the Australian House of Representatives,1901-1964*, Canberra: Australian National University.

Hughes, Colin A. and B. D. Graham 1975. *Voting for the New South Wales Legislative Assembly 1890-1964.* Canberra: Australian National University.

Hughes, Colin A. and B. D. Graham 1975a. *Voting for the Victorian Legislative Assembly 1890-1964*, Canberra: Australian National University.

Hughes, Colin A. and B. D. Graham 1976. *Voting for the South Australian, Western Australian and Tasmanian Lower Houses*, Canberra: Australian National University.

Hunt, Atlee Arthur 1914. *Memorandum by Secretary, Department of External Affairs, Relating to Norfolk Island*, Melbourne: Government Printer.

Hunt, Atlee Arthur 1916. *The Northern Territory of Australia. Memorandum by the Secretary, Department of External Affairs (Mr. Atlee Hunt, C.M.G.)*, Melbourne: Government Printer.

Hunt, Erling M. 1930. *American Precedents in Australian Federation*, New York: Columbia University Press.

Hunt, Lyall 2000. *Towards Federation: Why Western Australia Joined the Australian Federation in 1901*, Nedlands, WA: The Royal Western Australian Historical Society.

Huntington, Samuel P. 1968. *Political Order in Changing Societies*, New Haven: Yale University Press.

Inglis, K. S. 1968. 'Conscription in peace and war, 1911-1945', *Conscription in Australia*, Roy Forward and Bob Reece, eds, St Lucia, Brisbane: University of Queensland Press.

Jacobs, Joseph 1894. *The Fables of Aesop, Selected, Told Anew and Their History Traced by Joseph Jacobs*, London: Macmillan & Company.

James, Walter, A. Deakin, E. Barton, A. J. Peacock, J. Forrest, B. R. Wise, J. W Hackett, and H. Briggs 1949. 'The James' Papers – Letters on Federalism', *Australian Quarterly*, 21(4), 55-63.

Jay, Richard. 1981. *Joseph Chamberlain, a Political Study*, Oxford: Clarendon Press.

Jebb, Richard 1905. *Studies in Colonial Nationalism*, London: Edward Arnold.

Jenkins, Alan 1979. *Attitudes Towards Federation in Queensland*, MA thesis, University of Queensland.

Johnson, D. H. 1975. *Volunteers at Heart. The Queensland Defence Forces 1860-1901*, St Lucia, Queensland: University of Queensland Press.

Johnston, W. R. 1963. *The Role of the Legal Profession in Queensland in the Federation Movement, 1890-1900*, MA thesis, University of Queensland.

Joyce, R. B. 1974. 'S.W. Griffith: towards a biography of a lawyer', *Australian Historical Studies*, 16(63), 236-257.

Karskens, Grace 2013. 'The settler evolution: space, place and memory in early colonial Australia', *Journal of the Association for the Study of Australian Literature*, 13(2), 1-21.

Keel, Grace 1980. 'The early Bulletin and lyric verse', *Overland*, 81, 45-50.

Keenan, J. J. 1904. *The Inaugural Celebrations of the Commonwealth of Australia Compiled Under the Authority of the Prime Minister of New South Wales*, Sydney: W.A. Gullick, Government Printer.

Keith, Arthur Berriedale 1912. *Responsible Government in the Dominions*, Oxford: Clarendon Press.

Kell, Whaks Li 1893. *The Cornstalk. His Habits and Habitat*, Sydney: Troedel, Cooper & Co.

Kelley, Jonathan and Ian McAllister 1985. 'Class and party in Australia: Comparisons with Britain and the USA', *British Journal of Sociology*, 36(3), 383-420.

Kemp, D. A. 2018. *The Land of Dreams. How Australians Won Their Freedom, 1788–1860*, Carlton, Victoria: Miegunyah Press.

Kerwin, Dale 2013. 'The lost trackers: Aboriginal servicemen in the 2nd Boer War', *Sabretache*, 54(1), 4-14.

Kiernan, Brian 1989. 'Literature and Language', *Under New Heavens: Cultural Transmission and the Making of Australia*, Neville Meaney ed., Port Melbourne: Heinemann Educational.

King, Charles 2007. 'Imagining Circassia: David Urquhart and the Making of North Caucasus Nationalism', *Russian Review*, 66 (2), 238–255.

Kingston, C. C. 1897. *The Democratic Element in Federation*, Adelaide: J.L. Bonython.

Kingston, C. C. 2002. 'Charles Kingston's Draft Constitution', Appendix 2, *Sir Samuel Griffith. The Law and the Constitution*, Michael White and Aladin Rahemtula, eds, Sydney: Law Book Co.

Kirby Michael 2002. 'The mysterious word "sentences" in s 73 of the Constitution', *Australian Law Journal*, 76, 97-108.

Kirkpatrick, John 1903. *Supplement to Report of Royal Commission on Sites for the Seat of Government of the Commonwealth: Report on a Proposed Site for the Federal Capital at Dalgety with Plans*, Sydney: Govt. Printer.

Kirwan, John 1936. *My Life's Adventure*, London: Eyre & Spottiswoode.

Kitto, J. W. 1930. *History and Organisation of the Post Office: A Lecture*, Sydney: Commonwealth Post Masters' Association.

Kwan, Elizabeth Haydon 1995. *Which Flag? Which Country? An Australian Dilemma, 1901-1951*, PhD thesis, Australian National University.

Kyvig, David E. 2016. *Explicit and Authentic Acts. Amending the U.S. Constitution 1776-2015*, USA: University Press of Kansas.

La Nauze, J. A. 1957 *The Hopetoun Blunder: The Appointment of the First Prime Minister of the Commonwealth of Australia, December 1900*, Carlton: Melbourne University Press.

La Nauze, J. A. 1961. 'A day to remember: a fragment of narrative history', *Meanjin Quarterly*, 20(4), 453-455.

La Nauze, J. A. 1972. *The Making of the Australian Constitution*, Carlton, Victoria: Melbourne University Press.

Lang, Gordon, 2009. 'Hampden, Henry Robert Brand', *The Governors of New South Wales 1788-2010*, David Clune and Ken Turner, eds, Annandale, NSW: Federation Press.

Lang, John Dunmore 1850. *The Coming Event, or, The United Provinces of Australia: Two Lectures Delivered in City Theatre and School of Arts, Sydney*, Sydney: D.L. Welch.

Lang, John Dunmore 1870. *The Coming Event! The Freedom and Independence for the Seven United Provinces of Australia*, Sydney: John L. Sherriff.

Lang, John Dunmore 1875. *An Historical and Statistical Account of New South Wales: From the Founding of the Colony in 1788 to the Present Day*, 4th ed., London: Sampson Low, Marston, Low & Searle.

Langfield, Michelle 2001. 'Peopling of the Northern Territory. Part 1: a white elephant in a white Australia? The Northern Territory, 1901-1920', *Journal of Northern Territory History*, 12, 1-15.

Lawson, Ronald 1972. 'The political influences of the churches in Brisbane in the 1890s', *Journal of Religious History*, 7, 144-162.

Lawson, Sylvia 1983. *The Archibald Paradox: A Strange Case of Authorship*, Ringwood, Victoria: Allen Lane.

Livingston, K. T. 1994. 'Anticipating federation: the federalising of telecommunications in Australia', *Australian Historical Studies*, 26(102), 97-117.

Lloyd, C. J. 1988. *Parliament and the Press. The Federal Parliamentary Press Gallery 1901-1988*, Carlton, Victoria: Melbourne University Press.

Lloyd, Peter 2008. '100 years of tariff protection in Australia', *Australian Economic History Review*, 48(2), 99-145.

Lloyd, Peter 2015. 'Customs union and fiscal union in Australia at Federation', *Economic Record*, 91(293), 155-171.

Lloyd, Clem and Jolyon Sykes, 2001. 'George Houstoun Reid: "Dry Dog Days"', *1901, The Forgotten Election*, M. Simms ed., St Lucia, Queensland: University of Queensland Press.

Logan, W.S. 1968. 'The changing significance of the Victoria-South Australia boundary', *Annals of the Association of American Geographers*, 58(1), 128-54.

Lyne, Charles E. 1896. *Life of Sir Henry Parkes, Australian Statesman*, Sydney: George Robertson.

McCarty, J. W. 1970. 'Australian capital cities in the nineteenth century', *Australian Economic History Review*, 10(2), 107-137.

McCarty, J. W. 1973. 'Australia as a region of recent settlement in the nineteenth century', *Australian Economic History Review*, 13(2), 148-167.

McCarty, J. W. 1980. 'Melbourne, Sydney, Ballarat, Perth: the new city histories', *Historical Studies*, 19(2), 1-15.

McCormack, Patrick Martin 2009. *The Popular Movement to Federation in New South Wales 1897-1899*, PhD thesis, Australian National University.

MacDonagh, Oliver 1973. 'The Irish in Victoria 1851-91: a demographic study', *ANU Historical Journal*, 10, 26-39.

McFarland, Alfred 1885. *The Case of Norfolk Island Stated*, Sydney: Gibbs, Shallard & Co.

Mackay, Kenneth 1895. *The Yellow Wave: A Romance of the Asiatic Invasion of Australia*, London: Bentley.

Mackie, Thomas T. and Richard Rose 1991. *The International Almanac of Electoral History*, 3rd ed., London: Macmillan.

Macleod, Agnes Conor 1931. *Macleod of "The Bulletin": The Life and Work of William Macleod,* Sydney: Snelling.

McMinn, Trevor 1986. *A Political Biography of Sir John Robertson*, PhD thesis, University of New South Wales.

McMinn, W. G. 1989. *George Reid,* Carlton, Victoria: Melbourne University Press.

McMinn, W. G. 1994. *Nationalism and Federalism in Australia*, Melbourne: Oxford University Press.

McNaughton, W. R. n.d. *T.J. Byrnes*, thesis, St Lucia: University of Queensland.

McPhail, Isla 2016. *A Constrained and Cautious Liberalism: Western Australian Parliamentary Electoral History 1829-1901*, PhD thesis, University of Western Australia.

Markey, Ray 1988. *The Making of the Labor Party in New South Wales, 1880-1900*, Kensington, NSW: New South Wales University Press.

Marmion, Bob 2012. 'Gibraltar of the South: the evolution of the Victorian defences 1851-1945', *Victorian Historical Journal*, 83(1), 7-30.

Martens, Jeremy C. 2013. 'Pioneering the Dictation Test? The creation and administration of Western Australia's Immigration Restriction Act, 1897-1901', *Studies in Western Australian History*, 28, 47-67.

Martin, A. Patchett 1889. *Australia and the Empire*, Edinburgh: D. Douglas.

Martin, A. Patchett 1893. *True Stories from Australasian History*, London: Griffith Farran & Co.

Martin, A. W. 1969. 'Carrington, Charles Robert (1843–1928)', *Australian Dictionary of Biography*, 3, Melbourne: Melbourne University Press.

Martin, A. W. 1980. *Henry Parkes. A Biography*, Carlton, Victoria: Melbourne University Press.

Martin, A. W. 1990. 'Sir Henry Parkes and the 1890 Conference', *Canberra Historical Journal*, 26, 17-24.

Martin, Ged 2001. *Australia, New Zealand and Federation, 1883-1901*, London: Menzies Centre for Australian Studies.

Martin, Ged 2003. 'Explaining the sentimental utopia: historians and the centenary of Australian Federation', *Australian Studies*, 19(1), 211-230.

Meaney, Neville 2001. 'Britishness and Australian identity: the problem of nationalism in Australian history and historiography', *Australian Historical Studies*, 32(116), 76-90.

Megarrity, Lyndon 2001. 'Teething pains of the early Commonwealth: Barton, Philp and the end of the Pacific Islands labour trade', *The New Federalist*, 8, 54-65.

Megarrity, Lyndon 2017. 'Drake's progress: the political somersaults of J.G. Drake', *Journal of the Royal Australian Historical Society*, 103(2), 111-135.

Melville, W. B. 1913. *"Greatest Australians" the Keynotes on their Careers*, Sydney, NSW: Frank Adams Press.

Miller, Jack 1979. 'Tanker wreck led to racial controversy', *Port of Melbourne Quarterly*, 29(5), 9-13.

Milne, Tessa 1998. 'Barton at Bathurst: "front stage/backstage"', *Papers on Parliament*, 32, 103-107.

Milner, Colin 2013. 'Robert Randolph Garran and the creation of the Australian Commonwealth', *Australia and the World: A*

Festschrift for Neville Meaney, J. Beaumont and M. Jordan, eds, Sydney: Sydney University Press.

Mines, Francis John 1976. *Premiers' Conferences and Other Intercolonial Conferences in Australasia before Federation*, Fyshwick, ACT: Microdata.

Moore, Clive 1985. *Kanaka. A History of Melanesian Mackay*, Port Moresby: University of Papua New Guinea Press.

Moore, J. Sheridan 1888. *Memorials of the Celebration of the Australasian Centenary in New South Wales*, Sydney: Charles Potter, Govt. Printer.

Moore, W. Harrison 1902. *The Constitution of the Commonwealth of Australia*, London: John Murray.

Moran, H. M. 1939. *Viewless Winds: Being the Recollections and Digressions of an Australian Surgeon*, London: P. Davies.

Moran, P. F. 1897. 'Cardinal's Manifesto', *Cardinal Moran and the Federal Convention*, Sydney: F. Cunninghame and Co.

Morgan, Patrick 2012. *Melbourne Before Mannix*, Ballan, Victoria: Connor Court Publishing.

Morrison, A. A. 1950. 'The Brisbane general strike of 1912', *Historical Studies, Australia New Zealand*, 4(14), 125-144.

Morrison W. Frederic 1888. *The Jubilee History of Queensland*, Brisbane: Muir & Morcom.

Musgrave, Thomas 2003. 'The Western Australian secessionist movement', *Macquarie Law Journal*, 95-128.

Nairn, Bede 1967. 'The political mastery of Sir Henry Parkes: New South Wales politics 1871-1891', *Journal of the Royal Australian Historical Society*, 53(1), 1-51.

Nairn, Bede 1973. *Civilising Capitalism. The Labor Movement in NSW 1870-1900*, Canberra: Australian National University Press.

Nethercote, John 2000. 'Blunder put Barton in the box seat', *Canberra Times*, 21 December, 11.

Nicholas, F. W. and J. M. Nicholas 2008. *Charles Darwin in Australia*, New York: Cambridge University Press.

Nicolson, Harold, 1952. *King George the Fifth: His Life and Reign*, London: Constable.

Noone, Val 2009. 'Nicholas O'Donnell: "Australian born ... but a good Irish Scholar"', *Australasian Journal of Irish Studies*, 9, 93-111.

Norris, R. 1975. *The Emergent Commonwealth: Australian Federation, Expectations and Fulfilment 1889-1910*, Carlton, Victoria: Melbourne University Press.

O'Collins, Gerald 1965. *Patrick McMahon Glynn. A Founder of Australian Federation*, Carlton, Victoria: Melbourne University Press.

O'Collins, Maev 2002. *An Uneasy Relationship. Norfolk Island and the Commonwealth of Australia*, Canberra: Pandanus.

O'Connor, P. S. 1968. 'Keeping New Zealand white, 1908-1920', *New Zealand Journal of History*, 2(1), 41-65.

O'Farrell, Patrick 1986. 'Writing the history of Irish Australia', in *Ireland and Irish-Australia: Studies in Cultural and Political History*, Oliver MacDonagh and W.F. Mandle, eds, New Hampshire: Croom Helm.

Osborne, J. P. 1921 *Nine Crowded Years*, Sydney, NSW: George A. Jones.

Osborne, M. E. 1967, 'Thomson, Sir Edward Deas (1800-1879), *Australian Dictionary of Biography*, 2, Melbourne: Melbourne University Press.

Palazzo, Albert 2001. *The Australian Army: A History of its Organisation 1901-2001*, South Melbourne: Oxford University Press.

Palmer, E. V. (Vance) 1905. 'An Australian national art', *Steele Rudd's Magazine*, January, 75-76.

Parkes, Henry 1857. *Murmurs of the Stream*, Sydney: James W. Waugh.

Parkes, Henry 1885. *The Beauteous Terrorist and Other Poems, by a Wanderer*, Melbourne: George Robertson.

Parkes, Henry 1889. *Fragmentary Thoughts*, Sydney: Samuel E. Lees.

Parkes, Henry 1890. *The Federal Government of Australasia*, Sydney: Turner and Henderson.

Parkes, Henry 1890a. *United Australia: Public Opinion in England as Expressed in the Leading Journals of the United Kingdom*. Sydney: Charles Potter, Government Printer.

Parkes, Henry 1892. *Fifty Years in the Making of Australian History*, London: Longmans, Green, and Co.

Parkes, Henry 1895. *Sonnets and Other Verse*, London: Kegan Paul, Trench and Trübner.

Partlon, Anne 2004. 'How the west was won. John Waters Kirwan and the "Separation for Federation' campaign" ', *Australian Journal of Irish Studies*, 4, 105-116.

Patmore, Greg 1988. 'Systematic management and bureaucracy: the NSW railways prior to 1932', *Labour and Industry*, 1(2), 306-321.

Patterson, G. D. 1962. 'The Murray River border customs dispute, 1853-1880', *Australian Economic History Review*, 2(2), 122-136.

Peach, John 2008. *The Biggest Ever Mining Swindle in the Colonies*, Carindale, Queensland: Interactive Publications.

Pearl, Cyril 1979. *The Three Lives of Gavan Duffy*, Kensington, NSW: New South Wales University Press.

Penlington, Norman 1943. 'General Hutton and the problem of military imperialism in Canada, 1898-1900', *Canadian Historical Review*, 24(2), 156-71.

Penny, Barbara 1960. 'The Blake Case', *Australian Journal of Politics and History*, 6(2), 176-189.

Petrow, Stefan 1995. 'Modernising the law: Norman Kirkwood Ewing (1870-1928) and the Tasmanian Criminal Code 1924', *University of Queensland Law Journal*, 18(2), 287-30.

Phelps, Peter 2020. 'Federation: liberalism triumphant? Or liberalism thwarted?', *Agenda: A Journal of Policy Analysis and Reform*, 27(1), 163-176.

Phillips, A. A. 1963. *Bernard O'Dowd: Selection and Introduction*, Sydney: Angus and Robertson.

Phillips, A. A. 1971. 'The Cross-eyed Clio: McQueen and the Australian tradition', *Meanjin Quarterly*, 30(1), 108-113.

Phillips, A. A. 1980. *The Australian Tradition: Studies in a Colonial Culture*, 2nd ed., Melbourne: Longman Cheshire.

Piddington, Albert Bathurst 1929. *Worshipful Masters*, Sydney: Angus & Robertson.

Pike, Douglas 1967. *Paradise of Dissent: South Australia 1829-1857*, Melbourne: Melbourne University Press.

Pitt Cobbett, William 2019. *The Constitution and Government of Australia, 1788 to 1919*, Anne Twomey ed., Alexandria, NSW: Federation Press.

Plowman, David and Graham F. Smith 1986. 'Moulding federal arbitration: the employers and the High Court 1903-1935', *Australian Journal of Management*, 11(2), 203-229.

Portus, G. V. 1953. *Happy Highways*, Carlton, Victoria: Melbourne University Press.

Powell, Alan 1977. *Patrician Democrat: The Political Life of Charles Cowper, 1843-1870*, Melbourne: Melbourne University Press.

Pratt, Ambrose 1908. *David Syme: The Father of Protection in Australia, with introduction by the Hon. Alfred Deakin*, Melbourne: Ward Lock.

Pringle, Rosemary 1972. 'The 1897 convention elections in New South Wales – a milestone?', *Journal of the Royal Australian Historical Society*, 58(3), 217-225.

Pringle, Rosemary 1979. 'Public opinion in the federal referendum campaigns in New South Wales 1898-99', *Journal of the Royal Australian Historical Society*, 64(4), 235-251.

Pulsford, Edward 1903. *Commerce and the Empire*, London: Cassell.

Pulsford, Edward 1917. *Commerce and the Empire. 1914 and After*, London: P. S. King & Son.

Quick, John 1927. *A Classified Catalogue of Books and Writings by Australian Authors*, Melbourne: Australian Literature Association.

Quick, John 1965. *Sir John Quick's Notebook*, L.E. Fredman, ed., Newcastle, NSW: Pogonoski.

Quick, John and Robert Randolph Garran 1901. *The Annotated Constitution of the Australian Commonwealth*, Sydney: Angus & Robertson.

Quinlan, Michael and Margaret Gardner 1995. 'Strikes, worker protest and union growth in Canada and Australia, 1815-1900: a comparative analysis', *Labour/Le Travail*, 36, 175-208.

Rallings, Colin and Michael Thrasher 2000. *British Electoral Facts, 1832-1999*, England: Ashgate.

Reid, G. H. 1875. *Five Free Trade Essays: Inscribed to the Electors of Victoria*, Melbourne: Gordon & Gotch.

Reid, G. H. 1882. 'Our approaching centenary', *The Sydney University Review*, 2, 171-177.

Reid, G. H. 1891. 'The "Commonwealth" of Australia"', *The Nineteenth Century: A Monthly Review*, 30 (173) 145-153.

Reid, G. H. 1891a. 'The present stage of the federal movement', *Sydney Quarterly Magazine*, 8, 267-277.

Reid, G. H. 1899. *Public Demonstration in Honour of the Right Hon. G.H. Reid held at the Sydney Town Hall*, Sydney, NSW: Samuel E. Lees.

Reid, G. H. 1917. *My Reminiscences*, London; Melbourne: Cassell.

Reid, G. S. and Martyn Forrest 1989. *Australia's Commonwealth Parliament. 1901-1988. Ten Perspectives*, Carlton, Victoria: Melbourne University Press.

Reynolds, Henry 1971. 'Australian nationalism: Tasmanian patriotism', *New Zealand Journal of History*, 5(1), 18-30.

Reynolds, John 1948. *Edmund Barton*, Sydney: Angus and Robertson.

Rhodes, Glenn 1988. *The Australian Federation Referenda 1898-1900: A Spatial Analysis of Voting Behaviour*, PhD thesis, London School of Economics and Political Science.

Rhodes, Glenn 2002. *Votes for Australia: How Colonials Voted at the 1899-1900 Federation Referendums*, Nathan, Queensland: Centre for Australian Public Sector Management.

Richardson, Henry Handel 1948. *Myself When Young*, Melbourne: Heinemann.

Rickard, John 1976. *Class and Politics. New South Wales, Victoria and the Early Commonwealth 1890-1910*, Canberra: Australian National University Press.

Rickard, John 1984. *H.B. Higgins, the Rebel as Judge*, Sydney: George Allen & Unwin.

Rivett, Rohan 1965. *Australian Citizen: Herbert Brookes, 1867-1963*, Melbourne: Melbourne University Press.

Robertson, John 1887. 'Response to Henry Parkes', *The Introduction of Parliamentary Government in New South Wales, Sydney: Government Printer.

Roe, Michael 2001. 'In a state: Tasmania's polity under federal pressure, 1901-4', *Launceston Historical Society Papers and Proceedings*, 13, 18-24.

Rosa, Samuel Albert 1899. *The Federal Bill Analyzed: Being an Examination of the Federal Bill as Amended by the Secret Conference of Premiers*, Leichhardt, NSW: T.E. Colebrook.

Royce, Josiah 1891. 'Impressions of Australia', *Scribner's Magazine*, January, 75-88.

Rubinstein, W. D. 1979. 'The distribution of personal wealth in Victoria, 1860-1974', *Australian Economic History Review*, 19(1), 26-41.

Rubinstein, W. D. 1980. 'The top wealth holders in New South Wales, 1817-1939', *Australian Economic History Review*, 20(2), 136-152.

Rusden, G. W. 1883. *History of Australia*, London: Chapman and Hall.

Rutledge, Martha 1974. *Edmund Barton*, Melbourne: Oxford University Press.

Ryan, J. A. 1995. 'Bernhard Ringrose Wise', *Journal of the Royal Australian Historical Society*, 81(1), 70-88.

St Ledger, A., G. W. Power and J. J. Knight 1902. *Thomas Joseph Byrnes 1860-1898: Sketches and Impressions*. Brisbane: Alex, Muir & Co.

Salsbury, Stephen and Kay Sweeney 1992. *Sydney Stockbrokers: Biographies of Members of the Sydney Stock Exchange, 1871 to 1987*, Sydney, NSW: Hale & Iremonger.

Sawer, Geoffrey 1956. *Australian Federal Politics and Law: 1901-1929*, Melbourne: Melbourne University Press.

Scott, Ernest 1916. *A Short History of Australia*, London: Oxford University Press.

Serle, Geoffrey 1963. *The Golden Age. A History of the Colony of Victoria 1851-1861*, Melbourne: Melbourne University Press.

Serle, Geoffrey 1969. 'The Victorian government's campaign for federation', 1813-1889, in *Essays in Australian Federation*, A. W. Martin, ed., Melbourne: Melbourne University Press.

Serle, Geoffrey 1970. 'The gold generation', *Victorian Historical Magazine*, 41(1), 265-72.

Serle, Geoffrey 1996. 'Victorian Writers in the Nineties', *The 1890s: Australian Literature and Literary Culture*, Ken Stewart, ed., St Lucia: University of Queensland Press.

Serle, Percival, 1949. *Dictionary of Australian Biography*, Sydney: Angus and Robertson.

Shaw, A. G. L. 1990. 'Centennial Reflection on Sir Henry Parkes's Tenterfield Oration', *Canberra Historical Journal*, 25, 2-10.

Sherington, G. E. 1976. 'The politics of "state rights": J. H. Carruthers and the New South Wales state election of 1907', *Journal of the Royal Australian Historical Society*, 62(3), 179-188.

Shlomowitz, Ralph 1981.'Markets for indentured and time-expired Melanesian labour in Queensland 1863-1906', *Journal of Pacific History*, 16(2), 70-91.

Simpson, A. W. B. 1984. *Cannibalism and the Common Law: The Story of the Tragic Last Voyage of the Mignonette and the Strange Legal Proceedings to Which it Gave Rise*, Chicago: University of Chicago Press.

Sinclair, W. A. 2009. *Annual Estimates of Gross Domestic Product: Australian Colonies/States 1861-1976/77*, Monash University: Department of Economics.

Smith, Anthony D. 1991. *National Identity*, New York: Penguin.

Smith, Bruce 1888. 'Australian loyalty to the British Empire', *Sydney Quarterly Magazine*, 6(4), 369-377.

Smith, Bruce 1894. *The Ideal and the Actual in Politics*, North Sydney.

Smith, Bruce 1899. *Honour to Whom Honour is Due: A Federal Retrospect*, Sydney: McCarron, Stewart & Co.

Smith, Bruce 1908. *Some Thoughts in Regard to Anti-socialist-liberal-Programme for the Australian Federal Parliament*, Sydney.

Smith, Bruce 1924. *The Light of Egypt*, Sydney: Waite and Bull.

Smith, Bruce 2005 [1887]. *Liberty and Liberalism*, St Leonards, NSW: Centre for Independent Studies.

Smith, Francis Gould 1889. *Danger Ahead! Anti Imperial Federation of Australasia*, Melbourne: Australasian-American Trading Company.

Smith, James 1903. *The Cyclopedia of Victoria*, Melbourne: Cyclopedia.

Smith, Jim 2012. 'Aboriginal voters in the Burragorang Valley, NSW, 1869-1953', *Journal of the Royal Australian Historical Society*, 98(2), 170-192.

Smith, Simon 2016. *Judging for the People: A Social History of the Supreme Court in Victoria 1841-2016*, Crows Nest, NSW: Allen & Unwin.

Souter, Gavin 1988. *Acts of Parliament. A Narrative History of the Senate and House of Representatives*, Carlton, Victoria: Melbourne University Press.

Spence, Catherine Helen 1898. *Effective Voting, Australia's Opportunity: An Explanation of the Hare System of Voting*, Sydney: Brooks.

Stein, S. J and B. H. Stein 1970. *The Colonial Heritage of Latin America: Essays on Economic Dependence in Perspective*, New York: Oxford University Press.

Stenhouse, Paul 2018. *John Farrell. Poet, Journalist and Social Reformer 1851-1904*, North Melbourne: Australian Scholarly Publishing.

Stephens, A. G. 1893. *Why North Queensland Wants Separation*, Townsville Queensland: North Queensland Separation League.

Stewart, Ken 1996. 'Introduction', *The 1890s. Australian Literature and Literary Culture*, Ken Stewart, ed., St Lucia, Queensland: University of Queensland Press.

Stockings, Craig 2007. *The Making and Breaking of the Post-federation Army, 1901-09*, Duntroon, ACT: Land Warfare Studies Centre.

Strahan, Lynn 1984. *Just City and the Mirrors. Meanjin Quarterly and the Intellectual Front 1940-1965*, Melbourne: Oxford University Press.

Stretton, Pat & Christine Finnimore 1993. 'Black fellow citizens: Aborigines and the Commonwealth franchise', *Australian Historical Studies*, 25(101), 521-535

Stubbs, Matthew 2012. 'A Brief History of the judicial review of Legislation under the Australian Constitution', *Federal Law Review*, 40(2), 227-252.

Syme, David 1890. *On the Modification of Organisms*, Melbourne: George Robertson.

Symon, Josiah 1976. 'The dawn of Federation: some episodes, letters and personalities and a vindication', annotated by D. I. Wright, *South Australiana*, 15(2), 113-51.

Tanner, Thomas W. 1980. *Compulsory Citizen Soldiers*, Waterloo, NSW: Alternative Publishing Co-operative.

Taylor, Henry D'Esterre 1888. *The Advantages of Imperial Federation*, Melbourne: Kemp & Boyce.

Temby, Ian 1984. '"In this labyrinth there is no golden thread" – Section 92 and the impressionistic approach', *Australian Law Journal*, 58, 86-90.

Tennyson, Audrey 1978. *Audrey Tennyson's Vice-Regal Days*, Alexandra Hasluck ed., Canberra: National Library of Australia.

Thomson, James 2002. 'The Founding Father? Edmund Barton and the Australian Constitution', *Federal Law Review*, 30(2), 407-458.

Tulloch, Hugh 1988. *James Bryce's 'American Commonwealth': The Anglo-American Background*, London: Boydell and Brewer.

Turner, Henry Gyles 1911. *The First Decade of the Australian Commonwealth*, Melbourne: Mason, Firth and McCutcheon.

Twopeny, R. E. N. 1883. *Town Life in Australia*, London: Elliot Stock.

Tyrrell, James R. 1987 [1952]. *Old Books, Old Friends, Old Sydney*, Sydney: Angus and Robertson.

Vamplew, Wray, ed., 1987. *Australians, Historical Statistics*, Broadway, NSW, Australia: Fairfax, Syme & Weldon.

Viner, Jacob, 2014 [1950]. *The Customs Union Issue*, Paul Oslington, ed., Oxford: Oxford University Press.

Walker, Henry de Rosenbach 1897. *Australasian Democracy*, London: T. Fisher Unwin.

Walker, James Backhouse 1976. *Prelude to Federation (1884-1898): Extracts From the Journal of James Backhouse Walker*, P. B. Walker, ed., Hobart: O.B.D. Publishing.

Walker, J. T. 1898. *The Federation of British Australasia: A Sketch from a Political and an Economic Point of View*, Sydney: McCarron, Stewart & Co.

Walker, R. B. 1962. 'The Presbyterian church and people in the colony of New South Wales in the late nineteenth century', *Journal of Religious History*, 2(1), 49-65.

Walker, R. B. 1976. *The Newspaper Press in New South Wales, 1803-1920*, Sydney: Sydney University Press.

Walker, R. B. 1977. 'Some aspects of electoral reform in New South Wales 1858-1893', *Journal of the Royal Australian Historical Society*, 63, 149-166.

Ward, John M. 1950. 'The "germ of Federation" in Australia', *Historical Studies, Australia and New Zealand*, 4(15), 214-223.

Ward, John M. 1961. 'Charles Gavan Duffy, and the Australian Federation movement, 1856-70', *Journal of the Royal Australian Historical Society*, 47(1), 1-33.

Warden, James 1990. *Federal Theory and the Formation of the Australian Constitution*, PhD thesis, Australian National University.

Webb, Martyn 2003. 'John Forrest: Architect and founder of modern Western Australia', *Early Days: Journal of the Royal Western Australian Historical Society*, 12(3), 250-272.

Weir, George 1945. *50 Years of Labor in Politics*, Sydney: Industrial Publications.

Weller, Patrick 1974. 'The Labor Party and the defeat of Reid: a re-assessment', *Labour History*, 26, 14-18.

West, Francis 1968. *Hubert Murray: The Australian Pro-Consul*, Melbourne: Oxford University Press.

Wheeler, Edward 1982. 'The First ANZAAS Congress', *Search*, 13, 82-86.

Whittington, Helen 1986. 'Patrick McMahon Glynn, K.C. 1855-1931', *Law Society Bulletin*, 8(11), 337-341.

Wigmore, Lionel 1963. *The Long View: A History of Canberra, Australia's National Capital*, Melbourne: F.W. Cheshire.

Wilcox, Craig 1993. *Australia's Citizen Army, 1889-1914*, PhD thesis, Australian National University.

Willard, Myra 1967 [1923]. *History of the White Australia Policy to 1920*, Melbourne: Melbourne University Press.

Williams, John M. 1999. 'Samuel Griffith and the Australian Constitution: shaking hands with the new Chief Justice', *New Federalist*, 4, 37-44.

Willis, W. N. 1908. *The Life of W.P. Crick*, Sydney.

Willner, Ann R. 1984. *The Spellbinders: Charismatic Political Leadership*, New Haven, Conn.: Yale University Press.

Wise, Bernhard Ringrose 1913. *The Making of the Australian Commonwealth, 1889-1900: A Stage in the Growth of the Empire*, London: Longmans Green.

Wolskel, Augustus 1936. 'Pre-federation hopes and promises', *Victorian Historical Magazine*, 6, 13-30.

Wood, James 2006. *Chiefs of the Australian Army: Higher Command of the Australian Military Forces, 1901-1914*, Loftus, NSW: Australian Military History Publications.

Wright D.I. 1970. *Shadow of Dispute: Aspects of Commonwealth-State Relations, 1901-1910*, Canberra: Australian National University Press.

Wright, Reg 1998. 'Who was "Buckey" Jones?', *Descent*, 28(3),122-125.

Zetetic 1889. *Descriptive Australia and Federal Guide*, Port Adelaide: S.A. Bookstalls.

Zines, Leslie 1989. 'A legal perspective', *Australian Federalism*, Brian Galligan, ed., Melbourne: Longman Cheshire.

Endnotes

Chapter 1 (pp. 1-7)

1. Davison *et al* 2001, p.245.
2. Federation as a non-event is correlate with the judgement of Federation as a false and superficial remedy for the political ills which Federation idealists hoped to rid Australia of. As one disillusioned Federationist, G. B. Barton, suggested on the eve of Federation, 'The one thing needed in order to realise the dreams of Federal enthusiasts is a complete revolution in the character of Australian politics and politicians'. Barton 1901, p. 5.
3. Wise *CP* 1.10.10.
4. See Deakin 1944; Wise 1913; Scott 1916; Garran 1933.
5. Mock history to us, but not to them. Thus Garran: Tenterfield 'rang like a trumpet-call' (1958, p. 71). Or Wise: Tenterfield 'was the natural minaret from which to sound the trumpet blast that stirred the dry bones to life throughout the continent' (*CP* 1.10.10).
6. Crisp 1949.
7. Norris 1975.
8. Shaw 1990.
9. Was Sydney Australia's largest city at Federation? The point was contested by the respective Statisticians of NSW and Victoria. The answer is sensitive to the definition of boundaries. The most authoritative consideration of the question puts Sydney's population in 1901 at 496 000, and Melbourne's at 476 000 (McCarty 1970).
10. Crisp (1990), Botsman (2000) and Grimshaw (2002) are exceptions. But Crisp's dissatisfaction with Federation is simply that it did not go far enough, and produce unification: perhaps no student of the event has taken a more evident delight in '1901' than Crisp. Botsman's objection is not to the Commonwealth's creation, but to its conservation of the Imperial tie.
11. Birrell 2001.
12. Bolton 2000.
13. Most of the 422 788 Yes voters had no other memorial. Some had no other existence. See chapter 12.
14. Perhaps the brilliant essays of Martin (2001 and 2003) are the closest to a revisionist outlook.

Chapter 2 (pp. 9-35)

15 'That there was no logical imperative for federation in the 1890s is clear' (Bannon 1994, p. 3).

16 Headon and Williams 2000.

17 'The most striking thing about Australian Federation, compared to the political unification of Argentina (1864), Canada (1867) or New Zealand (1876) is that it appears to be an incidental or peripheral aspect of Australian economic development' (McCarty 1973, p. 156).

18 Ferry and Pennay 2000, p. 16.

19 Federationists preferred to dwell on the origins of the three smallest colonies. Of them Robert Garran wrote, 'All the earliest separations were ... due exclusively to Imperial action' (*Commonwealth* 1.10.94). But the suggestion that the settlers of SA or WA would be content with any prospect of being governed from Sydney is ludicrous. Tasmania? In April 1824 a 'Memorial to the King' of 102 of Tasmania's 'landholders, merchants and other free inhabitants' petitioned the Colonial Secretary to create a 'resident government ... not subject to control' of NSW. The grant of this wish was gazetted on 3 December 1825 and, in 1838, an annual Bank Holiday ('Regatta Day') was instituted at the approximate anniversary.

20 Ganter 1998, p. 1.

21 Bullen 1907, p. 87.

22 Details taken from Zetetic (1889). Another contemporary complained, 'It takes nearly as long to get from Melbourne to Brisbane by rail as it does from San Francisco to New York, although in the latter case the distance is 3 000 miles and in the former only 1 298' (*Age* 29.6.89).

23 In 1890 a telegraphic cable connected Sydney and Wellington. If New Zealand had joined the Commonwealth, might not this forgotten deed be carefully noted by historians as a symbol and sire of the coming trans-Tasman unity?

24 The data for this calculation is drawn from McCarty 1970. If Sydney in 1861 had 96 000 inhabitants, and Melbourne 125 000, then, of the total population of 221 000, 43 percent (namely, the Sydneysiders) are 714 km from 57 percent of the total population (namely, the Melbournians). And, correspondingly, 57 percent of the total (Melbournians) are 714 km from 43 percent of the total (Sydneysiders). Thus the average distance is 350 km = 43 percent of 57 percent of 714 km plus 57 percent of 43 percent of 714 km. The method can be generalised to the six capitals.

25 Jenkins 1979, p. 72.

26 The population of the 'northern division' of Queensland, as measured by the 1891 census, was 78 077, larger than that of WA in 1891 (= 49 792) shortly after it had obtained self-government.

27 Federationists who were at the same time separationists included J. M. Macrossan, 'a fervent advocate of North Queensland' who, in 1886, 'came out completely for separation'; Griffith, who claimed that Queensland would be divided into 'at least three' states (Johnston 1963, p. 5); and the *Bulletin*'s A.G. Stephens (1893). And did not Parkes predict Australia would have 'ten states in a very few years', and specifically recommend Western Australia break into three? (Crowley 1997, p. 291).

28 At the Australasian Federal Convention, the leader of the Federation movement, Edmund Barton, quashed the move of one of his fellow delegates, J. T. Walker, to accommodate constitutionally the separation of northern Queensland.

29 Logan 1968, p. 129.

30 Carney 2013, p. 10.

31 The words of the Rev. Dr Alexander Marshall, on the eve of the 1899 referendum (*Age* 24.7.99). In the same address he declared that anyone who voted No would be a 'traitor'.

32 Kingston 1897, p. 6.

33 *AFC* 16.2.98.

34 *AFC* 3.2.98.

35 No duties were imposed by either NSW or Victoria on each other. Instead, Victoria paid an annual lump sum to NSW, purportedly equivalent to the revenue which NSW sacrificed by the absence of duties, net of the revenue similarly sacrificed by Victoria (Patterson 1962).

36 Patterson 1962, p. 134.

37 Thus Andrew Garran, Reid's man in the Legislative Council: 'The gain if we establish inter-colonial free trade will be enormous. Australia as a whole will enter a fresh epoch' (*NSWPD* 5.6.90).

38 The tribulations of Canada's free trade agreements with the United States were the germ of this celebrated proposition in the economic theory. Viner 2014 [1950] is the classic reference.

39 See Coleman (2020).

40 Hirst 2000. In 1895 New Zealand and SA were on the verge of an agreement which would admit New Zealand hops to SA, and SA wine to New Zealand, free of duty. But although New Zealand

passed legislation, SA abandoned it, 'the natural result of the belief that it would give much to New Zealand but little to South Australia' (Pulsford 1917, p. 144).

41 Section 90 effectively forbad a mere free trade area: it makes the Commonwealth's possession of customs duty power conditional on a uniform tariff with respect to the rest of the world.

42 Jenkins 1979, p. 129.

43 Cave-Browne-Cave 1897.

44 Victoria's population stagnated during the 1890s. It was even measured to be falling at the time (*Commonwealth* 7.6.95).

45 Thus, in 1900, Victoria's tariff on footwear was 29.5 percent, on furniture 27 percent, on beer 28.1 percent (Lloyd 2015, p. 170). These rates may seem moderate by, say, the standards of modern income tax. But there is no analogy. An income tax may increase the supply of labour; a tariff must always reduce imports. An analytical inquiry suggests that, with import ratios in the region of 25 percent (or less), such rates would be destructive of revenue (see Coleman 2020b).

46 *Commonwealth* 7.11.94.

47 Cave-Browne-Cave 1897, p. 79.

48 *NSWPD* 8.12.91.

49 F. T. Crowder, WA, a manufacturer of carbonated water. Bannon 1998.

50 Rhodes 1988, vol. 2.

51 A 1970s estimate put 'high professional' and 'high clerical' occupations as absorbing 26 percent of Australia's workforce, compared to an average of just 12 percent in Great Britain, USA, Northern Ireland, the Netherlands, Scandinavia, and West Germany (Kelley and McAllister 1985, p. 388).

52 By one census based measure, 'professionals' amounted to 4.3 percent of NSW's workforce in 1871, and 7.3 percent 1901 (Markey 1988, p. 24). In 1900, 89 of the 154 barristers practising in NSW had been admitted in the years 1890-1900 (*NSW Statistical Register*).

53 'A strong and encouraging feature in the latter half of the famous 19th century is the ... social and legal status of solicitors' (*ACJ* 1.11.89).

54 At the close of the 19th century, lawyers and 'professionals' contributed about 30 of 125 members of the NSW Assembly, and about 22 of the 93 members of the Victoria's; about three or four times their incidence in the workforce (Data drawn from Rhodes 1988, vol. 2).

55 The Pharmacy Society sponsored the *Pharmacy Act 1897 (NSW)*,

which, in the condemnation of John Haynes, 'binds all the chemists of the country into the closest union' (*NSWPD* 6.10.92).

56 '... squatters are inclined to place their sons in urban professions' (Walker 1898, p. 300).

57 This ideology of professionalism is clearly voiced in *The Yellow Wave*, the 1897 invasion alarm novel by the Federationist soldier-politician, James Mackay. In the wake of the strikes and busts of the 1890s, Ada Cambridge, novelist and wife of the Reverend George Frederick Cross, laid a similar double curse on Labour and Capital. 'It was significant that our great Labour War developed with the Boom, and the defeat of the insurgents coincided with the downfall of the rotten edifice that towered so high. They were correlated forces the Boomsters and the Strikers' (Cambridge 1903, p. 221).

58 Smith 1991, pp. 120-21.

59 Glynn 1974, p. 28.

60 Parkes *NSWPD* 24.8.98.

61 Breward 2001, p. 68.

62 Breward 2001, p. 68.

63 Archbishop Carr; the Rev. Bertie Boyce; the Rev. William Curnow.

64 *Argus* 22.7.99.

65 *Argus* 31.1.99.

66 Mackay 1895.

67 L. F. Heydon *ACJ* 1.7.89.

68 Thus the Wentworth chambers housed Reid, Wise, O'Connor and, for a period, Barton (Tyrrell 1987).

69 As the historian of the NSW bar puts it, 'barristers ... came particularly at this time [end of 19th century] to develop a certain community of interests in their profession' (Bennett 1969, p. 105).

70 *SMH* 21.5.91

71 Joyce 1974, p. 251.

72 Griffith was entitled to be addressed as 'Your Excellency' whenever, as Chief Justice of Queensland's Supreme Court, he stood in for an absent Governor.

73 Graham 1939, p. 95.

74 Bennett 1969, p. 119.

75 Walker 1898, p. 7.

76 Reid, Braddon and Forrest. 'Forrest was, above all, an administrator

and master of files. ... Forrest's occupancy of the ministerial offices ... [was] perhaps more a measure of his skill as an administrator than of his standing as a politician' (Webb 2003).

77 Osborne 1967 and Ward 1950.
78 Australian Government 2020.
79 Garran 1958, p. 109.
80 Thus the NSW Government Railways, Australia's largest employer (and allegedly the largest industrial enterprise in the southern hemisphere), was 'a bureaucratic employer ... divided into departments and grades and administered by a hierarchical chain of command ... with comprehensive rules and regulations ... an appeals system and a pension fund' (Patmore 1988).
81 The Tasmanian Federationist, Inglis Clark, was another such 'consolidator'. A Federationist judge and Senator, N.K. Ewing, a younger brother of Thomas, attempted the codification of Tasmanian criminal law (Petrow 1995).
82 Pike 1967, p. 35.
83 Stein and Stein 1970, p. 58.
84 *SMH* 30.10.56.
85 Souter 1988, p. 4.
86 Cave-Brown-Cave 1897, p. 269.
87 Deakin 1968, p. 72.
88 Some delegates managed to identify federation with uniformity: to Quick any lack of uniformity was 'undoubtedly a departure from the Federal Principle' (*AFC* 26.3.97). Glynn commended the German constitution on the grounds it made railway rates 'uniform as far as possible' (*AFC* 24.2.98).
89 Livingston 1994.
90 *P&T* 1893, 1894.
91 *BC* 16.6.99.
92 Mines 1976.
93 The establishment in the 1890s of Australia's time zones, for example.

Chapter 3 (pp. 37-59)

94 In the same chamber of parliament Parkes stated, 'I trust and believe that we are in England now' (*NSWPD* 30.8.92).
95 Parkes' 'crimson thread' – one of Federationists' few memorable pieces of rhetoric – was a celebration of Britishness.
96 Parkes 1890, p. 139; Reid *Age* 29.1.95; William Copley one-time Chief

Secretary of SA and unsuccessful candidate for the Australasian Federal Convention. Bruce Smith articulated Copley's sentiment in words: 'the Union Jack, as the emblem of the British Empire, should *not* be supplanted by the Australian local symbol' (Smith 1908, p. 8).

97 Nationalism in this conception is a stinging, 'Who are you?', demanded of the outsider. The counter claim of those on the margin – the *'Civis Romanus sum'* expostulation – might be described as Populism. Thus, in the first century AD, Christianity was 'populist', while Judaism was 'nationalist'. In the 16th century, the Reformation was 'populist', and the Counter-Reformation 'nationalist'.

98 Moran 1939, p. 10.

99 Macrossan was 'a lifelong opponent of the Chinese, speaking vehemently against them with a Cato like persistence almost every time he opened his mouth' (Bryan 1954). Ewing was almost as preoccupied, and contributed three articles to *The Commonwealth*, a Federationist mouthpiece, on the obnoxiousness of 'The Alien' (7.11.94, 7.3.95 and 7.5.95).

100 *NSWPD* 30.8.92.

101 *NSWPD* 23.11.92.

102 *TN* 26.5.98.

103 To Reid the Commonwealth would be 'a colony within the Empire' (*AFC* 9.9.97). Soon after its proclamation, Deakin described the Commonwealth as a 'dependency' (1968, p. 64). Quick and Garran affirmed 'the Commonwealth ... is not an independent sovereign community' (1901, p. 367).

104 SA's constitution left the Privy Council to decide the space of 'royal disallowance' (Keith 1912, p. 29-30). Federationists troubled with no such qualification of this royal prerogative.

105 J. G. Gough *NSWPD* 22.5.90.

106 To rhyme with following line, 'Britons, hold your own!'. The words are Alfred Tennyson's.

107 The affairs of Blake (Penny 1960), Wright (Johnson 1975), Kitt (Harding 2000) and New Guinea. McIlwraith judged Britain's treatment of the annexation of New Guinea to be 'the grossest piece of treachery on the part of the English government to the colonies that has ever been perpetrated' (*QPD* 23.12.84).

108 Bavin 1941, p. 54.

109 In 1890 Victorian Federationists became concerned that Parkes may have been infected by republicanism, and so devised a test

of his loyalty (Bavin 1941). The essential resolution at the National Federal Conference would affirm that Federation must occur 'under the Crown'. Would Parkes refuse this phrase? He embraced it.

110 Martin 1980, p. 367.
111 Martin 1969, p. 358.
112 Martin 1969. Sir Henry Loch, Governor of Victoria until November 1889, and John Hope, the Earl of Hopetoun, thereafter until July 1895; and A. H. T. Keith-Falconer, 9th Earl of Kintore, Governor of SA until 1895. They were 'eager for Federation' (Martin 1990, p. 16). Later, Lord Hampden (NSW Governor, November 1895-March 1899) 'believed federation was vital' (Lang 2009, p. 373). Along with the entire British political class. In 1889 'immediately from all parts of England and Scotland there went up a newspaper chorus of congratulation' on Parkes's speeches (Smith 1899, p. 9). Parkes (1890a) carefully collected, and published, excerpts of such congratulations from 65 British newspapers.
113 A. G. Taylor.
114 King 2007, p. 238.
115 Other clear examples of the 'committed intercessor' conspicuous in Australia's Federationist cause would include J. D. Lang, David Christie Murray, Max Hirsch and A. W. Jose. James Bryce (1905), who pronounced his blessing on Federation at a distance, may also be so described.
116 Ward 1961, p. 1; Serle 1963, p. 314.
117 Pearl 1979, p. 201.
118 By successful resolutions of both the House and the Senate, on 26 October 1905.
119 'Recollections and reflections: the story of my life', *HCP*. The personal intersection between the causes of Irish Home Rule and Federation could be intense. Thus the Sydney-born (and Sydney University-educated) T. B. Curran was an Irish National Federation member of the House of Commons between 1895 and 1901. On returning to Australia shortly after Federation, he was admitted to the NSW bar on the nomination of Barton and O'Connor, and contested the seat of Paddington.
120 MP, 'Interview with Sunday Times'.
121 Glynn 1890.
122 That Hugh Mahon – an agent of the Irish National Land League, and Federationist – could express surprise that a 'colonial', such as

George Reid, could be a fine orator is one of a piece of Irish Catholic depreciation of the local society.

123 This claim might extend even to authors of purposively Australian patriotic verse, such as Marion Miller Knowles. 'Australia is her home, and Ireland her unexperienced romanticised source' (Morgan 2012, p. 83).
124 Moran 1939, p. 28.
125 Moran 1897, p. 29.
126 O'Farrell 1986, p. 108. In 1901, of 107 'secular priests' under Moran's authority, 94 were Irish born, and another 10 were of Irish parentage (Ayres 2007).
127 Quick 1927, p. 3.
128 Parkes 1890, p. 52.
129 For example, the 'very nice looking young ladies' Charles Darwin encountered in 1836 at Parramatta (Nicholas and Nicholas 2008, p. 94).
130 *Argus* 7.2.90.
131 *Empire* 14.5.56.
132 *AFC* 29.97. Lyne was another native-born who expressed the same sentiment. Notice that Downer and Lyne were asserting no more than that being native-born was not a handicap to being British. It did not actually make you British. Thus the villain in *The Yellow Wave* was Orloff, who 'though born in Australia, was in reality a Russian' (Mackay 1895). So the point was to be British; being native-born was a bit beside the point.
133 'Topophilia' – the attachment to local landscape, flora and fauna – was weak amongst Federationists. On one occasion, the corpses of shot koalas clinging to trees served Barton as the material of humorous comparison.
134 To Glynn, 'colonials' were 'no companions' (Glynn 1974, p. 40, p. 142). Perhaps they were poor stuff constitutionally; were not 'the heroes of the [American] revolution largely exiles from other countries'? (Glynn 1890, p. 12).
135 Serle 1970, p. 242.
136 Smith 1889.
137 Richardson 1948.
138 Cramp 1938, p. 210. *But oh the counter charm for home, Is not yet found, wher'er I roam.* 'Stolen Moments', Parkes (1857).

139 In Morrison 1888, p. 219.
140 Thus Barton, a few days after the Commonwealth's inauguration, declared, 'The firm of John Bull Liability Ltd is now the firm of John Bull and Family Liability Unlimited'.
141 'Throughout the length and breadth of Australia, the name of Benjamin Disraeli ... made the sunburnt settler glow with an unwonted patriotism' (Martin 1889). To this Australian author, the British Empire, rather than Australia, was his 'country'; 'we shall ever think of our country ... as the whole mighty Empire' (Martin 1893, p. 320)
142 Quick and Graran 1901, p. 20
143 In Melbourne a Gaelic League was founded in 1902 (Morgan 2012).
144 *CP* 22.7.99. The creation of the Irish Rifles did not trouble the Empire harmony of Federationists. O'Connor was full of reassurances of their loyalty to the British Empire: was not the Crown on their shoulder badges?
145 See Moore 1888.
146 Stewart 1996, p. 27.
147 Parkes, Deakin, Griffith, Piddington, Smith, Garran. Even Reid once attempted poetry.
148 Including, unlikely as it may seem, Bruce Smith. The admiring, 'astonishing', is his choice of adjective.
149 Kiernan 1989, p. 185.
150 Berryman 2016, p. 585.
151 Hadgraft cited in Cantrell 1976, p.13.
152 Keel 1980, p. 48.
153 Cantrell 1976, p. 109.
154 Lawson 1983, p. 190.
155 Serle 1996, p. 33.
156 See, for example, Walter Murdoch's dismissal of the 'pretensions' of 'The New School of Australian Poetry'. *Argus* 6.5.99.
157 *WC* 9.10.00.
158 Parkes 1890, p. 39.
159 If there was one thing that could be put in that empty box, it was Britishness.
160 McMinn 1994, p. 96. McMinn: 'the Young Turks of the ANA experienced ... difficulty ... in distinguishing between Victoria and

Australia' (1994, p. 96). Similarly, it has been suggested that in Higinbotham ' "the nation" and the country was defined as the part of Australia lying south of the Murray' (Bennett 2007, p. 232). Duffy's adopted nation was certainly Victoria, rather than Australia.

161 While Reid was an Australian 'in the widest sense, Mr Deakin's ideas seem unable to reach beyond the colony in which he was born' (Twopeny 1883, p. 180). This British visitor added, 'In all the Victorian papers, of whatever party, it is noticeable that Victorian topics ... occupy an almost exclusive share of both leading and news columns; while the New South Wales and South Australian papers devote far more attention to intercolonial and European affairs' (1883, p. 232).

162 Serle 1969. 'The men of Victoria run devotion to the soil to the extreme'. So speaks the herald of Tenterfield, David Christie Murray. Glynn in 1898: 'The Victorian spirit of exclusiveness and rivalry is as strong as when I arrived in 1880' (O'Collins 1965, p. 148).

163 Reid 1875, p. 55.

164 Serle 1969, p. 16.

165 Marmion 2012, p. 16.

166 Gordon 1965, p. 69. In 1900, Victoria's naval forces consisted of capital ships of a tonnage of 4 740 tons, along with 3 armed steamers, 3 torpedo launches and 3 torpedo boats. The rest of Australia's locally controlled naval forces consisted of capital ships of a combined tonnage of 1 950 tons, plus 3 torpedo boats. (Galloway 1899).

167 Even in Ballarat – apparently so rich in latent nourishment for a truly Victorian myth – the 'fealty to Britain was almost a fetish', in the words of one not unsympathetic historian, making 'it hard to see them as Australians' (Bate 1978, pp. 253-4). The *Cyclopedia of Victoria* referred to the Eureka Stockade as the 'Ballarat Rebellion'. To Ballarat, 'Eureka meant little or nothing to them as a democratic symbol' (McCarty 1980, p. 7).

168 Serle 1970, p. 265. 'Nearly every member of the Ministry who held office in 1883 had been educated at one or other of the universities in the Mother Country, or at one of its public schools' (*Cyclopedia of Victoria*, vol. 2, p. 14).

169 Serle 1970, p. 272.

170 Noone 2009, p. 99.

171 J. N. H. Hume Cook.

172 This analysis is indebted to the observations made and developed by Hall (1963).

173 'In his teens [William] Watt was a member of the Bouverie Street larrikin "push"' (Green 1969, p. 59).

174 HCP.

175 As one Bendigo-born Federationist recalled of his parents' generation, 'They extolled the fields, the woods, the fruits, the flowers and all the natural loveliness of the old country, and laughed at the suggestion of Australian fertility and beauty' (Cockerill 1943, p. 22).

176 Lawson 1983, p. 9 and p. 22.

177 See M. H. Ellis for one Federation contemporary's 1960s avowal of the falseness of any Australian nation until the Second World War (Australian Association of Cultural Freedom, 1963).

178 Reynolds (1971) and Bolton (1970).

179 Thus Rose Scott claimed of the six colonies that their 'interests are naturally as far apart as their geographical boundaries, and ... will in time develop racial distinctions such as even had marked the difference between an Englishman and an American' (*Worker* 11.3.99).

180 R. B. Wilkinson *NSWPD* 14.5.90.

Chapter 4 (pp. 62-68)

181 Abbott, Barton, Braddon, Cockburn, Forrest, Fraser, Hackett, Holder, Isaacs, McMillan, Peacock, Quick, Reid, Solomon, and Turner. One may add to these Copeland and Bavin (Cramp and Mackaness 1938). 33 of the 111 members of the inaugural Commonwealth Parliament were Freemasons.

182 Convention delegates with convict parents include William Trenwith and Carruthers. Brunker had a convict grandparent. One member of the inaugural House of Representatives was himself a convict. W. H. Groom, as a boy apprentice, was transported in 1846 for theft and, after pardon, convicted a second time for gold theft.

183 Three of the ten convention delegates from NSW could be classified under this head: Carruthers, Lyne and McMillan.

184 Smith 1888, p. 375.

185 '... the private letters of [colonial] liberal notables show the importance which these ambitious men attached to the outward signs of

respectability. Their letters are full of self-congratulation, 'Resentment of slights, caustic comments on the vulgarity of others ...' (Golder 1985, p. 23).

186 The words are put into Dalley's mouth by Daniel Deniehy (1860).

187 A favourite haunt of Barton's during his prime ministership.

188 See, for example, a remark of the author of an admiring salute of the Chief Justice: 'I sometimes think that Sir Samuel would be a greater man had life been less kind to him. To him success came so easily ...' (Graham 1939, p. 95).

189 In NSW in the years 1885-89, 34 estates in excess of £100 000 were probated; and 32 in 1895-99, despite the crash. By contrast, in Victoria there were 33 such estates in the first period, and just 20 in the latter (Rubinstein 1980, p. 143).

190 Portus 1953, p. 34.

191 Broinowski 2001, p. 30.

192 JP 3.8.05. As an aspirant gentleman one might further mention Henry Parkes, widower, 73, and Eleanor Dixon, 31 (and, later still, Parkes, 80, and Julia Lynch, 28). The NSW census of 1901 indicates that 0.3 percent of married men aged 45 to 59 were married to women under the age of 25.

193 Bolton 2000, p. 57.

194 Ryan 1995, p. 71.

195 Milner 2013.

196 Carruthers's father, a private in the 92nd (Highland) Regiment of Foot, was convicted in 1830 for drunkenness and theft, and sentenced to seven years transportation.

197 Quick, Dickson, McMillan and Symon received knighthoods on 1 January 1901. In the same January, Griffith was made a Privy Councillor. Forrest was elevated from K.C.M.G to G.C.M.G., and, later that year, Cockburn was appointed a knight of grace of the Order of St John of Jerusalem. Just prior to 'the day', the Colonial Office renewed an earlier offer of a knighthood to Deakin. Barton was knighted in 1902, as were Holder, Peacock and Neil Lewis. O'Connor declined a knighthood at about the same time.

198 W. B. Dalley was the first native-born Australian to be made a Privy Councillor. In 1897 Forrest, Kingston and Turner followed (along with Braddon and Reid). On 24 January 1901 Barton was made a Privy Councillor. A Privy Councillorship was formally offered to Deakin in 1900.

199 PHC 5.6.74.

200 *SA* 25.2.85.

201 Quoted in Keenan 1904, p. 117. Griffith is recorded as 'Griffith of Brisbane' in *Colonial Gentry*.

202 Thus Barker to a Governor's wife: 'I am not an Englishman, I'm a colonial'. 'I am so surprised', the lady recorded in her diary, 'at the way they are so proud of being colonials' (Tennyson 1978, p. 39). The Federationist program had one other linguistic price. In the late 19th century, the term, 'Australian', co-existed with 'colonial' as a term for native-born. Subsequent to 1901 the term was transferred to any British subject long resident within the Commonwealth; thus the term was removed from the native-born, and perhaps not to the advantage of Australian nationalism.

203 Thus section 109 of the Constitution (as contained in section 9 of the *Commonwealth of Australia Constitution Act 1900* (UK)) supersedes section 2 of the *Colonial Laws Validity Act 1865* (UK).

204 Deakin 1968.

205 Collis 1948 p. 26.

Chapter 5 (pp. 69-75)

206 Kell 1893.

207 *NMH* 24.5.98; *SMH* 27.5.98.

208 *AS* 27.5.98

209 *SMH* 30.5.98.

210 Stenhouse 2018, p. 150.

211 Reid 1917, p. 77.

212 Blackwell 1970 p. 27. In 1894 *The Australian Theosophist* commenced publication, edited by Federationist, Ernest Scott, a son-in-law of Annie Besant.

213 Haynes proposed that a chair in hypnotism at Sydney University be established.

214 Cockerill 1943, p. 129.

215 Grover 1993, p. 178. Reid: 'The Australian, in an audience, may be moulded like wax to your eloquence' (*NSWPD* 21.5.90).

216 Grover 1993, p. 179.

217 Mark J. Hammond was a Federationist, commended for his 'zeal' by Hunt, who coined the sobriquet 'Yes-No Reid' (Hammond

1988). Ninian Melville was a founder of the parliamentary protectionist party in NSW, and delegate to the Bathurst People's Convention.
218 *DT* 30.4.95.
219 *AS* 30.5.95.
220 *AS* 30.5.95.
221 Sydney-Phillip.
222 *DT* 15.5.96.
223 *Truth* 7.6.96.
224 Taylor 1888.
225 Parkes in Morrison 1888, p. 276.
226 Davison 1995.
227 Garran 1958, p.80.
228 Thus one anti-Federationist politician: 'It seems to be a popular superstition that days which are dead and gone should be regarded as days forgotten – that the golden age is ahead of us' (Fitzpatrick 1909, p. 1).
229 In 1881 Corowa's population was measured by the census at 495; in 1901 at 2 046.
230 *KH* 12.8.98.

Chapter 6 (pp. 78-91)

231 Martin 1980, p. 367.
232 Carrington 1889-1890, Part I.
233 *SMH* 22.1.89.
234 Obviously not all. Parkes landed in Sydney with three shillings in his pocket, and departed the world with less. He would disdain the (not completely puny) 'gifts' which second ranking MPs would complacently accept from their electoral associations; in 1892 Ewing accepted £50 from his grateful electors (*BGP*).
235 Hence the rail connection in 1901 to Willis's political 'capital', the now forgotten village of Brewarrina.
236 *SMH* 17.5.98.
237 Parkes 1892, p. 114.
238 Richard Cobden had led the successful crusade against England's protectionist Corn Laws.
239 Parkes 1892, p. 314.

240 In 1850 Parkes had been a prominent member of J.D. Lang's Australia League. In 1867, at an Intercolonial Conference, Parkes had announced, 'I think the time has arrived when these colonies should be united by some federal bond …' (Ward 1961, p. 15). In 1879 Parkes proposed NSW, Victoria and SA should unify (McMinn 1989, p. 91). In 1881 he announced, 'the time is now come for the construction of a federal constitution' (Burton 1973, p. 122).

241 Quoted in Ford 1966, p. 28.

242 The construction of a 'National Palace' in Centennial Park – a kind of Panthéon for the departed great of NSW. (In 1885 the Panthéon, with the funeral of Victor Hugo, had finally settled on its function as a temple to the illustrious deceased).

243 This proposal to rename New South Wales won the support of John Robertson, logically enough. In the event, Carrington induced Parkes to abandon this proposal in exchange for the elevation of Sir Henry's rank, from a 'Knight Commander' to a 'Knight Grand Cross' (Martin 1980, p. 369). The grandeur of NSW was, inevitably, subordinate to his own. As would be that of a federated Australia.

244 *FJ* 1.6.95.

245 *FJ* 2.11.95.

246 Martin 1980, p. 404.

247 Carrington 1889-1890, Part II, 17.2.90.

248 Dibbs: 'no greater attempt could be made to coerce the members of this House and the people of this country than this apparent conspiracy which exists between the Colonial Secretary [Parkes] and an imperial officer' (*NSWPD*. 15.5.90).

249 See Phelps (2020) for a contrary position.

250 Carrington 1889-1890, Part I, 19.10.89.

251 The *Federal Council of Australasia Act* licensed the Council to legislate for 'general defences' by the agreement of two colonies. The construction during the 1890s of the 'Princess Royal Fortress' at King George Sound in WA, and its garrisoning by South Australian forces, was part of the federalisation of defence before Federation.

252 Thus Carrington urged Victoria's governor, Sir Henry Loch, to mollify Victoria's Premier, Duncan Gillies (Wise 1913, pp. 26-27).

253 Charles Edden *NSWPD* 27.7.91. Reid *NSWPD* 27.7.91.

254 *NSWPD* 3.9.11.

255 *NSWPD* 13.1.92.

256 Barton was absent from NSW from 18 July to 8 September 1893. But, within a few years, he was an active mythifier of the event (or non-event?) at Corowa which he chose to miss. Already in 1898 he was seeking to build up the Corowa Convention as a stage of the 'Federation story', for the explicit purpose of diminishing Reid's role. On 30 November 1900, he attended a 'Recognition Banquet' in Corowa to honour the Convention. At about that time Barton's associate, Thomas Ewing, was co-authoring a history of 19th century Australia, in which the authors, tellingly, misrecord the Corowa Convention as taking place in May 1894 (Coghlan and Ewing 1903).

257 Burton 1973, p. 126.

258 Garran 1958.

259 For Parkes, see *NSWPD* 1.3.92.

260 This National Federal Party of 1894 recorded a total of 96 members in its brief existence (OP).

261 E. M. Clark. One of the 'Haynes five'. See chapter 12.

262 Barton received 24 percent of votes, David Storey 41 percent.

263 *DT* 18.7.94.

264 Thus the despondent outlook in 1894 of Barton and Deakin reported by the editor of the *Review of Reviews*.

265 *Commonwealth* 7.11.94.

266 *Commonwealth* 7.9.95.

267 A. B. Piddington to Higgins: 'Barton relies so much on free-trade supporters' (letter, HP 27.6.98).

268 West Maitland voted 65 percent free trade in 1898, and 67 percent Yes in the 1899 referendum. Newcastle East, 60 percent free trade in 1898, and 59 percent Yes in 1899. Sydney-King, 56 percent free trade and 61 percent Yes. But other free trade seats voted No; St George voted 72 percent free trade in 1898 but only 45.5 percent Yes in 1899. An examination of the 80 electorates in which free traders stood indicates no relation between the size of the free trade vote in 1898 and the Yes vote in 1898 or 1899 (Appendix 2, Table A2). Free trade voters, it seems, split roughly equally between Yes and No.

269 Haynes *NSWPD* 22.11.94

270 McMinn 1989, p. 109.

271 *Commonwealth*.

272 J. M. Proctor, Uralla, 33.9 percent; W. Taylor, St George, 17 percent; T. Jones, Marrickville, 17 percent.

273 The *Windsor and Richmond Gazette* (owned by the anti-Billite, J. C. L. Fitzgerald) claimed 'big tears rolled down Barton's cheeks' at the news of Parkes's defeat.

274 Thus Deakin: 'The position of the Federal movement up till January last [1895] was anything but reassuring ... We were faced by a helpless lethargy, by a paralysis of effort .... Now ... Mr Reid has stepped to the front' (*Commonwealth* 7.03.95).

Chapter 7 (pp. 93-131)

275 Parkes is an epitome of the syndrome. What here is called grandiosity, another describes as 'outrageous vanity' (McMinn 1989, p. 62); what here is termed 'vindictive', is articulated by another as Parkes being 'jealous of equals, bitter with rivals, and remorseless with enemies' (Gurner 1930, p. 294).

276 The grandiose-vindictive syndrome is also seen in some who played both sides of the field: Piddington and Norton. Some anti-Federationists (Want, Haynes) might seem of the same disposition; but their own 'warrior syndrome' displayed a capacity for self-sacrifice foreign to the narcissism of the 'grandiose-vindictive' syndrome.

277 Among Australian political leaders born in the last quarter of the 19th century, Jack Lang and H. V. Evatt may be classed as grandiose-vindictive. But both were, essentially, political failures, and their examples only buttress the asserted contrast.

278 Evatt 1945; McMinn 1989; Crisp 1990.

279 Freudenberg 2009, p. 384.

280 Piddington 1929, p. 123.

281 Grover 1993, p. 170, p. 175.

282 In 1901 Presbyterians amounted to 9.4 percent of the population in NSW, but supplied 16.6 percent of teachers, and 15.2 percent of 'superior' occupations (Walker 1962, p. 56).

283 See Hamer 1977.

284 Reid 1882.

285 Collis 1948.

286 Thus the 'customary dilatoriness' of Reid noted by one of his political collaborators (Boyce 1934, p. 105). Another sympathiser judged that Reid was 'often apparently wanting in definiteness of purpose' (Turner 1911, p. 90). A more critical observer noted of him 'little substantial capacity for constructive and painstaking work' (in Broinowski 2001, p. 56).

287 Barton *SMH* 13.2.79; Reid *EN* 13.2.79.
288 Martin 1980, p. 216.
289 *NSWPD* 21.5.90.
290 Quoted in Wise 1913, p. 138.
291 *NSWPD* 1.3.92.
292 *NSWPD* 21.5.90.
293 Reid 1891a, p. 276.
294 Quick 1965 p. 39
295 Evatt asserts that Reid's 'clear opposition would have wrecked the bill on either occasion' (Evatt 1945, p. 115).
296 McMinn 1994, p. 142.
297 McMinn 1994, p. 148.
298 Markey 1988, p. 233. See Reid's public and 'official' endorsement of Labor candidates in the in 1898 election (*DT* 27.7.98).
299 Reid 1899, p. 16. 'At the early age of 10 he discovered, to his great torture, that he was born to be premier of New South Wales' (*EN* 17.10.99, reporting Reid's speech). 'It is reported of Mr. G. H. Reid that when he was a member of the School of Arts Debating Society, in Sydney, he declared to a friend that he would one day be Premier of New South Wales' (*W&RG* 19.8.99).
300 Reid's Town Hall declaration in favour of Federation on 28 March 1898 'nauseated' supporters: Rosa 1899. Dibbs branded Reid 'a traitor to his own side' (*ST* 5. 6.98).
301 See Gorman 2016.
302 Reid's marriage, after an extended bachelorhood, to Flora Brumby, a beauty of 24, can easily be construed as a marriage of attraction, although some historians have judged it differently. Its concealment does not chime with ardour; the ceremony of November 1891 was kept secret until August 1892. The bride misspelt her name in the marriage register as Bromby, and they married 'over the border' in Wangaratta. In Beauchamp's opinion, Reid 'considered himself – perhaps like [John] Wilkes – a ladies man' (BD).
303 Kirwan 1936, p. 168; Deakin 1968, p. 120.
304 Carruthers 2005, p. 63.
305 Barton *LC* 1.6.92.
306 It was Beauchamp's belief that if he had invited Reid to propose the next premier, Reid would have suggested not Lyne but Barton (BD).

307 Lloyd and Sykes 2001, p. 67.
308 Deakin 1968, p. 275.
309 Turner 1911, p. 90.
310 *AFC* 27.1.98.
311 The *Customs Tariff Act* of 1902 had imposed a 20d per cwt tariff on hay imported from New Zealand and elsewhere. Before the drought a cwt of hay might sell for 60d: thus the severity of the new tariff on fodder. The Act also imposed a 50 percent tariff on sugar, compared to the zero rate which Reid's own NSW legislation had scheduled.
312 To one contemporary observer, he was 'plainly seen' to be seeking the prime ministership. Rosa, *LD*, 'Political History of Australia'.
313 Hirst 2000, p. 132.
314 'His detractors have been many …' (Reynolds 1948, p. 1).
315 William was from a family of perfumers with commercial links with Asia. His bride's family also apparently had trading connections. Mary's extremely rare surname, Whydah, is an old styling of the port of Ouidah, best known as the West African place of embarkation of slaves for the New World. The least unlikely supposition is that a forebear was connected with the port's commerce.
316 Salsbury and Sweeney 1992.
317 But as counsel rather than plaintiff. In 1899 Barton and Hunt represented an acutely unsuccessful Federationist candidate suing the *Sunday Times* for libel, and winning the miserable farthing. The Chief Justice refused to award costs to Barton's client, W.B. Melville, on the grounds that it was a 'very unfortunate thing that an action of this sort should have been brought' (*ST* 2.7.99).
318 *EN* 6.1.83.
319 *SM* 15.4.65.
320 *CP* 4.2.99.
321 *New South Wales Statistical Register*.
322 Carruthers 2005, p. 63.
323 *EN* 6.1.83.
324 Carruthers 2005, p. 63.
325 *EN* 6.1.83.
326 In 1891 Barton returned to the University Senate after a brief absence. But not all welcomed him. 'It is to be hoped that the graduates have not quite forgotten the way Mr. Barton conducted him-

self when he enjoyed the honour of holding a seat on the senate some time ago. He systematically failed to attend the meetings, and he forfeited his position in consequence' (*DT* 15.12.91).

327 'He may not have answered all letters sent to him. But he had set about to have accomplished what the writers of these letters requested, which he considered was better than writing and not doing' (*SM* 10.12.82).

328 In 1885 Barton had declared himself as a free trade candidate; protectionism was 'Chinese'. 'By 1887 Barton had become converted to Protection' (Rutledge 1974, p. 7).

329 The Speaker's salary of £1 500 came without the burdens of a ministry. Dibbs opined that Barton 'preferred the easy dignity and certain emoluments of the Speakership to the worry and uncertainty of office' (*BEP*, 19.2.86).

330 In 1885 Barton enjoyed an incumbency advantage in his seat of East Sydney: each of the other three winning candidates in the 1882 election had, in the subsequent years, either resigned or been removed.

331 October 1884 (Bolton 2000) and January 1887 (*SMH* 15.1.87).

332 Clune and Griffith 2006, p. 50.

333 *EN* 21.7.86. Carruthers later pronounced that Barton was 'probably the best Speaker we have ever had' (2005, p. 64). But Carruthers entered the Legislative Assembly only after Barton had relinquished the Speakership.

334 Barton's earnings at the bar averaged just over 850 pounds per annum between 1883 to 1886, 'little compared to the earnings of other barristers' (Rutledge 1974, p. 7). In 1898 Reid, a 'not a very deeply learned lawyer', having made himself Attorney-General, also made himself a QC (Blacket 1927, p. 12). Want was appointed QC while out of the office of Attorney-General.

335 One unimpressed Councillor's response to an appearance of Barton: 'It is the first time we have seen the honourable and learned member ... we seldom see the honourable member in the House at all ... the honourable gentleman seems to think that when he puts in an appearance he is going to be "boss of the show"' (*NSWPD* 14.8.90).

336 See Peach (2008, p. 153). Want Johnson and Co, the firm of Randolph Want, John Want's brother, represented the aggrieved shareholders.

337 *Worker* 9.7.98. 'Supreme Court processes may be tedious and expensive; but they are rapid and cheap compared with the process as illustrated in the Arbitration Court presided over by Mr. Barton' (*C&RE* 22.10.98). Smith was paid by the government, as its counsel, £8 201 6d, and Hunt £2 815 5s 6d.

338 Some mitigation for Barton's avarice might be sought in the sprawling legal fees charged by some of his Federationist colleagues. Thus Deakin received £1 711 10s, as a second counsel for Syme in the newspaper baron's legal combat with a former Railway Commissioner. But Deakin could at least plead he was paid, not by the taxpayer, but by perhaps the wealthiest man in Victoria. And Barton? Ensconced in 'Miandetta' in Kirribilli, he declared in 1899 to a fellow Federationist, 'I am a poor man' (James *et al* 1949, p. 58).

339 Bolton 2000, p. 120. This remarkable sum included some one-off expenses of a holiday to Canada.

340 DGP, letter, 23.12.91.

341 J.T. Walker in *SJP* 20.12.99.

342 WP 28.8.99.

343 During the formation of the Lyne ministry in 1899, the *Star* (15.9.99) reported that Barton 'had substantial private reasons for declining office at the present juncture'. But perhaps Lyne did not want him anyway. That Lyne offered Barton the position of Attorney-General is one element of the traditional history of Federation. There is good evidence that Lyne met Barton regarding the ministry, but where is the evidence he 'offered' him that position?

344 14 December 1892, for example. See the 'Hansard' for that evening.

345 The source is Piddington (1929). Hubert Murray, no abstainer by any stretch, was repelled by Barton's drinking (West 1968, p. 48). Beauchamp judged Barton 'overfond of a good glass' (BD).

346 Davies 1968, p. 85. Hunt on Barton: 'Too much work and late hours to say nothing of too much w[ine] which failing seriously detracts from his many fine qualities'.

347 Barton told the Assembly, in proud self-pity, that he had slept no more than three hours per night for ten months (*NSWPD* 20.9.92).

348 *DT* 31.5.93.

349 By 1900 Tarrant was regularly advertising his 'new method of healing which acts like magic' in removing, among other things, 'shortness of breath' and 'inclination to throw oneself down over water'.

350 BEP 21.6.93.

351 An annotation indicates the letter was never sent.

352 *DT* 18.7.94

353 Thus, in his last weeks as Prime Minister, Barton rose in the House of Representatives to protest the 'constant misrepresentation ... that I intend to appoint myself to be Chief Justice' of the High Court. 'I wish to state in the most emphatic terms that the idea of doing so has not been present in my mind' (*BS* 8.8.03). He was, certainly, not, then, in the process of appointing himself Chief Justice of the Court; he was in the process of appointing himself a Justice of the Court.

354 *CuFP* 30.1.97.

355 McMinn 1989, p. 171.

356 In the event, the first part of Reid's meeting was severely disrupted, but with eggs playing a minor part. The pro-Barton *Evening News* claimed 'two or three eggs were hurled up at the balcony but went under' (*EN* 19.9.98).

357 In the words of a one-time ardent Federationist, 'Sir Edmund Barton was ponderous in speech and appearance. His language was involved, and appeared given to him to conceal his thoughts' (Kirwan 1936, p. 163).

358 *C&RE* 11.3.98.

359 Reynolds 1948, p. 56.

360 Reynolds 1948.

361 According to Cockerill.

362 Collis 1948, p. 26.

363 *DT* 17.9.98,

364 Barton, like Reid, had many friends in the press. 'I'll tell you how Barton's got on', Foley told the *Evening News*. 'He keeps all right with the press. He never offends you fellows.'

365 *Age* 8.1.20. Francis Clarke attributed the epithet to Rev. R.H.D. Kelly, Vicar of All Saints, West Kempsey. Certainly, Kelly had publicly declared that 'Mr Barton had been appointed by God to carry out Federation' (*RRH* 30.9.98).

366 *DT* 20.9.98.

367 *DT* 23.9.98.

368 A devotee of Mussolini: 'He is like a god. Like a god? No he is a god'. A devotee of Roosevelt: 'To me you are a god in disguise' (Willner 1984, p. 7).

369 *NA* 3.6.98.
370 A nice example of the 'mirror hungry' narcissist and the ideal hungry mass. A palpable, even ludicrous, manifestation of Barton's narcissism was his attempt in 1911 to palm off on Rose Scott an (evidently) unwanted 'framed address' which English suffragettes had in 1902 presented him, to 'do honour' to Barton regarding women's franchise (*SRP*). That Scott would wish to adorn her walls with such an item is doubtful; she would presumably recall his long scoffing opposition to female suffrage.
371 *SMH* 3.6.98. In the face of imminent success in the Council of the amendment to raise the minimum to 80 000, Barton had himself moved raising the minimum to 60 000. This importunate concession belies his show of 'principled' opposition to the minimum.
372 The *Newsletter* (5.1.01) claimed that the call for cheers for Barton on the day of Proclamation 'met with little response'.
373 *DT* 8.2.01.
374 *MD* 15.3.01.
375 Fricke 1986, p. 27.
376 Bannon 2009, p. 193. Barton, with O'Connor, and Garran as best man, were among the guests at Downer's sparsely attended wedding in 1898. The bride and groom had first met at Barton's house. Barton would stay with the newly wedded couple when in Adelaide, before his translation to the High Court. Then the visits ceased.
377 *BEPNLA*, letter, 6.5.02.
378 Bolton (2000) invokes 'family legend' tending in the opposite direction.
379 McMinn 1994, p. 2.
380 Brooks 2004, p. 87.
381 Phillips 1980, p. 92.
382 Bolton 2000, p. 299.
383 Cited in Bolton 2000, p. 184.
384 One fount of this myth is Rosa's 'political history' (*LD* 22.9.28). The myth is repeated by Evatt (1945) and Crisp (1949, p. 12).
385 *ST* 14.2.97.
386 Willis made the same accusation against McMillan (*NSWPD* 21.7.91). In the argot of the Legislative Assembly, 'a Willis' was a lie. A few years later William Maloney alleged the same of Deakin (*NMG* 6.5.98).

387 Smith's words in the July 1900 issue of his journal, *United Australia*.
388 *SMH* 20.2.91.
389 But without Wentworth's practicality or, alternatively, expedience.
390 Smith 1894 p. 3.
391 Francis Herbert Bradley, *Appearance and Reality: A Metaphysical Essay*, 1893; John M.E. McTaggart, *Studies in the Hegelian Dialectic*, 1896; Josiah Royce, *The World and the Individual*, 1900; Bernard Bosanquet, *The Philosophical Theory of the State*, 1899. Philosophical idealism's conquest of academic philosophy within Australia in the late 19th century was rapid and complete (Boucher and Vincent 2000).
392 Phillips (1963) on Bernard O'Dowd.
393 *SMH* 6.11.02.
394 *CJP* 22.5.02.
395 *SBA* 22.4.04. Also *SMH* 6.11.02.
396 *CPD* 3.11.09.
397 Hirsch just prior to the first round of referendums: 'In all probability the federal tariff would be something like that of N.S. Wales' (*AB&WR* 27.5.98). In 1903 Pulsford could still write, 'no one in Australia will be surprised if the reins of power come into the hands of free traders' (1903, p. 2).
398 Rickard (1984): Higgins was a 'a father of federation (albeit an unhappy father)'. See Higgins 1900, p. 10, for his 'want'.
399 One observer judged Higgins to lack 'superficial cleverness'; 'a slow man with a muscle-bound brain' (Grover 1993, pp. 184-5).
400 Syme 1890, p. 54.
401 Higgins 1900, p. 135.
402 Higgins 1900, p. 91.
403 Higgins 1900, p. 17.
404 Higgins 1900, p. 19.
405 Higgins 1900, p. 7.
406 So there is a misrepresentation of his own position in Higgins's resonant declaration to the Convention: 'I simply want to give the next generations which follow us the same liberty to control the Constitution as we have ourselves' (*AFC* 9.2.98). More truly, his wish was that there be no constitution, simply a parliament ruling by majority.
407 *Toscin* 20.7.99.

408 The *Richmond Guardian*'s one paragraph obituary of Astley in 1911 makes no mention of any connection of his with the newspaper.

409 *LE* 13.7.80.

410 *LE* 17.5.81

411 4.4.87.

412 See Andrews 1976.

413 Conlon 1969, p. 43.

414 Wright 1998, p. 123.

415 Gibbney 1967.

416 'Rather than being shackled, the convicts had their chains *knocked off* after they arrived. They wore their own clothes ... Hideous floggings and hangings did occur, just as they did on ships [to sailors, marines and convicts alike], but ... not the general populace. ... There were no walls or bars around the settlement. ... Convicts did not live in gaol' (Karskens 2013, p. 3).

417 Bedford 1944, p. 4.

418 Thus the Government House *capriccios* of Beauchamp and Sydney bohemia in the Federation years.

419 'Had not Archibald felt so strongly about the system very probably Astley's stories would never have been printed' (Andrews 1976, p. 159).

420 Headon 1998, p. 83.

421 Milne 1998, p. 105.

422 John Norton, Francis Patrick Moran, 'Colonel' George William Bell, Edward Ellis Morris (a past headmaster of Melbourne Grammar School), and John Gavan Duffy (a past Postmaster-General of Victoria).

423 Andrews 1976, p. 33.

424 This was George Robertson of Angus and Robertson, not the George Robertson of Robertson and Mullens, who published Astley.

425 Barker 1982, p. 26.

426 Tyrrell 1987, pp. 100-101.

427 Consider the *Australian Federalist*'s jab at anti-Billites, who 'rage at every kindly mention of other colonies, just as their forebears did in times when Victorian pioneers were trampling down grass and herbage in the Darling Downs while they were disputing with chief constable Buggins about a ration of flour or a gallon of rum'(*AF* 23.4.98). This strange exercise in federal spirit was, unbelievably, distributed in Sydney.

428 Perhaps the closest to a 'successor' of Astley was Grant Hervey, 1880-1933, a 'Bulletin school' poet, who claimed convict origins, was a Federation enthusiast and several times imprisoned for forgery.

429 Hergenhan 1980, p. 339.

Chapter 8 (pp. 133-148)

430 Perhaps the closest precedent was the election in Massachusetts, in 1779 by all adult males, of the delegates to its constitutional convention (Kyvig 2016, p. 28).

431 And almost all delegates were gladly so bound. Perhaps the Convention delegate least committed to Federation was Douglas, whose conservatism and ardent free trade tenets put him on its very fringe: 'I myself am not in favour of federation, except conditionally' (*AFC* 14.9.97). Curiously, the one other delegate who voiced a frank doubt regarding the Federation project was an opposite number of Douglas ideologically, Isaac Isaacs (*AFC* 26.3.97). But he, like Douglas, was ultimately to support the cause.

432 *SAR* 17.2.97.

433 McMinn 1994, p. 164. Two of McMinn's Tasmanian non-entities were presumably C. H. Grant and William Moore. Perhaps the third was Matthew Clarke, a barrister, 'who made one general speech on the Resolutions and then, strangely for one of his profession, fell silent' (La Nauze 1972, p. 341).

434 Bolton and Waterson 1999.

435 Higgins: 'Sir John Forrest … is not elected by the People'. Forrest: 'I have not come here to represent the *Age*' (*AFC* 13.4.97). But who did Sir John represent?

436 Bergh 1956, p. 8.

437 Spence 1900, p. 23.

438 In Victoria and Tasmania the choice of a candidate was indicated by that candidate not being crossed out. In SA and NSW a voter's choice was indicated by crosses against the favoured candidates. Throughout this chapter, 'tick' is used to refer to the indication of the voter's choice of candidate.

439 Ashworth and Ashworth 1900, p. 178.

440 *TDT* 5.3.97.

441 With twelve rather than ten delegates each, Victoria and Tasmania would have sent four more conservatives to the Convention,

while NSW would have sent one more protectionist and one more free trader, and South Australia one more Kingstonite and one Labor.
442 *Australian Dictionary of Biography*. La Nauze judges Wrixon 'a distinct loss' to the Convention (La Nauze 1972, p. 101).
443 *Australian Dictionary of Biography*. Fitzgerald, ranked 13th, was also the 'missing Catholic'. MacDonagh (1973) has pressed the salience of Irish Catholics in Victoria's parliamentary politics of the day; but, like any other minority, they were vulnerable to the biggest takes all logic of the Convention's voting system.
444 Pratt 1908, p. 269.
445 Perhaps this made little difference; Charleston soon resigned from Labor, and was later a Liberal Union candidate for the Senate.
446 *LE* 5.3.97.
447 Pringle 1972, p. 223.
448 *DT* 18.2.97.
449 *DT* 23.2.97.
450 *DT* 23.2.97.
451 Dame Eadith Campbell Walker inherited her father's estate of £937 984, or about $150m in present values.
452 Under block voting, the greater the number of candidates, the greater the number of wasted votes. NSW had 49 candidates, SA 32 and Victoria just 29, reflecting the absence in NSW and SA of any deposit required of candidates. Victoria, by contrast, required fifty pounds, equal to about six months' wages of unskilled labour. It is on account of block voting that the commendably democratic profusion of candidates in NSW actually proved detrimental to the democratic value of its election.
453 60 voters of one opinion type dividing their two ticks between three candidates cannot yield more than 40 ticks for each of the three. If there are 40 voters of a second opinion type, their own favoured candidates will have a matching number of ticks.
454 Spence was one unsuccessful candidate in SA, receiving 7 500 'ticks', many fewer than the 18 463 received by the lowest polling winning candidate, Vaiben Solomon. Her protest (Spence 1898, p. 23) – 'We gave as much weight to the tenth man for whom we did not care, as for the first for whom we did' – could be expressed as her own personal grievance. Is it possible she might have been ranked first by a larger number than who put Solomon first?

455 On 5 May 1900 Kingston received 28.3 percent of the vote for the Southern district of SA's Legislative Council. In 22 September 1900 he won 51.6 percent for the Central district.

456 *AFC* 31.3.97. Reid had won all of the six multiple member contests he had entered in East Sydney, but had lost one of the two single vacancy contests there.

457 The prohibition of plumping amounted to compulsory voting; a voter who wished to vote solely for the ticket's head was required to vote for the entire ticket. Reid favoured no plumping (see Hirst 2000). Higgins unsuccessfully sought the abolition of plumping in Victoria.

458 Four delegates from WA were replaced during the Convention: Loton, Piesse, Sholl, and Taylor. Their absences are compounded with their replacements: Briggs, Crowder, Venn and Henning.

Chapter 9 (pp. 149-165)

459 Hunt 1930, p. 256.

460 Quoted in Stubbs 2012, p. 236. See also La Nauze 1972, p. 234.

461 Isaacs *AFC* 16.9.97.

462 Glynn *AFC* 24.4.97.

463 Quick was anxious that the anti-Chinese legislation that he and Berry (among others) had aggressively sponsored in Victoria would not be invalidated by the Constitution. 'While I am anxious to equip the Commonwealth with every power necessary for dealing with the invasion of outside coloured races, I do not see why, at the same time, the local Legislatures should not continue to enjoy local state rights within certain limits' (*AFC* 28.1.98).

464 Outside the Convention some Federationists expressed regret at the 14th Amendment to the US Constitution, and its constitutional auxiliaries. 'It was only after emancipation that it became apparent that the ballot in the hands of the negro was an instrument to inflict penalties on Southern whites. ... The alternative before the Southern white was either by force or fraud to obtain ascendancy in the State, or abandon it and their possessions to the hordes of savages' (Ewing, *Commonwealth* 7.3.95).

465 Reid 1891, p. 153.

466 *AFC* 30.3.97.

467 *AFC* 30.3.97. Inglis Clark, the one possible delegate well-equipped

to offer some counter to these contentions, deliberately excluded himself from the Convention. He did not stand for the Convention election, and embarked on a journey to the United States two days after it commenced. Both John Henry and William Moore offered their places at the Convention to Clark for the later Sydney session, but he declined.

468 Fraser *AFC* 17.2.98.

469 *AFC* 30.3.97

470 *Commonwealth* 7.2.95.

471 Glynn 1890.

472 In 1894 Garran complacently declared, 'Our relations with the Empire are so far Federal in spirit and have so familiarised us with Federal ideas, that when Australian Federation comes we shall glide into it as easily as a swan into water' (*Commonwealth* 1.10.94). He added, in a different tone, of Liberia, 'Even Africa has its little "Siberia" – that "black parody on white government," with a House of Representatives of 13 and a Senate of 8 members, to say nothing of a nigger President and a national debt of half-a-million dollars' (*Commonwealth* 8.4.95).

473 *Commonwealth* 1.10.94.

474 Tulloch 1988, p. 39.

475 Harvie 2004, p. 404.

476 Warden 1990, p. 48; Fredman 1989, p. 127.

477 Quoted in Warden 1990, p. 49.

478 Dicey and Rait 1920.

479 Dicey 1915, p. lxxvi.

480 A states' house may be interpreted as an attempt to foster political exchange over political diktat, by ordaining 'one interest, one value' rather than 'one voter, one value'. If a single interest claims a majority of the voters then political trade will be extinguished by 'one voter, one value'.

481 Isaacs *AFC* 9.2.98.

482 In Isaacs's view first chambers, too, were doubtful. Isaacs: 'My honourable friend asks what is the use of having parliament? Not much sometimes …' (*AFC* 9.2.98).

483 *AFC* 20.9.97.

484 Quoted in Aroney 2009, p. 101.

485 The Federal Council of Australasia legislated by majority. But the ideal of unanimity was observed in the principle that any mem-

ber colony of the Council could withdraw at its wish, and repeal the force, within its borders, of any previous enactment of the Council.
486 Deakin 1944, p. 15. Barton *Commonwealth* 1.10.94. Crisp 1990, p. 65. Garran 1958, p. 85.
487 Glynn told the Convention that railways gauges could be unified in a week (*AFC* 19.4.97).
488 Tennyson 1978, p. 102.
489 Wise narrowly missed winning a seat in the first Commonwealth parliament. Cockburn planned to contest, but failed on account of a mishap with nomination. There were only three delegates from Tasmania in the new parliament, but four if we count Lewis, who was appointed as minister without portfolio in January 1901, but declined to nominate for election. Only one delegate from WA entered the parliament (Forrest), reflecting the Constitution's near complete repudiation by that state's political class.
490 And would not unification produce unity? Unification, unity, union and uniformity all swirled in the minds of delegates. There was little recognition that unity, in the sense of the absence of dividers, did not require a central government, not even a federal central government. Simple 'mutual recognition' could have gone a long way to secure an absence of vexatious dividers. For example, the mutual recognition of naturalisations, as secured by the *Australasian Naturalisation Act 1897* of the Federal Council of Australasia.
491 *AFC* 15.9.97.
492 *AFC* 17.9.97.
493 Bryce 1889, vol. 1, p. 342.
494 Temby 1984, p. 86.
495 'Predictability' does not imply a strict invariance, but a regularity such that any unpredictable variation serves to reduce unpredictability henceforth.
496 See Coleman (2020a).
497 Subject to a free trade area within the Commonwealth. Griffith in the early 1890s had pressed the feasibility of the Commonwealth as a free trade area rather than as a customs union. *FCA* 1890, p. 19. But no more was heard of this.
498 The failed 'Simultaneous Elections' referendum of 1977.
499 A clause which appears not to have been applied to W. H. Groom,

a member of the inaugural House of Representatives, notwithstanding he being earlier convicted and imprisoned for more than one year (Carment 1977, p. 237).

500 Dicey 1915 p. 203. One modern commentator states, 'The Supreme Court of Victoria had comparable powers [to the High Court] in respect of Victorian legislation in the 1880s' (Bennett 2004, p. 123).

501 *AFC* 8.3.98. Most of 'left' hostility to judicial review was not a hostility to the thing in the abstract; the 'left' simply did not believe there should be much of a constitution to safeguard from a legislature in the first place. In their minds, the constitution should be no more than a device for articulating the 'sacred' will of the majority. 'Sacred' is Deakin's chosen adjective. 'The sacredness is in the principle that the majority should rule' (Deakin *AFC* 30.3.97).

502 At least to the extent that they did not conflict with UK law that extended to Australia.

503 The culpable sentence of section 13 stated, 'the election to fill vacant places shall be made in the year at the expiration of which the places are to become vacant'. But the root of the problem was the Convention's resolve to treat the Senate, not so much as a 'second chamber', but as an autonomous 'house' of parliament.

504 Quoted in Cave-Brown-Cave 1897, p. 27.

505 Reid judged of the Constitution, 'there is nothing original in it from its first word to last' (1891a, p. 274). An exaggeration, at least with respect to its form by 1898. The provision for the joint sitting of the Senate and the House of Representatives in the face of a 'deadlock' was almost without precedent. Regrettably, the delegates' preoccupation with 'deadlocks' was born of the bright but false light thrown off by the collisions of the Legislative Assembly and Legislative Council in Victoria and NSW. This preoccupation produced section 57 of the Constitution, with its schema of the dissolution of both chambers and their subsequent joint sitting; a course of proceeding which 'can almost be regarded as less a means of resolving a dispute as of prolonging it' (Howard 1978, p. 94).

506 Brunker recommended No in 1898. Higgins urged the same in both 1898 and 1899, as did Lyne.

Chapter 10 (pp. 167-200)

507 Lang 1850, p. 15.

508 In the first edition of the *Coming Event,* of 1850, 'nation' was only once mentioned.

509 Lang 1875, p. 466.

510 Lang 1870, p. 436.

511 Lang 1870, p. 453 and p. x.

512 *EN* 11.2.90.

513 *SMH* 4.2.90, and p. x.

514 Furphy in Driehuis 2000, p. 130.

515 *EN* 15.11.89.

516 'When he looked back to the old days, to the time when we had a Governor here ruling us without seeking the consent or the opinion of the people, he recognised a great change ... but he would sooner have a Governor controlling us than submit to the control of a certain progressive colony ...' (Robertson 1887, p. 12).

517 NSW's drive for self-government received an additional special warmth from its determination to exclude convicts. See Kemp 2018.

518 *EN* 3.2.90. See also Robertson's speech in 1887 to the 'surviving members of the first legislative assembly at parliament house': 'He could not say a word on this matter without almost being choked with the feeling of having lost all these men, and of having to speak now, as it were, over their bones. Most of those present had pretty well seen it out, and perhaps it was well that younger men should take their places; yet they might reflect with some degree of gratification upon the past history of these Colonies, especially when he said that within the walls of that building the liberties of Australasia were won' (Robertson 1887).

519 *DT* 21.3.91.

520 *SMH* 2.9.90.

521 Malcolm in *Macbeth*: 'So, thanks to all at once and to each one, Whom we invite to see us crown'd at Scone'.

522 *SMH* 7.4.65.

523 The Bogan 1877.

524 McMinn 1986, p. 344.

525 Parkes 1892, p. 117.

526 East Sydney, 10 April 1891.
527 Deniehy 1860.
528 McMinn 1986, p. 345.
529 W.B. Dalley, quoted in Barton 1866, p. 174.
530 Abbott 1944, p. 67.
531 McMinn 1986, p. 417.
532 Lyne 1896, p. 393.
533 McMinn 1986, p. 341.
534 Powell 1977, p. 111. 'Jack Robertson', Henry Lawson.
535 *EN* 5.3.91.
536 Douglas: 'Tasmania is independent. Victoria has tried to crush us and could not do it' (*AFC* 13.4.97).
537 By one estimate, pastoralists constituted 44 percent of members of the NSW Assembly in 1856, 32 percent in 1865, 24 percent in 1875, and 16 percent in 1889 (Barnard 1962).
538 Wise 1913, p. 46.
539 *NSWPD* 4.12.89.
540 But G. B. Barton was commissioned by the Parkes government to write *A History of New South Wales From the Records*.
541 See, for example, *AT&CJ* 16.5.91.
542 *NSWPD* 21.7.97 and *EN* 21.5.91.
543 *NSWPD* 10.12.91.
544 Simpson 1984, p. 20.
545 Blacket 1927, p. 9.
546 *NMH* 11.1.89.
547 John Garland. *SMH* 21.6.99
548 *EN* 12.1.99.
549 *NSWPD* 9.9.99.
550 Want: 'My medical man in England would not allow me to come out and take part in a severe campaign' (*NSWPD* 9.9.99).
551 O'Connor, already sitting in the Legislative Council, would have done everything which Barton might have wished done there. In November 1898 Want paid a visit to Barton laid up with a broken arm.
552 Bennett 1972, p. 109.
553 McMillan, MP.
554 *GI* 28.1.99.

555 Piddington 1929.

556 Walker 1976, p. 83.

557 A.G. Stephens, *SAGP*.

558 *Newsletter* 3.6.05.

559 *Newsletter* 27.7.05.

560 *NSWPD* 5.6.90.

561 *NSWPD* 6.7.90.

562 *MM* 23.8.88

563 Fletcher had spruiked the Taranganba 'gold mine', of which he was a director, and had publicly scoffed at suggestions of its salting. And yet his involvement in the conspiracy is speculative. In such frauds honest directors could be welcomed by the conspirators as cover (Hammond 1988). Fletcher resigned from parliament on 7 March 1889, the day before the court proceedings of aggrieved shareholders commenced.

564 *EN* 14.11.94. *RRH* 5.2.97

565 Haynes *SMH* 18.2.97 and *NSWPD* 22.3.91.

566 Dobson citing Quick *AFC*, 15.9.97.

567 Pringle 1979, p. 238.

568 '"What about Crick?" said an elector to Mr. Haynes. "Oh Crick's all right", said the irrepressible John. "I dealt with him quickly, and made him change his address in five minutes from Bondi to the Infirmary."' (*W&RG* 6.3.97). 'O'Sullivan ventured the remark that Protection was "founded on a rock." Quick as lightning came Haynes: "So it is – on a shamrock"' (*W&RG* 18.12.97). Haynes, in the opinion of the protectionist leader, John See, 'talks more about free-trade than any other member in the House' (*NSWPD* 16.7.91).

569 *NSWPD* 10.12.91.

570 Moran 1939, p. 29.

571 A.G. Stephens, SAGP.

572 *NSWPD* 29.8.99.

573 *AS* 30.6.96.

574 Haynes: 'Now we are all Federationists. No true man can be against union' (*AC* 23.7.98). A visiting British MP of the day observed, 'it is a curious feature of Australian federation that everyone is in favour of federation – even its most determined opponents' (Galloway 1899, p. 152).

575 *CM* 16.2.87.
576 *NSWPD* 24.8.01.
577 Walker 1976, p. 111.
578 www.parliament.nsw.gov.au/electionresults18562007/1904/Mudgee.htm
579 Walker 1976, p. 113.
580 St Ledger *et al* 1902, p. 17.
581 *CM* 16.9.29.
582 Bernays 1919, p. 194.
583 Thus Byrnes's ruling as Attorney-General regarding an apparent violation of the *Pacific Labourers Act 1884*. The case of a self-supporting Kanak was 'no doubt against the spirit of the Act', but he thought nothing in the Act prevented a 'man genuinely taking a piece of land and working it' (McNaughton n.d.).
584 Byrnes 1897, p. 12.
585 Byrnes voted against the limits on hours required by the *Shop and Factories Act 1896* (Qld).
586 *MaM* 15.9.94. Byrnes added, 'Speaking as Attorney-General of the colony, I say here to squatter and unionist, "A plague on both your unions."'.
587 *FCA* 28.1.97.
588 *BC* 8.2.97.
589 *FCA* 28.1.97.
590 *FCA* 28.1.97. New Guinea was, evidently, a different matter.
591 *LE* 29.1.97.
592 *FCA* 1.2.95.
593 St Ledger *et al* 1902, p. 73.
594 Byrnes's call was part and parcel of McIlwraith's support in 1893 of the Council's expansion in numbers, and his spurring Premier Dibbs to bring in NSW.
595 Byrnes never explicitly invoked Burke; but he did make a pilgrimage to John Morley, the keeper of Burke's flame in an essentially hostile 19th century mental universe.
596 Thus the post-1901 rapid transformation into a vehement anti-federationist of the enthusiastic Federationist and Byrnes ally, A. J. J. St Ledger.
597 O'Farrell 1986, p. 223.

598 Cahill 2001, p. 13. Moran's list goes on, not always accurately. 'Of 3 Public Service Board members, not one is a Catholic'. In fact, Timothy Coghlan, the government statistician, was one of the three members of the Board. Nevertheless, the Cardinal's point extends to professional classes more generally: thus, in 1897, no Catholics numbered among Sydney's 41 stockbrokers (Salsbury and Sweeney 1992).

599 Gill 1975, p. 179.

600 The points of controversy were the religion of appointments to the Department of Justice, and Byrnes's favour of government scholarships being available to Catholic schools (Lawson 1972, p. 157).

601 O'Connor in seventh place, Glynn in eighth place, Clarke in tenth; none from Victoria.

602 Byrnes, the Solicitor-General, acted as second counsel for the Crown, and received £2 968 13s in fees. But he earnt this fee in defending the public purse from a claim of £250 000 by the plaintiff, not, as O'Connor did, in laying siege to it (see Joyce 1974, p. 254).

603 *BC* 8.2.97.

604 Byrnes was aged 37 on becoming Premier. Andrew Dawson was 36 on commencing his one-week premiership of 1899.

605 McNaugton n.d.

606 *FCA* 27.1.97.

607 *MB* 30.8.98.

608 *SMH* 23.8.98.

609 *BC* 27.9.98

610 Bernays 1919, p. 82.

611 *BC* 8.8.91.

612 Australia endured 19 measles epidemics between 1874 and 1956. It was most prevalent in late winter and early spring.

613 Bernays 1919, p. 144. In the memory of one contemporary '... beyond a passing frown scarcely perceptible, even in the bitterness of debate, I have not seen Byrnes otherwise than smiling, but when one sat close ... and saw [his] eyes flashing fire could realise the strength and sincerity' (Corfield 1921, p. 137). But in later assessments Byrnes was 'rather unpopular' (Gill 1975, p. 189), with an 'arrogance of speech' (McNaughton n.d.).

614 'The clever man is prone to single out other clever men, and Byrnes recognised in Dawson a clever man ...' (Bernays 1919, p. 144).

Chapter 11 (pp. 201-238)

615 At the conclusion of the Governor-General's speech in Centennial Park, a *Te Deum* was sung by the Archbishop of Sydney's four hundred strong choir.

616 *GE* 31.3.98.

617 *DT* 29.3.98.

618 Rosa, 'Political History'; Piddington 1929.

619 *SMH* 2.4.98.

620 Pringle 1979, p. 237.

621 *SMH* 28.5.98. Edmund Barton to James shortly after the NSW referendum: 'Let me first thank you for your generous contributions to the funds of the Federal Cause. All the money subscribed was well spent …' (James *et al* 1949).

622 *NMH* 3.6.98.

623 *Worker* 11.3.99. *SMH* 31.5.98.

624 In 1894 Joseph Jacobs, Scott's Sydney contemporary, had rendered Aesop's fable thus: 'The frogs were living as happy as could be in a marshy swamp that just suited them; they went splashing about caring for nobody and nobody troubling with them. But some of them thought that this was not right, that they should have a king and a proper constitution, so they determined to send up a petition to Jove to give them what they wanted. "Mighty Jove," they cried, "send unto us a king that will rule over us and keep us in order" '.

625 *DT* 22.6.99.

626 The closing words of 'God give us men!', a poem by Josiah Gilbert Holland, which Scott would recite in full at the close of her address.

627 *SMH* 13.4.98.

628 Hunt: 'The Federal flag is, as you know, the ordinary Australian Ensign and can be obtained from any flag merchant'. NFLP, letter 30.5.99.

629 During the 1899 campaign, Lady Braddon presented a 'federal flag' to the Southern Tasmanian Federal League. The *Mercury* approvingly reported, 'The flag was subscribed to by 150 British-born citizens' (11.7.99).

630 Joseph Jacobs 1894.

631 Quick and Garran 1901, p. 976. In August 1899 an attempt to make possible, subsequent to Federation, a referendum on the secession of NSW was defeated in the Council 24 to 21, with the essential help of Reid's twelve appointees.

632 Did not Parkes, just eight days after the Tenterfield speech, write to the British prime minister urging creation of 'a "Council of Empire",' which would promote Australia's 'interfusion with the Empire'? (PHC 2.11.89). In 1907 Deakin pressed the project of a permanent 'Imperial Council' on the British government. He had been president of the Imperial Federation League in 1905.

633 *NSWPD* 25.6.90.

634 *FCA* 28.1.97. That Byrnes could also declare he would fight for 'Queensland's rights against Britain' brings out he was a 'localist' rather than an Imperial Federationist.

635 The illustration of the paradox also assumes other possible rankings had zero support. It supposes no one prefers both F to I and I to S. But some who ranked Australian Federation above all alternatives might have felt that, if Australian Federation proved unobtainable, then Imperial Federation would be better than the status quo (Barton?). And the illustration supposes no one judges S superior to F, *and* F superior to I; but many Labor supporters may have judged the matter so.

636 The 'principle of self-determination' is equally implied by the minimisation of the total number of votes disregarded.

637 If, in every seat, the majority favours what the overall majority favours, then this subset of seats will be zero in size, and 'minority regarding majoritarianism' is without effect. Going in the other direction, this subset of seats may, conceivably, be as large as the number of seats less one.

638 Proof. Let the number of Yes (No) votes be y (n) in one region, and y^* (n^*) in the other region. The total number of votes = $y + y^* + n + n^*$, and suppose $y + y^* > n + n^*$, so Yes is the overall majority, but $y^* < n^*$. Deferring to the simple majority implies $y + y^*$ of votes are heeded, and $n + n^*$ disregarded. Under 'minority regarding majoritarianism' $y + n^*$ votes are heeded, and $n + y^*$ disregarded. But, by the construction of the boundaries of the 'minority respected region', $n^* = y^*$, so $y + y^*$ votes are heeded, and $n+n^*$ disregarded.

639 East Adelaide, Port Adelaide, West Adelaide, West Torrens, Onkaparinga. The 'minority respecting principle' would imply the inclusion of the Northern Territory, even though it voted heavily Yes in percentage terms, since its majority for Yes was small in absolute terms. Consideration of contiguity would exclude it.

640 Sorell, Richmond, Glamorgan, Cumberland, Cressy, Oatlands, Queenborough, Brighton.

641 Albury, Deniliquin, Eden Bombala, Hume, Hay, and Wentworth.

642 *CoFP* 7.6.98. In 1911, William Watt, as Acting Premier of Victoria, lodged on NSW a formal claim to the Riverina (see Bevan 1912). Thus federal unity.

643 One observer records that when, for a few hours, it appeared that Yes would prevail in NSW in the 1898 referendum, the expression of Syme was 'grim'(Cockerill 1943, p. 103).

644 Bega, Monaro, Tumut, Wagga, Murrumbidgee.

645 'The working classes of New South Wales have hitherto been the greatest obstacle to the success of the Federation movement in this province': E.W. O'Sullivan, onetime president of the Trades Hall Council (*Commonwealth* 7.11.94).

646 Hume Cook, HCP.

647 Fitzgerald 1987, p. 25, p. 23.

648 To the west: Gipps, Pyrmont, Denison, Lang. To the east: Belmore, Bligh, Cook, Fitzroy, Flinders, King, Phillip.

649 The exception was Sydney-Fitzroy. As this district was essentially dockside Woolloomooloo, its No vote coheres with the thesis.

650 See also Coleman 2017.

651 All other socioeconomic variables are statistically insignificant, save one (see Table A.3). The negative impact of English birth suggests that, despite the absence of 'sunburnt country' nationalism from Federationist campaigning, the English-born perceived Federation as weakening of the Imperial link.

652 Coleman 2017. The absence of a pure gender effect does not mean female enfranchisement would not have made a difference. That both women and No voters were relatively concentrated in metropolitan areas suggests an adult franchise might have strengthened the No vote.

653 An exact calculation of the proportion of eligible voters who voted requires some niceness. In all colonies, save South Australia, eligible voters were, essentially, although not exactly, male British subjects of 21 years and over. This approximation has been used in the table.

654 David Storey *MD* 30.4.98.

655 Kirby 2002.

656 Pitt Cobbett 2019, p. 82.

657 *New South Wales v Commonwealth (1908)* HCA 68.

658 *Jumbunna Coal Mine NL v Victorian Coal Miners' Association (1908)*

HCA 95. The Jumbunna decision, which so enhanced the scope of compulsory arbitration, is an 'enigma' in the word of one later commentator. 'It is difficult to explain why Griffith and Barton (and to a lesser extent O'Connor) were prepared to make such wide pronouncements' (Plowman and Smith 1986, p. 213). In the Convention, O'Connor had decried arbitration as a 'disastrous failure' (AFC 27.1.98).

659 *New South Wales v Commonwealth (1915)* HCA 17. In 1915 'the court disposed of this invasion of its own area of interest by deciding that s. 101 did not mean what it said' (Howard 1978, p. 50).

660 *W& A McArthur Ltd v Queensland (1920)* HCA 77. In 1936 one observer opined: 'it is difficult for anyone who remembers the circumstances of pre-Federation days to believe that, had it then been pointed out that legal decisions [of the High Court releasing the Commonwealth from section 92] would prevent trade and intercourse between the states being absolutely free, there can be little doubt that the affirmative vote for Federation would have been a negative one' (Wolskel 1936, p. 27).

661 Colebatch 1951, p. 21.

662 *SMH* 31.5.98.

663 Reid voted *against* the amendment to increase the required minimum turnout to 80 000.

664 *AF* 18.6.98.

665 *AO* 4.6.98.

666 Collis 1948, p. 70.

667 The Bartonites also had little success with their string of lesser lights: Thomas Bavin, Francis Abigail, and William Traill all met defeat.

668 *EN* 19.7.98.

669 Reid's supporters smelled a rat, and Barton was moved to indignantly deny any responsibility for this doubtful candidacy. *EN* 22.7.98.

670 Francis Clarke resided in Carabella St, Kirribilli, where Barton was established at number 67.

671 *DT* 15.9.98.

672 *EN* 19.9.98.

673 CFP.

674 In the seat of Hastings Macleay, the protectionist majority in-

creased by 261 relative to the previous general election. The Kempsey booth alone provided 120 of this increase. The seat's 19 booths exhibit a statistically significant correlation between the percentage size of the free trade vote in 1895, and the percentage decline in the free trade vote in the 1898 by-election. The heavier the free traders came, the harder they fell.

675 CFP.

676 No one could accuse Reid of expecting the referendum to fail. Beauchamp recollected even 'his enemies declared the result of the first referendum had been a great surprise to him' (BD).

677 *WWA* 23.7.98.

678 Thus, in the midst of the 1898 election campaign, *The Patriot* hissed, ' ... we put it to Mr Barton as pleasantly as we can, that he would stand in a far better position with the great bulk of the [protectionist] party to which he belonged ... if he was not so fond of cutting himself apart from his old political associations ... we warn Mr Barton that if he persists in a wilful attempt to sink the fiscal question he will but bring his following to an ignominious fizzle' (*Patriot* 23.6.98).

679 At the very opening of 1899 Wise judged that Reid's 'aim through the session has been to raise the fiscal issue in order to split the Opposition ...' (James *at al* 1949, p. 57).

680 *NSWPD* 23.11.98.

681 Deakin 1899.

682 In conceding to the premiers' meeting of 1899 a minimum distance of the Commonwealth's capital from Sydney, Reid did not at the same time extract a matching *maximum* distance from Sydney. Did he overlook the possibility that the Parliament might select a remote corner of NSW for the 'seat of government'? His critics at the time did not. And did he overlook that no time frame was imposed on the establishment of the new capital? He had been very careful in imposing a time frame on the abolition of inter-state tariffs. Or was he content to gain at the premiers' meeting what would be widely seen as a concession in the eyes of the NSW public, regardless of its hollowness?

683 For all of Dickson's puffing, he obtained from the premiers no more than the right of Queensland to elect senators on a geographical basis for the inaugural parliament. In the event, this right was not exercised, despite Griffith's assurances to electors prior to Queensland's referendum (Griffith 1899).

684 The other two No majority seats were in Rockhampton. It may be estimated that, at a 100 km from Brisbane, every extra 10 km of distance from the capital increased the Yes share of the vote by about half a percent.

685 Byrnes's former seat, strangely.

686 Higgins's 'Memoir', HP.

687 'Had Jack Want been here I feel the result would have been different'. Dibbs to Higgins (HP 21.6.99).

688 The eight publicly declared anti-Billites who in 1898 lost the seats they were defending were T. Bavister, George Black, A. J. Gould, L. C. R. Jones, E. D. Millen, P. H. Morton, Sydney Smith and T. R. Smith.

689 Thus Deakin to Symon of the South Australian Federal League: 'Dear Mr Symon – I have just had a verbal request from Sydney to write you to see if your League can *in the strictest privacy* spare any funds or raise them to assist the fight in Broken Hill seats against their present occupants' (quoted in Symon 1976, p. 111).

690 Haynes was 'a persistent and bitter critic of Dibbs' (Campbell 1999, p. 244)

691 Barton 1901, p. 11.

692 Nairn 1973, p. 208. Much mid-20th century Laborist history sought to misrepresent or evade the vehemence of Labor opposition to the Bill. Fitzpatrick claimed there was 'no considerable Labor opposition to the idea of federation' (1941, p. 363). Crisp, with a copious understatement, writes of Labor that 'the majority seems to have been hostile' (1990, p. 462). Evatt (1945) presents Labor opposition as intended simply to make Federation more democratic. Labor's prompt conversion to Federation after the referendums' success is consistent with that suggestion. But William Holman, Evatt's hero, remained defiant.

693 Scott pinned her hopes on a protectionist. 'Dear Mr Lyne I do not know who is to save the country from that wretched Amended Bill unless it is you. ... The people are being sold for 25 pieces of silver instead of 30. Oh Mr Lyne, the women and their opinions are not to be despised any more than Pilate's wife was ... Having been with you in the last fight, and admired your courage and honesty of purpose, I appeal to you to save the country from those many evils yet remaining in the Bill, evils which I head you speak upon so ably' (SRP 27.2.99).

694 *C&RE* 17.6.99.

695 As in 1898, the aggregates of Yes and No disguise a remarkable range, with the Yes vote reaching as low as 24.4 percent (Northumberland), and as high as 93.3 percent (Albury).

696 See Rhodes' enumeration (1988).

697 The Yes campaign also had in the churches another important opinion leader firmly on their side: however much clerics had fought each other in 1897 Convention election, they now spoke in unison, in public, and in favour of Yes. In the wake of the referendum's success, Dibbs told the Anglican Archbishop of Sydney, 'I'll never enter a church again as long as I live' (*CA* 1.7.99). How influential were the clergy on their flocks is another question, but it was sometimes strong. Thus Pastor Friedrich Niemeyer of the Apostolic Church in Hatton Vale advocated Federation, and Hatton Vale proved to be 'a federal island in a vast anti-Billite Ocean' of southern Queensland (Jenkins 1979).

698 Gorman 2020.

699 Queanbeyan: E. W. O'Sullivan, Minister for Public Works in the Lyne ministry; Boorowa: J.A. K. Mackay, Vice-President of the Executive Council in the Lyne ministry.

700 *QA* 24.6.99. See also McCormack 2009.

701 See Nairn 1967 and Walker 1977.

702 MacLaurin, *NSWPD* 17.8.99.

703 In 1899 a record of absentee voters was not kept, so anyone unenrolled could vote by claiming to be absentee, and without fear of their ballot being repudiated.

704 'Double and even triple voting was common in suburban electorates'. Nairn 1967, p. 8.

705 Collis 1948.

706 Another ruse of corrupt officials was to fail to initial the ballot of a genuine, but unwelcome, voter, and thereby invalidate it.

707 In Queensland, by contrast, the *Enabling Act* prescribed that any elector, up to six per polling booth, was entitled to witness the count.

708 Pringle 1979, p. 239.

709 After the referendum Lyne protested, 'In some of the southern border electorates it is stated that a large number of rights have been applied for during the last few days by persons from Victoria who are still electors of Victoria — persons who have been in this colony ploughing and cultivating land, and will return to Victoria shortly' (*DT* 22.6.99).

710 The franchise is, obviously, limited to the living, and the living may make decisions for the much larger number of unborn. But in ordinary democratic processes the unborn will have their day.

711 The powers of self-government which Queensland held in 1899 can now only be restored by majorities in favour of their restoration in three states in addition to Queensland, and a majority in the Commonwealth's six states and territories over all. Queensland's electors of 1899 were privileging themselves with respect to electors of the future. T. J Byrnes: 'We have no right to give away, or barter, or exchange, the privileges of the Constitution we already possess' (quoted in St Ledger *et al* 1902, p. 89).

712 Jenkins 1979, p. 123.

713 Kingston 2002, p. 257

Chapter 12 (pp. 239-273)

714 *MC* 30.8.99. Reid *NSWPD* 30.8.99.

715 John Haynes, Frank Cotton, J. C. L. Fitzgerald, John Fegan, and Edward Clark.

716 That Reid's party without the Haynes group could not obtain a majority, even with Labor's support, is the conclusion of all scholarly examinations of the state of the chamber's 125 seats. Green (2007) puts free traders, inclusive of the Haynes group, at 47; or 42, exclusive of that group. Hughes and Graham (1968) put 'Ministerialists' at 46; or 41, excluding the Haynes faction. Both Green and Hughes and Graham put Labor at 19 seats. Thus Reid was short of the requisite 63. It is misleading for Evatt to write, 'In order to survive the censure, Reid had to obtain Labour's support' (1945, p. 70). Even obtaining Labor's support, Reid could not survive censure (see also Weller 1974, p. 9).

717 Weir 1945, p. 36.

718 Forced? Barton must have been forced to forgo even the small chance of Labor making him Premier of NSW, and thus the presumptive prime minister of the Commonwealth. An alternative interpretation supposes Barton chose to resign in order to ensure the Reid government did not fall. But Reid's government did fall. And Barton's resignation made possible the Lyne-Labor compact which felled it.

719 So it was not so much that Labor destroyed the Reid government – it was already destroyed – but that Labor created the Lyne gov-

ernment. It is not so surprising that Reid was all geniality towards the Labor party in the wake of his removal: 'I do not wish to speak harshly of the conduct of the Party during the recent crisis... Special thanks are due to our parliamentary allies the Labour Party' (Reid 1899, p. 23).

720 *AS* 18.8.99.
721 *NSWPD* 23.8.99.
722 *NSWPD* 30.8.99.
723 Roe 2001, p. 19.
724 W.D. Armstrong, W. Stephens, Andrew Petrie and George Thorn.
725 Thomas Burgoyne, land nationaliser and free trader.
726 Affleck 1916, p. 59.
727 Queensland also sent Dickson as a delegate.
728 Copeland was Agent-General of NSW from 14 May 1900, the day the Bill was introduced into the House of Commons.
729 Including Cockburn, who from 1898 was SA's Agent-General in London.
730 Rusden 1883.
731 A modest price. Other rumours had it that Lyne had agreed to recommend to the Governor-General that Barton be chosen as prime minister; or that Lyne, as prime minister himself, would appoint Barton chief justice (BD).
732 Deakin 1944, p. 103.
733 *PC*, p. 15. As the Colonial Office was to do throughout the 20th century, in spite of failure. Thus the Federation of Rhodesia and Nyasaland, the West Indies Federation, and the Federation of South Arabia. The Union of South Africa, although not 'federal', was obviously the agglomeration of the 'geographically contiguous' which the Colonial Office sought.
734 Jay 1981, p. 256.
735 Garvin 1932, p. 556.
736 Garvin 1932, p. 256.
737 And, dare one add, the same interest in irrigation, and 'being utterly incapable, as he admitted, of grasping the essentials of academic economics' (Jay 1981, p. 323)?
738 Crosby 2011, p. 2. 'The trappings of power had no attraction to him. He wanted and wielded its reality. He was the driving wheel of the Salisbury Cabinet, of the party behind it, and more than any

other man, of the British Parliament and people'. So writes Deakin of Chamberlain (Deakin 1944, p. 139). Substitute 'Barton' for 'Salisbury', and 'Australian' for 'British', and you have a resumé of Deakin.

739 Seddon, an advocate of unhampered rights of access to the Privy Council, complained that Chamberlain 'has proved a complete jellyfish' (James Thomson, 'The Founding Father? Edmund Barton and the Australian Constitution, *Federal Law Review*, 30(2) 2002, pp. 407-458).

740 J.T. Walker *SMH* 17.4.00.

741 *Argus* 21.7.90.

742 Deakin 1944, p. 156.

743 *SMH* 19.5.00.

744 Rosa: 'The unrestricted right of appeal to the Privy Council ... should be preserved at all hazards' (1899, p. 24). See also the *Toscin* 3.3.98.

745 Smith 2016, p. 119.

746 Dickson, in accordance with his government's wishes, indicated a willingness to concede to Chamberlain. Kingston henceforth refused to meet with Dickson (Deakin 1944). Thus the apostles of Australian unity dealt with each other.

747 GD. Divided, the premiers as a group could only produce a diplomatic formula: that they all agreed that to delay passage of the Bill would be worse than amending it (*DT* 23.5.00).

748 But who conceded the most? 'Achieving a substantial alteration of that text against Barton's no change position, Chamberlain clearly gained a victory' (Thomson 2002, p. 438).

749 Williams 1999, p. 40.

750 See Thomson (2002) for an adjudication.

751 *NSWPD* 20.6.00.

752 *NSWPD* 20.6.00.

753 In 1900 the average manufacturing wage was not quite £74 pa.

754 'It must have made a sad hole in that £1000 to buy off creditors': Haynes's *Elector*, 24.2.00.

755 *DT* 30.5.1900.

756 Jebb 1905.

757 Jebb 1905, p. 121.

758 La Nauze traces the excitement at the war to it being perceived as a

coming of age rite. The excitement, therefore, cohered with Federation. Doubtless there was some coming of age pride; but that does not by itself betoken Federationism. The excitement at the Sudan Expedition of 1885 also brought that pride, but was disconnected from any federal spirit. And to what extent is one 'coming of age' by serving a parent?

759 Meaney 2001, p. 82. Tellingly, the leaderships of Canada and Australia contrasted sharply regarding the war: 'To Laurier and his colleagues, South Africa was a country bristling with problems of no concern to Canada. Participation in a war was simply a subject that need not even be considered' (Penlington 1943).

760 *BI* 18.9.00.

761 Bolton 1970, p. 209.

762 Burton 1973. Corowa is one of the few Australian country towns where there stands a statue of Queen Victoria. Ballarat and Bendigo are other instances. Deakin was to request the Commonwealth parliament to spend £25 000 on a statue of the late Queen. *CPD* 10.10.05.

763 Bate 1978, p. 259.

764 *BA* 21.5.00.

765 Gill 1975, p. 100. Byrnes had not been permitted to ride in the same carriage as the Queensland premier, Hugh Nelson.

766 Including three Victoria Crosses.

767 *WM* 21.5.00

768 *WA* 21.5.90

769 Wheeler 1982.

770 Crowley 1997, p. 298.

771 Garis 1999, p. 307.

772 James *et al* 1949, 28.11.99.

773 Garis 1999, 310.

774 Garis 1999, p. 314,

775 Deakin 1899, p. 20.

776 Glynn 1974, p. 175.

777 Partlon 2004, p. 109.

778 Partlon 2004, p. 111.

779 Garis 1999, p. 310. Crowley 1960. Smith's resignation took effect on 29 June 1900, but he had returned to England by March.

780 Why gamble on the possibility of the Bill being negatived in a ref-

erendum, when the 'sure thing' effectively offered by Forrest's amended version was barely different from the unsullied Bill? Because the revised version would be 'owned' by Forrest; its victory would be his victory.

781 Section 95 of the Constitution conceded to WA a tariff for five years, amounting to, on average, 60 percent of her pre-Federation tariff.

782 And Forrest did stoop. See the rather pitiful expressions of submission in his correspondence with Deakin in the wake of the referendum of 1900 (DAP 28.10.00).

783 And miss out on the privileges of being 'an original' state.

784 4.8.99, cited in Jenkins 1979, p. 236.

785 Perth North, 1800; Northam, 1100; Murchison North, 300; Murchison South, 500; Nelson, 800.

786 Frederick Vosper and Charles John Moran, respectively. Vosper was previously a strike militant and editor of *Australian Republican*.

787 The offending assistant registrar, W. R. Burton, appears in a formal photograph of the officers of the League posing with the petition (see Kirwan 1936, p. 298).

788 Similarly, there is no evidence that the extent of ballot fraud in NSW could have overturned the 1899 Yes majority of 13 533 there. The most expansive interpretations of the results estimated in Table A5 will not allow that.

789 80.3 percent of votes in WA's 26 Yes majority electorates were cast for Yes.

790 The remainder consisted of the deep interior of WA.

791 In 1901, 89.8 percent of the inhabitants of the Central and Eastern Division were born outside of WA (Fraser 1904, p. 117).

792 In November 1900 O'Connor was already projecting his retirement from an as yet non-existent parliament upon his appointment to an as yet non-existent High Court (La Nauze 1957, p. 7).

793 Tennyson 1978, p. 130.

794 Anderson received in reply two 'long informative' letters from Barton indicating that the instructions were as wide as Barton and Deakin 'could have possibly wished' (DAP).

795 Cunneen 1973, p. 150.

796 BEP 20.12.00.

797 Federationists at a distance were also deployed. On 22 December 1900 Chamberlain cabled Hopetoun, 'Great surprise at the

choice of Lyne instead of Barton. Please give reasons' (Abjorensen 2015).

798 Thus Holder was summoned to Sydney, where O'Connor pressed him to decline Lyne's offer of a cabinet post, as a precondition for an appointment in Barton's ministry. Holder refused, and Holder was frozen out. Barton, with a characteristic effrontery, publicly declared that the 'furious and disappointed' Holder (Glynn in Souter 1988, p. 29) 'did not claim, nor press any claim to inclusion in the Ministry. I don't even know if he has any ambition to be satisfied in the affairs of federation' (*MM* 18.1.01).

799 See Nethercote 2000; see also Hirst 2000, pp. 280-81.

800 Barton had resigned from the seat of Hastings Macleay on 7 February 1900. It was now filled again by Frank Clarke who, having conveniently made way for Barton in the first place by accepting an (unpaid) position in the Legislative Council, now relinquished that appointment to return to his old (paid) seat in the Assembly on 1 March 1900. But not for long: on 11 June 1901 he relinquished the seat of Hastings Macleay a second time, now to contest (successfully) the first Commonwealth election. The electorate's forbearance of this game of musical chairs is another indication of its forbearance of the political class.

801 McPhail 2016, p. 25.

802 'Mr. Glynn. Does the Leader of the Convention suppose that the Governor-General would be justified in selecting executive officers before Parliament meets? ... it would be opposed to all our notions of parliamentary government' (*AFC* 31.1.98).

803 Quoted in La Nauze 1957, p. 50.

804 *FJ* 14.7.00

805 *DT* 3.1.01

806 Barton: 'My Right hon friend [Samuel Griffith] has not been properly listened to .... I heartily condemn, those who prefer to listen to ordinary conversation rather than the elevated words of that distinguished gentleman' (Keenan 1904, p. 117).

807 Keenan 1904, p. 89.

808 Hirst 2000, p. 308.

809 La Nauze 1961, p. 455.

810 O'Collins 1965, p. 16.

811 The first day of the new century naturally occasioned festivities worldwide. Federationists avoided the suggestion that the Procla-

mation was timed to coincide with such celebrations. In July 1900 Barton publicly stated that 'his ideal of a date [for Proclamation] would be the first day of the 20th century ... just as Prussia commenced her career as a kingdom in the first year of the 18th century' (*SMH* 5.7.00). An unexpected comparison. And Prussia did not 'commence her career' on the first day of the first year of the 18th century.

812 *ST* 15.12.01; *SM* 21.12.01.

813 The Melbourne Cup? Reliable measures of attendance begin in 1906, with the crowd put at 42 385 (Vamplew 1987, p. 386).

814 That 68 000 travelled by rail between 2 pm and midnight on 1 January is unsupportive of vast numbers at Centennial Park in the middle of the day (Keenan 1904). In any case, *Dymock's Views of Sydney* puts Redfern station as averaging, over a year, 63 000 passengers per day.

815 Wright 1970. p. xiii.

816 *Truth* 6.1.01. 'Silence at the Park; silence *en route*, and dead silence at the *News* office when the photo was displayed at night' (*Newsletter* 5.1.01).

817 Drake 1896, p. 35.

818 Barton *MM* 18.1.01.

819 Misleading because it suggests a tariff may be a 'revenue tariff' without being a 'protection tariff'. And if the motive was to raise revenue, why was about 33 percent of imports completely un-tariffed by the subsequent legislation (Lloyd 2008, p. 123)? Flattening the tariff structure ordained by the *Customs Tariff Act* of 1902 would have increased revenue, as well as benefitting consumers. The un-level structure of the Act's tariff shows how heavily the interests of certain protected producers weighed in the counsels of Barton's government. Leake: 'the tariff that had been placed before them by the Federal Ministry was neither a free trade nor a revenue tariff, but was an all round protectionist tariff. ...Victoria under the circumstances of the Federal tariff would be able to trade where she liked in Australia, while all the other states would only be able to trade with Victoria' (*WM* 26.10.01).

820 *Mercury* 4.2.95.

821 *OC* 9.3.01.

822 *Argus* 20.3.01.

823 *Advertiser* 6.3.01. 'Contamination' in the period was connotative of

mixed race children. Thus one of Barton's lieutenants in the first parliament: 'Can you allow your children to blend their blood with that of the alien races? Can you imagine anything more pathetic than sad-looking almond eyes peeping out of the Caucasian faces. That sight is sufficiently repugnant enough for us to say, "We are going to have a White Australia"' (Littleton Groom, *TC* 29.8.01).

824 *BC* 2.02. 01.

825 This calculation discounts Barton's election to the NSW Assembly in 1879 to represent the University of Sydney; only University graduates could vote in that stagey affair. Apart from the largely *pro forma* by-election for a single vacancy in East Sydney in 1891, the only single vacancy contest Barton ever entered and won was the Hastings Macleay by-election of 1898.

826 A. P. Matheson, Separationist, Federationist, land developer and company director. He publicly repudiated his endorsement by the Free Trade Association.

827 The number of senators elected in 1901 who were former MLCs: NSW, four (Pulsford, Millen, Gould and O'Connor); Queensland, two (Drake and John Ferguson); Victoria, three (Fraser, Zeal and Sargood); SA, three (Charleston, Baker and Gregor McGregor); WA, 1 (Matheson); Tasmania, one (Dobson).

Chapter 13 (pp. 275-319)

828 Nicolson 1952, p. 79.

829 William Gurr. 11 months earlier, the minister had opened a Parliamentary Patriotic Concert by singing, 'I am an Englishman'.

830 Kwan 1995, p. 96.

831 Whittington 1986, p. 337.

832 Kwan 1995, p. 86.

833 *Age* 4.9.01.

834 Burton 2008, p. 87.

835 *NSWPD* 8.12.05. Carruthers had in the Convention protested, '... it has been seriously proposed that the federal capital should be established in the interior of Australia'. Forrest: 'Only by lunatics' (*AFC* 3.3.98). But see Gale (1907) for Forrest's subsequent about turn.

836 Deakin 1968, p. 131. Deakin's reference is to Bombala: 75 kms closer to the coast than Dalgety, 75 kms further from Albury.

837 Kirkpatrick 1903, p. 2.
838 Cockerill 1943, p. 148.
839 Cockerill 1943, p. 139.
840 *SMH* 2.5.99.
841 Of 31 accredited journalists, 23 represented Victoria newspapers, seven NSW papers, and one a Queensland paper. And none acted for the newspapers of SA, WA or Tasmania. (Lloyd 1988, p. 40).
842 Lloyd 1988, p. 41.
843 Rivett 1965, p. 94.
844 Following Huntington 1968.
845 American historians have sometimes used the categories of 'Federalist' and 'Anti-Federalist' to interpret a later revolutionary transition of American history, virtually coincident with the creation of the Commonwealth: the transition from a Populist insurgence in the last decade of the 19th century to a Progressivist ascendancy in the first decade of the 20th. The Populists are the anti-Federalists (that is, anti-centralists), and the Progressives are the Federalists (that is, centralists).
846 The notion that Federation had two phases – a populist phase before 1901 and nationalist one after 1901 – faces no great difficulty in the fact that the metropolitan working class was one of the groups least attracted to Federation before 1901. They lacked wealth and status, but not centrality: 'It is impossible for the inland districts to have the same political power as a given number of persons in any Sydney electorate'. So spoke Henry Copeland, the member for Sydney-Phillip (*NSWPD* 30.9.91).
847 Deakin 1968, p. 239.
848 Franklin 2004, p. 257.
849 Palmer 1905.
850 Bedford 2007, p. 56.
851 Strahan 1984, p. 61.
852 Palmer 1905, p. 75.
853 Serle 1996, p. 65.
854 Phillips 1971, p. 112.
855 Wigmore 1963, p. 45. The *Bulletin* claimed that Dalgety, as capital, would be 'the greatest and cheapest manufacturing city in Australia' (Green 1965, p. 16).
856 Drake 1896.

857 But in accord with the black letter of section 111.

858 In 1909-10 the annual deficit of the government of the Northern Territory was £157 285, or £18 016 excluding interest charges (*Register* 9.11.10). Although discharging this burden on the rest of Australia would gratify SA, nevertheless parting with the Territory extinguished the prospect of the state being a 'Western Australia' of the centre of the continent. 'As predicted, South Australia became a minor state like Tasmania' (Cross 2011, p. 333).

859 Canada's federal government acquired its territories from the United Kingdom, not its provinces.

860 The *Commonwealth Franchise Act 1902* and the *Immigration Restriction Amendment Act 1905*. In March 1901 there dwelt in the Northern Territory 902 Europeans, 4 886 Asians and 'well over' 10 000 Aboriginals (Langfield 2001, p. 4).

861 Donovan 1984, p. 36.

862 Hunt 1916, p. 38.

863 Hunt 1916, p. 38.

864 Langfield 2001, p. 11.

865 Donovan 1984, p. 38.

866 Quoted in Serle 1969, p. 31.

867 Thus the informal network of informants which Hunt organised to assist the enforcement of the *Immigration Restriction Act* (Fahey 2018, p. 11).

868 To rule, but not always to benefit: 'Practically every product that Papua and New Guinea can produce, except copra and rubber, is debarred from access to our markets in the interests of North Queensland' (Eggleston, *Forum* 27.9.22).

869 So may speak the voice of natural justice. The teaching of positive law requires a more particular inquiry. But in 1885 one NSW District Court Judge pressed this opinion: 'The "seizing" or "legal estate" in it remains in the Crown (for it has not been formally transferred), but no lawyer can doubt, and no Court in Equity would hesitate in holding upon the documentary evidence, acts and circumstances ... that, since 1856, the Crown has been, and now is, a mere trustee for the descendants of the mutineers of the *Bounty*, who are at present resident at Norfolk Island, in all the land and buildings within in or on it ...' (McFarland 1885).

870 Hunt 1914, p. 15.

871 O'Collins 2002.

872 Deakin 1968, p. 97.

873 Deakin 1968, p. 104.

874 A sense of federation is probably not to be expected from an imperial proconsul. One commentator has written of Anderson that he 'clearly had an imperfect knowledge of the Australian Constitution'; and, dispensing with understatement, that Lord Northcote, Governor-General, had 'an abysmal knowledge of the Australian Constitution' (Wright 1970, p. 4, p. 7). 'Throughout his letters runs a fundamentally centralist attitude to the Australian Federation' (Cunneen 1973, p. 245). 'By 1910 the attitude of the Colonial Office had certainly helped the Commonwealth consolidate its power and importance relative to the States' (McMinn 1994, p. 209).

875 Wright 1970, p. 27.

876 Cunneen 1973, p. 245.

877 And Barton's annual protest, between 1912 and 1917, to the NSW Commissioner of Taxation against his liability to pay state income tax (BEP).

878 See Sherington 1976.

879 One legal colleague of Griffith adjudged, 'I think the greatest enjoyment he got from the exercise of his judicial functions came when he found himself able to sit, in 1913, for six weeks as a member of the Judicial Committee of the Privy Council' (Graham 1939, p. 58).

880 Megarrity 2001, p. 55.

881 Queensland's Premier Kidston (1908-11) claimed he could 'raise the whole of Queensland in a flame against federation' (Wright 1970, p. 28).

882 Tennyson 1978, p. 207.

883 Foster 1986, p. 28.

884 Similarly, in 1902, Langdon Bonython, proprietor of the *Adelaide Advertiser*, and MHR for SA in the inaugural parliament, expressed the belief Federation would have been better delayed. Inglis Clark: 'I must confess that I have become disillusioned about the higher and more patriotic level of political life and conduct that I expected to see under Federation' (in Roe 2001, p. 191). In 1905 Hackett recorded that Deakin 'is not very cheerful about federal politics, evidently believing in his heart the great effort is so far failing ...' (JP 22.3.05).

885 Walker 1898, p. 278.

886 Reid and Forrest 1989, p. 400: 'In its critical first year those elected parliamentarians who were not members of the Executive played very little part in the development of overall administrative arrangements that have survived almost unchanged to the present day'.

887 Hawker 1971, pp. 115-119.

888 Hawker 1971, p. 99.

889 Hawker 1971, p. 98.

890 Reid and Forrest 1989, p. 36.

891 Hamer 1993, p. 14.

892 Cook, as Postmaster-General of NSW (Hawker 1971, p. 70).

893 Crisp 1978.

894 And, almost by implication in a 'two party' system, its democracy was made plebiscitary. Since 1910, on only one occasion (in 1941) has the Commonwealth's House of Representatives, rather than a general election, changed the prime minister. By contrast, of the 29 NSW ministries between 1856-1901, 19 were unmade by the Assembly (Clune and Griffith 2005, p. 34).

895 Reid and Forrest 1989, p. 52.

896 'Our Governors General have made little impression on the community at large' (Collis 1948).

897 The phrase is Hume Cook's. HCP.

898 Cockerill 1943, p. 54.

899 The first twelve years of the Commonwealth saw, in varying degrees of tangibility, the Australian Liberal Association, the Australian Free Trade and Liberal Association, the National Liberal Organisation, the Commonwealth Liberal Party, the People's Liberal Party, the Federal Liberal Party, the Australian Liberal Union, the Australian Liberal League and the Liberal Democratic League.

900 Crick was a key figure in constructing O'Haran's defence. Reid puttered at the margins of the case. In court, he successfully defended Ernest Abigail, a solicitor with Orange connections, who had been charged with importuning witnesses to perjure themselves against O'Haran. Abigail had been entrapped by P.F. Meagher, a son of John Meagher, MLC, an ally of Barton and doyen of Bathurst Federationists. Want prosecuted Abigail and defended O'Haran.

901 *NS* 19.08.05.

902 *Bulletin* 5.12.05.

903 Clarke identifies Reid as political party leader, 'Mr R'. CFP.
904 Affleck 1916, p. 66.
905 Union membership was 55 100 in 1901 by one source (Vamplew 1987) and 97 134 by another (Rickard 1976). Both sources put union membership in 1911 at 364 700.
906 As one organiser recalled, 'had it not been for the introduction of Arbitration legislation in 1901, there would have been no shop assistants' union' (Osborne 1921, p. 4). This union was important in transforming Paddington, a former free trade citadel, into a safe Labor seat. Alternatively, Labor's explosion may be traceable to the extinction of an independent voice for the retail, rural and property sectors, and the narrowly protectionist base of Deakin's rickety Commonwealth Liberal Party. Its platform formally committed itself 'to maintain the policy of effective protection'. The first of the 'rules' of the Party was that its head office would be in Melbourne.
907 Bryce 1921, vol. 2, p. 289.
908 Legislation in NSW and SA allowed private bodies to effect conciliation (Walker 1898, p. 285). The NSW Act permitted strikes if a reasonable time had elapsed without the matter being referred to the court.
909 Holt 1980.
910 Morrison 1950.
911 A Denis McCarthy was charged with the murder of one George Smith, found guilty of manslaughter, and sentenced to 15 years imprisonment.
912 See Quinlan and Gardner 1995.
913 Moran 1939, p. 18. Bryce 1921, vol. 2, p. 273.
914 '... the problem of industrial relations wrecked governments, split parties ...': Sawer 1956, p. 330.
915 At the time of Federation something under half of Kanakas worked under contract (as 'time-expired') rather than under 'indentures' (Shlomowitz 1981, p. 75). Even ten years before 'there were 2,879 time-expired men in the colony, and north of Townsville they could demand and receive £1 per week' (Burgmann 1980, p. 57). It was believed there was 'a sort of union amongst them'.
916 Kanakas resident in Australia since 1879 were exempt from deportation. An amendment in 1905 further exempted those of 'extreme age', those married to whites, and those who were freeholders. Deakin declined to exempt those who had been schooled in Aus-

tralia.
917 *Commonwealth* 7.3.95.
918 Moore 1985, p. 279.
919 Corris 1973, p. 128.
920 Corris 1973, p. 127.
921 Parkes 1890, p. 18.
922 *CPD* 2.10.01
923 Hunt was an appropriately punctilious enforcer of bureaucratic brutality. In 1903, when *Petriana* grounded heavily on rocks at Portsea Back Beach, he warned its Chinese seamen that if they abandoned their wrecked craft and landed on Australian soil, they risked a £100 fine 'at the minister's discretion'. In the ensuing uproar Deakin publicly and emphatically endorsed Hunt's action (Miller 1979, p. 12).
924 Martens 2013.
925 Langfield 2001, p. 9.
926 Section 3(n) of the *Immigration Restriction Act 1901* had exempted prior residents of Australia from its provisions. But the Amendment Act of 1905 removed this laxity.
927 That Aboriginals served in Australia's armed forces in South Africa has been established (Kerwin 2013). That in 1907 certain Aboriginals resident in South Africa were refused permission to return to Australia is also established (Bakker and Rogers 2019). That these persons were also formerly part of Australian forces in South Africa during the Boer War is unproved. But every likelihood is that they were.
928 Deakin 1968, p. 70.
929 The Immigration Restriction Acts of the late 1890s of NSW, Tasmania and New Zealand only required the arrival be able to write in some European language a certain 50 word statement laid down in their acts. 'The applicant … seems to have been able to choose the European language himself' (Willard 1967, p. 115). The WA legislation required the arrival to write in English a passage chosen by the customs officer; not, as in the Commonwealth's Act, in some European language chosen by the officer. SA avoided tests, and simply required a permit, to be granted at the discretion of authorities; a discretion which could obviously be exercised either in a race-blind or race-conscious way.
930 *CPD* 30.10.01.
931 Higgins: 'By herself Victoria would not have sufficient weight to

legislate against the influx of Asiatics. But what about the Federal Parliament? Is the Federal Parliament to be still in leading strings, as the different State Parliaments were' (*CPD* 6.9.01).

932 O'Connor 1968.

933 Higgins *CPD* 24.04.01.

934 *Argus* 25.4.02.

935 The force of this section of the *Commonwealth Franchise Act 1902* could have been much limited, thanks to the Convention having side-stepped the question of female suffrage by means of section 41, which affirmed that anyone entitled to vote in a state would be entitled to vote federally. But Garran recommended that this simply be taken as mandating the 'grandfathering' of existing Aboriginal voters. In practice, the administration of the Act was committed to the removal of Aboriginals (see Stretton and Finnimore 1993).

936 In WA Aboriginal voters were required to be freeholders.

937 Smith 2012.

938 *C&RE* 24.6.99.

939 *FJ* 15.8.91 and *NSWPD* 12.8.91.

940 *Worker* 22.4.99.

941 There is food for thought in the contrast with the United States Congress, which, in 1900, despite the heated opposition of some Southern members, conferred a non-racial suffrage on all male residents of Hawaii (Basson 2005).

942 Higgins 1910, p. 12.

943 *SMH* 12.12.11, 10.01.08.

944 Higgins 1910, p. 12.

945 Hirst 2000, p. 192.

946 Coleman 2020c.

947 *SMH* 30.5.98.

948 Fricke 1986, p. 17.

949 On Barton's 'circuit' of 1900 he appears to have presided over a single 'cause tried'. See the *New South Wales Statistical Register*.

950 And John Quick.

951 But the *Daily Telegraph* judged the appointments 'deplorable'. Glynn in the Convention had moved that the High Court be composed of a Chief Justice augmented by the Chief Justices of the state supreme courts, so as 'to stop the probable elevation of some

conventionists to the first Bench' (GD, 28.1.98). The motion was easily defeated.

952 Only 45 delegates, because, putting aside Baker, only 45 delegates attended all three sessions.

953 The data of the Australasian Federal Convention assigns a spectrum position value to the hypothetical delegate 'Majority' of minus 16; that is, closer to Douglas than Deakin.

954 Graham 1939, p. 61.

955 *Age* 19.03.98.

956 Higgins 1900, p. 134.

957 Musgrave 2003, p. 102.

958 *AFC* 10.9.97.

959 *AF* p. 2.

960 Forrest: '... to hand over the telephones of a state to the Commonwealth seems to me an absurdity' (*AFC* 28.1.98); Holder: 'I do not see any reason why we should hand over the posts and telegraphs' (*AFC* 26.3.97).

961 Kitto 1930, p. 20.

962 *Australasian* 7.9.01. The *Commonwealth Public Service Act 1902* sought to provide some relief from such abuses.

963 Caiden 1965.

964 Also unwelcome were competitors, in the matter of telephone books or anything else. The *Post and Telegraph Act* of 1910 made it an offence to 'circulate' any 'list' of telephone subscribers.

965 Caiden 1965, p. 97.

966 Anderson 1915, p. 13.

967 Johnson 1975, p. 195.

968 Johnson 1975, p. 127.

969 'Nothing could have been more satisfactory to Admiralty pundits than the plans of Barton and Forrest' (Gordon 1965, p. 157).

970 Penlington 1943. E.T.H Hutton, while in Canada during the Boer War, had expressed 'vehement opposition to the raising of a volunteer brigade' (Wood 2006, p. 22).

971 In 1893 Hutton had pressed himself as the head of a 'federalised' army in Australia, but 'the idea of appointing a British military commander was unthinkable to the colonists' (see Johnson 1975, p. 183). Not, however, to the Commonwealth.

972 Wilcox 1993.

973 Wilcox 1993, p. 261.

974 The 'rising sun' motif devised by the Commonwealth's planners is effective, but almost 'fascist' in emotional register. It contrasts with the fond, flora and fauna imagery favoured by the older local units, as well as with the gentler 'rising sun' imagery of 1890s vernacular Australia. Here we encounter a daring question that cannot be quickly answered: was the Commonwealth fascist? The Young Australia National Party, of the five years before the First World War, was plainly pre-fascist in general ambience, including in its zealous devotion to the cause of a unitary Australia.

975 Wilcox 1993, p. 327.

976 Wilcox 1993, p. 221.

977 Wilcox 1993.

978 Stockings 2007, pp. 81-82.

979 Wilcox 1993, p. 288.

980 The Act's only significant exemptions were a disbarring illness, not being of European descent, and not being a British subject.

981 *Age* 21.4.13.

982 Neglecting occasional appeals to make military training part of the school curriculum; and the roars of a few editorials in the wake of the 'Black Week' of the Boer War.

983 Barrett 1979, p. 68.

984 Pratt 1908, p. 239.

985 Wood 2006, p. 137.

986 At the opening of the 20th century, County Durham, UK, had a population of 1.2m, Victoria 1.2m and NSW a touch below 1.4m.

987 The *Defence Act 1911* (section 3) imposed a fine of £100, equal to about one year's earnings of unskilled labour.

988 Barrett 1979, p. 213.

989 See Fletcher and Hills 1919, p. 144.

990 *Advertiser* 24.4.13.

991 Inglis 1968, p. 28.

992 Palazzo 2001, p. 57.

993 Palazzo 2001, p. 65.

994 Coulthard-Clark 1984.

995 By 1930 there was 'widespread rejection' of Federation in Tasmania

(Roe 2001, p. 245).

996 Even W. R. Burt, who had earlier done his bit for the federal cause through ballot fraud in 1900, now made a public appeal for secession (*KM* 25.3.33).

997 A. L. Mahon, surgeon captain of HMAS *Brisbane*; Lieutenant A. I. Mahon, Military Cross.

998 Franki 2001.

Chapter 14 (pp. 321-327)

999 Walker 1898, p. 13.

1000 The Australasian Federal League of NSW's annual report of 1899 expressed the belief that 'a majority of members of the [New Zealand] House of Representatives are also now in favour of New Zealand joining the Union'.

1001 Jebb 1905, p. 88.

1002 One newspaper counted 20 New Zealand MHRs as favourable, 19 unfavourable, and the remaining 31 as uncertain or uncontacted (Martin 2001).

1003 Conservatives of myth pondering the internal decay of the Commonwealth might pause to ponder if the red, white and blue state-nation of 1901 has brought forth, in its own image, a putative state-nation of red, black and gold. Notice the recurrence of a new 'two flag state', in curious parallel with the two flag state of the original Commonwealth.

General Index

Aboriginals 131, 285, 300-1 en 860, en 927, en 935

'Advance Australia Fair' 53

Anti-Convention Bill League 203, 231

anti federation organisations
See Anti-Convention Bill League, Democratic Federal Union

architecture and architects 50, 51, 63

armed forces 24, 83, 299, 310, 312, en 166

Australasian Federal Conference xiii, 84

Australasian Federal Convention xiv, 27, 29, 40, 45, 54, 62, 70, 148, 192, 197, 269, 337, en 28, en 953
election of, 135-6, 137-144
attitude to British Empire, Canada, Great Britain and USA, 149, 150, 152
attitudes to High Court 303
delegates to,
absences of 147-8
concord and discord between 304-6

Australasian Federation Enabling Act Amendment Act xiv, 219, 220, 396

Australian Natives' Association 53-5, 57-8, 226, 315

Bathurst People's Convention 130, 294, en 217

Boer War 79, 252-54, 310, 317, 333, en 927, en 982

Brisbane 10, 12, 13, 74, 113, 226, 296, en 22, en 684

bohemia 127, 129, 131, 283

borders 14, 15, 125, 161, 302

British Empire 41, 153, 209, 253, 287, 288, en 141, en 144

Bulletin, The 48, 51, 52, 58, 73, 129, 185, 190, 284, 294, 329, en 27, en 428, en 855

bureaucracy 28, 31-3, 310, 325

Canada 78, 150, 152, 271, 296, en 17, en 38, en 759, en 859

Canberra xvi, 284

capital of Commonwealth, see Dalgety and Canberra

China 83,

Chinese 80, 114, 125, 194, 270, 299, en 99, en 463, en 923

civil service 28, 30, 221

clergy 23-4, 142, 190, 266, en 697

Colonial Office 31, 247, 251, 259, 262, 277, 288, en 197, en 733, en 874

Commonwealth Conciliation and Arbitration Act 1904 xvi, 295, 296

Commonwealth Franchise Act 1902 xvi, 300, en 860, en 935

compulsory arbitration of workplace disputes 32, 103, 125, 126, 218, 269, 294-5

compulsory military training 314-317, en 987

confederalism 158-9
Coningham case 293
conservatism 196, en 431
Constitution of the
   Commonwealth of Australia
   Bill 218, 225, 240, 247, 255-7,
   307, 323
   Section 13 en 503
   Section 41 en 935
   Section 44 163-164
   Section 57 en 505
   Section 59 40
   Section 90 161, en 41
   Section 92 161, 218, en 660
   Section 94 218
   Section 95 256, en 781
   Section 101 218
   Section 109 en 203
   Section 111 en 857
   section 123 284
   section 125 279, 280
   section 128 162
Convention election 137-44, 245
Conventions, see
   Australasian Federal
   Bathurst People's
   National Australasian
convicts and convictism 96, 98, 128-9, 176, 331, en 182, en 196, en 416, en 428, en 499, en 517
Corowa 74, 86, 254, en 229, en 762
Corowa Conference xiii, 86, 87
corruption 79, 187, 192
cricket 47, 70, 96, 98, 106, 107, 267

crowds 70, 74, 75, 96, 102, 115, 116, 185, 255, 267-8, en 813, en 814

Dalgety 103, 279-80, 284, en 855
Dean case 71-3
Democratic Federal Union 126

East Sydney, electoral district 88, 98, 102, 107, 174, 303, en 330, en 456, en 526, en 825
elections
   by-elections 174, 187, 198, 223, 303, en 674
   Commonwealth 1901 268-73
   NSW
      1887 82, 178, 120,
      1889 78, 82,
      1891 84, 88, 175, 189
      1894 xiii, 87, 88, 89, 113, 223
      1895 xiv, 90, 100, 221, 223, 230-231
      1898 xiv, 113, 181, 192, 197, 220, 221, 230, 231, 317, en 298, en 678, en 688
      1901 102
electoral finance 203, 260, en 621, en 689
electoral fraud 234-7, 260-1, en 709, en 788
Enabling Acts xiv, 134, 238, en 717

fascism en 974
Federal Council of Australasia 66, 83, 159, 195, 196, 251, 331, en 490

GENERAL INDEX

federalism
- States' rights 34, 126, 125, 150, 162, 188, 287-8, 307, en 874
- See also Senate

Federation Historiography 4-7, 85, 87, 94, 104, 106, 119-120, 167, 170, 178, 184, 245, 264, 266, 388, 256, en 758

Federationist organisations 24, 75, 86, 87, 90, 99, 127, 131, 203, 231, 230, 232, 261, en 1000
- See also Australian Natives Association

First World War 4, 7, 317, 319

flags
- NSW Ensign 38, 176, 205, 277, 278
- Victorian Ensign 277, 278
- 'Federal Flag' 38, 205, 230, en 628, en 629
- Australian National 59, 277, 326
- Union Jack 38, 275, 276, 277, 278

franchise
- Aboriginal 300-1, en 935
- manhood 173, 184, 214
- women's 79, 141, 173, 191, 204, 217, 269

Free Trade and Liberal Association 190, 230, 269, 272

Freemasonry 61, en 181

gentlemanly class 62-5, en 192
Germany 271, en 51, en 88
goldfields 74-5 256, 260-2, 324

Hawaii 194, en 941

High Court of Australia xvi, 26, 27, 67, 100, 127, 162, 247, 248, 249, 250, 280, 289, 323, 325
- appointments to 304-6, 307, 310, en 353, en 792, en 951
- Constitutional review 163-4
- decisions 218, 298, en 657, en 658, en 659, en 660

idealism, philosophical 121-2

immigration 19, 46, 56, 57, 79, 194, 270, en 860
- *Immigration Restriction Act 1901* 122, 298-9, en 867, en 926, en 929

Imperial federation 41, 59, 66, 68, 208-10, 247, 254, en 632

Ireland
- Home Rule 43, 155, 319, en 119
- Federation 44, 152, 319
- nationalism 48, 55, 193

Irish 39, 43, 44, 125, 190, 196

Japanese 194

Kanakas 39, 194, 268-70, 298, en 915, en 926

Labor Party xvi, xvii, 23, 84, 85, 90, 100, 103, 120, 139, 141, 143, 146, 181, 189, 199, 203, 215, 231, 241-4, 249, 272, 285, 291, 292-5, 300-1, 303, 309, 315, 316, 317, 337, en 692, en 716, en 719

legal profession 23, 27, 30, 84, 130, 175, 188, en 334

liberal parties 190, 191, 220, 230, 269, 272, en 899, en 906

liberalism 119, 121, 123, 189
literature 51, 52, 282

majoritarianism 125, 126, 158, en 501
   vs self-determination 211
   vs 'minority-respecting' majoritarianism 211-2, 213-4, 227, 233-4, 261, en 637 to 640
marriage and divorce 62, 64, 105, 117, 181, 191, en 192, en 302
Melbourne 52, 55. 63, 182, 215, 240, 279-80, 282, 283, en 22, en 813, en 906
miners and mining 18, 84, 109, 262. See also goldfields

National Australasian Convention xiii, 20, 84, 86, 89
nationalism and nationalists 5, 23, 37-47, 50-5, 58-9, 66-7, 169, 171, 172, 248, 253, 281-3, 326-7, en 97, en 202, en 425
naval forces 311, 318, en 166
newspapers
   Age 139-41, 277, 280
   Argus 139-41, 280
   Daily Telegraph 26, 142 , en 951
   Evening News 96, 179, 184, 221, 232, en 356, en 364
   Freeman's Journal 265
   Star 232, 242, 334
   Sydney Morning Herald 24, 96, 142, 174, 178, 197, 221, 232, 301, 331
New Caledonia 195, 205, 299
New Hebrides 95, 195, 298

New Zealand xiii, 17, 55, 59, 271, 291, 295, 300, 315, 323, en 17, en 23, en 40, en 311, en 929, en 1000
Newfoundland 150
Norfolk Island 128, 286-7, en 869
Northern Territory 83, 284-5, en 639, en 858, en 860

Papua 41, 200, 286, en 868
parliament 244, 256
   House of Representatives 100, 102, 165, 188, 272, 284, 292, 300, 303, en 118
   Senate 100, 158, 164-165, 188, 197, 205, 259, 272-3, en 118, en 505
   NSW Legislative Assembly 82, 89, 99, 102, 111, 121, 138, 187, 192, 219, 243-4, 250, en 54, en 518, en 537
   NSW Legislative Council 181, 182, 232, 239, 240, 246,en 631
   Victorian Legislative Assembly 21, 244, en 54
parliamentarism 34, 10, 121, 15, 195, 241, 243, 289-92
parties
   see Labor Party, liberal parties, protectionist parties
population
   Australia 169, 316; projected 73; distribution between colonies 13, 134, 157, 194
   Melbourne 63, en 9
   New South Wales en 986
   North Queensland en 9
   South Australia 63

Sydney 63, en 9
Victoria 57, en 44, en 986
Western Australia en 26
populism 184, 188, 189, 281, 282, en 97, en 845, en 846
Post Office xv, 33, 86, 110, 168, 192, 265, 269, 289, 308-10, 315, 334
Privy Council 66-8, en 197, en 198
   judicial subcommittee 66, 67, 68, 108, 182, 187, 247-51, 288, en 104, en 739, en 744, en 879
Proclamation of Commonwealth 201, 265-6, 267-8, en 372, en 811
progressivism 2, en 845
protectionist parties and protectionism 5, 19-21, 22, 85, 88, 90, 99, 100, 103, 107, 108, 120, 123, 125, 170, 173, 174, 190, 203, 209, 223, 225, 232, 240, 241, 247, 260, 272, 294, 300, 315, en 217, en 328, en 674, en 678, en 906
   See also tariffs
'provincial patriotism' 59, en 179
   New South Wales 176, 177
   Victoria en 161

railways 10, 12, 21, 34, 35, 79, 100, 187, 238, en 80, en 487
referendums on the Bill
   origins xiii, 86-7, 89, 257
   dates xiv, xv
   campaigns 33, 39, 70, 115, 124, 130, 181, 188, 197, 202-7, 230-1, 302, en 31, en 621, en 697
   results in 1898 201, 206, 212, 213, 221, 223, 229, 338, en 268, en 676

results in 1899 226-8, 232, 338
result in WA 75, 135, 260
see also electoral fraud, Enabling Acts, *Australasian Federation Enabling Act Amendment Act*

religion
   Catholicism and anti-Catholicism 81, 82, 107, 142, 173, 189, 190, 193, 196, 197, 266, 294, en 443, en 598
   Church of England 24, 143, en 697
   Congregationalism 131, 142
   Orange lodges 142, 143, 242, 294,
   Presbyterianism 95, 154, 167, 168, en 282
republicanism 40, 41, 208, 318, en 109, en 786
responsible government, principle of 165
'Rule Britannia' 230, 255

schools 29, 30, 106, 184, 193, 277, en 168
secession and separation 200, 214, 240, 257-9, 261, 289, 318, 333, en 19, en 27, en 28, en 631
Second World War en 177
sinkers in politics 81, 83, 84, 88, 90
socialism 100, 120, 142, 182
South Africa 247, 286, 301, 302, en 733
sovereignty and independence 38, 39, 40, 45, 154, 168-70
Speaker 102, 107, 108, 248, 290, 291, en 329, en 333

squatters 18, 21, 175, en 56, en 537, en 586

strikes 84, 120, 176, 295-7, en 57, en 908

Sydney 5, 52, 63, 73, 74, 86, 128, 129, 189, 211 215-6, 227, 232, 249, 280-1, en 9, en 268, en 649, en 682, en 846

Taranganba 'gold mine' 109, 187, en 563

tariffs 16, 19, 20, 83, 85, 99, 103, 125, 269, 302, en 45, en 819

    Constitution 161-2, 225, 256, 257, 259, 330, en 41, en 781

    Customs Duties Act 1895 15, 99, 225, 302

    Customs Tariff Act 1902 (Cth) xvi, 15, 103, 302, en 311

Tenterfield, address at by Henry Parkes xiii, 4, 5, 83, 98, 255, en 5, en 632

'The Nineties' 50-2, 282

trade unions 140, 163, 215, 280, 295, 309

United States 2, 26, 99, 144, 150, 154, 162, 164, 271, 273, 288, 295, en 38, en 941

voting, 'paradox of' 209-10

'Waltzing Matilda' 53

wedges in politics 80, 81, 83, 84, 88, 89, 90

Western Australia 255-62, 324

White Australia policy 270, 299-300

women

    anti-federationists 204-5, 219, 231, 335, en 179, en 626

    federationists 231

Women's Federal League 231

Names Index

Abbott, J. H. M. 129, 304, 329
Adams, John 286
Archibald, J. F. 55, 58, 129-30, 185, 329
Ashworth, T. R. 136
Astley, William 127-31, 329

Bailes, Alfred 18
Baker, Richard 27, 153, 165, 329
Barton, Edmund ix, x, xi, xii, 104-18,
  absence from Corowa Conference, 85, en 256
  alcohol 111, en 345, en 346
  compulsory arbitration of workplace disputes 126, 269, en 658
  Dean case 72-73
  education 106, en 326
  electoral contests, xiv, xv, 87, 107, 112, 113, 114, 146, 147, 221, 223, 224, 246, 272, en 300
  England and Empire, 66, 253, 254, en 140
  Hastings Macleay by-election en 800, en 825
  honours en 197, en 198
  Justice of High Court 26, 116, 298, 303, en 353, en 376
  McSharry case 109, 110, 189, 197, en 337
  myths about 104
  'noblest son' epithet 114, 271, en 365
  Parramatta River murders 261
  personal finances 109, 110, 111, 246, 248, 249, 251, en 338, en 877
  personality 93, 115, 116-118
  protectionism 22, 85, 107, 225, 269, 302, en 328, en 678
  Proudfoot case 109,
  race 39, 80, 107, en 328
  rivalry and friendship with Reid, 94, 98, 101, 102, 221, 222, 223, 230, 240
  rivalry and partnership with Parkes, 108, 111, 112
  Speaker 107, 108, 187, 248, en 329, en 333
Barton, Jane 64, 110, 117, 231, 251, en 378.
Bavin, Thomas 27, 30, 117, 142, 282, 329
Beauchamp, see William Lygon
Bedford, Randolph 129, 282-3, 329
Berry, Graham 54, 86, 141, 147
Bevan, Llewelyn 24, 284-5
Bigge, John Thomas 128
Bird, Stafford 244
Braddon, Edward 45, 244, 300, 329
Brockman, Deborah 64
Broinowski, Leopold 286, 318
Brunker, James 143, 330
Bryce, James 153-55, 160, 164, 295, 330
Burke, Edmund 147
Burnett, Alice 64
Byrnes, Thomas 193-199, 209, 225,

254, 322, 330, en 634, en 685, en 711, en 765

Carrington, see Wynn-Carington, Charles
Carruthers, D. 142
Carruthers, Joseph 64-5, 142, 147, 250, 287-8, 304, 330, en 182, en 183, en 196, en 393, en 835
Chamberlain, Joseph 244-50, 254, 257-9, 262, 286-7, 298, 323, 330
Charleston, David 141
Clark, Inglis 27, 39, 65, 84, 123, 133, 153, 284, 303, 330, en 81, en 467, en 884
Clarke, Andrew 245
Clarke, Francis 117, 221, 224, 294
Cockburn, John 150, 245
Coghlan, Timothy 82, 330
Collis, E. H., 64
Cook, Joseph 231, 315, en 892
Copeland, Henry 90, 123, 143, 245, 330
Crick, William 26-27, 72, 79, 93, 123, 130, 192, 224, 241
Crisp, Fin 5, 159
Curzon, George 64

Dalley, W. B. 62, 175, 331
Dawson, Andrew 199, 200, 301, 331
Deakin, Alfred xv, xvi, 331
  campaign finances 23, 260, en 689
  Chamberlain 247, 248, 249, 257, 259, 287, en 738
  Chinese, Kanakas and Aboriginals en 916, en 923
  declines Honours en 197, en 198
  Defence 30, 311, 314, 316
  England and Empire en 632, en 762
  Federal constitution 68, 150, 159, 165, 195, 287, 288
  Federation historiography 4, 43, 170, 245, 264
  legal career 27, en 338
  pessimism about Federation en 884
  proposes statue of Queen Victoria en 720
  Victorian patriotism 54, 280, 283, en 161
Dean, George 71-2, 109
Dibbs, George xiii, 40, 70, 85, 87-9, 108-9, 126, 185, 203, 250, 331, en 284, en 256, en 697
Dickson, James 198, 227, 238, 244, 254, 259, 331
Dicey, A. V. 153-5
Douglas, Adye 41, 175, 196, 305, 331
Dowling, Edward 131
Downer, John 27, 46, 64, 117, 160, 163, en 376
Drake, James 27, 64, 230, 253, 272, 284, 331
Duffy, Charles Gavan 42-3, 130, 170, 331

Edwards, James 83
Esson, Louis 282
Evatt, H. V. en 277, en 295, en 384, en 692, en 716

Ewing, N. K. en 81
Ewing, S. A. 75
Ewing, Thomas 30, 298-300, 311-2, 314, 316, 331, en 99, en 256, en 464

Fisher, Andrew 291, 316
Fitzgerald, J. C. L. 140-1
Fitzpatrick, Brian 5, en 692
Foley, Larry 116, 221
Forrest, John 84, 135, 147, 199, 255-7, 259, 300, 308, 311, 318, 324, en 76, en 81, en 197, en 198, en 490, en 782, en 833, en 960, en 962
Franklin, Miles 50, 104, 282
Fraser, Simon 150
Freeman, E. A. 153-5
Furphy, Joseph 50-1, 282
Fysh, Philip 147, 245

Garran, Andrew 99, 331
Garran, Robert 4, 27, 29-30, 40, 47, 64, 73, 86, 99, 106, 113, 123, 131, 149, 153, 158-9, 161, 191, 286, 332, en 103, en 376, en 472,
Gillies, Duncan 83, 332
Glynn, Patrick 27, 43, 48, 54, 64, 123, 150, 158, 165, 257, 265-6, 277, 332
Golding, Belle 231
Gould, A. J. 231, 415
Grey, George 70, 72
Griffith, Samuel 25-7, 31, 61, 65, 67, 70, 84, 93, 116, 119, 193, 197-8, 250-1, 266, 288, 303-5, 307, 321, 332, en 27, en 72, en 197, en 497, en 658, en 685, en 806, en 879

Hackett, John 64, 165, 196, 332
Hammond, Mark 72
Haynes, John 142, 184-193, 197, 225, 231, 240, 242-3, 254, 317, 332, en 55, en 213, en 690, en 716, en 435, en 457, en 506, en 931
Henzell, Arthur 316
Heydon, L. F. 176, 209
Higgins, Henry 27, 93, 124-126, 141, 150, 158, 244, 254, 295, 300-1, 305, 307, 334, 336, en 388, en 406, en 435, en 457, en 931
Higinbotham, George 130, 163, 332
Hirsch, Max 123
Hirst, John 6
Holder, Frederick, 332, en 181, en 798, en 960
Hope, John (7th Earl of Hopetoun), 263-4
Hopetoun, 7th Earl, see John Hope
Hordern, Samuel 63
Hughes, Robert 129
Hughes, Thomas, 66, 294, 315, 321, 332
Hughes, William 254, 315, 332
Hume Cook, James 332, 428
Hunt, Atlee 30, 109, 111, 230, 285-7, 299, 332, en 337, en 346, en 628, en 867, en 923
Hutton, Edward 30, 312, 317

Isaacs, Isaac 27, 54, 93, 152, 154, 158, 163, 305, 307, 333, en 181, en 431, en 482

James, Walter 27, 64, 147, 256, 318

Kingston, Charles 15, 26-27, 84, 93, 101, 141, 146, 229, 238, 244-6, 248, 250, 253, 262, 264, 268, 270, 303, 314, 323, 333, en 198, en 455, en 746
Kitchener, Herbert (Lord) 314-5
Knox, Adrian 289
Knox, Edward 106

Lalor, Joseph 318
Lalor, Peter 318
Lang, John Dunmore 95, 167-70, 333
Larkin, Ted 317
Lawson, Henry 50-2, 174, 282-3
Leake, George 147, 256-9, 333, en 819
Legge, James 30, 314, 317, 333
Lewis, N. E. 27, en 197, en 489
Lygon, William (Seventh Earl of Beauchamp) 243, 329, en 302, en 306, en 345, en 418, en 676
Lyne, William xv, 333
   condemns delegates to London for arrogance 249
   Convention, often absent from 147
   declares for unification 160
   free trade and protection 15, 22, 241
   Hopetoun incident 264-5
   marriage 64
   protests ballot fraud en 709
   refuses to pay state income tax 288

Scott, appealed to by en 693
votes against Dalgety as capital 284

Macarthur, James 246
Macarthur, John 316
Macarthur-Onslow, John 316
Mackay, James 333, en 699, en 132
MacKellar, Dorothea 46
Macky, W. M. Dill 315
MacLaurin, Normand 231, 250, 333
McEacharn, Malcolm 63, 66
McGonagall William 253
McGowen, James 143, 203, 249, 333
McIlwraith, Thomas 32-3, 41, 333, en 107, en 594
McInnes, George 142
McLean, Allan 244, 333
McMillan, William 43, 84, 89, 95, 122-4, 220, 333, en 181, en 197, en 386
Macrossan, John 333, en 27, en 99
Mahon, Hugh 300, 319, en 122
Maloney, William, 315, 334, en 386
Manning, William 87,
Meagher, Richard 72-3, 79, 93, 99, 109, 243, 334
Melville, Ninian 72, en 217
Melville, W. B. 336, en 317
Millen, E. D. 231, en 688, en 827
Milner, Alfred 64
Moran, Patrick (Cardinal) 24, 44, 48, 142-4, 190, 196, 293-4, 315, 334

Murdoch, Walter 253
Murray, Hubert 286

Neild, John 231, 242
Norton, John 70, 112, 130, 181, 272, 334

O'Connor, Richard 26-7, 31, 43, 48, 72, 87, 95, 107, 109, 117, 123, 130, 202-3, 208, 220, 230, 264, 272, 303-5, 334
O'Donnell, Nicholas 55
O'Dowd, Bernard 282
O'Malley, King 93, 284

Palmer, Nettie 131
Palmer, Vance 131, 282
Parkes, Henry xiii, xiv, 334
    Aboriginal suffrage 301
    absent from Corowa Conference 86
    antagonistic relations with Reid, 101, 221, en 273
    Australia as 'one of the greatest peoples on God's earth' 73
    Australia as 'wicked' 37
    crimson threads and veins 10, 46, en 95,
    Dean case 72
    England and Empire, 37, 38, 44, 46, en 94, en 112, en 138, en 632
    free trade and protection 21, 81, 82, 83, 100,
    honours 388 en 243
    invokes English Civil War 34
    marriages en 192
    proposes second convention plus referendum 87
    religion 23, 81-2, 173
    republicanism en 109
    Tenterfield, address xiii, 83, en 5
    vinedresser 110
    White Australia 298
Paterson, Andrew Barton 'Banjo' 50-1
Patterson, James 86
Peacock, Alexander 54, 87, 277, 334
Pearl, Cyril 129
Philp, Robert 288-9
Pulsford, Edward 112, 123, 270, 272, 334

Quick, John 27, 40, 47, 54, 86-9, 91, 99, 153, 158, 161, 280, 334, en 181, en 197, en 463

Redmond, John 43
Reid, Flora 231
Reid, George xiii-xiv, 94-104, 335
    absent from parliament 292
    appoints twelve legislative councillors 232, 240
    Barton, rivalry and friendship with 101, 230
    buggy accident 223
    cricket riot 96
    Coningham case en 900
    Dalgety, supports as capital 279
    England and Empire 38, 151, 152, en 103
    forced to resign from parliament 187

free trade and protection 15, 21, 225
in Federationist historiography 94
honours en 198
and Labor 240, 241, 391 en 298, en 716, en 719
loses no confidence motion in his Premiership 242-244
marriage 64, en 302
Parkes, bad relations with 21
on United States 99, 150
prorogues parliament 203, 243
so-called 'Yes-No' speech 100, 202

Reid, John 95
Richards, Edwin 192
Robertson, John 46, 63, 95, 98, 101, 130, 168, 170-177, 179, 184, 186, 209, 335
Ronald, J. B. 23, 335
Rosa, Samuel 249, 250, 335, en 312, en 384
Royce, Josiah 121
Rudd, Steele 199
Russell, Una 64

Salmon, Carty 291
Sargood, Frederick 140-1, 275, 335
Scott, Ernest 4, en 212
Scott, Rose 204, 205, 219, 231, 309, 335, 384 en 179, en 370, en 626, en 693
Seddon, Richard 323, en 739
See, John 38, 335, en 568
Smith, Bernard 5, 51, 84, 90, 93
Smith, Bruce 27, 45, 84, 87, 90, 93, 95, 106, 109, 119-124, 208, 220, 269, 335, en 96, en 112, en 148, en 337, en 387
Smith, Gerard 259
Smith, Sydney 231, en 688
Solomon, Vaiben 141, 147
Spence, Helen 146, 191, en 454
Stawell, William 163
Stephens, A. G. 131
Storey, David 251, 335, en 262
Street, Mary 64
Stuart, Charles 128
Syme, David 93, 124-5, 141, 213, 264, 284, 315, 335, en 338, en 643
Symon, Josiah 26-27, 93, 123, 134, 336, en 197, en 689

Tarrant, Harman 111, en 349
Taylor, Adolphus 186-7, 336
Thomson, Edward 28, 32
Toohey, J. T. 48
Tozer, Horace 245
Trenwith, William, 20, 215, 336
Turner, George 54, 126, 195, 220, 244, 246, 264, 279, 336, en 181, en 198

Walker, J. T. 110, 123, 143, 235, 250, 272, 336
Want, John 72, 101, 175, 178-184, 197, 203, 230, 336, en 334, en 550, en 687, en 900
Ward, E. J. 269
Ward, Russel 5, 26
Watson, Chris xvi, 220, 250, 301
Watson, George 178

NAMES INDEX

Watt, William 54, 253, 317, 336

Webb, Beatrice 191

Wentworth, William 40, 65, 103, 120-1, 178, 246

Willis, William 79, 120, 192, 234, 336

Windeyer, William 70, 72

Wise, Bernhard 4, 27, 84, 90, 93, 95, 101, 147, 158, 196, 202, 220, 336, en 5, en 489, en 679,

Wrixon, Henry 140-1, 336

Wynn-Carington, Charles (Lord Carrington), 41-2, 78, 83, 330

Zeal, William 65, 141, 266, en 827